AFRICAN PRESENCE
in
EARLY ASIA

Edited by Runoko Rashidi

Co-Edited by Ivan Van Sertima

From the Library

of _____

TRANSACTION PUBLISHERS
New Brunswick (U.S.A.) and London (U.K.)

Second printing 1999
Tenth Anniversary Edition, 1995.
Copyright © 1985 by the Journal of African Civilizations Ltd., Inc.

This book is printed on acid-free paper that meets the American National Standard for Permanence of Paper for Printed Library Materials.

ISSN:0270-2495
Library of Congress Catalog Number: 85-8529
ISBN: 0-88738-637-7 (paper)
Printed in the United States of America

Library of Congress Cataloging-in-Publication Data

Main entry under title:

The African presence in early Asia.

    (Journal of African Civilizations, 0270–2495; vol. 7, no. 1)
    1. Africans—Asia—History—Addresses, essays, lectures. 2. Asia—Civilization—African influences—Addresses, essays, lectures. 3 Asia—History—Addresses, essays, lectures. I. Van Sertima, Ivan. II. Series.
DT14.J68 vol. 7, no. 1 [DS28.A35} 950   85-8529

    ISBN 0-88738-637-7 (pbk.)

AFRICAN PRESENCE IN EARLY ASIA
(TENTH ANNIVERSARY EDITION)
Incorporating Journal of African Civilizations
August, 1995 (Vol. x, No. x)

CONTENTS

Acknowledgements

In addition to the authors listed in the table of contents, as is the case with any major undertaking, it is the collective contributions of many people, organizations and institutions that guarantee a successful final product. *African Presence in Early Asia* is no exception, and although it would take an entire book to acknowledge everyone's input, the *Journal of African Civilizations* would like to formally recognize the following persons and organizations for special work done or special permission given to make this book possible:

Dr. Joseph E. Harris, for permission to reprint the chapter "Malik Ambar" from *The African Presence in Asia: Consequences of the East African Slave Trade,* published by Northwestern University Press in 1971.

The *Journal of the Interdenominational Theological Center,* for permission to reprint "Blacks and Jews in Historical Interaction," by Dr. Charles B. Copher, which appeared in its Fall 1975 issue.

Scientific American, for permission to reprint "The Script of the Indus Valley Civilization," by Dr. Walter A. Fairservis, which appeared in its March 1983 issue.

Lee Williams, Dorothy Retamar, Kenneth Mitchell, Danita Redd-Terry, Dr. Regina L. Blackburn, Dr. Omowale Fowles, Njeri Khan, Naeem Deskins and Jacquetta Y. Parhams, for assistance in critically reviewing and proofing important sections of the text.

Laurence Rozier, Pili-Masani Anwabwile and J. Montgomery Pratt, for technical assistance.

Clara Mann, Cris T. Clay and the Amon-Rah: African People's Community Church, for material support.

Ndugu James Cage, for his assistance and cooperation in the John G. Jackson interviews.

Rev. Raju Thomas, Rev. Masilamani Azariah, David Patrick, R. Elumalai, Bhagwan Das, Dr. Velu Annamalai and the Dalit Sahitya Akademy, for interviews and background materials on the Dalit.

Shiho Fukui, for the translation of reference materials.

Larry Obadele Williams, C. Martin, Jim Roberts, W. Paul Coates, Warren Jones III, Amani Anu, Peter E. Dawson, M.D., Jeff Jackson, Paris Williams, Osagyefo Kojo Ansante, Legrand H. Clegg II, Roman Bunker, Lee Williams, Laurice Elaine Smith, Dr. Michael Hooser, Adisa Banjoko, Vulindlela I. Wobogo, Dr. Asa G. Hilliard III, Karen A. Johnson and the African Elders Tribute Foundation, for reference materials, background information and bibliographic data.

Larry Obadele Williams, Wayne Richardson, Gaynell Catherine and Naja L. Naji, for photographs.

Black Classic Press, for allowing us to use an extract from *Wonderful Ethiopians of the Ancient Cushite Empire*, by Drusilla Dunjee Houston.

The *Journal of African Civilizations* is particularly grateful to art historian James E. Brunson and anthrophotojournalist Wayne B. Chandler for their research efforts, technical skills and invaluable photographic contributions to all three editions of this anthology.

PREFACE TO THE TENTH ANNIVERSARY EDITION

The Essence and Evolution of the African Presence in Early Asia

In 1984 at the Nile Valley Conference at Morehouse College in Atlanta, Georgia, Dr. Ivan Van Sertima, founder and editor of the *Journal of African Civilizations* and one of our greatest living scholars, requested that I coordinate and edit a special volume of the *Journal of African Civilizations* on the African presence in early Asia. It was to be the first of a trilogy of books on the Global African Community focusing on the African presence in early Asia, Europe and America. It was also the first volume of the *Journal of African Civilizations* to be edited by anyone other than Dr. Van Sertima himself. I was honored by the request and set about my assignment with determination and vigor. The first edition of the *African Presence in Early Asia,* incorporating the *Journal of African Civilizations* Volume 7, Number 1, consisted of 165 pages and was published in April 1985. A revised and expanded edition of 256 pages was published in 1988. The current product is the second revised and expanded edition. It is dedicated to departed scholars John Glover Jackson and Chancellor James Williams, and comes during the tenth anniversary year of the initial publication of *African Presence in Early Asia.*

In his editorial to the 1985 volume, Ivan Van Sertima provided an excellent overview of the original essays by Runoko Rashidi, Drusilla Dunjee Houston, Walter A. Fairservis, R.A. Jairazbhoy, Wayne B. Chandler, John G. Jackson, James E. Brunson, Gershom Williams, Kilindi Iyi, Graham W. Irwin and Joseph E. Harris. Unfortunately, however, no such overview was provided for the 1988 edition. This brief preface, therefore, is intended a highly capsuled synopsis of the evolution and expansion of the *African Presence in Early Asia* since its initial publication in 1985.

It should be stated at the beginning that the coordination and editing of this text in three main phases was a formidable and sometimes daunting task, presenting both advantages and dangers. Among the advantages was the opportunity for examination and inclusion of materials that previously were either unavailable or unknown. On the other hand, from the editor's perspective, there was the difficult job of reducing and reconciling the inevitable unevenness and inconsistencies inherent in such a project. Part of this problem was stylistic, ranging from the use of *B.C.* for the recording of dates in the early editions of the text to the more consistent use of *B.C.E.* in the 1995 edition, changes from lower to upper case in the use of the word *Black,* relatively minor alterations and corrections in the spelling of proper names, the selection and utilization of source materials, and variations in the organization and placement of end notes.

At the same time, however, ten years allows for a considerable degree of retrospection on the nature, definition and complexities of our work. This factor, combined with new discoveries and developments in the field, in concert with our own evolution and maturation, has had a modifying effect on our viewpoints, even though it did not fundamentally alter our initial perspectives and conclusions. Our purpose here has been an earnest quest for truth, not the maintenance of dogma, and we readily admit honest mistakes. This anthology is not offered as, nor does it pretend to be, a flawless document, and we openly invite and solicit constructive criticism. Although it has been no easy task, we have tried to be as scrupulous and careful in the overall process as well as in the harmonic weaving of all the strands of the text. In spite of our own limitations and the enormity of the subject itself, we believe that we have been generally successful in our efforts.

Additions to the current volume of *African Presence in Early Asia* include works by Dr. Chancellor James Williams and Professor John Glover Jackson, Dr. Charles B. Copher, Runoko Rashidi, James E. Brunson, Wayne B. Chandler, Charles S. Finch III, M.D., V.T. Rajshekar, Dr. Omar Khalidi and Wallace Magsby, Jr. Both collectively and individually these scholars document African aspects within, and influences upon, classical Asian civilizations. Their works underscore many of the African elements and underpinnings of the major religious and philosophical movements of early Asia, and highlight and demonstrate many of the relationships that form the basis of the African presence in Asian antiquity. The new additions to the book (including materials on Central Asia, Southeast Asia, Japan and the Philippines, sometimes taking the form of relatively brief research notes with extensive bibliographic references), have helped to make the text a truly continent-wide survey.

One of the most provocative aspects in the evolution of the anthology is the inclusion of background materials on the Dalit. The Dalit are arguably the descendants of India's original settlers and civilizers and are sometimes referred to as "the Black Untouchables of India." Although it is a highly controversial thesis, our thrust is that the Dalit form a critically important but insufficiently known component of the Global African Community and are demonstrating a rapidly expanding awareness of their African roots. The contribution of South Indian journalist V.T. Rajshekar is particularly critical here, and helps to bring a measure of comprehensiveness to the text that otherwise might not have been realized.

Finally, we have placed great emphasis on the writings of many of the early and sometimes unheralded scholars whose works illuminated critical elements of the African presence in early Asia. This component of the book is presented in the form of commentaries, tributes, assessments, selected bibliographies, interviews and extracts from their works.

Runoko Rashidi
May 1995

INTRODUCTION TO THE TENTH ANNIVERSARY EDITION
AFRICAN PRESENCE IN EARLY ASIA

By Runoko Rashidi

We now know, based on recent scientific studies of DNA, that modern humanity originated in Africa, that African people are the world's original people, and that all modern humans can ultimately trace their ancestral roots back to Africa. Were it not for the primordial migrations of early African people, humanity would have remained physically Africoid, and the rest of the world outside of the African continent absent of human life. Since the first modern humans (Homo sapiens sapiens) in Asia were of African birth, the African presence in ancient Asia can therefore be demonstrated through the history of the Black populations that have inhabited the Asian land mass within the span of modern humanity. But not only were African people the first inhabitants of Asia. There is abundant evidence to show that Black people within documented historical periods created or influenced some of ancient Asia's most important and enduring high-cultures.

African Presence in Early Asia, edited by Runoko Rashidi and Ivan Van Sertima, is the most comprehensive publication of its type in existence. It is a project involving the work of more than twenty contributors. It is ambitious in its scope, and pioneering in its approach, in the sense that there were few real blueprints or detailed guidelines to follow. It is an effort of reconstruction and definition. It is a distinct and essentially unique publication in the sense that *by the African presence in Asia, we are referencing all of the Black populations that have peopled Asia within both the prehistoric and historic periods. We are using the words "African" and "Black" interchangeably, as synonyms.* This includes African people as the first modern humans in Asia, the subsequent migrations and movements of African people impacting the essential character and content of classical Asian civilizations, and the later involuntary arrival of African people in Asia resulting from slavery.

For well over a century, Western historians, ethnologists, anthropologists, archaeologists and other such specialists have generally and often arbitrarily used such terms as *Negroid, Proto-Negroid, Proto-Australoid, Negritic* and *Negrito* in labeling populations in Asia with Africoid phenotypes and African cultural traits and historical traditions. This has especially been the case with Black populations in South Asia, Southeast Asia and Far East Asia. In Southwest Asia, on the other hand, terms like *Hamites, Eurafricans,*

Mediterraneans and the *Brown Race* have commonly been employed in denoting clearly discernible Black populations. In this work, we have chosen to reject such deliberately confusing nomenclature as obsolete and invalid, unscientific and racially motivated.

Dr. Cheikh Anta Diop, whose work has in so many ways formed a model for much of our research efforts, expressed a keen understanding of the nature and ramifications of the phenomena. In a November 1985 interview with the *Journal of African Civilizations,* Charles S. Finch (one of our major contributors) pointed out that, "There seems to be a growing consensus or idea in the literature of anthropology that there is no such thing as race." Continuing, Dr. Finch noted that "One consequence of this thinking is the idea that Black people in India, Asia and the Pacific Islands who have almost the identical physical characteristics as Africans—that is, black skins, kinky hair, full lips, broad noses, etc.—are said to be totally unrelated to Africans." In his response, Dr. Diop, speaking deliberately and uncompromisingly, pointed out that:

> A racial classification is given to a group of individuals who share a certain number of anthropological traits, which is necessary so that they not be confused with others. There are two aspects which must be distinguished, the phenotypical and the genotypical. I have frequently elaborated on these two aspects.
>
> If we speak only of the genotype, I can find a black who, at the level of his chromosomes, is closer to a Swede than Peter Botha is. But what counts in reality is the phenotype. It is the physical appearance which counts. This black, even if on the level of his cells he is closer to a Swede than Peter Botha, when he is in South Africa he will live in Soweto. Throughout history, it has always been the phenotype which has been at issue; we mustn't lose sight of this fact. The phenotype is a reality, physical appearance is a reality.
>
> Now, every time these relationships are not favorable to the Western cultures, an effort is made to undermine the cultural consciousness of Africans by telling them, 'We don't even know what a race is.' What that means is that they do not know what a black man is, they do know what a white man is, they do know what a yellow man is. Despite the fact that the white race and the yellow race are derivatives of the black which, itself, was the first to exist as a human race, now we do not want to know what it is. If Africans fall into that trap, they'll be going around in circles. They must understand the trap, understand the stakes.
>
> It is the phenotype which has given us so much difficulty throughout history, so it is this which must be considered in these relations. It exists, is a reality and cannot be repudiated.

It is in this light and with this in mind that we present the current anthology. It is a search for answers. Inside this context and within our studies, this anthology examines and surveys several core areas. Among the most fundamental of these areas are:

1. The peopling and settlement of Asia from Africa. identifying African people as Asia's first modern human populations. That African people—*Black people*—are the aborigines of Asia, and that subsequent and periodic migrations and movements of African people into Asia occurred throughout antiquity.
2. The impact and extent of the African presence in the human cultures and classical civilizations of early Asia.
3. Discernible African elements and underpinnings of the major religions and philosophical movements in Asian antiquity.
4. Historical, anthropological and linguistic relationships between Asia's Africoid, Mongoloid, Caucasoid and Semitic populations.
5. The enslavement and subjugation of African people in Asia.
6. Ancient and modern documentation and historiography of the African presence in Asia.
7. Major population centers and geographic locations of African populations in Asia from antiquity to modern times.
8. Nomenclature and designations for African people in Asia.
9. The numbers and proportions of African people in Asia from antiquity to modern times.
10. The status of the Global African Community in Asia today.

In summation, in brief, we contend that the history of the African presence in Asia is one of the most significant, challenging and least written about aspects of the global African experience. It covers a time span of more than 90,000 years, and encompasses the largest single land mass on earth. As the first modern humans, as hunters and gatherers, primitive horticulturalists and sophisticated agriculturists, kings and queens, poets and prophets, sages and scientists, servants and slaves, African people have known Asia intimately from the very beginning. Even today, after an entire series of holocausts and calamities, the African presence in Asia may exceed two-hundred million people.

The questions we pose are simply these: Who are the Black people of Asia? What is their significance in the annals of history? Precisely what have they done and what are they doing now? These are extremely serious and fundamental questions. We hope that our readers will conclude that this anthology, *The African Presence in Early Asia,* offers serious and fundamental answers to those questions.

EDITORIAL

(Introduction to the First Edition, 1985)

This issue, entitled *The African Presence in Early Asia*, is the first in series of books on the African physical and cultural presence in world civilizations. It is followed by the *African Presence in Early Europe* (1986) and the *African Presence in Early America* (1987).

Asia is one area in which I, as editor, have never done any substantial research and it is the first time in the six years of my editorship that I have delegated responsibility to another to solicit relevant articles and coordinate the research effort of a body of scholars in a particular field. The result has been most reassuring and makes me confident that the work of the *Journal* will continue on the same level of competence when the burden of building a responsible new school of African civilization history is finally lifted from my shoulders.

The Nile Valley Conference held at Morehouse College in Atlanta (September 1984) made me very aware of the growth and vitality of that new school. Our guest editor of this special issue on Asia belongs to that new school. He is Runoko Rashidi, known to readers of the *Journal* through his excellent essays on "The African Presence in Ancient Sumer and Elam" in *Egypt Revisited* and "Nile Valley Presence in Asian Antiquity" in *Nile Valley Civilizations*. He is the founder of research organizations and think-tanks, like *Amenta* and *Southern Cradle* in Los Angeles. He is also author of the monograph *Kushite Case-Studies*. He brings to this symposium not only a comprehensive awareness of the multiple time-levels and places of African migration and influence but a scholarly rigor in his summaries and analyses, qualities which should accompany an original perspective for it to be both revolutionary and responsible.

He does not downplay, for example, the complexity of the question of racial composition in ancient Sumer, the first formative civilization of West Asia, admitting that the population was not racially homogeneous. But he demonstrates forcefully, with pictorial, cultural and skeletal evidence, that a major element in Sumerian civilization were black migrants from the Nile Valley who called themselves "the blackheads." He poses the question: if they were Mongoloid types and this was simply a term for black hair (as some historians argue) why should they seek to distinguish themselves in this way from other Asiatics, who would also be black-haired? Their blackness or African-ness, which is glorified in this term, may be seen in the skeletal evidence. Rashidi shows that craniologists, finding roughly the same headshape, nasal index, brow-ridge variations in Ethiopic or Africoid skulls in interior Africa as skulls found in excavations in ancient Egypt and Sumer, try to create new and nebulous classifications, such as "Eurafricans," "Mediterraneans," and "Hamites." These, he identifies, as "ethnocentric synonyms for black people."

He also introduces us to the blacks in Elam and in Susa, its capital. Elam was the first high-culture in what is now Iran or Persia. He shows how Elamite cultural forms, their goddesses, art-motifs, weapons and scripts, link them back to the Nile Valley so that one could actually speak of Elam as "a Kushite colony with its Susiana heartland." Extremely dark populations still hover on the borders of modern Persia. "The whole country," according to one authority, were "originally Negritos who probably stretched along the northern shores of the Persian Gulf to India."

Arabia also, like much of Asia, was initially populated by blacks. Some of the surviving black populations, known as Veddoids, are the major portion of the Mahra population found still in the southern extremities of Arabia. There are also the Sabeans, a mix of East Africans and nomads from the north and central sections of the Arabian peninsula. Out of this mix came the most famous black queen in history—Makeda, the queen of Sheba—who placed her son by Solomon on the throne of Ethiopia, starting a line that was to last until the late Haile Selassie. Another mix—of Ethiopians and South Arabians—occurs in the Tigre province of Ethiopia and led to the powerful kingdom of Axum, whose rise to power over South Arabia is briefly outlined. Readers who seek further details on the very early peopling of Arabia by Africans should read Drusilla Houston's essay "Ethiopians in Old Arabia" which was condensed by Rashidi for the purposes of our 1985 issue. The African presence in Arabia is of particular interest in a much later period since Arabia was the home of Islam and Mohammed. While some have speculated that Mohammed may have been of African lineage (some say his mother was Nubian), we know for certain that Bilal, one of his disciples, certainly was. Bilal was a pivotal figure in the development of Islam and has been referred to as a third of the faith.

The African presence in the Indus Valley civilization occupies the attention of the two major essayists in this issue, Runoko Rashidi and Wayne Chandler. They both present their case with persuasive eloquence and well-researched data but are in strong disagreement over the role played by the Dravidians in the Indus Valley civilization. I think it is necessary for me to restate the case in order to clarify the nature of the disagreement and perhaps to resolve it, following the light of my own experience of similar archeological and historical problems.

Rashidi portrays the Dravidian as an ethnic type characterized by straight to wavy hair texture with distinct Africoid features. He takes the view (now widely accepted) that these Dravidians were the founders of the Indus Valley complex. He identifies them with the hated Dasas or Dasyus (blacks) of the Rig Veda, the adversaries of the invading Aryans (whites). They were the same people who later became the Sudras, the conquered black masses reduced in Aryavarta (Aryan Land) to the status of slaves. He contends that these people provided the stimulus for the Indus Valley civilization which reached its height between 2200 and 1700 BC. This is known as the Harappan phase. The Indus Valley was dominated by two great cities: Harappa and its sister city, Mohenjo-Daro.

Chandler, however, argues that although blacks were the foundation of the Indus Valley civilization they were *not* the later Dravidians but the original layer of Ethiopian blacks (known as Negritos) and the Proto-Australoid. The Harappans he contends were a fusion of just these two Africoid types. He feels that the Dravidians came in too late to have affected Harappan civilization, since the occupation of the Indus Valley sites go back 9,000 years.

There is a middle distance between these two points although they appear to be in clear opposition. It is obvious that the Dravidians did not originally occupy these sites and that the aboriginal blacks were responsible for the first cultures of the Indus Valley. It is equally obvious that it is not until about 2,200 B.C. that a sudden leap in the Indus Valley occurs and an aboriginal *culture* with low technology explodes overnight into a highly advanced *civilization*. Chandler himself states that the bricks of Mohenjo-Daro are as late as circa 2,000 B.C., even though the actual occupation of the site goes back several millenia before that. We must, therefore, conclude that, upon an aboriginal layer or native base, an outside force built the Harappan phase. The evidence of cultural loans from the Dravidian in this period are too concrete to be dismissed. Walter Fairservis Jr. in "The Script of the Indus Valley," reprinted in this volume from *Scientific American* (March 1983), states that the language of Harappa and Mohenjo-Daro was an early Dravidian tongue. What we have, therefore, is the blend of early aboriginal black with a later, more advanced, African or African-Asiatic element, the Dravidian.

Chandler's brilliant photography not only vivifies the African faces of these ancient times but his dramatic narrative conveys to us a sense of the modernity of these African-Asiatic cities. We learn of the creation of a central sewage system, bathrooms with drains that carry waste to the sewers under the main streets, every house with its own private well, a great public bath with carefully made floors that empty into the undergound sewers, the bathwater changing at regular intervals. He even evokes the dust of passing traffic on the 30-foot wide streets and the privacy of the people whose windows open only on their central court-yard, not on the street.

We enter early China with the black dwarfs. James Brunson introduces us to the first Chinese emperor, Fu-Hsi (2953–2838 B.C.) who is a wooly-haired negro. He is probably half-historical, half-legendary, like Osiris, his achieve-ments (creation of government, social institutions like marriage, writing) far too broad and sweeping to be credited to a single individual. But this is the usual story with first dynasties where the plural becomes fused into the singular as the time-distance between the event and its much later recording tends to turn *several* real leaders into a mythical or divine *one*. It is significant, however, that he should be represented as a divine black in recognition of the African beginnings of culture in certain parts of China. What is particularly interesting is that the Shang dynasty (1766-1100 B.C.) was largely a black dynasty and that the Shang were given the name of *Nakhi* (*Na*-black, *Khi*-man) by the Moso, because of their very dark complexion. The Chou who conquered the Shang described the inhabitants of the area as having black skin.

We are fortunate to have Rafique Jairazbhoy contribute for the first time to a publication of the *Journal of African Civilizations*. The main thrust of his essay "Egyptian Civilization in Colchis on the Black Sea" is that Colchis may have been established *not* by the black armies of Sesostris but by blacks in a later ex-pedition by Ramses III. Colchis is where Jason sailed with the Argonauts in the Greek myth and Jairazbhoy presents a close set of parallels which link the major elements of the Argonaut myth with cultural traits and artifacts datable to the Ramses III dynastic period. Most striking of these Ramessid traits is that of the golden ram of Phrixus with a snake overlooking it, a most unique design which exactly matches the prow of the solar ship of Ramses III.

John G. Jackson, in "Krishna and Buddha of India: Black Gods," presents startling parallels between the lives of Krishna (1200 B.C.) Guatama Buddha (600 B.C.) and Jesus (100 B.C. or 33 A.D.?) The parallels between Krishna, the Black Christ of India, and the Jesus of the Gospels, are so remarkable that the latter almost seems to be a reincarnation of the former. Some of the major mythological elements surrounding these men surround the Buddha also, who is represented in early statuary as a man with wooly hair and Africoid features. Jesus, himself, as we have shown in the *Nile Valley Civilizations* issue, appear in his first physical representation as a man with wooly hair with what we would de-scribe as Afro-Semitic features. This is on the back of a coin struck in the time of the Roman emperor Justinian II. These Christ-figures or prophets are all related to the same tradition although each appears roughly six hundred years after the other. What these parallels are meant to suggest we do not know. Some feel that they prove Jesus is a fiction and the story of his life is a reworked version of earlier Christ figures. But it seems to us that the uniquely individual style of the sayings of Jesus, rather than the duplicatable drama of his actions (the main actions of a prophet, after all, tend to follow a pattern) establish that Jesus did exist as a historical figure, who, after death, was clothed in a mythological raiment best suited to make him universally acceptable.

We close with two essays on Africans in the later slave period. Graham Irwin brings a new light to bear on the nature of slavery in certain parts of Asia. It is not confined to the familiar context with which we usually associate it in the Americas. Irwin informs us in his essay "African Bondage in Asian Lands" that Muslim societies from the Middle East, India and Central Asia adopted the practice of using people from other lands for various specialized occupations who would be called "slaves" but who might achieve high rank and status, as high as commander or even general in the military, and as high as the rank of prime minister itself in the bureaucracy. The rationale behind this is that "if you have a slave that comes from somewhere else, and you put him in a position of authority, he does not have kinship ties with the local people. That means that he tends to be loyal rather than disloyal. That means that he is unlikely, other things being equal, to head a coup d'etat. Because how can he rely on local support?". This is not to deny that many blacks were brought in also in the lowliest positions, as house servants and concubines and eunuchs. But beyond the familiar relegation of the black to the role of inferior, we must still see a significant and qualitative difference in a system which allowed several of the Abbasid Caliphs of Baghdad to be African and an African palace guard to become ruler of Bengal. Irwin cites an instance where a community of great African sailors, known as the *Sidis*, dominated the northwest coast of India and their commander was appointed admiral of the Indian Ocean by the Mughal emperor.

The most celebrated of all African rulers in India is Malik Ambar, the subject of Joseph Harris' essay. Ambar was brought to India in 1575. Born in Ethiopia, he had been a slave in the Middle East. In India he became a trader, he recruited followers and built an army as his trading made him prosperous. He eventually developed such a strong army that he was able to establish himself as the power behind the throne. He invented highly innovative guerilla warfare tactics, making him formidable and feared by those who challenged his state. He was a brilliant soldier, diplomat and administrator. He appointed his own African ambassador to the court of Persia. He encouraged manufactures, he built canals, mosques, a post office. He supported poets and scholars with pensions from the treasury of the state. Harris' chapter on Ambar is indeed one of the most inspiring in the history of an African in Asia.

And on that note we close. The black role in Asia, as elsewhere in the world, has been submerged and distorted for centuries. But it has not been totally eclipsed and it rises now like a star which was hidden by a cloud but never faded into the oblivion of the night. As Godfrey Higgins says in *Anacalypsis*, quoted in our book review by Gershom Williams, we have found the black everywhere "whenever we approached the origin of nations."

Ivan Van Sertima

NOTE: This editorial relates only to the first 1985 edition of African Presence in Early Asia.

DEDICATION AND TRIBUTE
THE PASSING OF GIANTS: JOHN G. JACKSON AND CHANCELLOR WILLIAMS

By Runoko Rashidi

The *Journal of African Civilizations* deeply laments the passing of two of our greatest scholars—John Glover Jackson (1907–1993) and Chancellor James Williams (1893–1992). John Glover Jackson was born on 1 April 1907 in Aiken, South Carolina. At the age of fifteen he moved to Harlem, New York, where he entered Stuyvesant High School. During his student days Jackson began to do active research, and was soon writing short essays about African-American culture and history. These essays were so impressive that in 1925, while still a high school student, Jackson was invited to write articles for the Honorable Marcus Garvey's *Negro World.*

We are fortunate to have interviewed and worked with John G. Jackson on the subject of the African presence in early Asia. Professor Jackson authored a number of pamphlets and books particularly relevant to our studies. These texts include, *Ethiopia and the Origin of Civilization* in 1939, *Introduction to African Civilizations* in 1970, *Man, God, and Civilization* in 1972, *Christianity Before Christ* in 1985, and *Ages of Gold and Silver* in 1990.

John Glover Jackson was one of the major influences in my life, and I was blessed to know him personally. I met Professor Jackson for the first time in 1982 while working at Compton College. After our initial encounter, we spent many hours on the phone and in person dissecting history, scholarship and politics. The twilight years of John G. Jackson's life were spent in a nursing home in Southside Chicago. On my last visit with Elder Jackson I was accompanied by James E. Brunson. It was about three weeks prior to his death. This was for me a very difficult, almost tearful occasion. Jackson was more distant and despondent than I had ever seen him. The news of his passing came as a serious personal loss.

Dr. Chancellor James Williams, an acclaimed writer, educator and historian, was born in Bennetsville, South Carolina, on 22 December 1893. His father had been a slave; his mother a cook, a nurse, and evangelist. Dr. Williams received a Bachelor of Arts degree in Education from Howard University in 1930, a Master of Arts degree in History from the same institution in 1935, and a Ph.D. in Sociology from American University in Washington, D.C. in 1949. In 1956, he began to direct field studies in African history, while based at University College, which later became the University

of Ghana. Williams was actually in Ghana when it gained independence from
Britain under the leadership of Kwame Nkrumah on 6 March 1957. The final
phase of the field studies, which covered twenty-six countries and 105 language groups, was completed in 1964.

Chancellor Williams is best known as the author of *The Destruction of
Black Civilization: Great Issues of a Race from 4500 B.C. to 2000 A.D. The
Destruction of Black Civilization* is a seminal work, with a distinct and
perceptible quality that is evident from the beginning, where Dr. Williams
reproduces an anonymous Sumer legend. The Sumerians, an ancient people
who flourished in the fertile river valley of the Lower Tigris-Euphrates, were
the architects of the earliest identifiable high-culture in Asia. According to the
epigraph:

> 'What became of the Black People of Sumer?' the traveller asked the
> old man, for ancient records show that the people of Sumer were Black.
> What happened to them?' 'Ah,' the old man sighed. 'They lost their
> history, so they died. . . . '

It is this very epigraph, by the way, simple though it may seem to some, that
has so captivated and sustained a number of researchers engaged in reconstructing the history of the African presence in early Asia.

Chancellor Williams was the father of fourteen children. Blind and in poor
health, he died on 7 December 1992. His legacy, however, remains distinct,
vibrant and alive.

AFRICANS IN EARLY ASIAN CIVILIZATIONS: A HISTORICAL OVERVIEW

Runoko Rashidi

The Black-heads of Sumer

Ancient Sumer, the Biblical land of Shinar, was the formative civilizing influence of early West Asia. Flourishing during the third millennium B.C., Sumer set the tone and established the guidelines for the kingdoms and empires which succeeded her. Frequently designated as, or linked with, Chaldea and Babylonia, Sumer embraced the Tigris/Euphrates river valley from the base of the Persian Gulf north to Akkad, a distance of about 300 miles.

While Sumer's many cultural achievements are much celebrated, the important question of her ethnic composition is frequently glossed over or left out of the discussion altogether. While it would be foolish to assert that Sumer's inhabitants were homogeneous or exclusive to any particular racial type, it seems rather obvious that the bright light of Sumerian civilization can only be attributed to the arrival of Black migrants from Africa's Nile Valley.

In their own literature the Sumerians called themselves "the black-heads," and were only one of the numerous Nilotic Kushite colonies implanted in early Asia. A survey of the available Sumerian anthropological data is strongly supportive of this. In 1926, and again in 1928, the Field Museum and Oxford University conducted extensive joint excavations in northern Sumer. At the dig's conclusion they stated that:

> The earliest historical crania (hyperdolichocephalic) are from Jemdet Nasr, 18 miles northeast of Kish and those from 'Y' trench at Kish . . . The forehead is retreating, the brow-ridges are always prominent, and the cheekbones rather wide. The nose is broad, in some cases inclining to extreme platyrrhine, although the face has seldom survived. This is the type described by Sergi, Giuffrida-Ruggeri and Fleure and named the 'Eurafrican' type . . .[1]

In an additional publication on the excavations at Kish, T.K. Penniman lists three distinct cranial groups:

> First, there is the Eurafrican . . . In ancient times, the type is found in Mesopotamia and Egypt, and may be compared with the Combe Capelle skull. It is possibly identical with men who lived in the high desert west of the Nile in palaeolithic times, and is the type seen in the familiar portrait statues of Ramses II . . .[2]

Plate 1. Africoid governor, Gudea of Lagash, circa 2,150 B.C. Courtesy of the Metropolitan Museum of Art.

Secondly, there is the Mediterranean type, whose variants occur all the way from Java through India and Mesopotamia, and on both sides of the Mediterranean. These people are of medium stature, with complexion and hair like those of the Eurafrican, to which race they are allied, dark eyes, and oval faces. They have small ill-filled dolichocephalic skulls, with brow-ridges poorly developed or absent, bulging occiputs, orbits usually horizontal ellipses, broad noses, rather feeble jaws, and slight sinewy bodies. In ancient times their distribution was much the same as today.[3]

Thirdly, there is the Armenoid type, whose relatives are found all over the Eurasiatic plateau and mountains from the Persian highland and Asia Minor.

Although both reports, through their very terminology, reflect the narrow and pervasive thinking of their day and unfortunately ours as well, the information to be derived from them provides solid verification for the historical traditions and eye-witness accounts of the black presence in ancient Sumer. We can find no substantial difference between the crania of the "Eurafricans" and "Mediterraneans" referred in these statements and the crania of the modern blacks of Africa and Asia. This data, albeit limited, leaves no doubt as to the racial identity of the region's early population. Of the 14 crania from "Y" trench at Kish which Penniman examined, two he described as brachycephalic, eight dolichocephalic (Eurafrican), two Armenoid and two mixed. Buxton and Rice studied 26 crania which, according to their own report, consisted of 17 Eurafricans, five Mediterraneans, who are by their own description Austrics, and four Armenoids. Incredibly they conclude that there were no traces of Negroid, i.e., African, inhabitants. Fortunately we are in a position to form our own conclusions and we can only conclude that we are dealing with ethnocentric synonyms for Black people.

The Third Dynasty of Ur

For most of her history, Sumer consisted of a number of largely independent city-states. Each such entity contained a comparatively large urban center around which were the smaller satellite towns and villages. At frequent intervals however the Sumerian city-states coalesced to form powerful unified kingdoms led by provincial leaders endowed with divine status. Such was the case during Ur's Third Dynasty. Ur itself, while not the earliest of the great Sumerian cities, was arguably the most important. At her height Ur covered more than four square miles, quite large for the time, and while the Third Dynasty was her most illustrious era, written records acknowledge her existence until 440 B.C. The third Dynasty itself lasted for nearly a century, 2112-2015 B.C., under the reign of five brilliant rulers who elevated Ur to the status of a great empire.

The Third Dynasty rulers of Ur assumed the titles of "King of Sumer and Akkad" and this was not the first time a Sumerian city-state had reached out to

Plate 1a. Jewish Prisoners taken captive in Palestine by the Assyrians c. 700 B.C.
(Photo: James Brunson).

embrace the surrounding regions. During the reign of its powerful governor
Gudea, 2142-2122 B.C., Lagash subjugated Susa and much of Elam. From a
series of inscriptions we learn of Gudea' conquests, his lack of acknowledgement
of a superior, and of the Susians and Elamites who came to Lagash, '' . . . to aid
him in reconstructing the temple of his god.''[4] Gudea's god was Anu, a name
found seemingly whenever the ancient blacks themselves are found. In spite of
the scarcity of stone, classical Sumer was an age of colossal construction projects, and each of the major urban centers erected tremendous multiple levelled
brick structures called ziggurats.

Ur's Third Dynasty empire, grown expansive and wealthy, unfortunately was
built on a very fragile base. First of all, the coalition that constituted the core of
the empire was a loosely arranged affair, and there does not appear to have been
any genuine efforts towards long term, concrete regional centralization. Secondly, through decades of soil abuse, the agricultural productivity of much of
Sumer had become severely limited creating an increasing dependence on food-
stuffs grown in the northern provinces of Sumer and Akkad. Thirdly, the continuing spread of Indo-European and Semitic peoples after the mid-third millennium
B.C. had begun to isolate Sumer and seriously challenge not only her dominance
of Lower Mesopotamia but her existence itself. The powerful rulers of the Third

Dynasty had initially been able to hold these nomadic and half savage tribes at a distance, but by the end of the third millennium B.C. the dam was ready to burst. The northern food producing regions first attracted the attention and then the violent assaults of the interlopers, who through the early domestication of the horse, afflicted the Sumerians with wave after wave of lightning swift attacks, creating both panic and famine in the populous southern city-states. The Sumerians called these roving tribes:

> . . .the MAR.TU who know no grain . . . The MAR.TU who know no house or town, the boors of the mountains . . . The MAR.TU who does not bend (to cultivate the land), who eats raw meat, who has no house during his lifetime, who is not buried after his death . . .[5]

Is this how the now mighty Semites and Indo-Europeans entered history? If so, as seems apparent, it is quite ironic. Any of these factors might have caused the decline of Sumer. Combined, they spelled their doom. The seemingly stable empire rapidly fell apart and Sumer's former vassals turned on her with a vengeance.[6]

By 1700 B.C. the Sumerian Black-heads, who for a thousand years had dominated the Mesopotamian center stage and laid the foundation for every near eastern civilization that was to come after it, had, in essence, vanished from history. Over the Black-headed people the winds swept.[7]

Heroic Elam

Elam was the first high-culture of Iran. It had many affinities with Sumer and shared her eastern border. The country was divided into two parts; Anshan and the mountainous north, and Susiana with its capital of Susa in the south. The early Elamites seem to have titled their land Anzan-Sousounka, with the term Elam perhaps introduced by the early Hebrew writers.

As is to be expected, a number of scholars, e.g., Elliot Smith, demonstrate numerous similarities between the material cultures of early Elam and the Nile Valley, including: arrow-heads, polished stone implements, pressure-flaking, mace heads, scripts, pottery forms, stone vases, female figurines, art motifs, and metal mirrors.[8]

The women of Elam, like their Nile Valley contemporaries, and women in early Black societies in general, held significant stature both as mortals and goddesses. The Elamitic woman's sphere of activity was not limited to the home. She signed documents, conducted important business transactions, inherited and willed fortunes, brought suits to the courts of law, and controlled servants. In early Elamite documents there is frequent mention of the mothers, sisters and daughters of the ruler. The existing evidence points to a matrilinear character of the royal succession.

Plate 2. Citizens of Susiana/Elam. Gaston Maspero describes the Elamites as "a short and robust people of well-knit figure with brown skins, black hair and eyes, who belonged to that Negritic race which inhabited a considerable part of Asia. . . . George Rawlinson records that, "In Susiana . . . there was . . . a very decided prevalence of a negro type of countenance. . . . The head was covered with short crisp curls; the eye large, the nose and mouth nearly in the same line, the lips thick."

Elamitic scholar George C. Cameron calls attention to Kirisha, a form of the mother-goddess, and claims that the " . . . hundreds of clay statuettes of this deity found in the course of the Susa excavations bespeak her whom the common people of Elam really worshipped."[9] Walther Hinz, in a significant work, *The Lost World of Elam*, is in complete harmony with Cameron:

> Pride of place in this world was taken by a goddess and this is typical of Elam. The treaty we have just mentioned opens with the following appeal: 'Hear, Goddess Pinikir, and you good gods of heaven!' Later, too, the Elamites saw Pinikir as the mistress of heaven endowed with the power to curse, and her name often forms a part of proper names . . . The very fact that precedence was given to a goddess, who stood above and apart from the other Elamite gods, indicates a matriarchal approach in the devotees of this reli-

gion . . . In the third millennium, these 'great mothers of the gods'; still held
undisputed sway at the head of the Elamite pantheon.[10]

Elam's Final Battle

The beginning of the seventh century B.C. ushered in the twilight of Elam.
This was the epoch marked by the wars with the Assyrians, whose imperial ambitions cast a giant shadow over all of western Asia and northern Africa. In all the
annals of human history, it is difficult to find any people with an appetite for
bloodshed and carnage to rival that of the Assyrians. The civility they did possess
was borrowed from the Sumerian Black-heads. Their chief contribution to the
modern world was their ability to preserve the religious and secular texts of their
predecessors.

The Assyrian state with its capital of Nineveh was a vast military machine.
The Assyrians introduced the first large armies with iron weapons, and unlike
many nations of antiquity, placed no dependence on foreign mercenaries whose
loyalties might shift at any time. The bulk of the Assyrian armies consisted of ar-
chers and heavily armed spearmen and shield bearers, horsemen and heavy
chariotry. These armies were well trained, absolutely ferocious, and utterly mer-
ciless, and employed battering rams and formidable siege machines.

The Assyrians elevated warfare to an exact science. They were not content to
merely conquer peoples; they must completely destroy them. Around the smok-
ing ruins that had been cities would stretch lines of tall stakes, on which were impaled the bodies of the defeated community leaders, flayed alive. Scattered about
were huge mounds of the viciously mutilated bodies of the dead and dying.
Those who survived the holocaust were deported to other regions of Assyrian
control.

Under the reign of Ashurbanipal, 669-626 B.C., the Assyrians reached their
destructive zenith. In 667 B.C. Egypt was invaded. In 663 B.C. she was again
invaded; this time with Ashurbanipal himself at the head of what must have
seemed like the legions of Hell. The Egyptian countryside was wasted; its splendid cities plundered. The many magnificent temples of Thebes, living re-
positories of the greatness that was Egypt, were looted and set ablaze. On his return to Nineveh, Ashurbanipal besieged the great Phoenician city of Tyre. In a
panic Tyre's ruler sent to Nineveh his own family heavily burdened with rich tribute and his own daughter for Ashurbanipal's harem.

After the Egyptian and Phoenician conquests, and the defeat of a host of lesser
states, the Assyrians directed their attention towards Elam. Elam, a highly formidable state in her own right, who had often struck terror in the regions of the
near east, had long contested the territorial ambitions of the Assyrians and, seiz-
ing the initiative, took the war to Nineveh's doorstep. So much of Assyria's

energies were directed to the Elamitic wars that Egypt, in 655 B.C., was able to regain her independence. At any other time Ashurbanipal would have led an army to stamp out the revolt. The Elamitic war effort however had grown so intense and exhausting that the Assyrians had to give up Egypt to maintain Asia.

In 639 B.C., after a prolonged resistance, Susa was overwhelmed. Her ziggurat was destroyed. The royal family was sent to its fate in Nineveh. The Assyrians made an example out of Susa. For 25 days their armies marched over Susa's remains, scattering salt over the ruins. "Wild beasts," declared Ashurbanipal, "would now be her occupants."[11] To a people conscious of a proud past there could be no greater humiliation.

Albeit in a severely diminished capacity, after the devastation of Susa, the Blacks of Elam remained an important regional factor. Herodotus finds them represented as Persian auxilaries in the Greco-Persian wars.[12] During this same period southern Baluchistan, extreme eastern Iran and western Pakistan, was known as Gedrosia, "the country of the dark folk." The Persian ruler Cyrus erected his winter capital at a rebuilt Susa, and it was in this now Persian city that the Biblical prophet Daniel resided. Even today the very same site is thought to house the tomb of Daniel.

In spite of the early and continued incursions of new peoples in the north, and the decisive defeat at the hands of the Assyrians, the ancient Susian Elamites distinguished themselves as a highly advanced and aggressive people who developed their land, and defended it from conquest again and again. Like the Sumerians of Mesopotamia they established a standard for civilization that the kingdoms and empires that followed could only imitate. 2500 years after its last national defense, reports of the remnants of this Kushite colony called Elam, with its Susian heartland, persist. In his *History of Persia*, Percy Sykes writes:

> Some years ago during the course of my travels, I was puzzled by the extremely dark populations of Baskakird and Sarhad, very remote and mountainous regions bordering on Persian Baluchistan. The solution may be that the whole country was originally peopled by Negritoes, the Anariakoi or Non-Aryans of the Greeks, who probably stretched along the northern shores of the Persian Gulf to India and that their descendants have survived in those distant parts.[13]

Massey describes this group, whom he calls Lumluns, as anthropologically allied to the Bisharis of the Egyptian/Sudanese border region.[14] According to George Rawlinson, "Even now the ancient Susiana is known as Khuzistan, the land of Khuz, or of the Cushite."[15]

Africans in Early South Arabia

The Arabian Peninsula, first inhabited over 8,000 years ago, was, like much of Asia, initially populated by Black people. Their descendants can still be found,

Plate 3. Remains of the famed Marib Dam, once capable of irrigating 4,000 acres.

in fact, in the peninsula's southern extremities. Generally classed as Veddoids by anthropologists, these Blacks today form numerically significant portions of the region's Africoid Mahra population. They are the earliest Arabians that we are aware of, and derive their name from essentially identical peoples, culturally and physically, in nearby Sri Lanka (Ceylon). Their hair varies from slightly wavy to curly; their skin complexions from light to dark brown. These were the first Arabians. They were black in the beginning and remain so to this day.[16]

When we speak of Arabian civilization, and particularly so in the pre-Islamic phase, we speak most prominently of the peninsula's southwestern regions (Yemen, P.D.R. of Yemen and western Oman). Here lies perhaps the most fertile land in all of Arabia. This was the Arabia Felix (Happy Arabia) of Greek and Roman literature. In this region geometric objects of obsidian composition, with East African origins survived well into the first millennium B.C.[17]

In addition to the arrival of East African settlers, there were at least two major migrations, the first before 1500 B.C., the second around 1100 B.C., into southern Arabia by nomadic peoples from the northern and central sections of the peninsula.[18] The consequence of the resulting physical and cultural interaction was the Sabean culture, or, more precisely, the Sabean civilization. The Sabeans, named after their capital of Saba, are the first clearly distinct, and by far the most famous, dwellers of pre-Islamic Arabia.

We first hear of the Sabeans in the tenth century B.C. through the fabled exploits of its semi-legendary queen known as Bilqis in the *Koran*, Makeda in Ethiopia's *Kebra Negast (Glory of Kings)*, and the Biblical Queen of Sheba. Each of these documents provides a relatively clear picture of a highly developed and prosperous state marked by the pronounced general status of women. Bilqis/ Makeda was not an isolated phenomenon. Several times, in fact, do we hear of prominent women in Arabian history; the documents they are mentioned in making no commentary on husbands, consorts or male relatives. Either their deeds, inheritance, or both, enabled them to stand out quite singularly.

Around the beginning of the first millennium B.C., the period in which Makeda is thought to have lived, we find the emergence of a number of large urban centers with highly developed irrigation systems. With the domestication of the camel, the southern Arabians could effectively exploit the region's greatest natural resources-—frankincense and myrrh—which from the earliest historical periods were in constant demand from the eastern to the western extremities of the world's major civilizations. The best and most abundant sources of both these products were centered in southern Arabia and Somalia, just across the Red Sea.

Both frankincense and myrrh played a tremendously important role in the life of the great Nile Valley civilizations. Frankincense, for example, while extensively utilized for its perfume-like fragrance in religious observances, was equally valued for its medicinal properties. It was used both in the stoppage of bleeding, and as an antidote to poisons. Myrrh was employed for cosmetic purposes and formed an essential element in the all important mummification process.

It should also be pointed out that due to its very geographic location, southern Arabia was in a position to supplement her profits from the incense trade, as an exchange point and haven of safety for the numerous ships involved in the trade in luxury items from east to west. This centuries-old and highly lucrative trade involved vast quantities of products from silk to produce and spices, ebony and ivory, precious metals and fine jewels. The kingdoms of southern Arabia, of which Saba was the first and most important, understandably waxed rich in their roles as intermediary between regions. She carefully guarded all knowledge of her commerical enterprises and created the impression that she was the actual source of the great wealth which passed through her hands, and of course other than frankincense and myrrh she was not. One can easily understand why the region was known as Arabia Felix or Happy Arabia.

We hear of Saba again in the eighth century B.C. during the reign of the powerful Assyrian king Sargon II, 721-705 B.C. In a series of inscriptions detailing Assyrian military successes, we find specific mention of "Piru, the king of Musru, Samsi, the queen of Arabia, It'amra, the Sabean. The(se) are the kings of the seashore and from the desert. I received as their presents gold in the form of

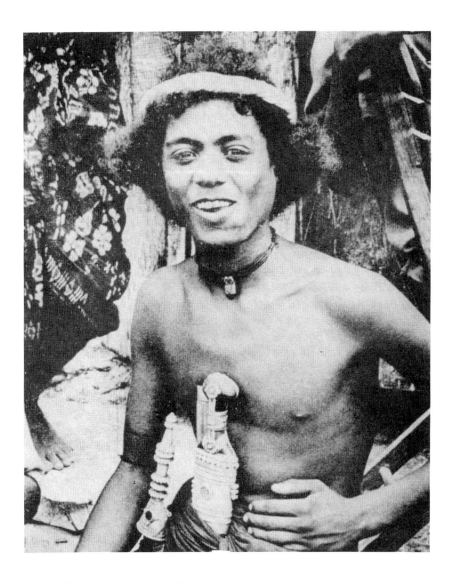

Plate 4. Southern Arabian youth.

dust, precious stones, ivory, ebony-seeds, all kinds of aromatic substances, horses (and) camels.''[19]

It was during this era that Sabean rulers were known as mukarribs, or priest kings. The earliest known Sabean construction projects are dated to this epoch, with the building materials consisting mainly of basalt, granite, and limestone, as the Awwam temple, frequently compared to the stone monuments of Zimbabwe, attests. The temple consisted of an oval wall enclosing an area approximately 300' east-west and 225' north-south. It was entered from the north through a large peristyle hall, containing a paved court surrounded by a series of rooms on all sides except the south. Beyond the court stood a line of eight monolithic pillars.[20]

The first constructions of the great Marib Dam were also begun at this time when two mukarribs, Sumuhu'alay Yanaf and Yithi'amara Bayyim, cut deep watercourses through the solid rock at the south end of the site. The Marib Dam, traditionally believed to have been conceived by Lokman, the great sage of Arabia, was Saba's greatest technical achievement, and served its builders and their descendants for more than a thousand years. In effect, the dam was an earthen ridge stretching slightly more than 1700' across a prominent wadi. Both sides sloped sharply upward, with the upstream side fortified by small pebbles established in mortar. The dam was rebuilt several times by piling more earth and stone onto the existing structure, with the last recorded height over 45'. Although the Marib Dam has now practically disappeared, the huge sluice gates built into the rocky walls of the wadi are very well preserved and stand as silent witnesses to the creative genius of the South Arabian people. When the great but periodic rains did come, the mechanism divided the onrushing waters into two channels which ultimately sustained the area's populace. Such was the force generated by the turbulent waters, however, that the dam was washed out from time to time. Reconstruction was a formidable task, and in one such operation 20,000 workmen were employed, many coming from hundreds of miles away.[21]

Our relatively sharp view of this early period in Sabean history is much more obscure in the succeeding centuries, as her power begins to gradually decline. At some point during this period, and perhaps even earlier, we find evidence of South Arabian settlement in Ethiopia's Tigre province. The resulting co-mingling of Ethiopian and South Arabian cultures produced the soon to be powerful African kingdom of Axum. The earliest Ethiopian alphabet is of a South Arabian type,[22] and the Axumite script is apparently a derivative of Sabean.[23] The name Abyssinia itself is taken from the Habashan, a powerful southwestern Arabian family which ultimately sojourned and settled in Ethiopia.[24] From this period Ethiopia, which itself is a Greek term, is known in Arabic scripts as Habashat and its citizens Habshi. This early Ethiopian-Sabean epoch lasted about a hundred years, beginning around the first part of the fifth century B.C., the remains of actual South Arabian settlements having been found principally at Yeha, Matara, and Haoulti, all in Tigre province.[25]

As the sceptre of South Arabian supremacy passed from Saba's hands, and also Ma'in, an early rival of Saba and apparently governed by a grand council, Qataban, another regional state, emerged as the area's foremost power. Timna, one of the more archaeologically explored sites in South Arabia, was Qataban's

Plate 5. Colossal Africoid head near Medina, Saudi Arabia.

capital and major urban center. Qataban reached its zenith about 60 B.C. during the reign of King Shahr Yagil Yuhargib, but afterwards went into a period of rapid eclipse. The power in South Arabia then shifted back to Saba in the west, albeit in a lessened form, and Hadramaut in the east, which occupied and destroyed Timna. Ausan, a lesser known state, also became distinct at this time. Ausan had such commercial ties with Africa, that in the *Periplus of the Erythraean Sea*, c. 60 A.D., the entire East Africa seaboard is known as the "Ausanitic Coast."[26]

Following the rise of Axum, Africans assumed a highly aggressive role in

Ethiopian-South Arabian relations. Between 183 and 213, for example the Ethiopian king Gadara, followed by his son, appear to have been the dominant figures in South Arabia.[27] Less than a century later, the Ethiopian king Azbah sent military contingents to South Arabia and apparently settled Ethiopian troops there as well.[28]

Saba was again occupied by Ethiopia from 335 to 370. The effects of this occupation were perhaps more long lasting than those preceding it, in that this one firmly implanted Christianity on South Arabian soil, with the Sabean rulers themselves adopting the faith. Christianity had already made considerable inroads in Arabia, as is evidenced by the attendance in 325 of six Arabian bishops at the historic Council of Nicea.[29] Christianity was to play a critical part in the remaining years of pre-Islamic Arabia. Initially, for example, the church suppressed the age-old burning of incense in religious rituals by deeming that it was a pagan tradition, and consequently an impediment to Christianity itself. When combined with the establishment of direct sea routes linking Asia with the west, South Arabian fortunes sharply diminished.

After a brief resurgence of Sabean power under the leadership of Malikkarib Yuhad'in, South Arabia, which in addition to its Christian population had attracted large numbers of Jews, witnessed an increasingly antagonistic relationship between the two religions and their adherents, soon resulting in a violent period of Christian persecutions and church burnings. This particularly virulent epoch of Christian martyrdom provoked an immediate response in Ethiopia, then headed by King Ella Asbeha, known as a formidable advocate of "Christian enlightenment." It is said, in fact, that a total of seven different saints lived under Ella Asbeha's patronage.[30]

In 524 a powerful coalition composed of the Eastern Roman Empire, South Arabian Christian refugees, and the Kingdom of Axum, was organized for the specific purposes of invading South Arabia and dethroning its ruling class. Byzantine supplied the ships, the South Arabians the advance guard, and the Ethiopians the bulk of the fighting forces. The coalition soon achieved their goals, and in the *Book of Himyarites* and the *Martyrdom of Arethius* we read of a great battle on the Arabian seashore where the Ethiopians were triumphant and the South Arabian king literally lost his head. Ethiopia once again possessed South Arabia's strongholds.

After seven months Ella Asbeha returned to Africa, leaving behind him a joint government of the South Arabian nobility and the Ethiopian military. This arrangement lasted until 532 when Abreha, a junior Ethiopian military officer, seized the South Arabian throne. The 3000 man Ethiopian army sent to suppress the revolt quickly defected to Abreha. A second expeditionary force Abreha rapidly and soundly smashed. Abreha's stunning success apparently was facilitated by the deep class contradictions within Ethiopian society, including the military, creating a base from which a former junior officer could rise to become one of the great personalities in Arabian history.

Although officially acknowledging Ethiopia's overall supremacy, Abreha worked unendingly to strengthen South Arabia's autonomy, extending her influence into the northern and central portions of the peninsula. Domestically, Abreha is known to have inaugurated major repairs on the Marib Dam. After his death in 558, Abreha's exploits were recorded and embellished in Arabic, Byzantine and Ethiopian literature, and no history of pre-Islamic Arabia is complete without him.

It was during this long series of wars involving Ethiopia, and later Persia, and the Islamic jihads themselves, that many of the major monuments in South Arabia were either damaged or destroyed. Such was the case with the fortress of Ghumdan, a truly superb construction, described most vividly in the tenth century by Al-Hamdani. Standing twenty stories high, the upper levels were composed of polished marble. The roof was made of stone so transparent that a crow could be seen flying overhead from underneath the building. On top of the fortress stood four bronze lions which roared when the winds blew.[31]

Before the arrival of Islam South Arabia had large and influential Christian and Jewish communities, upon which we have commented. In addition, she also possessed the sacred Kaaba sanctuary, with its black stone, at Mecca. The Kaaba was a holy place and the destination of pilgrims long before Mohammad. At the same time Allat, the Arabian goddess supreme, was worshipped at Ta'if, in Mecca's immediate proximity. Allat, quite simply, was the ultimate reality in female form, and was worshipped in the medium of an immense uncut block of white granite, as firm as the earth she represented. The most solemn oaths were sworn to Allat beginning with the words, ''by the salt, by the fire, and by Allat who is the greatest of all.''[32]

It was in this rich religious tradition that Muhammad, who was to unite the whole of Arabia, was born. The seeds of Islam were already ripe and Africa and Black people were instrumental in its nurturing. Black Bilal was such a pivotal figure in the development of Islam that he has been referred to as a third of the faith. Many of the earliest converts to Islam were African, and a number of the Muslim faithful sought refuge in Ethiopia because of initial Arabian hostility. As a parting note, we might add that according to Uthman Amr Ibn Bahr Al-Jahiz, the brilliant black writer and historian, the prophet Muhammad himself was of African lineage.[33]

Africans in Early Asia: 19th Century Perspectives

The story of the Black presence and heavy intermittent influence in Sumer, Elam, and Arabia are only a portion of the much wider story of Africans in early West Asia. This includes the Black role as the first Asian hominids, the first modern human populations, and the builders of the first and greatest Asian civilizations. The critical elements in the bold and adventurous Phoenician city-states; Sumer, the seminal high-culture of West Asia; and Elam, with its capital of Susa,

the home of Memnon and the tomb of the Biblical prophet Daniel, can each be
traced ultimately back to Africa's Nile Valley. The claim of modern "scholarship" that these were "Semitic" civilizations, or civilizations of "mysterious"
origins, is one of the great frauds of recent times. This has not, however, always
been the case, and this is particularly true of the 19th century. Ironically, it was
in this period, the zenith of European imperialism, with most of the world's surface conquered in the name of white supremacy and manifest destiny, that history, archaeology, and related sciences, as we currently know them, made giant
strides. European and American scholars now had an almost unprecedented and
unhindered access to the treasures of the world's past, largely hidden up to then.
Some of the most interesting postulations in respect to the place of the Black race
in the formation of early civilizations, in fact, were made during this transitional
period, before the modern standardizations of history's major themes.

Godfrey Higgins, 1772-1833, comes under this category. Through the publication of *The Celtic Druids* in 1829, and a much more massive work, *Anacalypsis*, published posthumously in 1836, Higgins was able to show an initial and all
pervasive Black presence and influence upon early Asia's major civilizations.
His numerous references to the Black Buddhas of India, the Black god Krishna,
and the Black Memnon, along with many others, establish Higgins as basic
reading material for students searching out the story of the Black presence in
Asian antiquity. Higgins was convinced, along with many others, that mankind
itself, of which the Black race was the first representative, owed its origins to
Asia, and specifically India, rather than Africa. The ugly face of racism can also,
unfortunately, be found in Higgins' work, for while he vociferously argued that
the Black man was the original man, he was equally emphatic in his insistence
that while first, he had subsequently become obsolete and utterly incapable of
competing with newer and more evolved races. Cited below are Higgins' exact
words:

> Now I suppose, that man was originally a Negro, and that he *improved* as
> years advanced and he travelled Westwards, gradually changing from the jet
> black of India, through all the intermediate shades of Syria, Italy, France, to
> the fair white and red of the maid of Holland and Britain. On the burning
> sands and under the scorching sun of Africa, he would probably stand still, if
> he did not retrograde. But the latter is most likely to have happened; and, ac-
> cordingly, we find him an unimproved Negro, mean in understanding, black
> in colour.[34]

What could be more explicit?

Francois Lenormant, 1837–1883, was a French archaeologist and member
of the Academy of Inscriptions and Belles-Lettres. Lenormant was a very
bright fellow who at the young age of fourteen published a major paper on
Greek inscriptions at Memphis. In the 1869 publication of volume one of
Ancient History of The East, Lenormant asserts an influential Kushite presence in early West Asia:

Of these two great nations who constituted the mass of the population of Chaldea, one was of the race of Ham and of the Cushite branch. The presence of Cushites in Chaldea and Babylonia is attested by the Bible, by Berosus, and by the universal testimony of antiquity.[35]

In this state, the first regularly organised government in the world, the preponderance and dominion among the various tribes belonged at first to the Hamites of the Cushite race.[36]

In volume two of *Ancient History of The East*, which appeared in 1871, Lenormant continued his established theme with the early Kanaanites, and ultimately the Phoenicians, and in another section, the southern Arabians. The following statements are typical of Lenormant:

The Phoenicians, as we read in the tenth chapter of Genesis, as they themselves asserted, and as their descendants informed Saint Augustine, belonged to the race of Canaan, who were, according to the biblical tradition, of the posterity of Ham. They were but a branch however, not the whole of the race, a branch among the most celebrated and the most permanent. In this book we shall speak specially of the Phoenicians, because they alone of their race played an important part in history; but first of all, by way of introduction, we must say a few words on the Canaanites in general, on their origin and their migrations, up to the time when the Sidonians or Phoenicians separated themselves from the other nations sprung from the same source, and organized themselves into distinct communities.

The Canaanites at first lived near the Cushites, their bretheren in race, on the banks of the Erythraean Sea, or Persian Gulf.[37]

Of the southern Arabians:

We may perceive the remembrance of a powerful empire founded by the Cushites in very early ages, apparently including the whole of Arabia Felix, and not only Yemen proper.

Circumcision established in Yemen from remotest antiquity, and several other pagan usages, still practiced in our days, appear to be of Cushite origin. Lokman, the mythical representative of Adite wisdom, resembles Aesop, whose name . . . seems to indicate an Ethiopian origin. In India, also, the whole literature of tales and apologues apparently come from the Sudras. Perhaps this style of fiction . . . may represent a style peculiar to the Cushites.[38]

John D. Baldwin, an American antiquarian, was the next writer to make significant additions to our knowledge of an ancient and overwhelmingly preeminent Ethiopian impact on the development of Asian high-cultures. 1872 saw the publication of Baldwin's most relevant work, that being *Pre-Historic Nations; or, Inquiries Concerning Some of The Great Peoples And Civilizations of Antiquity, And Their Probable Relations to a Still Older Civilization of the Ethiopians or Cushites of Arabia.*

Pre-Historic Nations, still interesting reading today, contains chapters on early Arabia, the Phoenician city-states, Mesopotamia, India, Egypt and North Africa, and western Europe. According to Baldwin, "The Cushite race appeared first in the work of civilization." And in further detail: "The Hebrews saw nothing geographical more ancient than this land of Cush. . . . The people described in the Hebrew Scriptures as Cushites were the original civilizers of Southwestern Asia; and that, in the deepest antiquity, their influence was established in nearly all the coast regions, from the extreme east to the extreme west of the Old World.[39]

Although written at a time when archaeology and related sciences were still in their infancy, *Pre-Historic Nations*, like *Anacalypsis* before it, is a tremendous repository of eye-witness accounts, both ancient and modern, of black history in early Asia. *Pre-Historic Nations* does contain, however, major drawbacks which are obvious and cannot be overlooked. Baldwin, like Higgins, had major problems with geography, as the text's lengthy subtitle suggests. The following statement nearly sums up Baldwin's position: "The original Ethiopia was not in Africa, and the ancient home of the Cushites or Ethiopians, the starting point of their great colonizing and civilizing movements, was Arabia."[40] "At that time Arabia was the exalted and wonderful Ethiopia of old tradition—the centre and light of what, in Western Asia, was known as the civilized world."[41]

Pre-Historic Nations, following tradition is also marred by racist thinking, through which Baldwin, when pressed, transforms as if by magic history's great Ethiopians into dark Caucasoids:

> In modern times, it has commonly been assumed, without proper inquiry, that the Ethiopians were of course Africans. This grave mistake has been the source of much misunderstanding and confusion . . . Careful students of antiquity now point out that 'the people of Ethiopia seem to have been of the Caucasian race,' meaning white men . . .[42]

Gerald Massey, 1828–1907, stands head and shoulders over even the most erudite 19th century antiquarians. Massey grew up in an atmosphere of intense intellectual activity, and it is interesting to note that among his London contemporaries were Karl Marx and Charles Darwin. Much to Massey's credit, his works are also refreshingly free of the blatantly racist commentaries so often included in antiquarian works. Massey was consistent in his geography and dedicated to truth irrespective of the consequences. Indeed, his statement, "Africa the birthplace and Egypt the mouthpiece," succinctly summarizes his philosophy, and is just as profound today as when it was originally penned.[43]

Massey's largest emphasis on the black foundations of Asian history and religions is contained in volume two of *Book of Beginnings*, published in 1881. Over two thirds of the text is devoted solely to Hebrew origins in Egypt. Moving east, *Book of Beginnings* includes a comprehensive comparative vocabulary of Akkadian/Assyrian and Egyptian words, followed by a telling chapter entitled "Egyptian Origines in Assyria."[44]

Marcel-Auguste Dieulafoy, 1884-1920, was a French archaeologist who, from 1884 to 1886, conducted major excavations at the ancient site of Susa, in what is now Iran. The results of the digs were published successively from 1890 to 1892 under the title *L'Acropole De Susa*.[45] In the first section, on Susa's history and geography, Dieulafoy devotes considerable space to the region's early Black inhabitants.

Dieulafoy's legacy is significant in that he focused on only one area; concluding that the black element in ancient Iran was highly prominent and has survived even into modern times. The text is accompanied by a set of extremely rare and quite distinct photographs of Susians with clear Africoid features, i.e., thick lips, broad noses, and tightly curled hair.

L'Acropole De Susa was unfortunately printed in limited quantities which are now extremely scarce. There has never been an English translation that we are aware of.

The last of the major 19th century writers whose works prominently address the black presence in early Asia are Henry C. Rawlinson, 1810-1895, and George Rawlinson, 1812-1902. The former is perhaps best known for his work from 1835 to 1844 in deciphering Mesopotamia's cuneiform scripts. Through his linguistic background Rawlinson was able to effectively identify the Kushite roots in West Asian scripts. The following passage, taken from his commentary to the 1858 publication of the *History of Herodotus* is representative of Rawlinson's views:

> Recent linguistic discovery tends to show that a Cushite or Ethiopian race did in the earliest times extend itself along the shores of the Southern ocean from Abyssinia to India. The whole peninsula of India was peopled by a race of this character before the influx of Arians; it extended from the Indus along the seacoast through the modern Beloochistan and Kerman, which was the proper country of Asiatic Ethiopians; the cities on the northern shores of the Persian Gulf are shown by the brick inscriptions found among their ruins to have belonged to this race; it was dominant in Susiana and Babylonia, until overpowered in the one country by Arian, in the other by Semitic intrusion; it can be traced, both by dialect and tradition, throughout the whole south coast of the Arabian peninsula, and it still exists in Abyssinia, where the language of the principal tribe (the Galla) furnishes, it is thought, a clue to the cuneiform inscriptions of Susiana and Elymais, which date from a period probably a thousand years before our era.[46]

George Rawlinson merely echoed his brother's assessment on the Asiatic Ethiopians, utilizing Biblical references as the primary evidence. In one of his finest works, *Origins of Nations*, published posthumously in 1912, Rawlinson's surveys trace the geneaologies of the races of man, with special emphasis on the Black or Hamitic race. His conclusions: ''The author of Genesis unites together as members of the same ethnic family the Egyptians, the Ethiopians, the Southern Arabians, and the primitive inhabitants of Babylon''[47]

Indus And India: Ethiopia's Eastern Bastions

As has been noted, the early African presence in Asia extended, and still exists in limited degrees, from the furthest western points to the continent's southern and eastern reaches, and far into the Pacific. The existence of an isolated Dravidian or South Indian language, namely Brahui, in Baluchistan, is one of the strongest datums in support of ongoing black migrations into the Asian interior in long distant times. In conjunction with this, extensive studies suggest that Elamite is cognate with the Dravidian family of languages.[50] The commentary of Diodorus Siculus, who wrote during the time of Augustus, reflects the same theme:

> From Ethiopia he (Osiris) passed through Arabia, bordering upon the Red Sea as far as to India, and the remotest inhabited coasts; he built likewise many cities in India, one of which he called Nysa, willing to have remembrance of that (Nysa) in Egypt where he was brought up. At this Nysa in India he planted Ivy, which continues to grow here, but nowhere else in India or near it. He left likewise many other marks of his being in those parts, by which the latter inhabitants are induced, and do affirm, that this god was born in India. He likewise addicted himself to the hunting of elephants, and took care to have statues of himself in every place, as lasting monuments of his expedition.[51]

The pronounced cultural developments of the Indus Valley complex, with its vast extensions into Central Asia and peninsular India, where its legacy remains distinct, owe their origins to Asia's early black presence. Based primarily on trade, the Indus Valley complex was at its height from about 2200 B.C. to 1700 B.C. This particular phase is called Harappan, the name being derived from Harappa, in the Punjab, one of the earliest known Indus Valley sites. Harappa actually attracted attention as long ago as 1856. No excavations were undertaken however until the 1920s, by which time Harappa had been savagely pillaged for building materials for a British engineered railway line. The severe damage inflicted upon the site through this callous indifference to one of the great cities of ancient times is incalculable.

In 1922 in Pakistan's Sind province, about 350 miles northeast of Harappa, her sister city, Mohenjo-daro (Mound of the Dead) was identified. Mohenjo-daro was almost an exact duplicate of Harapa, and in this case excavations began the same year. Mohenjo-daro and Harappa were apparently the chief administrative centers of the Indus complex, and since their discoveries several additional sites including Chanhu-daro, Kalibangan, Quetta, and Lothal, have been excavated.

The decline of the Harappan civilization has been attributed to several factors, including diminishing agricultural returns due to over cultivation; increased flooding due to tectonic disturbances in the Lower Indus; and increasing incur-

Plate 6. Ruins of Mohenjo-Daro, Indus Valley Civilization.

sions from aggressive and highly warlike nomads from Central Asia. By about 800 B.C. these nomadic Aryan tribes had conquered Pakistan and all of northern India, naming their newly won territories after themselves, Aryavarta, or the Aryan Land. Throughout Aryavarta a rigid, caste-segmented social order was established with the conquered blacks, the Sudras, relegated to the very bottom and imposed upon for service, in any capacity required, to the higher castes. These higher castes were the Brahmins, the Aryan elite, and identified with the color white; the Kshatriyas, the military and administrative sector, identified with the color red; the Vaisyas, merchants and farmers, and identified with the color yellow; and of course the Sudras themselves, identified with the color black. Beneath even the Sudras were the outcastes or untouchables, composed of the unfortunate offspring of Brahmin-Sudra unions, and long established Indian populations which had retreated into the hinterlands to escape the Aryan advances, but ultimately coming under the Aryan sphere of influence.

For the maintenance of the new order a detailed religious and legal code was implemented which regulated even the most minute aspects of daily life. In respect to the Sudras and outcastes the code was quite simply draconian, with few if any ambiguities about it. Because of the critical nature of this subject which is arguably the study of early race and cultural relations, several illustrative passages from *The Law of Manu* (Manu being a mythical Indian sage and lawgiver and supposedly a descendant of Brahman) are offered for critical examination:

> Twice-born (Brahmins, Kshatriyas, Vaisyas) who, in their folly, wed wives of the low (Sudra) caste, soon degrade their families and their children to the state of Sudras.

> He who weds a Sudra woman becomes an outcast, according to Saunaka on the birth of a son, and according to Bhrigu he who has (male) offspring from a (Sudra female, alone).

> A Brahmana who takes a Sudra wife to his bed, will (after death) sink into hell . . .[52]

> Let him not allow a dead Brahmana to be carried out by a Sudra, while men of the same caste are at hand; for that burnt-offering which is defiled by a Sudra's touch is detrimental to (the deceased's passage to) heaven.[53]

> A Brahmana . . . may, at the king's pleasure, interpret the law to him but never a Sudra.[54]

> A Kshatriya, having defamed a Brahmana, shall be fined one hundred (panas); a Vaisya one hundred and fifty or two hundred; a Sudra shall suffer corporal punishment.

> A Brahmana shall be fined fifty (panas) for defaming a Kshatriya; in (the case of) a Vaisya the fine shall be twenty-five (panas); in (the case of) Sudra twelve.[55]

> A once-born man (a Sudra), who insults a twice-born man with gross invective, shall have his tongue cut out; for he is of low origin.

> If he mentions the names and castes of the (twice-born) with contumely, an iron nail, ten fingers long, shall be thrust red-hot into his mouth.[57]
>
> If he arrogantly teaches Brahmanas their duty, the king shall cause hot oil to be poured into his mouth and into his ears.
>
> A low-caste man who tries to place himself on the same seat with a man of high caste, shall be branded on his hip and be banished, or (the king) shall cause his buttock to be gashed.
>
> If out of arrogance he spits (on a superior), the king shall cause both his lips to be cut off; if he urinates (on him), the penis; if he breaks wind (against him), the anus.[58]

For the Sudras and Outcastes, as we have noted and followed with the evidence, the Law of Manu was brutal and vicious and designed to keep them in their lowly caste position from generation to generation unto eternity. The very name for caste in Sanskrit is *varna*; literally, color. However there was a way upward, for the Sudras at any rate, and Manu himself articulates the method: "[A Sudra who is] pure, the servant of his betters, gentle in speech, and free from pride, and always seeks a refuge with Brahmanas, attains [in his next life] a higher caste."[58]

As the very name implies, the life of the Indian outcaste was full of misery and impoverishment. Food and drink, if seen by them, were not to be taken. Generally they lived in settlements on the outskirts of villages and towns. In certain periods in Indian history outcastes, or untouchables, were not allowed to enter the adjoining Hindu community at night, in other periods, in daylight. Indeed, the outcaste's very shadow was polluting. Outcastes were required to attach a broom to their backs to erase any evidence of their presence. A cup was tied around their necks to capture any spittle that might escape their lips. The sole untouchable possessions consisted of dogs and donkeys. Their meals were consumed from broken dishes. Their clothing was taken from corpses. The Principal functions of the outcastes included street sweeping, the removal of dead animals and human corpses, and the clean-up of cremation grounds; all of which was regarded as impure even by the Sudras.

The inevitable reactions to the social order were soon in coming and took diverse forms including the humanitarianism of the Jains and also Buddhism, which was much more pervasive and connected with Siddhartha Gautama in the sixth and fifth centuries B.C. An African or Black origin for the Buddha and Buddhism has been vigorously promulgated for centuries. Even the briefest glimpse at the early Buddha statuary of India and Southeast Asia, in particular, would seem to bear this out. Whether or not Gautama Siddhartha himself was born in Africa or Asia offers no significant obstacle to this assertion. Ktesias, for example, the first European to write a comprehensive general account of India, known to posterity as the *Indika of Ktesias*, mentions large concentrations of Blacks in the regions of the eastern Himalayas and the upper Ganges, where most accounts place the birthplace of Gautama.[59] As a final note on the Buddha's emergence, one cannot help but reflect upon the interesting parallels between immaculate conceptions in the Nile Valley, e.g. Isis and Horus, and India itself.[60] The mother of the Buddha, Maya, was said to be so pure, in fact, that neither man nor god could look upon her with lust. Buddhism placed little emphasis on caste, and was most popular in the central, eastern and southern portion of India, all of which were teeming with black populations.[61]

The Nanda Dynasty of fourth century B.C. India was of Sudra origin, and is quite downplayed in Indian histories. The Nanda Dynasty, like the Jains and Buddhism was another child born of India's rigid caste antagonisms. The apparent lack of popularity surrounding the Nanda family may be the result of the Sudra founder's determined seizure and consolidation of power, as revealed in early Indian literature:

> A son of Mahanandin by a sudra woman will be born a king, Mahapadma (Nanda), who will exterminate all ksatriyas. Thereafter kings will be of sudra origin. Mahapadma will be sole monarch, bringing all under his sole sway. He will be 88 years on the earth. He will uproot all ksatriyas, being urged on by prospective fortune. He will have 8 sons, of whom Sukalpa will be the first; and they will be kings in succession to Mahapadma for 12 years.

While we are limited in our knowledge of Mahapadma, by most accounts he was certainly a highly remarkable man, and is credited with halting Alexander's eastern advance with an army of 80,000 horses, 200,000 foot soldiers, 8,000 war chariots, and 6,000 elephants trained for battle. The center of his powerful, but short-lived dynasty, was Magadha, in what is now the East Indian state of Bihar, which then and now was dominated by black peoples. Until quite late in its history it was also notably absent of Aryan settlers, who regarded the region's populace with contempt. It could be pointed out here, to establish the region's stature, that Gautama himself not only travelled Bihar frequently but also received enlightenment here, as well as the friendship of its early rulers. Mahavira, a contemporary of Gautama and identified as the Jain's founding figure, was born in Bihar in 599 B.C. The Nandas were quite favorably disposed towards the Buddhists and Jains, and were widely known for their patronage of scholarship.

The Nandas were succeeded by the Mauryan Dynasty which was also of Sudra origin. The dynasty's founder was Chandragupta Maurya whose opportunity for power came as a result of the withdrawal of Alexander's expeditionary forces around 320 B.C. Stepping into the resulting vacuum in the Punjab and western India, Chandragupta assembled a huge army with which he marched east to confront the Nanda forces, who were ultimately vanquished.

During a 24 year reign Chandragupta considerably swelled the already large empire seized from the Nandas. Ultimately the Mauryas would rule what was then the largest empire in the world, from the Magadha kingdom's capital city, Pataliputra. Under Mauryan control Pataliputra became a magnificent and highly prosperous city. According to Fa-hien, " . . . the royal palace and the halls in the midst of the city, the walls and the gates and the inlaid sculpture work seemed to be the work of super-human spirits." [62]

Chandragupta was succeeded by his son Bindusara about 300 B.C. Bindusara's reign was one of economic expansion, with ever growing plots of land coming under cultivation.

Bindusara was succeeded by his son, Ashoka, the most singularly distinct personality of the Mauryan dynasty and one of the great kings in India's long history. Ashoka was coronated around 268 B.C. after the ouster of several rival princes. Buddhist accounts say that while he began his reign in the militaristic traditions of Chandragupta and Bindusara, in 261 B.C. Ashoka underwent a profound transformation. The great human suffering brought on from his successful suppression of a major revolt in Kalinga, in what is now Orissa, caused Ashoka to renounce violence and adopt Buddhism as his personal religion.

Through Ashoka's new vision, a series of social reforms were instituted which were exceedingly humane and even radical for the time. Through Ashoka's own words we read: "There is no better work than promoting the welfare of the whole world. Whatever may be my great deeds, I have done them in order to discharge my debt to all beings." [63]

By Buddhist accounts we learn that in his later years Ashoka became so involved in the Buddhist council of monks that the affairs of state were neglected and the king was overthrown in a palace coup. Ashoka's lasting impact upon the world, however, has been extensive. Buddhist diplomats were far and wide including Egypt, Libya, Greece, Rome and Southeast Asia, and probably China as well. To Sri Lanka Ashoka sent his own son with a branch of the Bodhi tree, under which Gautama received enlightenment, as a peace gesture.

The Mauryan dynasty went into a period of rapid decline following Ashoka's reign, and it seems fairly clear that it was a direct result of his very own foreign and domestic policies. Combined, however, the Nanda and Mauryan dynasties represent the spectacularly abrupt seizure of power by the lowly Sudra caste, and their subsequent unbroken rule for more than 150 years. Following the destruction of the Indus Valley civilization, the Nanda and Mauryan dynasties were the next major examples of Black power in India and Pakistan. This tradition of black greatness was maintained after the fall of the Mauryas in the far south of India among the newly emerging Dravidian kingdoms. The Dravidians were the "Eastern Ethiopians" mentioned in Greek literature, and only distinguished from the blacks of the west because of their straight hair. The Venetian traveller Marco Polo, who visited extensively in South India, made a number of vividly detailed observations on the Dravidians, with the following passage indicative of the blatant racial pride among them:

> It is a fact that in this country when a child is born they anoint him once a
> week with oil of sesame, and this makes him grow much darker than when

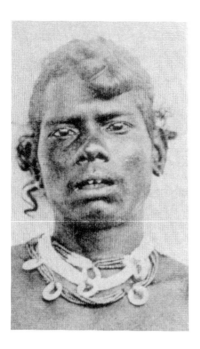 

Plate 7. Modern South Indian   Plate 8. Modern South Indian

he was born. For I assure you that the darkest man is here the most highly
esteemed and considered better than the others who are not so dark. Let me
add that in very truth these people portray and depict their gods and their
idols black and their devils white as snow. For they say that God and all the
saints are black and the devils are all white. That is why they portray them as
I have described. And similarly they make the images of their idols all
black.[64]

The above passage speaks for itself and needs little elaboration. The term
"Dravidian" itself is apparently derived from an Aryan corruption of Tamil, and
encompasses both an ethnic type characterized by straight to wavy hair textures,
combined with distinct Africoid physical characteristics; and a family of languages spoken by more than a hundred million people, including of course Tamil
itself, Telegu, Kannada, Malayalam (from which the name for the Asian country
Malaya is derived) and Tulu.

It is now the widely prevalent view that the Africoid Dravidians were the
founders of the great Indus Valley complex. They were the hated Dasas and

Plate 9. Sathya Sai Baba, "Sage of Southern India."

Dasyus of the *Rig Veda*; the perpetual adversaries of the invading Aryan nomadic tribes. These were the very same peoples, Dasas and Dasyus, that later became the Sudras, the conquered black masses reduced in Aryavarta to the status of slaves. As has been pointed out, the Harappan phase of the Indus Valley complex was already in decline when the Aryan incursions began to grow from a small trickle to a mighty torrent. The Aryans were undeniably responsible for the ultimate, and amazingly complete, destruction of the Indus Valley complex, and most of the identified Indus sites cease to be inhabited after this time. Those blacks who had continued to people the Indus sites during the decline but prior to the massive Aryan influx, either lost their lives during the holocaust or fled the region entirely with their remarkable cities ablaze behind them. The evidence is difficult to challenge on this point and the Aryans were cognizant of the ruins around them. The following Aryan passage illustrates our point most succinctly: "The people to whom these ruined sites, lacking posts, formerly belonged, these many settlements widely distributed, they, O Vaisvanara, having been expelled by thee, have migrated to another land."[65]

The lands the blacks migrated to were both within and without India. Thus for example we might point to the tradition preserved by the early Christian writer Eusebius who states that, "in the reign of Amenhotep III a body of Ethiopians migrated from the country about the Indus and settled in the Valley of the Nile."[66] The profundity of the just quoted passage is magnified when one considers that the reign of Ame III, 1417–1379 B.C., in the Nile Valley is contemporaneous with the Aryan incursions in the Indus Valley.

The Dravidians, on the other hand, are the living descendants of the Indus Valley migrants who journeyed south into the interior of India. This is certainly consistent with Dravidian traditions which recall flourishing cities that were lost or destroyed in ancient times. One might also see the links in the early seafaring posture of the Indus Valley people and the later Dravidian kingdoms of south India which were the great Indian maritime powers of their era. In the Indus Valley the mother goddess figure was conspicuous and this is most consistent with the early black civilizations of Africa and Asia as well. South India is no exception here and it has been noted that the Dravidian village deities are nearly all female, with the few exceptions in the Tamil country. In the Telugu districts, on the other hand, male deities are almost unrecognized in the Dravidian pantheon, the few who are, being relegated to the position of subordinate attendants upon the female divinities who hold the supreme power.

> This dominance of the female sex among the village divinities of the Dravidians who represent the main racial element present in India when the Aryan influx took place, is characteristic and is the converse of what we know was the case in Brahmanism and, to a lesser degree in modern Hinduism. In the latter the supreme deities who divide between them the devotional, adherence of the great mass of orthodox Hindus are both male-Siva and Vishnu. It is true that their various energies or active principles, their saktis, are deified in the persons of their wives, but this seeming exception is to be explained by the modifying influence exerted upon the orthodox Brahman faith by long and intimate contact with the aboriginal culture of the land, a culture which held mother goddesses as the most important divinities in its pantheon.[67]

From a remote period in Indian history three major kingdoms existed in South India which were Pandya, Chola, and Chera. Pandya was the southernmost kingdom, stretching from coast to coast. The major city of Pandya was Madura, flourishing as early as the beginning of the Christian era. In Madura is the famous chapel of the Tamil Sangam. The Sangam, of which there were three, were bodies of 48 learned scholars who established standards and ruled over all literary productions. The Pandyan kings received these intellectuals with great honors.

To the northeast of Pandya lay the Kingdom of Chola, said to house the resting place of Saint Thomas the Apostle. To the northwest of Pandya lay the Kingdom of Chera, which was later followed by a fourth power, the Pallava Kingdom.

The kingdoms of South India were quite well known in the west, having sent several embassies to Rome in particular, in spite of the great distance involved. During the height of their commercial relations South India was said to extract 100 million sesterces annually from the Roman economy.

Plate 10. Portion of Angkor Temple, 12th century.

Plate 11. Malaysian youth.

Black Power in Southeast Asia

The initial kingdoms of Southeast Asia emerged by the third century; the region first attracting attention as a rich source of coral, forest and mineral products, all of which were extremely valuable. In order to secure regular access

Plate 13. Buddha from early Thailand.

Plate 12. Buddha, 7th century Thailand.
Sandstone.

to these products, small colonies of Indian merchants were gradually established at strategic points throughout the area. With these Indians came their ideas about government, architecture, literature, religion, etc. Through the impetus of these Indian colonies, including strong Dravidian elements, and the native genius of the indigenous Mon, or Austric, populations, which were both highly Africoid and numerically significant, came the first Southeast Asian states. There is no evidence of large-scale migrations, armed invasions or forced conversions.

The first kingdom of Southeast Asia is called Funan, and located in what is now southern Kampuchea (Cambodia) and Vietnam. Chinese historians who visited the area described the Funanese men as "small and black," and detailed a picture of the safe anchorage and large warehouses offered to the numerous merchant fleets which frequently passed through the area.

Besides Funan's commercial activities, the most critical element to her existence, and the succeeding kingdoms as well, was an elaborate network of waterworks and canals designed to control both the annual flooding and the encroachments of the sea. The major Funanese cities, of which Oc-Ec, Hundred Roads, and Angkor Borei were the most important, were laid out along these canals, with boats used to sail into them. All of this of course precedes the famed canals of Venice by centuries.

Plate 14. Buddha protected by the naga Mucilinda, Thailand, circa 7th-8th century. Limestone relief. National Museum, Bangkok.

Funan began to decline in stature in the sixth century due to loss of the vital trade routes coupled with major agricultural reverses. Her last king, Rudravarman, 514–539, was a devotee of Vishnu and sent several diplomatic missions to China whose influence in the region was then expanding.

Chen-La was the successor kingdom to Funan, and emerged as the result of a political marriage between the grandson of Rudravarman and a Chen-La princess, following which the center of regional power was shifted north, where stone was abundant and utilized as the major building material for the first time. The history of Chen-La is much the same as that of Funan. At some point late in the eighth century trade with India was disrupted, resulting in an

Plate 15. Head of Buddha, Thailand, 14th century. Bronze.

administrative break down while Chen-La collapsed into a feuding group of small and insignificant states, and for a short time the regional power shifted to Indonesia where the Shailendra dynasty was ruling with vigor. The most significant and long-lived of the South Asian states was centered at Angkor, Kampuchea, and was much more empire than kingdom. The roots of Angkor can be traced back to Funan, Chen-La, and the Shailendras of Indonesia, Indianized states all. Angkor was designed to be completely self sufficient, and was filled with great stone temples and a large and thriving population. The key factor was a magnificent irrigation project, the basis of which was a series of huge artificial reservoirs fed by the local rivers and linked to each other by a rectangular grid system of canals. The reservoirs, called barays, were placed at the highest point in the river system, and were utilized to supply an immense chain of irrigation channels spreading out over the low lands.

During the more than 640 years of Angkor's life, great rulers emerged one after the other, leaving their marks upon the world in the form of stupendous temple islands, the vast artificial lake known as the Indratataka, and the temple mountains of Angkor Wat and Angkor Thom and Bayon, among the most conspicuous.

Even during her greatness Angkor was afflicted with ongoing battles with the Champa kingdom to her southeast. Champa was a central Indian colony and shared many elements of Angkor's material culture, but was somewhat weaker and less fortunate in location and natural resources.

The ultimate fate of the black kingdoms of Southeast Asia can be effectively linked to the rising influx of Mongoloid racial types from the north. Even the Mon kingdoms of Thailand and Burma, possessors of the most Africoid statuary of Buddhas and Bohdisattvas in the world, were ultimately overwhelmed.

The story of the black kingdoms of Southeast Asia is, in essence, the story of the black race in early Asian history; builders of the earliest kingdoms, only to be overwhelmed in the end. The early and intermittent Black influence in Asia, however, is permanent and everlasting, and the Asian nations of today, whether conscious of it or not, have merely raised themselves under an African tutelage.

Notes

1. Henry Field, *Ancient And Modern Man in Southwestern Asia* (Coral Gables: University of Miami Press, 1956), pp. 84-85.

2. Diop illustrates the common physiognomy of the now famous portrait statue of Ramses II, in the Turin Museum, and a modern Watutsi from Central Africa. Cheikh Anta Diop, *African Origin of Civilization* (Lawrence Hill & Co.: New York, 1974), p. 19.

3. T.K. Penniman, "A Note on The Inhabitants of Kish Before The Great Flood," *Excavations at Kish*, Vol. 4, pp. 65-72.

4. George C. Cameron, *History of Early Iran* (Chicago: University of Chicago Press, 1936, rpt. 1976), p. 55.

5. E. Chiera, *Sumerian Epics And Myths*; Chicago, 1934, nos. 58 & 112.

6. "The death blow came at the hands of the Elamites from the eastern," (One must remember

that there were different racial and cultural elements in Susa/Elam. By the beginning of the second millennium B.C. non-Africoid types became predominant in Iran's mountainous regions)'' . . . hills, who overran Sumer and carried off the last king of the Third Dynasty, the temples plundered of their treasures. At the same time, Amorite tribes led by the ruler of Mari occupied the land of Akkad. This disaster marks the end of Sumerian political leadership in Mesopotamia. The territories of the Third Dynasty broke apart into city-states, such as Isin and Larsa; and the empires to follow in Mesopotamia, down to the Persian, were run by Semites.'' William H. McNeill, *The Origins of Civilization* (Oxford University Press: London, 1968), pp. 67-68.

7. ''Over the black-headed people the winds swept. The people groan . . . Covered Ur like a garment, enveloped it like linen . . . The raging storm has attacked unceasingly. The people groan . . . In its boulevards where the feasts were celebrated they were viciously attacked. In all its streets where they were wont to promenade, dead bodies were lying about; In its places where the festivities of the land took place the people were ruthlessly laid low. Mothers and fathers who did not leave (their) houses were overcome by fire. The young lying on their mother's bosoms like fish were carried off by the waters. The nursing mother—pried open were their breasts. The black-headed people wherever they laid their heads . . . were carried off.'' ''Lamentation Over the Destruction of Ur,'' S.N. Kramer, ed. *Assyriological Studies*, No. 12, Oriental Institute (Chicago: University of Chicago Press, 1940).

8. G. Elliot Smith, *Human History* (New York: Norton & Co., 1929), pp. 365-368.

9. Cameron, p. 21.

10. Walther Hinz, *Lost World of Elam*, trans. J. Barnes (New York: New York University Press, 1973), pp. 42-43.

11. D.D. Luckenbill, *Ancient Records of Assyria And Babylonia*, V. 2 (Chicago: University of Chicago Press, 1927), pp. 309-312.

12. Herodotus, *The Histories*, trans. Aubrey de Selincourt (New York: Penguin Books, 1972), p. 468.

13. Percy Sykes, *History of Persia*, v. 1 (London, MacMillan, 1930), p. 51.

14. Gerald Massey, *Book of Beginnings*, v. 2 (Secaucus: University Books, 1881, rpt. 1974), pp. 518-519.

15. George Rawlinson, *Egypt And Babylon* (New York: John W. Lovell), p. 10.

16. ''Non-Mediterranean Veddoids live as a minority in parts of the southern Yemen and the Western Aden Protectorate; in the Hadhramaut they become numerically important, while still farther east they are the chief factor in the tribes of Mahra-land, at the extreme end of the Aden Protectorate, and the Shahara, Qara, and other tribes in the Sultanate of Oman. All these tribes speak pre-Arabic Semitic languages.'' Naval Intelligence Division, *Western Arabia And The Red Sea* (June, 1946), pp. 368-369.

17. Naval Intelligence Division, pp. 213-214.

18. Wendell Phillips, *Oman* (Reynal & Co., n.d.), p. 2.

19. James B. Pritchard, *Ancient Near East* (London: Oxford University Press, 1958), pp. 196-197.

20. Phillips, p. 233.

21. L. Sprague & Catherine De Camp, *Ancient Ruins And Archaeology* (New York: Doubleday & Co.).

22. Yuri M. Kobisachanov, *Axum* (Moscow: Nauka, 1966).

23. Kobisachanov.

24. J. Doresse, ''Ethiopia and Southern Arabia,'' *Kush*, v. 5, 1957, p. 59.

25. Kobisachanov.

26. *Periplus of The Erythraean Sea*, trans. W. Schoff (London: Longmans, Green, & Co., 1912), p. 23.

27. Kobisachanov, pp. 48-49.

28. Kobisachanov, pp. 67-68.

29. Phillips, p. 225.

30. Kobisachanov, p. 97.

31. DeCamp, p. 100.

32. Patricia Monaghan, *The Book of Goddesses And Heroines* (New York: Dutton, 1981), p. 10.

33. Uthman 'Amr Ibn Bahr Al-Jahiz, *The Book of The Glory of The Black Race* (Los Angeles: Preston Publishing Co., rpt. 1981), p. 52.

34. Godfrey Higgins, *Anacalypsis*, v. 1 (London: Longman, 1836), p. 284.

35. Francois Lenormant, *Ancient History of The East*, v. 1 (London: Asher & Co., 1869), p. 342.

36. Lenormant, p. 348.

37. Lenormant, v. 2, p. 144.

38. Lenormant, pp. 296, 318.

39. John D. Baldwin, *Pre-Historic Nations* (New York: Harper & Brothers, 1872), pp. 17-18.

40. Baldwin, p. 21.

41. Baldwin, p. 47.

42. Baldwin, p. 48.

43. Gerald Massey, *Ancient Egypt*, v. 1 (New York: Samuel Weiser, 1970).

44. Gerald Massey, *Book of Beginnings*, v. 2 (Secaucus: University Books, 1881, rpt. 1974).

45. Marcel A. Dieulafoy, *L'Acropole De Susa* (Paris: Hachette, 1892).

46. George & Henry Rawlinson, *History of Herodotus*, v. 1 (London: John Murray, 1858), p. 650.

47. George Rawlinson, *Origin of Nations* (New York: Charles Scribners' Sons, 1912), p. 214.

48. Quoted by T.K. Joseph, "India, a Continuation of Egypt and Ethiopia," *Journal of Indian History*, Vol. 26, 1948, pp. 201-207.

49. Quoted by W.R. Halliday, *Folklore Studies* (London: 1924).

50. David W. McAlpin, "Toward Proto-Elamo-Dravidian," *Language*, V. 50, No. 1, pp. 89-101; see also David W. McAlpin, "Elamite And Dravidian: Further Evidence of Relationship," *Current Anthropology*, V. 16, No. 1, pp. 105-115. The most fruitful efforts in the decipherment of the Indus Valley script have come as the result of utilizing modern Dravidian scripts as the foundation. Linguistic proof: In a combinatory analysis (A2 to 4) the linguistic type of the language of the Indus inscriptions appears to be agglutinative: of the languages known from the Indian subcontinent only the Dravidian languages belong to this type. The declension paradigm discovered fits to the declension of Dravidian. The alternation of a zero suffix and the genitive suffix which is attested in the Indus inscriptions is a characteristic of Dravidian. The decipherment displays an earlier stage of development of Dravidian, which corresponds to expectations (etymologies of suffixes). The word order is the same in Dravidian and the Indus inscriptions. The homophony laws are in accordance with the morpheme structure of Dravidian. *Journal of Tamil Studies*, Special Number on The Decipherment of The Mohonjo-daro Script, V. 2, No. 1, May 1970.

51. Diodorus Siculus, Book 1, 11, 12.

52. *The Law of Manu*, trans. G. Buhler (Delhi: Motilal Banarsidas, 1979), pp. 78, 15, 16, 17.

53. Manu, pp. 187: 104.

54. Manu, pp. 255: 20.

55. Manu, pp. 301: 267, 268, 270.

56. Manu, pp. 302: 271, 272.

57. Manu, pp. 303: 281, 282, 283.

58. Manu, pp. 401: 335.

59. *Ancient India as Described by Ktesias The Knidian*, trans., ed. J. McCrindle (London: Trubner & Co., 1882), pp. 84-85.

60. Kersey Graves, *The World's Sixteen Crucified Saviors, or Christianity Before Christ* (New York: Truth Seeker Co., 1875; rpt. 1960).

61. "Maya, the mother of Buddha, and Devaki the mother of Crishna, were worshipped as virgins, and represented with the infant Saviours in their arms, just as the virgin of the Christians is rep-

resented at the present day. Maya was so pure that it was impossible for God, man, or Asura to view her with carnal desire . . . Crishna and his mother are almost always represented black, and the word Crishna means the black.'' T.W. Doane, *Bible Myths*, (New York: Truth Seeker Co.; rpt. 1970), pp. 326-327.

62. B.N. Puri, *Cities of Ancient India* (Meerut: Meenakshi Prakashan, 1966), p. 64.

63. Romila Thapar, *Asoka And The Decline of the Mauryas* (Oxford University Press, 1977).

64. *The Travels of Marco Polo*, trans. R. Latham (Middlesex: Penguin Books, 1982), p. 276.

65. Quoted by T. Burrow, in ''Early Imperial India,'' *The Encyclopedia of Ancient Civilizations*, ed. Arthur Cotterell (New York: Mayflower Books, 1980), p. 184.

66. Quoted by George Rawlinson, *Ancient Monarchies*, v. 1 (New York: Dodd, Mead, & Co., 1881) p. 49. There is the story of the Ethiopian king Ganges, conveyed by Samuel Purchas, ''who with his Ethiopian army passed into Asia and conquered all as far as the River Ganges . . .'' *Purchas: His Pilgrimage*, Bk. 7, Africa, p. 551; ''In the last century, in regards to Denderah, before the Suez Canal was cut, Indian army troops passed by long journey from Calcutta to Portsmouth. Much to the amazement of their British officers, the Sepoys identified the huge images of Hathor as one of their own Hindu gods, and worshipped in the great empty temple.'' John Romer, *People of The Nile*, p. 214

Some Hindus claim the Nile to be one of their sacred rivers; they also regard as sacred the Mountains of the Moon (in Uganda-Congo) and Mount Meru (in Tanzania). In both India and the Indianized kingdoms of Southeast Mount Meru was regarded as the mythical dwelling place of the gods. Each of these statements reflect millenia old relationships between the blacks of Africa and South Asia. The Ethiopian *Kebra Negast* regarded Western India as a portion of the Ethiopian Empire. ''Murugan, the god of mountains, the son of the mother goddess is a prominent and typical deity of the Dravidian India. It is interesting to note that at least twenty-five tribes in East Africa worship 'Murungu' as supreme god, and like the Dravidian god Murugan, the African Murungu resides in sacred mountains.'' U.P. Upadhyaya, ''Dravidian And Negro-African,'' *International Journal of Dravidian Linguistics*, v. 5, No. 1, January 1976, p. 39.

67. James Hornell, ''The Ancient Village Gods of South India,'' *Antiquity*, vol. 18, No. 69, March 1944, pp. 82-83; ''Even today, in almost all villages of Southern India a form of the mother goddess is worshipped as a village deity and she is specially worshipped to ward off the evil spirits and contagious diseases or epidemics and the rituals associated with this worship do not bear any influence of the Aryan customs and the Brahminical ways of worship. The word amma used to refer to this village goddess as well as the disease of smallpox etc. caused or cured by her will have its parallel in the same word amma used by the Dogons of French Sudan. As in Dravidian India, altars are built in those parts of Africa also for sacrifice and communal worship for deity amma.'' Upadhyaya, p. 40.

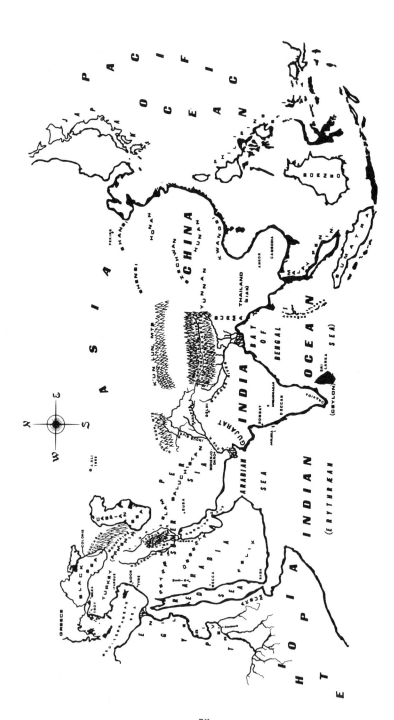

Map of Asia.

EGYPTIAN CIVILIZATION IN COLCHIS ON THE BLACK SEA

R.A. Jairazbhoy

The Greek historian Herodotus makes extraordinary assertions about Colchis on the eastern shores of the Black Sea, the same where Jason sailed with the Argonauts. He says that "there can be no doubt that the Colchians are an Egyptian race. Before I had heard of any mention of the fact from others, I had remarked it myself."[1] Herodotus goes on to say that he investigated the matter on both sides, and found that the Colchians had a more distinct recollection of the Egyptians than the Egyptians had of them. According to him the latter believed that the Colchians were descended from the army of Sesostris. Herodotus says that his own conjectures were "founded first on the fact that they are black-skinned and have woolly hair." And he offers two more evidences of his claim—the practice of circumcision, and the art of linen weaving, both of which he elaborates.

Herodotus is quite categorical that the Egyptians are the only people in the world who use circumcision, apart from "those who have learned the practice from them.[2] The Palestinians themselves confess that they learned the practice from the Egyptians, and the Syrians say that they have recently adopted it from the Colchians. Now these are the only nations who use circumcision, and it is plain that they all imitate here the Egyptians."[3] How likely is it that Herodotus is correct in this matter? The case can be tested against the Jews, most famed of all the ancients for the practice of this rite. From Biblical evidence itself we learn that they adopted it from the Egyptians. According to Joshua (Verses 2-9) "all the people that came out of Egypt were circumcised, but those born in the wilderness were not." And an obvious connection appears to be that both used stone knives for the purpose, according to Pliny.[4] If the Jews adopted circumcision from the Egyptians, it is hardly surprising that the Pre-Colombian Indians would have in turn adopted it from them also. That they did so they readily admit when they say that the practice of circumcision was introduced "by a visitor."[5]

On the second of his evidences Herodotus is equally firm. He insists that Colchian linen (which the Greeks call Sardinian) is woven in exactly the same way as the Egyptian, and both are different from the rest of the world.[6]

But is Herodotus correct in his information that Sesostris sent the Colchians? Sesostris I built ships and sent them to the region of Bia Punt, and his port of the Red Sea was discovered just the other day.[7] And Sesostris III certainly made many conquests in the 19th Century B.C. Margaret Murray has suggested that the soul houses of the Tripolye culture on the Dneiper of the same period are influenced by those of 12th Dynasty Egypt.[8] Nevertheless other evidences suggest

Plate 1. The description of Phrixus' *golden ram with a snake
overlooking it* exactly matches the prow of the solar ship of
Rameses III. Note that this is the only Egyptian pharaoh to
claim that he sent naval expeditions to the far corners of the
world. (Reconstruction of Bjorn Landstrom, *The Ships of the
Pharaohs*, 1970, pp. 120-121.)

that the Greek contact with the East Coast of the Black Sea took place in or
around the time of Rameses III. Archaeologically this is attested by sub-
Mycenaean fibula of the 12th-11th Century B.C. found in excavations in West-

ern Georgia,[9] and from literary sources. The date given for the Argonautic expedition is 1225 B.C. by Eratosthenes, and 1263-1257 B.C. by Eusebius.[10] Now I shall attempt to show that some of the chief elements of the Jason legend have an Egyptian origin.

The Ram

Jason was in search of the golden ram of Phrixus, and this is why he undertook the voyage to the river Phasis.[11] He is said to have worn a cloak pictured with Phrixus's ram.[12] The tale told about Phrixus, the Minyan from Orchomenos in Boeotia, is that his mother gave him a golden-fleeced ram, and he fled, taking this with him to Colchis. The fleece had been spread on an oak in front of Aeetes' city at the mouth of the Phasis.[13] The fleece is described as being "watched over by a serpent."[14] Such a golden ram's head overlooked by a serpent occurs nowhere else than on a prow of a ship of Rameses III (and of one of his predecessors). The ship was named Userhet, it was 130 cubits long (about 200 feet), and had golden rams on both prow and stern, each with a uraeus serpent overtopping it surmounted with the sun's disk.[15] Below is a grand collar, which could have been mistaken for its fleece.

The Fleece

Neither Homer nor Hesiod mention the golden fleece. However a lost passage of Hesiod preserved by the Scholiast on Apollonius' poem does say that Jason was seeking Phrixus' golden ram.[16] So this suggests that the ram was primary and the fleece secondary. But even the fleece in a special context has Egyptian undertones. Herodotus describes the festival of Jupiter (Amun) when they slay a single ram, and strip off its fleece to cover the statue of that god. They then mourn for the ram and bury it in a holy sepulchre. Otherwise, he says, the Thebans do not sacrifice rams but consider them as sacred animals.[17] This leads us back to Phrixus, for we are told that at the oracular shrine founded by him, a ram was never sacrificed.[18] Strabo has a more prosaic explanation for the golden fleece, and suggests that it arose through the gold washed down by mountain torrents being collected using fleecy skins.[19] Which of us is correct remains to be seen. I submit that his is a pure guess, while mine is backed by a close set of parallels.

The Sun King

The king Aeetes who ruled at the mouth of the Phasis was given the epithet 'son of Helios.'[20] He was thus 'son of the Sun' which is the exclusive title in antiquity of the Pharaohs of Egypt.

Plate 2. Map of Western Asia.

The Solar Shrine

   The sanctuary of Phrixus appears to have been a sun temple. Strabo cites Min-
nermus (as preserved by Scepsis) to the effect that Jason's voyage extended to the
lips of Oceanus where the sun lies in a chamber of gold.[21] This again recalls the
same ram-emblemed Barge of the Sun of Rameses III which had "its great shrine
in the midst of fine gold."[22] In siting this temple on the *confines* of Colchis
Strabo says that it was a small well fortified city in Iberia, the present Idëwesa.[23]
There must have been the intention to place it on the edge of Oceanus, for there
was a very real belief in Oceanus surrounding the inhabitable world: it is attested
by Homer, and confirmed by Strabo who says that the sun rises and sets in

Oceanus.[24] This is 'the Great Circuit of the Ocean' (*sn-wr*) of Rameses III's inscriptions.[25] And when Apollonius says that the Egyptian pirests of Thebes knew of another way back for the return of the Argonauts[26] he is evidently referring to the streams of the Ocean, for one Greek variant does say that they ascended the river Phasis, got to the streams of the Ocean, and so sailed around till they reached the Mediterranean.[27]

Strabo records that the once rich shrine of Phrixus had recently been robbed by invading rulers, but if a protracted search succeeds in finding the site, it would no doubt reveal (perhaps in a dramatic way) why here in this remote place the Sun and Leucothea, the white goddess of the sea, may have been both worshipped together.[28]

Postscript

Classical texts can help in the search for ancient Colchis sites. Strabo[29] and Pliny[30] describe the location of the chief towns on the Phasis (later known as Rioni). Since mileages are given and some geographical features, they may be of some help in identification. It appears that the ancient site of Phasis has been recently identified by Soviet archaeologists (the problem having been aggravated by a substantial amount of silting at the mouth of the river). The site of Vani (60 miles from the sea) has yielded rich classical remains. When there were 120 bridges over the Phasis,[31] and 70 languages were spoken in the area,[32] there can be no doubt that in due course a rich sequence of cultures will emerge as a result of strenuous efforts by the Georgian Academy of Sciences.[33]

References

1. *History*, 2, 104.
2. *History*, 2, 36.
3. *History*, 2, 104.
4. *Natural History*, XXXV, 46.
5. Jairazbhoy, R.A., *Ancient Egyptians in Middle and South America*, London, 1981, p. 33.
6. *History*, 2, 105.
7. Abd el Monem A.H. Sayed, "The recently discovered port on the Red Sea shore," *Journal of Egyptian Archaeology*, 1978, pp. 69f.
8. Murray, M.A., *The Splendour that was Egypt*, (Four Square ed.), London, pp. 259-60.
9. Lordkipanidze, O., *The Antique World of Ancient Colchis* (in Georgian), 1966, p. 176.
10. Bacon, J.R., *The Voyage of the Argonauts*, London, 1925, p. 143.
11. Apollonius, *Argonautica*, 4, 284.
12. *The Voyage of Argo*, tr. F. Rieu, 1959, pp. 56-7.
13. *Argonautica*, 1959, *ibid*, p. 84.
14. *Argonautica*, 1959, *ibid*, p. 84.
15. Reconstruction of B. Landstrom, *Ships of the Pharaohs*, 1970, pp. 120-1.
16. *Argonautica*, 4, 284.
17. Herodotus, *History*, II, ch. 41-3.

18. Strabo, *Geography*, XI, 2, 17-18.
19. Strabo, *Geography*, XI, 2, 18-19.
20. *Argonautica*, 1959, *ibid*, p. 106.
21. Strabo, *Geography*, I, 2, 40.
22. Breasted, J., *Ancient Records*, IV, §209, and Landstrom, *op. cit.*, p. 120.
23. Strabo, *Geography*, II, 2, 18-19.
24. Strabo, *Geography*, I, I, 1-3.
25. Breasted, J., *op. cit.*, IV, p. 25, Jairazbhoy, *op. cit.*, 1974, pp. 12-13.
26. *Argonautica*, 1959, *ibid*, p. 154.
27. See Janet R. Bacon, *The Voyage of the Argonauts*, London, 1925.
28. Strabo, *Geography*, tr. H.L. Jones, 1932, V, p. 213.
29. Strabo, *Geography*, XI, 2, 17-18.
30. Pliny, *Natural History*, VI, 4, 11-14.
31. Pliny, *Natural History*, loc. cit.
32. Strabo, *Geography*, tr. H.L. Jones, vol. 5, pp. 209, 211, 241.
33. It could be that the Egyptians of the Black Sea colony influenced the Scythians of the Altai mountains who embalmed their bodies. Although they evidently did not use natron, they did remove the brain and internal organs, and the men wore artificial beards.

THE SCRIPT OF THE INDUS VALLEY CIVILIZATION

Walter A. Fairservis, Jr.

The oldest civilizations are those of Sumer, Egypt, China and the Indus Valley in the northwestern part of the subcontinent now occupied by India, Pakistan and Bangladesh. The writings of the first three civilizations can be read; the inscriptions of the fourth one remain largely enigmatic. As a result what is known of the Indus Valley civilization comes solely from the material objects brought to light by archaeology. It is ironic that in a part of the world noted for the antiquity of its literature even the most ancient accounts contain no valid reference to the first great culture that thrived there.

The culture of the Indus Valley civilization is called Harappan, after one of its two great cities: Mohenjo-Daro and Harappa. The difficulties that face those who would decipher Harappan writing seem at first virtually insurmountable. They derive in large part from the Harappans' limited use of their script. Their "texts" consist almost exclusively of brief inscriptions on seals and equally limited graffiti on pottery. No known inscription consists of more than 21 signs and the average text numbers only five or six. This, coupled with the fact that many of the signs are pictographic, has let the imagination of more than a few scholars run riot. Earnest attempts have been made to relate Harappan to Minoan, Canaanite, Hittite and even to the peculiar "writing" of Easter Island. Studies in recent years building on what the archaeological record reveals about Harappan life have now yielded a more rewarding approach to the decipherment problem. It is my intent to outline some of these achievements here.

In the decades since the two great Harappan cities were discovered in the 1920s, and particularly since the end of World War II, archaeologists in India and Pakistan have located nearly 1,000 other Harappan sites. They are spread in a wide arc from western India in the vicinity of the Narmada River northward across Gujarat and Kutch, through the Pakistani regions of Sind and the western Punjab and on into Indian Rajasthan and the eastern Punjab up to the vicinity of Delhi. Other settlements have been found along the coast of the Arabian Sea almost as far as the Iranian border and in Baluchistan; one settlement was even discovered close to the Oxus River, deep in central Asia, by a recent French archaeological mission.

Most Harappan sites are small, covering between two and five acres, and are

This article originally appeared in *Scientific American*, March 1983. Copyright 1983 by Scientific American, Inc. Reprinted with permission.

near rivers or streams. There appear to have been three phases of settlement. Sites of the early phase are in or near the borderlands between the subcontinent and Iran. Those of the mature phase are more widespread. Most are in the valley of the Indus River itself, but such far-flung sites as those in Baluchistan and the one near the Oxus also belong to the mature phase. Those of the later phase tend to be far to the south and east of the Indus. Findings at these later sites also contain evidence that the older Harappan culture was in the process of merging with local pastoral and agricultural peoples. Such findings suggest Harappan civilization did not come to a sudden end but played a role in the development of the style of village life that is so characteristic of the subcontinent today.

What does the archaeological record tell us about Harappan life? First, it indicates that its mainstay was farming. Both grains and garden vegetables were grown, and cattle husbandry was central to the farm economy. Second, it indicates that the material culture of the Harappans was simple but not lacking in rich goods. They used copper and bronze for some tools and weapons and occasionally worked gold and silver into the beads that were their principal form of jewelry. At the same time the bulk of their artifacts consist of wood and bone, shell, flint and clay, all materials that were locally abundant. Among the beads, however, were some skillfully fashioned out of rarer semiprecious stones such as agate, carnelian and lapis. (The site near the Oxus was also close to early lapis mines.)

A further striking aspect of Harappan life was the extent of standardization. In architecture, building bricks were standard in size and were laid in standard ways. Drainage and sewer systems were standard in pattern. Dwellings were standard in dimensions and special structures (possibly public) were positioned with respect to private ones according to standard plans. Other aspects of the same phenomenon included standard weights and measures, pottery that was standard in shape and ornamentation and standardized artifacts such as ladles, loom weights and even toy carts. At the same time certain aspects of Harappan life suggest the later culture of India, for example the use of distinctive headdresses and of multiple bangles and necklaces and even the style of Harappan figurines.

So much for a broad summary of what is known. What is not known may be of equal significance. There is no evidence of rivalry between different Harappan states, of warfare, of major international trade or of the kings and courts and great temple complexes so characteristic of the other ancient civilizations of the Old World. The archaeological evidence reveals next to nothing about Harappan religion or political and social organization. Yet Harappan civilization was important to the civilizations that succeeded it. The Harappans cultivated cotton and perhaps rice, domesticated the chicken and may have invented the game of chess and one of the two great early sources of nonmuscle power: the windmill. (The other was the water wheel.)

When did this enigmatic civilization flourish? Although there is some con-

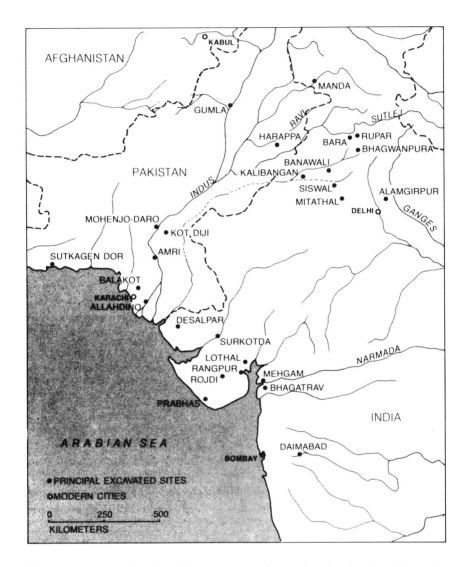

Harappan sites have been found from almost as far south as Bombay to as far north as central Asia and from as far east as Baluchistan to as far west as Delhi. Twenty-five of the principal excavated sites are shown on this map, including the great cities of civilization: Mohenjo-Daro and Harappa. Most Harappan sites are small, covering between two and five acres.

troversy on the point, the mature Harappan phase seems to have extended from about 2200 to 1700 B.C. Most Harappan sites appear to have been occupied for no more than 200 years; they give the impression of a short-lived development characterized by substantial group organization and regular interaction between contemporaneous settlements.

The task of "reading" the Harappan inscriptions is sufficiently difficult to make many scholars believe it is impossible. The first difficulty arises from the fact that the inscriptions represent the unknown writing of an unknown language for which there is no bilingual texts, such as the Rosetta stone of Egypt or the Behistun monument of Iran. A second difficulty is the absence of long texts. The entire corpus of Harappan writing consists of some 4,000 seals, seal impressions (that is, impressions of seals) and graffiti on pottery; moreover, many of the seals are damaged and many of the pottery graffiti are interrupted by breakage. Still a third difficulty arises from the fact that Harappan civilization was not only geographically remote from the other civilizations of its time but also historically remote from later cultural developments on the subcontinent.

Fortunately the Harappan seals are inscribed with both writing and pictures, and the pictorial motifs can yield clues to what the writing means. Most Harappan seals are square or rectangular pieces of soapstone, a material that is easy to carve. On the back of most of the seals is a raised boss pierced with a hole for a carrying string; on the front is a combination of a negative picture and an inscription. The carvings presumably identified the owner of the seal, so that when the seal was pressed into soft clay, the imprinted object was recognized as somehow associated with the owner.

A majority of Harappan seals display one or the other of two distinct pictorial motifs. The first involves an animal. It is usually a long-horned bull, but humped zebus are also portrayed, as are water buffaloes, goats, short-horned bulls, rhinoceroses, tigers, gavials (the river crocodiles of India) and elephants. Whatever the animal, an object was shown in place before it. The object shown with wild or dangerous animals is platterlike. The object shown with the domestic animals is either a basket or (particularly in front of the long-horned bull) a "stem" emblem such as one also shown being carried in processions.

A few of the animal seals show their subjects in groups. One well-known example is centered on an anthropomorphic figure, sometimes called the "Lord of the Beasts," seated cross-legged and wearing a water-buffalo headdress. To the right of the figure are an elephant and a tiger; to the left are a rhinoceros and a water buffalo. The seal is damaged but below and to the left of the central figure's feet can be seen a goat looking over its shoulder and to the right are what may be the horns of a matching goat figure, otherwise obliterated. A less elaborate seal centers on a pipal, or sacred fig tree (*Ficus religiosa*); the heads of two long-horned bulls are shown growing up from its trunk.

Another "animal group" depiction appears on one prismatic seal. (A few Harappan seals were made in the shape of a prism and a few others were cylindrical.) In a row on one of its three faces are an elephant, a rhinoceros and a tiger; a fourth figure in the row is too worn to identify. Presumably this is the "wild animal" face of the seal. On the second face is another four-animal procession,

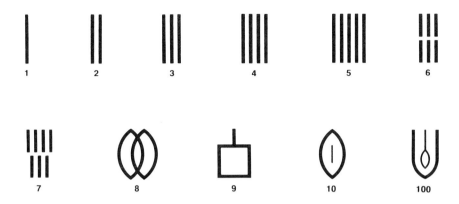

Harappan numerals, perhaps originally part of a system with a base of eight, are a plausible set of vertical strokes for 1 through 5 and a sextuplet of short strokes for 6. The sign for 7 is a similar set of short strokes. The signs for 8 and 9 are respectively pictographs of a double sun and a "foundation post." The sign for 10 is a single sun with a short stroke inside it. One other identified numeral, the sign for 100, is a pictograph of a mortar and pestle.

none of them apparently "wild." On both faces, however, a fifth animal is depicted above the animal procession. It is a gavial, self-evidently a member of the "wild" group. On the "wild animal" face the gavial is shown with a recognizable fish in front of its snout and what may be a fish behind it. On the second face no recognizable fish appears.

A fourth seal, even more elaborate than the "Lord of the Beasts," introduces a "worshipper" element. It repeats the depiction of a pipal tree, this time at its upper right corner. Between the branches of the tree stands a horned anthropomorphic figure. Facing the horned figure is a kneeling one, skirted and thus presumably female; to the left of the kneeling figure is a large goat. Seven skirted figures occupy the bottom half of the seal, their hair dressed in some kind of long "ponytail." A rather gruesome depiction on a fifth seal shows several similarly coiffed figures, one of them wearing a skirt, being attacked by a water buffalo.

These motifs suggest something about Harappan social organization: that individual seal-bearers belonged to groups that transcended normal familial lines. For example, all individuals with a rhinoceros on their seal may have had some social tie in common. What was held in common could have been membership in some superfamilial group such as a clan or a club. The existence of procession scenes on a few seals, where animal effigies seem to be carried as standards, adds strength to this concept of superfamilial groups. The groups in turn may have been part of a larger two-part grouping, as is suggested by the motif of the "Lord of the Beasts" on the one hand and the motif of the "Pipal-deity worshippers"

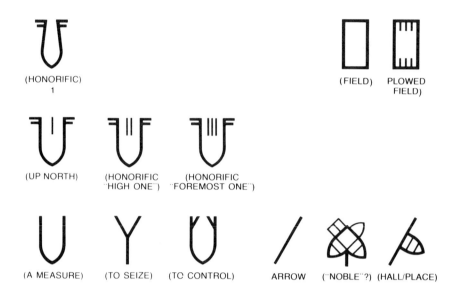

(HONORIFIC)   (FIELD)   PLOWED
1   FIELD)

(UP NORTH)   (HONORIFIC   (HONORIFIC
                   "HIGH ONE")   "FOREMOST ONE")

(A MEASURE)   (TO SEIZE)   (TO CONTROL)   ARROW   ("NOBLE"?) (HALL/PLACE)

Combined signs make up half of the total of the 200 signs most frequently encountered in the Harappan script. Four examples are given here. At the top left is one of
the commonest script signs, a pictograph of a pot with handles (labeled with the
Arabic numeral 1). Below it are three combined signs: the sign labeled *1* plus signs
like those for the Harappan numerals 1, 2 and 3 but consisting of short strokes.
Under each of these three signs appears its sense in English. Below the combined
signs are seen, from left to right, the pictographs for a container and for a forked
stick, and a third sign combining them. At the top right is the pictograph for a field,
a simple rectangle. Beside it is a sign that combines the field sign with the strokes of
the Harappan numeral 6 to form a new pictograph with the apparent sense of
"plowed field." At the bottom right, from left to right, are pictographs for "arrow"
and for "pipal-tree leaf." The third sign, combining "arrow" with a partial "pipal
leaf," seems to indicate "hall" or "place."

on the other. Such a possible structure is familiar to anthropologists as what is
termed a moiety: a society characterized by the classification of clans or similar
subsidiary organizations into two groups, "halves" that usually intermarry.

If one accepts the working hypothesis that the pictorial material on each seal
identifies its bearer as to clan and moiety, it logically follows that the part of the
seal devoted to Harappan script could be concerned with identifying the bearer as
an individual. The script might, for example, give the individual's name, occupation, place of residence, rank or title and similar information. In support of
such an interpretation the study of seal texts reveals considerable variation in the
sequence of individual signs and yet a frequent repetition of certain of them. The
hypothesis gives the would-be decipherer some basis on which to proceed. Just
as Michael Ventris knew that at least some of the Linear B texts found on Crete

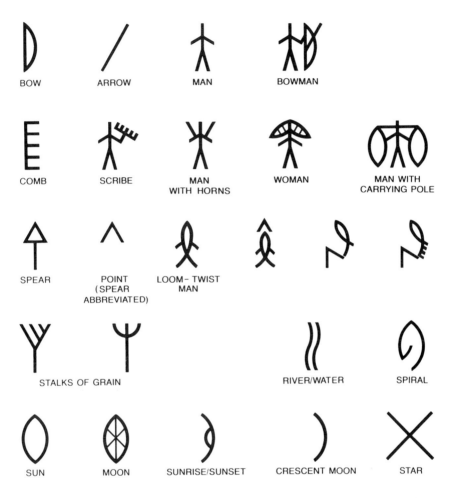

Additional pictographs to be found on the grid on the following pages include those illustrated here together with some combined forms. In the top row, from left to right, are "bow," "arrow," "man" and the combination "bowman." In the second row are "comb," a third human stick figure holding a comb (a combination that appears to indicate "scribe"), a fourth stick figure with "horns," a fifth stick figure with an elaborate coiffure ("woman") and a stick figure with a loaded shoulder pole (a combination appearing to indicate "guardian"). In the third row, from left to right, are "spear" and the shorthand for "spear," "point" (*color*), an honorific; a "loom twist" plus human arms, a second honorific pertaining to rulership, and the two signs combined. In the fourth row are two stalks of grain (both signs have the interchangeable sense of "grain" or "month"), a sign with the sense of "river" or "water" and a spiral with the sense of "surround" or "surrounding." In the bottom row are five astronomical pictographs. From left to right are seen the sun, the moon, sunrise or sunset, the crescent moon and a star.

were inventories of material objects, so the decipherer of Harappan script can assume that what to search for are proper names and their embellishments or other statements identifying the individual.

As long ago as the 1930s the British scholar G.R. Hunter had identified a total of 396 separate Harappan signs. More recent work has added another 23, so that the script is now known to incorporate a total of 419 signs. Statistical analysis shows that they occur 13,376 times in 2,290 known texts. Of the 419, 113 signs occur only once, 47 occur twice and 59 occur fewer than five times. In effect this means that the remaining 200 signs were in more or less general service, and analysis shows that fully half of them are combinations of the remaining half.

These findings demonstrate that Harappan writing was neither alphabetic, as Sanskrit is, nor logographic (that is, having one character for each word), as Chinese is. This places Harappan writing in the category known as logo-syllabic, meaning that some signs represent words and others serve purely for their syllabic values, or sounds. Other examples of this kind of writing are Egyptian hieroglyphs, early Sumerian ideographs and modern Japanese. The fact that half of the Harappan signs in common use were combinations of other commonly used ones suggests that the writers exploited such combinations to express ideas (as the Chinese do when they pair the characters for sun and moon to represent the word "brightness") and to combine syllabic sounds to "spell out" a word.

A crucial part of any writing system is the series of devices used to indicate gender, to distinguish between singular and plural, to establish the case of a verb and so on. The identification of these devices goes a long way toward establishing the relations between the graphemes, or individual components, of words and the language the graphemes represent. Now, the Harappan texts exhibit certain regularly paired signs, much as in the English reiteration of titles such as "His Majesty" and "Her Grace." It is also notable that certain signs appear in the middle of a text but rarely at the beginning or the end, whereas with other signs the reverse is true.

The usual ordering of signs and the identity of characteristic pairings may be established with a grid. Since the Harappan inscriptions are commonly brief, such a grid can consist of a relatively limited number of vertical columns. In fact, 14 columns were found to be sufficient. Of the first 17 inscriptions selected for horizontal grid display, most consisted of only five or six signs; thus they were entered near the center of the column array, allowing any longer lines to extend to the right or the left.

On entering the texts on the grid it became evident that certain signs appeared regularly in most of them. Consider the "pot" signs in column 5, the "loom twist" signs in column 8 and the "two-stroke" signs in column 10. When two of these three signs appear in the same text (as in lines b, e, h and p), they are always in the same right-to-left order with respect to each other no matter what other signs are included in the inscription. Regularity of position evidently gov-

		14	13	12	11	10
a	FEMD 606					
b	HAR 16				⊕	I
c	HAR 99			O		
d	HAR 72		(sign)	(sign)	(sign)	I
e	FEMD 590				◇	II
f	MD-31 121			⊞	(sign)	II
g	MD-31 46					
h	MD-31 26	‖	(pot sign)	‖		II
i	HAR 110				X	(sign)
j	HAR 102					I
k	FEMD 111			⫴	(human figure)	II
l	MD-31 69		(sign)	(sign)	(sign)	
m	HAR 69	(sign)	(sign)	⫴	(sign)	
n	MD 650				(sign)	(sign)
o	MD 405				(sign)	(sign)
p	FEMD 48				(oval)	II
q	ME-31 110		⊕	(sign)	(loom twist)	

Analytical grid 14 columns wide contains 17 seal texts that range in length from two signs to nine. When "pot" signs were all assigned to column 5, "loom twist" signs and their variants to column 8 and the signs made up of two short vertical dashes to column 10, it became apparent that when two or more of these three signs appeared in an inscription, they always appeared in the same right-to-left order with respect to one another regardless of what other signs might appear in the text. Lines b, e, h and p provided four examples. The single short vertical dashes in column 10 (lines b, d and i) reveal an inflectional quality. The same sign also appears in combining form in column 12, line d, as an addition to a "sun" sign; in column 11, line k, as an addition

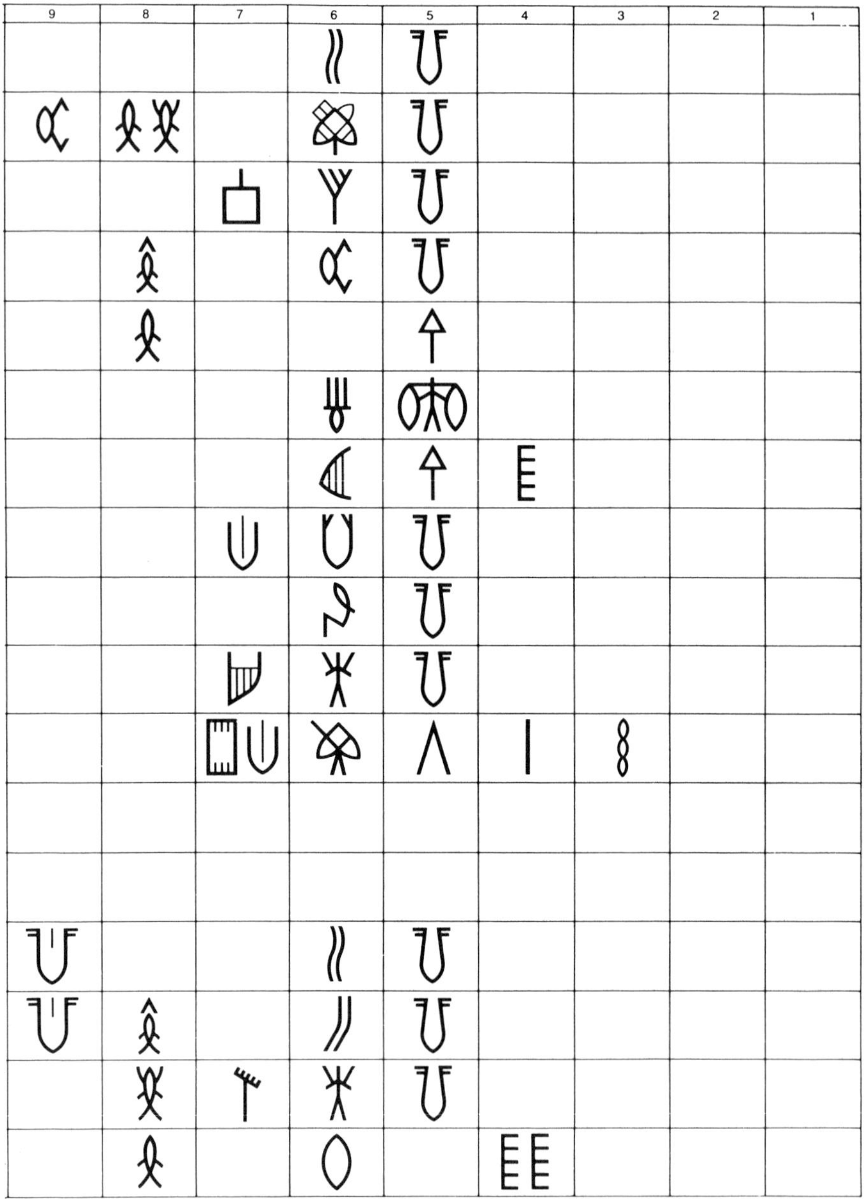

9	8	7	6	5	4	3	2	1

to a "man" sign, and in column 9, lines *n* and *o*, as additions to "pot" signs. The sense of the single sign and its combination (lines *i, n* and *o*) appears to be that of a possessive; the sense of the double-dash sign appears to be that of a locative. Two of the texts, lines *l* and *m*, do not fall within the "normal" central grid distribution. Thus it can be assumed that they are not texts of the usual formulation. When two signs are found in one grid cell, the placement indicates that the signs are regularly found paired in seal texts. Readings of four of these 17 texts (lines *d, e, g* and *k*) are shown at the bottom of the next figure.

erned their relations. Accordingly in setting up the Harappan grid such signs were placed in the columns noted above even when only one of them appeared in a particular text.

What then became clear was that these signs were the most numerous among those in the 17 selected texts.

The pot sign in column 5 appears there 10 times, and three variants appear in two other columns. The loom-twist sign in column 8, variants included, appears six times, and the two short vertical strokes of column 10, variants included, appear eight times. Certain other signs utilizing vertical strokes are not as fixed in their relative positions. Whereas the group of one or two short single strokes can be accommodated in column 10, those groups consisting of one, two, three or more long strokes fall outside the central columns of the grid.

By now, acquainted with the appearance of some 50 Harappan signs as they are displayed on the analytical grid, the reader may be wondering in which horizontal direction they are to be "read." On the basis of seal inscriptions alone this might have been a hard question to answer. Fortunately the graffiti inscribed on pottery supplied an answer. Studies by B.B. Lal and I. Mahadevan of the Archaelogical Survey of India have shown that some graffiti have overlapping strokes. The overlaps demonstrate that the direction of writing was from right to left. This is why lumn 14 of the grid appears at its left margin and lumn 1 at its right margin. The reversal puts the reading order in the more familiar left-to-right pattern.

We now come to the most complex part of the decipherment problem: What was the Harappan language? When Ventris identified the language of Linear B as Greek, he had overcome his greatest difficulty. The archaeological record of the region offers something of the same kind of help to those trying to pick a candidate for the unknown tongue. For example, the record shows that Harappan civilization was no sudden development. It had a long ancestry in the Indo-Iranian borderland, spread widely and eventually made its own contribution to the emergence of village India. This sequence suggests that the language spoken by the Harappans cannot have completely disappeared from the subcontinent.

Accepting such an assumption, which of the three principal families of languages spoken in the region might be related to Harappan? One candidate is Munda, a family of languages (spoken largely in eastern India) that seems affiliated with certain languages of Southeast Asia. Studies of the earliest forms of Munda, however, find little in its vocabulary that comports with what archaeology tells us about the culture of the Harappans. Another candidate is Indo-Aryan, a family of languages that traditionally came to India in the middle of the second millennium B.C. Its earliest literary expression, the Rig-Veda, however, describes a basically central-Asian culture quite different from the Harappan. The third candidate is Dravidian, a language now spoken mostly in southern and southeastern India but also still found in pockets in northern India and in Baluchistan.

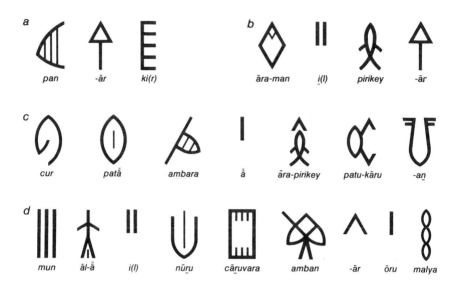

Four seal inscriptions appear together with the syllabic value of each sign in Dravidian, a surviving family of early languages of the region. The shortest inscription (*a*), in the author's reading, is "The singer's mark." The next inscription (*b*), which repeats the third-person honorific "spear" sign, *ār*, is read as "Belonging to the noble house (of the) Pirikeyar." The next inscription (*c*) is seven signs long and includes a variant of the "loom twist" sign of inscription *b*. It is read as "Patukaran, powerful (noble) chief of the surrounding settlements." The last inscription (*d*) is nine signs long and includes the two-stroke sign *i(l)* of inscription *b* and an abbreviation of the "spear" signs in both *a* and *b* (*color*). It is read as "Belonging to Munala, mistress of 100 plowed fields, noble first lady." More than 100 seal texts have now been read. The majority of the readings accord with the hypothesis that the seal signs identify individuals.

A fourth possibility, of course, is that Harappan is related to none of the above. It is nonetheless worthwhile to consider the candidacy of Dravidian more closely than that of either Munda or Indo-Aryan. In addition to the northern forms (Kurukh, Malto and Brahui) about 25 Dravidian languages are still spoken. Indeed, the major families (Tamil, Malayalam, Kannada and Telegu) are spoken by more than 100 million people. Thanks again to the archaeological record it is not necessary to accept the candidacy of Dravidian blindly.

In 1974 excavations at the Harappan site of Allahdino, near Karachi, unearthed an ivory fragment with a half-circular cross section. There were holes on one side, apparently drilled to hold pegs; on the other side were two lengthwise parallel grooves. The object was similar to a large number of ivory rods or sticks excavated in the 1930s by one of the later workers at the great Harappan city of Mohenjo-Daro, E.J.H. Mackay. The Mohenjo-Daro ivories were not, as has been asserted, merely gaming pieces. For example, one of them, square in cross section, had a series of alternating circles and crescents cut into one side.

On some of the Mohenjo-Daro ivories is a sign in the grid (column 6, line *c*) and another sign resembling some form of plant. In various seal texts these two signs are associated with vertical strokes that range from one to seven in number and with five other signs. (Two appear on the grid at column 7, line *c*, and column 11, line *q*). Like the second sign on the Mohenjo-Daro ivories, the sign at column 6, line *c*, appears to represent a plant, probably a stalk of grain. Considering the association of both signs in the seal inscriptions with what appear to be numbers and the marking of one of the ivories with circles and crescents that approximate in number a lunar (crescent) month of 30 solar (circle) days, the two plant signs might logically be taken to represent a word meaning both grain and month (or moon). Furthermore, the vertical strokes associated with both signs end after reaching a total of seven, suggesting that some other sign served for the number eight and possibly that the Harappan number system was to the base eight.

What language has a word for grain that also means month or moon and is associated with a base-eight numerical system? On the first point *nel* means rice in five Dravidian languages and *nilā* or *nela* means moon in three of the same five and in five others as well. It is also the word for month in some of the same languages. On the second point, a student of Dravidian language, Kamir V. Zvelebil, has pointed out that the original Dravidian number system was indeed probably to the base eight: the count to 10, used for conformity with the base-10 number system today, goes literally (in translation) "one," "two," "three," "four," "five," "six," "seven," "number," "many minus one" and "many."

Over the years scholars have noted in Dravidian a number of homophones: words with the same sounds but with different meanings. For example, the word for the shoulder pole from which pots are suspended is *kā*. It is also the word meaning guardian, or protector. The common word for fish is *mīn*, which is also the word for star. The word for 100 is *nūru*, which is also the word meaning to grind or to powder.

The homophonic, or rebus, principle is found in a number of ancient languages, including the hieroglyphs of Egypt. The key aspect of the homophonic principle is that it seeks a syllabic equivalent (say a picture of an eye to mean "I") rather than merely being a picture of something. For example, an early Egyptian ruler, Nr-mr, was represented in hieroglyphs by the sign for a catfish (*nr*) and the sign for a chisel (*mr*). The representation was not meant to suggest that he be called "the catfish-chisel one" but rather that his name sounded like "catfish-chisel."

Does this suggest a basis for deriving a Harappan syllabary? I shall put the point to trial in what follows, first warning that the acid test of any decipherment is its consistency. If a decision is made to declare a certain symbol equivalent to a selected sound or sense, it cannot later be shifted to represent some other sound or sense. Inner logic is basic to all writing systems; when decipherers arbitrarily alter the values of symbols in order to fit the model they prefer, their work is spoiled.

For a start consider the sign shown in column 7, line *h*. Pictographically it could be taken to represent a mortar and pestle. Linguistic reconstructions suggest that this utensil was given the syllabic value *nūru* in Dravidian. This, as we have seen, is also the sound of the verb to grind or powder and the numerical noun "100." Next consider the sign that figures so prominently in column 5 of the grid. Some years ago Mahadevan conjectured that this sign, which most frequently appears at the end of seal texts, was a pictographic representation of a pot with handles. He went on to point out that various Dravidian words for this kind of pot were homophones of words meaning male, including the common honorific suffix *an* used with male personal names at least as long ago as early in the Christian Era. The fact that such a sign terminates seal texts hypothesized to contain personal names strengthens Mahadevan's conjecture.

Now, another terminal sign on the grid (column 5, line *f*) is a pictograph of a human figure carrying a shoulder pole with a pot at each end. As we have seen, the syllable for a pole with pots alone, *kā*, is a homophone of the Dravidian words meaning "to guard" or "to protect." Furthermore, a common Dravidian word for man is *āl*. The combination of these would allow the reconstruction of the sign at column 5, line *f*, as a two-syllable word, *kā-āl*. In the Dravidian languages, for the sake of euphony, such adjacent vowels are separated by a consonant, either a *v* or a *y*. Thus the restored word, *kāvāl*, could be translated as "one who guards or protects," a statement of personal identity suitable for entry on a private seal.

To give two further examples before turning to trial readings of some of the seal texts on the grid, two of the "number" signs—the sign in column 12, line *k*, presumably meaning three, and a second sign consisting of four vertical strokes, presumably meaning four—also have plausible homophones. The first homophone, *mu(n)*, equates with the Dravidian word meaning "foremost" (*mun*); the second homophone, *nāl*, equates with the word meaning "good" (*nal*), both logical titular adjectives.

Let us now consider two short and two longer seal texts from the grid. The text designated Mohenjo-Daro 3146 (line *g*) consists of three signs, putatively a musical instrument, a spear and a comb. The assigned Dravidian syllabic values are, in the same order, *pan, ār* and *ki(r)*, in translation the word "sing," a third-person honorific and the word "mark," read as *Panār-ki(r)*. The proposed translation is "Panar's seal," or literally "The singer's mark." Next, the text designated FEMD 590 (line *e*) consists of four signs. The first sign, a diamond shape, has the three-syllable value *āra-man*, the second, two short vertical lines, has the value *i(l)*, the third, a "loom twist," has the three-syllable value *piri(key)* and the fourth is the same honorific *ār* as in the preceding text. This is read as

Āra-man-i(l) pirikeyār, with the proposed translation "Belonging to the noble house (of the) Pirikeyar" ("pirs" and "pirikeys" are chiefs). The third text, Harappa 72 (line *d*), consists of seven signs: an initial spiral (*cur*), an oval enclosing a short vertical dash (*pată*), a pipal leaf and an arrow combined (*ambara*), a short vertical dash alone (*ă*), a twist with a point above it (*āra-pirikey*), pincers combined with the sign for the sun (*patu-kāru*) and, as the terminal sign, the pot with handles (*an*). This is a mouthful: *Cur patăm-bara-ă āra-pirikey patu-kāran*. The proposed translation is "Patukaran, powerful (noble) chief of the surrounding settlements." The fourth text, FEMD 111 (line *k*), is one of the longest of the translated seal inscriptions, consisting of nine signs. In the interest of brevity, only the syllables and their proposed translation will be given: *Munălă-i(l) nūru cāruvara amban ārōru malya*, or "Belonging to Munala, mistress of 100 plowed fields, noble first lady."

So far syllabic values have been assigned to nearly 100 seal and pottery signs and appropriate Dravidian homophones have been found for each. Translations such as those given here have been proposed for more than 100 seal texts. They range from such simple statements as "water-holder" (probably a proper name) to such sonorities as "Arasamban, High Chief (of) Chiefs of the Southwest, lineage of the Moon."

What such readings demonstrate about the Harappans is that a number of individuals (Arasamban among them) traced their lineage to such major figures of the cosmos as the Sun, the Moon and the Stars and perhaps also the Monsoon Rain. These may represent distinctions within each clan. Chiefs were associated with *aramani*, or chiefs' houses, which may have had both residential and administrative functions. In addition there was a high place (the "citadels" identified by archaeologists?) that served a special but so far undetermined function. An assembly area—an open court or a pillared hall (both known archaeologically)—suggests that an assembly of chiefs was a basic part of Harappan political organization.

Among other kinds of leaders known from the seals were heads of associations (guilds?) such as that of the coppersmiths, storehouse overseers, irrigation supervisors and landowners, a category that as we have seen included women. Religious references, however, are scarce. There is a possible "horned deity," referred to as "the copper one" or "the red one," and a possible "mother deity," but at the moment these distinctions are not confirmed. Lesser figures included drummers and singers, the drummers perhaps to summon assemblies and the singers prehaps to entertain or perform at ceremonies.

The seals attest further to a class of scribes, to people in charge of weights and measures and to supervisors of the distribution of stores, the grinding of flour and probably hunting operations. There were also captains of boats and custodians of fire. Many seals bear the sign *kā*, referring to guardianship, not in a military sense but more in terms of a responsibility for the care of crops and the preservation of herds and flocks. One of the gratifying near-proofs that the decipherments are on the right track comes from the prismatic seal where a gavial is twice seen above an array of "clan" animals. In Dravidian the word for crocodile is *mutalai*. The Dravidian word for first chief, *mutali*, is a close homophone.

Thus it appears that the language of Mohenjo-Daro and Harappa some 4,000 years ago was an early Dravidian tongue and that the Harappan scribes struggled to put that language into graphic form as a method of identifying the elite of the Indus Valley civilization. The Harappan civilization, however, was geographically so widespread that a number of non-Dravidian words must have entered the language, just as Dravidian words were later borrowed by the speakers of Indo-Aryan.

A great deal of additional decipherment remains to be done and no doubt what has been put forth here will be found to have flaws. What remains to be done is even more exciting. It leads toward a goal that until recently seemed impossible to attain: cohesive information on Harappan polity, social organization and ideology, and perhaps even stronger evidence that, as the parent of the village India of today, the Harappan culture never did disappear.

THE JEWEL IN THE LOTUS: THE ETHIOPIAN PRESENCE IN THE INDUS VALLEY CIVILIZATION

Wayne B. Chandler

> *And upon his return to Greece they gathered around and asked, "tell us about this great land of the Blacks called Ethiopia." And Herodotus said, "There are two great Ethiopian nations, one in Sind (India) and the other in Egypt."*
>
> —Godfrey Higgins,
> *The Anacalypis*

The ancient civilization of India is unique in that its cultural and philosophical traditions have been maintained without a break from antiquity down to the present day. Some claim that this connective cultural filament is rooted as far back as the 7th millennium B.C. In contrast, Ethiopia, Egypt and Iraq were ignorant of their history until the advent of the archaeologist; relatively modern explorers excavated cryptic ruins in order to unearth the cornerstones of our present day sciences, philosophies and religions. As A.L. Basham states: "the peasant of Egypt or Iraq had no knowledge of the culture of his forefathers, and it is doubtful whether his Greek counterpart had any but the vaguest ideas about the glories of Periclean Athens—on the other hand, the earliest Europeans to visit India found a culture fully conscious of its own antiquity."[1] The flowers of contemporary Indian philosophy, science and religion are rooted in this ancient past.

No other nation can lay claim to this sense of history. Even Egypt, land of great dynastic empires, had only a fragmented understanding of its past. During the 12th dynasty, massive excavations were made around the Sphinx and the pyramids by Amemhemet III. The pyramids of the early kingdoms, long neglected, had been partially consumed by the encroaching desert; the inhabitants of the middle kingdom were studying their predecessors' monuments with the same nebulous perspective modern man applies to them today. The people of the middle kingdoms could not fathom the minds of a nation who conceived and constructed these great monoliths, whose sphere of comprehension included advanced metaphysics, astronomy, and mathematics; they had lost the cultural continuity that would have enabled them to fully appreciate the greatest accomplishments of their forebears.

Using "keys of knowledge" to unlock ancient mysteries, H.P. Blavatsky in *The Secret Doctrine* maintains that "India (not in its present limit but including its ancient boundaries) is the only country in the world which still has among her

Plate 1. The Buddha. India—First century AD.

sons adepts, who have the knowledge of all the seven subsystems and the key to the entire system. Since the fall of Memphis, Egypt began to lose those keys one by one and Chaldea has preserved only three . . .''[2]

In his literary masterpiece *The Wonder That Was India*, A.L. Basham poses the question: "Who were the people who built this great civilization?" After sixty-four years of study, historians are still unable to come forth with a consensus regarding the racial makeup of the Indus Valley civilization; consequently, despite much discovery, little has been released to the general public. The growing likelihood that the culture of Indian Asia was born out of the Black race is a bitter pill for many to swallow; therefore, a controversy exists among historians even today. Basham continues, " . . . some Indian historians have tried to prove that they were the Aryans, the people who composed the Rg Veda, but this is quite impossible."[3] (Note: Aryans—"the noble ones"; Caucasian invaders from the central steppes of Asia. Rg Veda—earliest of the Vedas, spiritual hymns of the Aryan priestly class.)

Basham's outright rejection of the notion of Aryan or Caucasian paternity of the Indus Valley civilization stems from huge discrepancies between the age of the Indus Valley cities and the dates of the Aryan influence in India. Mohenjo-Daro and Harappa, the greatest examples of Harappan architecture, were built between 3000 B.C. and 2500 B.C.; these masterpieces of Harappan city planning were the culmination of towns and villages which date from 6000 B.C. to 7000 B.C. In contrast, the earliest evidence of the Aryans as a major force in India is their destruction of Mohenjo-Daro, estimated to have taken place circa 1500 B.C. The Aryan influence occurs too late to be credited for generating the Indus Valley civilization; to the contrary, the Aryan entrance upon the ancient east Indian stage caused the violent destruction of a civilization already more than a thousand years old.

In the Rg Veda, the Aryan invaders gave their own testimony regarding their bitter war upon the Harappan foe, known to them as Dasas and described as "dark and ill favored, bull-lipped, snub nosed worshippers of the phallus . . . they are rich in cattle and dwell in fortified places called Pur."[4] Although the light-skinned Nordic race had waged war for many years on the black, by then "native" people, one can infer from the Rg Veda that their conquest was long incomplete. "Though many hymns refer to battles between one Aryan tribe and another, there is underlying this intertribal rivalry a sense of solidarity against the Dasas who evidently represent the survivors of the Harappan culture . . ."[5] The fact that the Harappans or Dasas were still capable of amassing armies of 10,000 men even after the destruction of their main settlements[6] speaks volumes for the prowess of the beleaguered civilization.

Given the fact that the Black race is by far the oldest,[7] the presence of Black culture at the dawn of Indian history should not be surprising. Bharatiya Vidya Bhavan, Indian historian and anthropologist, suggests: "We have to begin with the Negroid or Negrito people of prehistoric India who were its first human inhabitants. Originally they would appear to have come from Africa through Arabia and the coastlands of Iran and Baluchistan . . ."[8]

In the India of today the presence of people resembling the ancient Ethiopian negritos is rare enough though it does exist. Sparse pockets of these Negrito descendants can be found among the Kadar and Ragahmal Hill cultures in Eastern Bihar and the Andamans.

Bharatiya, though in agreement with most authorities as to the identity of the first racial presence, nevertheless feels strongly that this Negrito or African presence was culturally insignificant. He later claims that "owing to their very primitive state, the negritos do not appear to have contributed anything of importance to the civilization of India."[9] Such a statement appears incongruous to the point of absurdity. Only ignorance could prevent a historian from seeing the indelible connection between the original African presence and later civilization. For, as the mighty Kushite nation was to Egypt, as Egypt was to Greece and as Greece was to Renaissance Europe, so was the Ethiopian race to Harappan civilization.

In fact, Bharatiya later sows the seeds to his own counterargument: in reference to Gupta sculpture and the Ajanta frescoes he states: "Negrito elements or traits, judging from some racial types depicted in the art of Gupta and post-Gupta India, seem to have survived to a very late period, but now they have been almost wholly eliminated."[10] Through his acknowledgement of the willful and systematic destruction and mutilation of Negrito art, he apparently unwittingly supports the very point he seeks to deny. The Negrito images he refers to were created by the Negritos themselves, in their own image, during the time that the Negritos constituted the dominant race of India.

The Mathurian school of iconography responsible for many of the frescoes had very disciplined standards regarding proportion. "The stone workers drew upon two main traditional sources: Firstly their own experience in the making of images . . . whether gods or royal heroes, and secondly, upon the indications given in literary traditions."[11] Thus, the statues' kinky hair, whether tightly curled, locked or braided, thick lips and broad noses can be accepted as accurate portrayals of existing people. In spite of defaced statues, it is nevertheless apparent that these elements occur regularly in artistic renditions dating from the Bronze Age to those of the 6th century A.D.; even later statues from medieval India occasionally show Negrito features. The prevalence of Negrito traits over many millenniums cries Bharatiya's disparagement of their influence.

At this juncture, clarification must be made as to the racial stratifications arranged within Indian history. As previously noted, the original layer consisted of Ethiopian Blacks known as Negritos. The second element, later introduced, was that of the Proto-Australoid. Bharatiya describes these people as Black and platyrrhine (having a broad nose with widely separated nostrils). With the Negritos, this race may once have covered the whole of India; a genealogical offshoot would later generate the aborigines of Australia. The merging of these two culturally diverse but monoracial groups—the Ethiopian Negrito and the Proto-Australoid—produced the people of the Indus Valley civilization.

In the text, *The Vedic Age*, Bharatiya informs us of two major subgroupings of the third element, a mongoloid race. The first or Paleo-mongoloid category is further divided into two subgroups. The first was characterized by a "peculiar head resembling dolichocephal;" this long-headed group, thought to be the ear-

Plate 2. Vishnu. Negrito Art, 6th century AD.

liest mongoloid type, formed a "dominant element in the tribes living in Assam and the Indo-Burmese frontiers." The second Paleo-mongoloid subgroup was round-headed; examples of this racial type can be found even today among the primitive tribes in Burma and in Bangladesh. This round-headed type is believed to represent a less advanced subdivision of the Paleo-Mongoloid race. The second Mongoloid group is that of the Tibetan mongoloids, who possessed more pronounced and articulated mongoloid features. This racial group, still found today in Sikkim and Bhutam, "must have infiltrated from Tibet in comparatively later times."[12]

The fourth racial strata has come to be generally known as the civilized or advanced Mediterranean; however, some anthropologists refer to this group as letorrpine or dolichocephalus. The advanced Mediterranean element is also marked by several variations. In *The Vedic Age*, Bharatiya describes two: "We have in the first instance the Paleo-Mediterranean type, medium statured, dark-skinned and of slight build . . . secondly the true Mediterranean or European type, taller and fairer than the Paleo-Mediterranean . . ."[13] The first or Paleo-Mediterranean type which represented a mix of Black and Mongoloid races, occurs in the Kannada, Tamil and Malayan regions.

Plate 3. Terracotta found at Harappa, 2300 BC.

The second, or true Mediterranean, which resulted from a mix of Black and Caucasian races, can be found in the Punjab and the Valley of the Upper Ganges. The Mediterranean influence entered the Indus Valley circa 500 B.C. We infer that they came from the West and travelled by sea. As Basham states, ''The Mediterranean element spread throughout the subcontinent and, . . . mixing with the indigenous peoples, formed the Dravidians . . .'' [14]

At this point, a common misconception must be addressed. Several historians have mistakenly identified the Dravidians as the racial element represented in the Indus Valley civilization. For example, in his account of the ethnic background of India, W.E.B. DuBois identifies ''first a prehistoric substratum of Negrillos; then the pre-Dravidians, a taller, larger type of Negro; then the Dravidians, Negroes with some mixture of Mongoloid and later of Caucasian stocks. The Dravidian negroes laid the basis of Indian culture thousands of years before the Christian era.'' [15] DuBois is correct of course in his identification of the Harappans as Black; however, the Harappans represented a meshing of the Ethiopian Negrito and the Proto-Australoid solely. The racial parentage of the Harappans becomes more apparent when one considers the dates involved. The Mediterranean influx which was to father the Dravidians has been tentatively placed within the ''latter half of the first millenium B.C.''; this is inferred from the age of the Dravidian megaliths. [16] The Harappan civilization, of course, is much older. (Due to apparent similarities between the Harappan script and the writing of certain Dravidian sub-groups, some historians believe that the terms Harappan and Dravidian should be synonymous. Due to the relatively late construction of the Dravidian megaliths, I believe that the Dravidians were the inheritors of the Harappan script rather than its originators. Similarly, Harappan science and philosophy far predates the Dravidian's arrival in India; although they later absorbed these elements, yoga and Jainism originated thousands of years prior to the Dravidian migration. We will return to this point later.)

Little is known about the fifth element or racial influence. The Armenoids, or Western Brachycephals, represent a specialized offshoot of Alpine or European stock; however, the Armenoids apparently arrived in India with the ''true Dravidians'' or Mediterranean race and spoke their language.

In the sixth racial stratum we find a new and significant element. The Vedic Aryans, or Nordics, introduced the Sanskrit language to India and created a dynamic cultural synthesis between themselves and the indigenous people. The Aryans represent the latest major racial influence on India.

To summarize, six groups have been identified, with all three major races represented. They are as follows: the Ethiopian Negrito and the Proto Australoid: Black race; the Paleo Mongoloid: Mongoloid race; the Mediterranean: Black/ Mongoloid and Black/Caucasian (the Dravidians are of this racial mixture); the Armenoids and the Aryan or Nordic: Caucasian race. These racial and ethnic factors converged in one geographical location, each one adding new elements which in turn created fresh cultural syntheses. From the Indus Valley basin, successive waves of influence spread throughout the Indian subcontinent.

Examination of the evidence provided by the skeletal remains confirms the identity of the race that gave birth to the Indus Valley civilization.

Since excavations have been suspended for over two decades, three-quarters of the two main cities are still underground. Consequently, the sample of skeletal remains available for analysis is not as large as it could be. Nevertheless, the trend of the results is compelling.

In their volume, "Comparative Study and Racial Analysis of the Skeletal Remains of the Indus Valley Civilization", B.K. Chatterjee and G.D. Kumar examine 18 skeletons from the city of Harappa. As to the racial identity of this sample, they found the type to be "akin to the Veddoid or (Proto) Australoid type."[17]

Chatterjee and Kumar compared the mean values of different cranial, facial, nasal and orbital measurements with those of prehistoric skulls found in other countries. Several comparative tables note variations between the Harappan mean and the other pre-historic skulls; the authors list variations in maximum cranial length, maximum cranial breadth, auricular height and basion bregmatic height for both male and female skulls. To recapitulate the tables here would be tedious, since deviations are reported between Harappan skulls and those of up to twenty-five other types, for each of the four categories of measurement, and for both sexes. However, Chatterjee and Kumar report close comparisons between the Harappan skulls and crania found in the following pre-historic sites: Kish (Mesopotamia), Alishan (Copper Age), Anan, Hissar III (Mediterranean), Egypt Naqada, Egypt Badari, Kerma (Egypt 12th-13th Dynasty), Ur, Sakkara and Palestine. In summary, Chatterjee and Kumar found "very close relation with the before mentioned cranium materials excavated in Egypt, areas of Mesopotamia and Sumer, Ethiopia and Asia."[18]

In addition, Chatterjee and Kumar make an interesting point regarding some "Mediterranean" skulls found at Chanhu-Daro, the third largest city of the Indus Valley: "On the basis of cranial measurements, indices and certain morphological features, long head, broad face, low orbit, and broad nasal aperture, Chanhu-Daro skulls were placed with the Proto-Mediterranean type. But long-head is not the only characteristic feature of the Proto-Mediterranean type nor is it solely an attribute to the Caucasic groups; it is also the characteristic feature of the Negroid type."[19]

Chatterjee and Kumar also note that two archaeologists, Friederichs and Muller, have identified three skulls of Mohenjo-Daro as "Hamitic." These same skulls were identified as "Mediterranean" by a different team of archaeologists, Sewell and Guha. Chatterjee and Kumar go on to state that "This type was classified by Sergi as Mediterranean, Hamitic by Poch, the Predynastic by Giuffrida-Rugger, the Proto-Egyptian by Elliot Smith, Iranic by Dirr, the Orien-

tal by Fischer, the Nordoide by Lebzelter, and the Eastern Mediterranean and In-
dide by Eickstedt.'' Finally, Chatterjee and Kumar report that, in their opinion,
''this type of skull is similar to Ariba skulls . . . from Nubia during the third to
second millennium B.C.''[20]

After considering this archaeological doubletalk, one must recognize the di-
lemma existing in communities of anthropologists around the world. Evidence
requires that these scholars accept the fact that black people, in ancient times,
populated and influenced areas of the world other than Africa. This reality has
been difficult for many to accept. Consequently, the somewhat fraudulent practice of creating unnecessary names and categories has evolved. In my opinion,
the other appellations only serve to obscure the true racial identity of the skulls at
hand. Thus we have encountered nine different categorizations for a skull which
had its origins in Nubia 5000 years ago.

Sir Mortimer Wheeler offers a calm, clear-sighted perspective. In reference to
the skeletal remains, he states: ''As for those specimens reserved for study, fifteen represent adult males, nineteen adult females and two juveniles. A majority
of them are grouped in two main classes, twenty-one adult skulls in Class A and
ten adult skulls in Class A1 with four unclassified and one aberrant . . . without
emphasis Class A is compared with the Proto-Australoid or Eurafrican of earlier
writers, whilst Class A1, which is of slighter build, recalls the conventional
Mediterranean or Indo-European.''[21] (Interestingly enough, the Rg Veda agrees
with Sir Mortimer Wheeler: the ancient text mentions only two races: the Dasas
and the Aryans themselves. Brief mention is made of tribes of cattle thieves
known to the Aryans as Panis. These people may have been Semitic traders.)

My first objective has been to demonstrate that the first inhabitants of India
were Black. Since this premise has come to be generally accepted by scholars
and laymen alike, this task proved not particularly difficult. My next and greater
challenge is to make evident the tremendous contribution made by the Black race
to Indian civilization and culture.

The first step in demonstrating this connection is to examine the Indus Valley
civilization itself. Evidence of this civilization was uncovered only relatively recently: the year was 1856. While the British were building a railway system, two
brothers, William and John Brunton, engineered the Indus Valley portion of this
massive project. The brothers, working in different areas of the Indus Valley
basin, encountered the same problem: laying railway tracks directly on top of the
sandy alluvial soil was virtually impossible. A layer of gravel or broken stone,
then called ballast, was necessary in order to stabilize the ground sufficiently for
the laying of the rail bed. Brunton heard rumors of an ancient city, called
Brahminabad, in the vicinity of the railway line. Eager to find a source for ballast, John Brunton visited the ruins, and found in the bricks of its buildings an inexhaustible supply. The pillage of the city for its brick commenced, and, ironically, bricks fired thousands of years ago secured the ground for modern railway
tracks.

William Brunton, working to the north of his brother, experienced the same obstacle and availed himself of the same solution. While John Brunton in the south mined Mohenjo-Daro for its brick, William Brunton drew upon Harappa. The ancient city of Harappa had already been pillaged for brick to build the modern city of Harappa on the same site. Nevertheless, William Brunton successfully plundered Harappa for 93 miles of ballast, obtained for only the cost of transportation.

As workmen destroyed the city walls, artifacts were uncovered. Among these artifacts were soapstone seals which aroused the interest of General Sir Alexander Cunningham, an archaeologist as well as a soldier. Cunningham was intrigued by the fact the script on the seals was completely unfamiliar to him. In 1892, Cunningham became Director General of the Indian Archaeological Survey and commenced excavations on the cities. Intensive examination pushed back the date of the oldest archaeological site in India by 2000 years, since the bricks of Mohenjo-Daro were over 4000 years old, and the stone walls at Rajagrika, previously identified as the oldest Indian site, dated from the 6th century B.C.

Reconstructing Harrapan history has been an arduous challenge; our greatest impediment in this endeavor has been and remains our inability to decipher Harrapan script. But our findings so far have profound and mind-boggling implications. The Harrapan civilization flourished in the midst of a time period still considered by some as prehistoric, since it "has no history in the strict sense of the term."[22]

As far back as the 4th century before Christ the climate of North West India was much the same as it is today. When Alexandar of Macedon crossed the Indus in 326 B.C., he found fertile river basins, dense with forests, although the coastal stretch west of the Indus was already arid wasteland. But in the 3rd millennium B.C. the climate was very different; the whole Indus region was well forested, providing fuel for brick-firing and food for man and beast alike. The earliest Indian settlements, which date from the 6th millenium B.C., existed in Baluchistan and in lower Sind, to the north and west of present day Karachi. This area, then well-watered and capable of supporting many village communities, is now riverless desert.[23]

As the Nile was to Egypt, and the Tigres and Euphrates were to Sumer, so the Indus River was to the Harappan civilization. It is appropriate that India's name derives from the river which nourished her earliest peoples. (Interestingly enough, early Indians knew this river as the Sindhu, and the region around it the Sind. Persians, who had difficulty pronouncing the letter S called it Hindu. From Persia to Greece the word spread and in time the land became known as Hindustan and its inhabitants Hindustanis or Hindus.) The Indus and its tributaries cover almost 100 miles over the northwest corner of India. The Indus itself nutured Mohenjo-Daro, while its tributaries supported Harappa and smaller village outposts of the Harappan civilization.

Mohenjo-Daro was located on the western bank of the Indus about 200 miles from the coast; Harappa, on the south side of the tributary Ravi river, lay almost 400 miles to the northeast of its sister city. The area on which the Harappan civilization is located, long considered part of northwest India, is now located in Pakistan. The territory once dominated by this bronze age empire is astonishing. If this can be considered to be the shape of an irregular triangle, its apex lay almost as far northeast as the western elbow of the Ganges River while its base extended along the coast from the western cap of the Arabian Sea, now the border between Iran and Pakistan, to the Gulf of Gombay, near modern Bombay, which formed its eastern extremity. The land mass included in this triangle is greater than the combined kingdoms of Egypt and Mesopotamia. Within this vast area, archaeologists have already uncovered fifty-three communities, ranging in size from the cities of Mohenjo-Daro and Harappa to medium-sized towns such as Chanhu-Daro and smaller villages.

The population of Mohenjo-Daro and Harappa are estimated to have been 40,000 apiece. The discovery of these two cities has given us a new opportunity to increase our understanding of the earliest human settlements. The most striking aspect of these city ruins is their undisputable evidence of sophisticated city planning. The founders of the Harappan cities are undeniably the world's first urban planners. The two major cities are similarly laid out, again demonstrating the Harappans deliberate city planning. As one author put it, the city was "Built in a gridlike fashion with a large main street; it seems almost a minute version of Manhattan Island."[24] Both capitals were masterpieces of urban planning. A few thousand years transpired before the Romans began to construct towns along similar patterns and then another millennium passed before municipal planning would be seen on the earth again.

Harappan homes were two or more stories high. Although they varied in size, all were based on the same principles of design, each unit consisted of a square courtyard surrounded by graciously arranged rooms. Each household had a side street entrance, and all windows faced the central courtyard rather than the main street; it appears that the Harappans valued their privacy and made an effort to remove the family unit from prying eyes. Since many streets were not paved, traffic would have stirred up the dust; this may have been another reason for the arrangement of the windows. Lined with shops and restaurants, some main boulevards were as much as thirty-feet wide. The thoroughfares of the two main capital cities were laid out in a rigid mathematical pattern; as previously stated, avenues ran north to south and east to west.

One indication of the Harappans' sophistication as builders and also of their understanding of hygienic principles is the fact that most private homes, both large and small, were equipped with a special kind of chute used to dispose of debris. This chute was built into one of the outside walls and filtered trash and debris into small tunnels which in turn emptied into a covered central sewerage system. At intervals along the central system there were sumps, or drainage pits,

Plate 4. The Great Bath at Mohenjo-Daro.

designed to collect the heaviest waste so that it would not obstruct the main chan-nels.

Virtually every household was equipped with what much of the modern western world still thinks of as "modern conveniences." In addition to the trash chutes, each household had bathrooms with drains which carried waste to the sewers under the main streets. Almost every dwelling had its own private water well from which fresh water was drawn. Apparently, prosperity was not as elusive to the Harappans as it was to their contemporaries in Egypt and Sumer. Although the average size of a house's ground floor was 30 square feet, A.L. Basham states that " . . . there were many bigger; obviously there were numerous well to do families in the Indus cities."[25] As Sir Mortimer Wheeler notes, the planning and sanitary arrangements of the Harappan cities convey a picture of "middle class prosperity with zealous municipal controls."[26]

Examination of the ancient city of Mohenjo-Daro brings to light other achievements of the Harappans. One of these is the structure archaeologists call the Great Bath. This rectangular 20 + 40 foot structure has a depth of eight feet. Its filling and emptying system is remarkable along with the meticulous joining of the bricks in its walls. The bricks of the bottom and sides of this pool were set on edge in gypsum mortar and covered with a layer of bitumen, which in turn was covered with more bricks. This ensured that the bath was watertight. A series of small bathing rooms, each with a narrow entrance set to one side, had carefully made floors connected to a drain 6 feet in height which emptied into the city's sewerage system. This drainage system also allowed the Harappans to change the bathing water at regular intervals. A similar but smaller bath existed at Harappa.

Both Mohenjo-Daro and Harappa possessed structures known to us as the Grainary and the Citadel; these constitute other architectural accomplishments. In all probability, the Grainary functioned as a public treasury for warehousing taxes. It seems likely that grain was used both for payment of taxes and also as renumeration for government employees. The Citadel, an artificial platform oblong in its dimensions and ranging in height from 35 to 50 feet, covered an area approximately 400 by 200 square yards in size. The Citadel was defended by notched walls; all of the public buildings resided atop the Citadel, while below it lay the private dwellings and shops of the city's residents.

As A.L. Basham points out in *The Wonder That Was India*, "pre-Aryan India made certain advances in husbandry for which the whole world owes her a debt."[27] The people of the Indus cultivated wheat, corn, barley, peas, and sesame, the latter still holding its position as an important crop, mainly for its seeds and oil. We are uncertain as to whether rice was cultivated in the Indus Valley region in Harappan times, but clear evidence indicates that cotton was cultivated.

At the time Basham was writing, prehistoric India was thought to be the earliest cultivator of cotton. But, as Dr. Ivan Van Sertima notes in *They Came Before Columbus*, "the agricultural revolution came to West Africa and particularly to the Mande people much earlier than was formerly supposed (as early as 5000 B.C.) and . . . cotton cultivation in Sudanic Africa was of considerable antiquity."[28] Dr. Van Sertima then quotes George Peter Murdock, an American anthropologist, "one of the major contributions of the Nuclear Mande people to the welfare of mankind was the domestication of cotton. Originally ennobled in the Western Sudan, this textile plant was transmitted early to India . . ."[29]

Having established Africa as the oldest cultivator of cotton, and India as the second, we can infer that the African Negritos introduced cotton to the Indus. Basham puts the earliest possible period for the development of agriculture, towns and villages between 10,000 B.C. and 6,000 B.C. Since the cultivation of cotton would presumably follow food crop cultivation rather than precede it, and since cotton bolls are relatively useless without the knowledge of how to process them, it is more than plausible that the three elements—basic agricultural science, cotton cultivation, and hand-weaving technology, were all brought to India at the same time by African Negritos.

Evidence indicates vigorous trading between the Indus Valley and Mesopotamia. Cotton appears to have been the chief commodity, although Harappan traders also dealt in gold, copper, turquoise, lapis lazuli, and timber from the Himalayas. Many seals and some Indus pottery have been found as far away as Mesopotamia, thus leading to speculation that merchants from India actually lived there.

At the head of the Gulf of Cambay in India lies Lothal, a busy commercial port with extensive connections into inland central India. This seaport measures about 230 by 40 yards. The enclosed shipping dock is made of brick and measures 700 feet in length; this dock was controlled by a sluice gate which enabled the loading of ships during high or low tide.

Active traders in several commodities, the Harappans developed a system of weights and measures. Found at most major sites, along with ceramic or metal pans, these weights varied in size; some were so large that they were lifted and suspended by copper rings, while others were so minute one author speculates that "they might have been used by jewellers."[30] Weights uncovered so far have been cylindrical, conical and cubular. Since the scales used with these measures were wooden, and consequently prone to disintegration over the years, few scales have been found.

Historians and archaeologists can only puzzle over the organization of the Harappan governing body or social structure. We speculate that the Indus Valley civilization consisted of a federation of self-governing cities.

As to the religious and spiritual beliefs of the Harappans, their principles were fully incorporated in their everyday existence. There is evidence of a deep spiritual sensitivity that permeated their culture to its very core; the author speculates that such an understanding may not have been seen upon the earth since the fall of the Indus Valley civilization.

Two major spiritual influences governed the Indus Valley culture: the philosophy of Jainism and the science of yoga. Contemporary historians underestimate the age of both of these disciplines; Vardhanana Mahavira, a contemporary of the Buddha who lived in the fifth century B.C., is said to have founded Jainism, while a grammarian named Patanjali is held to have written the first yoga sutras in the 2nd century B.C.

Evidence unearthed at Mohenjo Daro and Harappa bears testimony to a far greater antiquity. The genesis of these philosophies occurred during the days of the Indus Valley civilization.

Like a major artery, Jainism runs through the body of India's philosophical traditions. The Jaina philosophy was borne out of the people who were indigenous to the Indus Valley, and is not to be found in any of the other civilizations that were contemporary with Harappa. Therefore, we can infer it was not imported by any other people or race.

Contrary to popular knowledge, Mahavira was not the founder of the Jaina school of thought. Ironically Jainism acknowledges Mahavira as the *last* of its twenty-four Tirthankara's or Saints; the earliest Tirthankara, according to tradition, lived in the dawn of time, when men were as giants, during a period so old we cannot calculate even the geological date.[31]

Plate 5. A *lingam*, India. Symbol used for fertility worship.

However old that may be, it certainly predates the Aryan conquest. Joseph Campbell, editor of the literary works of Heinrich Zimmer propounds the eminent historian's ideas: "Dr. Zimmer regarded Jainism as the oldest of the non-Aryan groups . . . He believed that there is truth in the Jaina idea that their religion goes back to a remote antiquity, the antiquity in question being that of the pre-Aryans, so-called Dravidian [read: Harappan] period which has recently been dramatically illuminated by the discovery of a series of great late stone age cities in the Indus Valley dating from the third and perhaps even the fourth millennium B.C."[32] (Note that Zimmer, like Du Bois, used the term Dravidian rather loosely.) I feel that the antiquity of which the Jaina tradition speaks far exceeds the Harappan civilization; in any case, it is safe to say that the Jaina philosophy existed during the Harappan age at least.

Tracing the lineage of the Tirthankara's backwards from Mahavira will take us to the civilization of Harappa. Mahavira's immediate predecessor, the 23rd Tirthankara, was known as Parsvanatha or the Lord Parsava. Parsava was born in 872 B.C. and achieved enlightenment in approximately 772 B.C.; thus he would have lived during the great wars for the supremacy of India, being waged between the descendents of the Harappan culture and the Aryans.

There is little doubt as to the racial identity of this saint. In his text, *Philosophies of India*, Dr. Zimmer quotes a passage from the life of this Tirthankara, "When the son [Parsava] was born, the thrones of all the Indras trembled, and the gods understood that the Lord had seen the light of day. With pomp they descended for the celebration of the Second Kalyana, 'the salutary event of the Savior's birth.' The child was of a beautiful blue-black complexion, grew rapidly in beauty and young strength."[33] In his footnotes, Zimmer adds that Parsava "was a scion . . . of the non-Aryan, aboriginal stock of India."[34]

From this statement, we see that Parsava, like Mahavira and the Buddha, was a saint of pre-Aryan philosophical belief. This Jaina savior was the second to the last of its spiritual warriors, and lived in the 8th century B.C. How far beyond this penultimate Tirthankara does the lineage extend?

Tradition holds (though this cannot be substantiated by historical fact) that Parsava's immediate predecessor Aristanemi lived 80,000 years before his time; this would take us back to the lower Paleolithic period. The prior Jaina saint, Nami, who preceded Aristanemi, taught and preached the faith fifty thousand years before that. This date extends the lineage to the Eolithic period. His predecessor, Survata, the twentieth Tirthankara, is said to have lived eleven hundred thousand years before Nami. The list goes on, down to the earliest Tirthankara, who is said to have lived in a period more ancient even then the three and a half million year old Ethiopian female known as Lucy. Tradition holds that the Jaina faith is truly eternal and boundless; even if only a fraction of this principle is true, it would surely be enough to support the existence of Jainism in the Indus Valley civilization at 3000 B.C., if not before. Thus, Jainism may be as old as the Black race's presence in India and consequently appears to be indigenous to it.

Plate 6. Yogi from Mohenjo Daro. Indus seal, 3000-2500 BC. Transcription reads: "The Black One, The Black Buffalo."

Images in Harappan artwork corroborate the existence of Jainism in the Harappan civilization. One of the characteristics of the Jaina monks is that upon initiation they would become gymnosophist. Several of these nude religious images have been unearthed in terra cotta form; these constitute powerful evidence of the Jaina presence in Mohenjo-Daro and Harappa. A.L. Basham describes these images to be of ''nude men with coiled hair; their posture, rigidly upright, with the legs slightly apart, and the arms held parallel to the sides of the body but not touching it, closely resembles the stance called by the Jaina's Kayotsarga in which meditating teachers are often portrayed in later times.''[35]

As stated earlier, yoga, known also as the "Supreme Science," is held to have developed in the 2nd century B.C. by an Indian grammarian named Patanjali. In composing the earliest sutras of yoga, he earned the appellation of the father of yoga. History, however, has given him too much credit. The science of yoga was born out of an antiquity just as mysterious as Jainism. There is reason to believe that these disciplines have co-existed side by side for several millennia. Speaking of yoga and its counterpart Sankhya, Dr. Zimmer states, "These ideas do not belong to the original stock of the Vedic Brahmanic tradition [Aryan thought]. The two ideologies are of different origin . . . Yoga being related to the mechanical system of the Jainas, which we have seen can be traced back in a partly historical, partly legendary way through the long series of the Tirthankaras, to a remote aboriginal non-Vedic [Harappan] Indian antiquity. Yoga therefore must be immensely old." [36]

In his assertion as to the age of yoga, I believe Zimmer to be absolutely correct. There is no doubt that this spiritual science was born out of Black ancestry. Evidence of its impact on Harappan culture is visible in the soapstone seals found at Mohenjo-Daro and Harappa. The images on several excavated seals clearly depict an individual sitting in what is traditionally classified as Padmasan or "Lotus" posture and a similar posture known to practitioners as Bhadrasana or the adepts pose. Both of these "asanas" or postures are heralded as the most advanced in meditation poses since the practitioner must maintain the posture for two hours at least to achieve meditative benefits.

Another interesting fact one may note is that some of the seals depict a yogi (one who practices yoga) surrounded by animals of the forest. Herein is reflected a deep kinship with the animal kingdom that seeped into the science of yoga. Many of the postures are named after animals, i.e., crane, cobra, crocodile, lion, frog, fish, etc. Here we see a deep integral oneness with nature. Zimmer says, "A feeling of profound fellowship and comradeship with the beast and with all living things has inspired Indian thought throughout the ages. The most significant ethical outcome of the attitude was the commandment not to injure any living thing . . ." [37] Basham's ideas support Zimmer's in a different but convincing approach pertaining to diet. "When Fa-hsien visited India in the early 5th century he reported that no respectable person ate meat. The growth of vegetarianism was of course linked with the doctrine of nonviolence . . . It was known in the days of the Upanishads and was elaborated by Buddhism and Jainism . . ." [38]

The seal dramatized on the following page is known as "Lord of the Wilderness." His horned headdress, though seemingly abstract, may very well be a prototype to later Indian symbolism. Quoting again Dr. Heinrich Zimmer, "the curious headdress resembles to a striking degree one of the most common symbols of early Buddhist art. The posture is associated also and even more characteristically with the Buddha . . . The cross-legged posture of the meditating

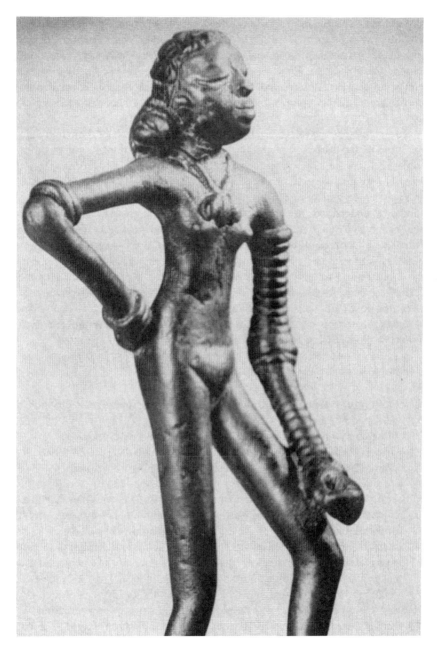

Plate 7. Bronze woman, Mohenjo-Daro. 2500 BC (characteristic of indigenous types).

yogi."[39] Thus it is through these images we discover a new and different interpretation to the origins of the cross-legged pose so often seen in Oriental Art. We are now at a point where the civil, spiritual, and cultural, patterns begin to enlighten one as to the tremendous contribution made by the African race to India and the world at large. From Harappa to Parsava to Krishna then Buddha; from Jainism to Yoga to Sankhya and the Gita, the investment the Black race has made in Indian culture and civilization affects one with a profound and sobering clarity.

For me to elaborate further on the Yogic and Jaina schools of thought would at this time be too vast an undertaking. There are many volumes written on both subjects. But what I will attempt to do is to give a general overview as to the internal structure of both.

Yoga by definition in the English language means to "yoke" or unite. It should be understood that yoga is not a religion or dogma and has no "ism's" attached to it. Yoga is categorized as a science, a practical and scientifically prepared method of gaining mastery over one's self, i.e., controlling body and mind. Hinduism is not a part of yoga though yoga may become a component of the Hindu faith. Swami Vishnudevenanda once said, "A yogi is not a Hindu but a Hindu may become a Yogi."[40] Using a metaphor to describe the unition of yoga and religion, Yoga is to philosophy and religion what oil is to a lamp. Without oil a lamp is a receptacle with a wick, no light. Without Yoga (or union), philosophy becomes rhetoric and religion is taken for granted.

The Training Course of the Yogi

1. Self-control (yama): the practice of non-violence, truthfulness, chastity, and avoidance of greed.
2. Observance (niyama): to create awareness of the above principle.
3. Postures (asana): sitting in certain postures of which there are 840,000; 84 are major. They condition the body and prepare it for meditation.
4. Breath Control (pranayama): it is said a Yogi gauges his life not by the number of years he lives but by the number of breaths he takes. In pranayama the breath is controlled and the respiration forced into bio-dynamic rhythms which are believed to be of great physical and spiritual value.
5. Restraint (pratyahara): sense withdrawal; this involves disciplining the sense organs (hearing, sight, smell, etc.) so to take no note of their perceptions and thereby curtail temptations of these organs, i.e., food, sex, intoxicants, etc.
6. Steadying the Mind (dharana): cultivating the ability to focus on one object for a length of time so as to develop profound skills of concentration.
7. Meditation (dhyana): when the object of concentration engulfs the entire mind.
8. Deep Meditation (samadhi): the whole personality is dissolved temporarily. Superconsciousness.

Jainism

The philosophy of the Jaina differs from Hinduism in that it is void of the many gods and goddesses which exist in the latter. Though there is no overt-denial of these gods, Jainism does not acknowledge any special role for them. The world and cosmos for the Jaina practitioner is not created, maintained, or destroyed by a personal god or deity, but functions in accord to universal axioms or laws. Jainism in many ways is akin to what has come to be known as the Hermetic Philosophy, given to Egypt by Thoth, who later was called Hermes Mecurius Trismegistus (Master of Masters) or Mercury by the Greeks.

Principles of the Jain

1. The Qualities of Matter: the universe is a living organism but imperishable in its essence.
2. The Mask of Personality: personality is derived from the Latin persona which literally means the mask worn over the face. One must separate true self from personality (the Mask).
3. The Cosmic Man: materialized spirit is the First Man. Spirit is eternal and the universe, being permeated within and without, never had a beginning and will never end.
4. The Doctrine of Bondage: Karma or the law of Causation—every cause has its effect, every effect has its cause, and everything happens according to law. Chance is but a name for law not recognized. Spoken in Biblical terms as an eye for an eye, and as ye sow so shall ye reap.
5. The Doctrine of Release: progress to purity, self detachment and finally enlightenment.

Through the principles of both Yoga and Jainism, obviously the Indian people were able to achieve high levels of spirituality. This resulted in a God-inspired existence that was quite simplistic, as evidenced in their art and sculpture.

The Indus Valley culture appears to have been rather austere. Their building endeavors, while incredibly functional, are completely lacking in ornamentation. However, the Harappans did indulge in the art of creative appliance. Some soapstone seals have quite complex designs, and smaller terracotta statues and toys have also been found. Many of these toys are jointed and have moveable heads which can nod or be moved side to side. One of the most interesting works of art found is a bronze statue of a young girl (see illustration). This statue is the only one of its kind so far unearthed. Cast in bronze, the subject's features are more distinct than those of the terra cotta statues.

Perhaps the bronze dancing girl statue represents an initial Harappan foray into more sophisticated art work; as the civilization evolved, it may be that their desire to experiment more deeply in the creative arts was just being kindled. Unfortunately, fate had set a different mandate, one which was to drastically alter the face of Indian civilization. The excavated site of Rana Ghundai shows that horse riding barbarians had begun to raid villages in the Baluchistan area during the 3rd millennium B.C. These would-be invaders mixed and were apparently absorbed by the indigenous people, and disappeared.

But later, about 1800 B.C., barbarians again came out of the Western Steppes to assault the Indus. The villages of Baluchistan were the first to fall prey to the marauding barbarians. As word spread through the Indus region, Harappans who lived in villages and small towns in the path of the invaders uprooted themselves and sought protection that only the major cities could provide. Basham assesses the impact this migration had on the cities as follows: "After the barbarians had conquered the outlying villages, the ancient laws and rigid organization of the Indus cities must have suffered great strain. At Mohenjo-Daro large rooms were divided into smaller, and mansions became tenements; potters' kilns were built within the city boundaries and are even in the middle of a street.[41]

Defenses were strengthened, and of the four great gateways, one was wholly blocked—danger threatened from the west. Thus the sun began to set and the Indus Valley civilization entered the twilight of its destiny.

The day finally arrived and horse riding barbarians engulfed the land. Converging on the Indus cities with superior weapons and steeds, they consumed them and slaughtered people by the hundreds—men, women and children, none were spared. And so it was written in the Rg Veda that Indra their war-god had destroyed hundreds of the Dasa's fortified places called Pur.

The positions of the skeletons found in the cities leave little doubt as to the violent manner of their deaths. The archaeologist Mackay discovered two skeletons lying on a short flight of brick steps and two more just outside the steps. He recorded that "There seems no doubt that these four people were murdered . . . It can be regarded as almost certain that these skeletal remains date from the latter end of the occupation of Mohenjo-Daro and are not later intrusions." [42] Mackay describes another group of nine skeletons, five of them children, lying "in strangely contorted attitudes and crowded together," as though "thrown pell-mell into a hurriedly made pit." It appears, comments Mackay, that this group "tried to escape with their belongings at the time of the raid but were stopped and slaughtered by the raiders." [43]

Another archaeologist, Marshall, described a similar violent scene. Some fourteen skeletons, all unfortunately in bad condition, were found. A couple of skulls showed signs of violent injury, including "a straight cut 136mm in length" which "could only have been done during life with a sharp and heavy weapon, such as a sword, and that this was in all probability the cause of death." [44]

Finally, Dr. George F. Dales describes five sprawling skeletons "not buried in any normal way but the victims of some disaster." [45] Seven other skeletons were found but detailed descriptions are not available. However, we can say that a

Plate 8. Parsava, the 23rd Jaina (savior). Tirthankara.

total of thirty-eight skeletons have been found, with only nine of them receiving even a scanty funeral covering. From the layering of the earth over the remains, we can also verify that twenty-two of these individuals died at approximately the same time.

Thus we have construed the violent collapse of the Indus Valley civilization. Although the cities were destroyed and hundreds died in the wake of the disaster, thousands survived. They migrated to the northeast where kindred villages awaited their coming. With them they brought their sciences and culture and in time they again began to flourish. This initiated a series of wars which raged through the northwest of India. These wars lasted 1,000 years and finally climaxed in the great battle of Kuruksetra on the Kuru River, in the 5th century B.C. This battle was known as the Mahabharata.

There comes the appearance of Krsna the ultimate warrior, of whom Basham describes as "the Black one . . . the name means Black."[46] Along with Krsna were five central figures known as the Pandavas, one of which was Arjuna, another great Ksatriya (warrior). All nations and people's gathered for this devastating battle: Greeks, Persians, Bactrians, and more. Each siding with the Pandavas (the Black kings) or the Kuravas (the Aryan kings), to see who would reign supreme on the Indian sub-continent.

To quote a passage from the Mahabhrata epic, as the armies amassed, "Arjuna said: 'Place my chariot O changeless one between the two armies, so that in this moment of impending battle I may behold those standing eager for war, with whom I have to fight.'"[47] (See cover.)

Thus addressed, Krsna drove the incomparable chariot between the two armies drawn up for battle, "facing Bhisma, Drona and all the rulers of the earth."[48]

"Then Arjuna gazed upon the two peoples: fathers, grandfathers, teachers, uncles, brothers, sons, grandsons . . . and he was overcome with horror . . ."[49] He was afraid to fight, for he did not want to lose those who were of his own people. But being a Ksatriya he was bound by code "to avenge the injuries that he and his brothers had sustained . . . and to assist his brethren in their just effort to recover their dominion."[50]

Not knowing what he should do, unable to distinguish right from wrong, Arjuna in despair turns to Krsna. The divine warrior conveys to him the dual principles of right and wrong and puts Arjuna's mind to rest.

Krsna then stands upright and in a great voice says to Arjuna "Time am I, the Destroyer great and mighty, appearing here to sweep all men away. Even without thee none of these warriors here, in their ranks arrayed shall remain alive. Therefore, do thou arise, win glory, smite your foe, enjoy in prosperity thy lordship . . . 'Thou dost feel pity,' speaks the mighty warrior, 'where pity has no place. Wise men feel no pity either for what dies or for what lives. There never was a time when I and thou were not in existence, and all these princes too . . . Be assured (Arjuna) that the very tissue of this universe is imperishable; it lies in no man's power to destroy it—Fight then, O Bharata.'"[51]

So began one of the greatest battles said to be witnessed upon the Earth. A battle that literally ended the Aryan Vedic age and ushered in a new and major cycle in India's history. It was soon after, Vedic thought and the non-Aryan philosophies of the indigenous inhabitants merged as one, creating a spiritual and philosophical synthesis that remains to this day. This is especially exemplified in the Hindu faith. Dr. Zimmer speaks on this cultural unition; "Following a long history of rigid resistance the exclusive and esoteric Brahmin mind of the Aryan invaders opened up . . . and received suggestions and influences from the native civilization. The result was a coalescence of the two traditions. And this is what produced in time, the majestic harmonizing systems . . . of contemporary Indian thought."[52]

Other developments took place as well. Omnipotent Black sages such as the Buddha, Mahavira, and Gosala came into being. India saw its first great Black empire since the fall of the Indus Valley civilization—the Mauryan Dynasty. From this dynasty arose a Black king who would reshape Indian history named Asoka. As A.L. Basham states, "Asoka was the greatest and noblest ruler India has known, and indeed one of the greatest kings of the world."[53]

India would experience many magnificent 'transformations,' spurned and perpetuated by the race which gave India her first civilization and culture—the Black race.

But this is another time and another story . . .

Notes

1. A.L. Basham, The Wonder That Was India (Grove Press, Inc., New York, 1959), p. 4.
2. H.P. Blavatsky, The Secret Doctrine (The Theosophy Company, Los Angeles, 1949), p. 311. The keys to the seven sub-systems of which Blavatsky speaks are those originally contained within the Hermetic Philosophy. They are as follows: Principle of Correspondence, Vibration, Polarity, Rhythm, Causation (cause and effect), Gender, and the Principle of the All or Mentalism. An adept is one who aspires for the ultimate in spiritual revelation, i.e., Sons of God.
3. A.L. Basham, p. 24.
4. A.L. Basham, ibid., p. 32. It must be understood that ancient India, Egypt and Kush were all absorbed in the science of procreation metaphysically and spiritually as well as physiologically. This gave use to the tantric schools in India, Egypt and China. For further information, see the Tao of Love and Sex, Jolan Chang, E.P. Dutton, New York, 1977; or Sexual Secrets, by Nick Douglas and Penny Slinger, Destiny Books, New York, 1979.
5. A.L. Basham, p. 32.
6. A.L. Basham, p. 32.
7. New York Times, November 16, 1984, and Cheikh Anta Diop, Origin of the Ancient Egyptians (Transaction Periodicals Consortium, Rutgers University), p. 9.
8. Bharatiya Vidya Bhavan, The Vedic Age, Vol. 1 (S. Roma-Krishnan and Bhavan Bombay, India 1962), p. 148.
9. Bharatiya Vidya Bhavan, p. 149.
10. Bharatiya Vidya Bhavan, p. 149.
11. Marshall Snellgrove, Icons of the Buddha (Freer Gallery, National Smithsonian Institute, 1978), p. 48.
12. Bharatiya Vidya Bhavan, p. 151.

13. Bharatiya Vidya Bhavan, p. 151.
14. Bharatiya Vidya Bhavan, p. 151.
15. W.E. Burghardt DuBois, The World and Africa (International Publishers, New York, 1972), p. 176.
16. A.L. Basham, p. 25.
17. B.K. Chatterjee and G.D. Kumar, Comparative Study and Racial Analysis of the Human Remains of Indus Valley Civilization. (Calcutta, Sol Distributors, W. Neuman, 1965), p. 17.
18. Chatterjee and Kumar, p. 17.
19. Chatterjee and Kumar, p. 23.
20. Chatterjee and Kumar, p. 23.
21. Sir Mortimer Wheeler, The Indus Valley Civilization (Cambridge, 1953), p. 68.
22. Editors note: Because the script of the Harappan culture has not been deciphered, there are no written records as such and therefore must be classified as prehistoric, i.e., before writing.
23. A.L. Basham, p. 13.
24. Mario Rossi, A Lost Civilization Vanishing Again? (Christian Science Monitor, 1984), p. 25.
25. A.L. Basham, p. 16.
26. Sir Mortimer Wheeler, Civilizations of the Indus Valley and Beyond (McGraw-Hill, 1966), p. 33.
27. A.L. Basham, p. 25.
28. Dr. Ivan Van Sertima, They Came Before Columbus (Random House, 1977), p. 187.
29. Dr. Ivan Van Sertima, p. 188.
30. Robert Davreu, The Lost Empire of the Indus Valley: The World's Last Mysteries (Readers Digest, 1976), p. 128.
31. Editors Note: It is interesting to note all of the major civilizations of Old have recorded somewhere in their sacred text the legend of giants. Even the Bible acknwledges the same in Genesis, "There were giants on the earth in those days; and also after that when the sons of God came in unto the daughters of men..." (The Bible, Genesis, chapter 6, verse 4), and Heinrich Zimmer, Philosophies of India (Princeton University Press, 1969), p. 226.
32. Heinrich Zimmer, Philosophies of India (Princeton University Press, Bollinger Series XXVI, 1969, edited by Joseph Campbell), p. 60.
33. Heinrich Zimmer, p. 196.
34. Heinrich Zimmer, p. 196.
35. A.L. Basham, p. 22.
36. Heinrich Zimmer, p. 281.
37. Heinrich Zimmer, The Art of Indian Asia, completed and edited by Joseph Campbell, Vol. I (Princeton University Press, Bollinger Series XXXIX, 1983), p. 31.
38. A.L. Basham, p. 213.
39. Heinrich Zimmer, p. 27.
40. Swami Vishnudevenana in a personal statement made by himself to the writer.
41. A.L. Basham, p. 26.
42. Sir Mortimer Wheeler, The Indus Civilization (Cambridge, 1968), p. 130.
43. Sir Mortimer Wheeler, p. 130.
44. Sir Mortimer Wheeler, p. 130.
45. George F. Dales in (Archaeology, vol. 18, no. 2, 1965), p. 147.
46. A.L. Basham, p. 305.
47. Heinrich Zimmer, Philosophies of India, pp. 382-384.
48. Heinrich Zimmer, pp. 382-384.
49. Heinrich Zimmer, pp. 382-384.
50. Heinrich Zimmer, pp. 382-384.
51. Heinrich Zimmer, pp. 382-384.
52. Heinrich Zimmer, p. 281.
53. A.L. Basham, p. 53.

KRISHNA AND BUDDHA OF INDIA: BLACK GODS OF ASIA

John G. Jackson

The classical home of the ancient Ethiopians was the Eastern Sudan, although Homer and Herodotus mentioned other Ethiopians dwelling in Egypt, Arabia, Palestine, Western Asia and India. To cite Lady Lugard: "The fame of the ancient Ethiopians was widespread in ancient history. Herodotus describes them as the tallest, most beautiful and longlived of the human races, and before Herodotus, Homer, in even more flattering language, described them as the most just of men, the favorites of the gods. The annals of all the great early nations of Asia Minor are full of them. The Mosaic records allude to them frequently; but while they are described as the most powerful, the most just, and the most beautiful of the human race, they are constantly spoken of as Black, and there seems to be no other conclusion to be drawn than that at that remote period of history, the leading race of the Western World was a Black race" [*A Tropical Dependency*, p. 221].

The ancient Kushite or Ethiopian culture may be called the Archaic Civilization. Even before the rise of the culture of Egypt, there was the great Kushite, or Ethiopian civilization, which was widespread in both Africa and Asia. One of the greatest African Ethiopian temples was located at Abu Simbel, or Ipsambul, in Nubia. When an English traveler named Wilson visited this temple, he saw sculptured on its walls the story of the Fall of Man as told in Genesis. Adam and Eve were shown in the Garden of Eden as well as the tempting serpent and the fatal tree. Commenting on this fact, Godfrey Higgins asked: "How is the fact of the mythos of the second book of Genesis being found in Nubia, probably a thousand miles above Heliopolis, to be accounted for?" [*Anacalypsis*, Vol. I, p. 403]. Higgins then added that: "The same mythos is found in India." For evidence he cited Colonel Tod's *History of Raputana* as follows: "A drawing brought by Colonel Coombs, from a sculptured column in a cave-temple in the south of India represents the first pair at the foot of the ambrosial tree, and a serpent entwined among the heavily laden boughs, presenting to them some of the fruit from his mouth" [*Anacalypsis*, Vol. I, pp. 403-404]. The ancient peoples of

Plate 1. Krishna raises Mount Govardhana, 16th century.

India were Asiatic Ethiopians and it should not surprise us that they shared common traditions with their brothers in Africa.

Krishna and Buddha of India

Krishna was the 8th Avatar of the Hindu pantheon and is said to have lived about 1200 B.C. The parallels between the life of Krishna, as recorded in the sacred books of India and of the life of Jesus Christ, as related in the sacred anthology of the Christians, is so close that some scholars have believed that the Christian writers copied their account from the Hindus. This opinion, though plausible, has little to recommend it; the most we can say is that both traditions seem to be traceable to a common source. In this brief sketch only a few of these parallels can be discussed (for an exhaustive treatment the reader is referred to *Christianity and Mythology*, by John M. Robertson):

"The Hindu Christ like many other savior gods was born of a virgin. Krishna was the son of the Virgin Devaki. An angelic voice from heaven announced to the Virgin: 'In thy delivery O favored among women, all nations shall have cause to rejoice.' The nativity of Krishna was heralded by a star at the time of his birth in a cave, where he was visited by wise men, who brought him valuable presents. In the Apocryphal Gospel 'Protevangelion,' a work attributed to James the brother of Jesus, we have been told that the Christian Savior was also born in a cave. At the time of the birth of Krishna the cave was mysteriously illuminated. Similarly, at the birth of Jesus there was such a bright light in the cave that the eyes of Joseph and the midwife could not bear it [This tradition has been recorded in *The Apocryphal New Testament: Gospel of Protevangelion*, Chapter 14:11]. The infant Krishna began speaking to his mother soon after his birth. In the *New Testament Apocrypha* we read a similar story about Jesus. In this document we have been told that: 'Jesus spake even when he was in the cradle, and said to his mother: Mary, I am Jesus, the Son of God, that *WORD* which thou didst bring forth according to the declaration of the angel Gabriel to thee, and my Father hath sent me for the salvation of the world' [*The First Gospel of the Infancy*, chapter 1:263].

"The birth of Krishna occurred while his foster father, Nanda, was in the city to pay his tax to the King. Likewise, Jesus was born while his foster father, Joseph, was in the city to pay tax to the governor.

"King Kansa sought the life of the Hindu Christ by ordering the slaughter of all male children born on the same night as was Krishna. This is paralleled by the story of the slaughter of the innocents, ordered by King Herod, as related in the Gospel according to Matthew: 11-16.

"A heavenly voice warned Nanda to flee across the Jumna River with the infant Krishna, in order to escape from King Kansa. In this instance, we recall that Joseph was warned in a dream to flee into Egypt with the Virgin Mary and the Christ-child to escape from King Herod.

"Krishna performed numerous miracles in Mathura. While in Egypt Jesus performed similar miracles in Matarea. The lame walked, the blind saw, the sick were healed, the dead were raised, demons were expelled, and the laws of Nature were frequently suspended for the benefit of the Church. But the sages of Greece and Rome turned aside from the awful spectacle and, pursuing the ordinary occupations of life and study, appeared unconscious of any alteration in the moral or physical government of the world. Under the reign of Tiberius, the whole earth, or at least a celebrated province of the Roman Empire, was involved in a preternatural darkness of three hours. Even this miraculous event, which ought to have excited the wonder, the curiosity, and the devotion of mankind, passed without notice in an age of science and history. It happened during the lifetime of Seneca and the elder Pliny, who must have experienced the immediate effects or received the earliest intelligence of the prodigy. Each of these philosophers in a laborious work, has recorded all of the great phenomena of nature, earthquake, meteors, comets, and eclipses, which the indefatigable curiosity could collect. Both the one and the other have omitted to mention the greatest phenomenon to which the mortal eye has been witness since the creation of the globe. A distinct chapter of Pliny is designed for eclipses of an extraordinary nature and duration; but he contents himself with describing the singular defect of light which followed the murder of Caesar, when, during the greatest part of a year, the orb of the sun appeared pale and without splendor. This season of obscurity, which cannot surely be compared with the preternatural darkness of the Passion, had been already celebrated by most of the poets and historians of that memorable age.'' [*History of Christianity*, pp. 200-202, by Edward Gibbon].

The descent into hell was one of the exploits of Krishna; where he raised the dead before returning to the abode of the gods. On the return from hell he brought with him two boys, whom he restored to their parents on earth. In the New Testament Apocrypha is an account of the descent of the Christian Savior into hell, from whence he led a party of saints back to earth, and besides them, two sons of the High priest, who were returned to life on earth. The story of the descent into hell is related in the Gospel of Nicodemus, from which the following extracts are taken:

"Satan, the prince and captain of death, said to the prince of hell, 'Prepare to receive Jesus of Nazareth, himself who boasted that he was the Son of God, and yet was a man afraid of death'. . . . To this the Prince of hell replied to Satan; 'Who is that so powerful prince, and yet a man who is afraid of death?' . . . . And while Satan and the prince of hell were discoursing thus to each other, on a sudden there was a voice as of thunder and the rushing of winds, saying, 'Lift up your gates, O ye princes; and be ye lift up, O everlasting gates, and the King of Glory shall come in.' . . . . When the prince of hell heard this, he said to Satan, 'Depart from me and begone out of my habitations; if thou art a powerful warrior, fight with the King of Glory. But what hast thou to do with him?' And then he cast him forth from his habitations. And the prince said to his impious officers, 'Shut the brass gates of cruelty and make them fast with iron bars, and fight courageously lest we be taken captives.' . . . . But when all the company of the saints heard this they spoke out with a loud voice of anger to the prince of hell, 'Open thy gates that the King of Glory may come in'. . . . Then there was, as of the sound of thunder, saying 'Lift up your gates, O princes; and be ye lifted up, ye gates of hell, and the King of Glory will enter in.' . . . . The prince of hell perceiving the same voice repeated cried out . . . 'Who is that King of Glory?' David replied to the prince of hell, . . . 'I say unto thee, the Lord strong and powerful, the Lord mighty in battle; he is the King of Glory, and he is the Lord in Heaven and earth. He hath looked down to hear the groans of the prisoners and to set loose those that are appointed to death. And now thou filthy and stinking prince of hell, open thy gates, that the King of Glory may enter in; for he is Lord of heaven and earth.' . . . . While David was saying this, the mighty Lord appeared in the Form of a man, and enlightened those places which had ever before been in darkness, and broke asunder the fetters which before could not be broken; and with his invincible power visited those who sat in the deep darkness by iniquity, and the shadow of death by sin. . . . Then the prince of hell took Satan, and with great indignation said to him. 'O thou prince of destruction, author of Beelzebub's defeat and banishment, the scorn of God's angels and loathed by all righteous persons! What inclined thee to act thus?'. . . . While the prince of hell was thus speaking to Satan, the King of Glory said to Beelzebub, the prince of hell, 'Satan, the prince shall be subject to thy dominion forever, in the room of Adam and his righteous sons, who are mine. Then Jesus stretched forth his hand, and said, 'Come to me, all ye saints, who are created in my image, who were condemned by the tree of the forbidden fruit, and by the devil and death; live now by the word of my cross; the devil, the prince of this world, is overcome and death is conquered' " [The Gospel of Nicodemus, chapters XV-XVI, cited by Dr. Paul Carus in The History of the Devil, pp. 174-179.

Gautama Buddha, the 9th Avatar of India, flourished around 600 B.C. The Stories relating to his life and death are similar to those recorded concerning Krishna. He was said to have been born of the Virgin Maya, or Mary. His incarnation was accomplished by the descent of the Holy Ghost upon the Virgin Maya. The infant Buddha, soon after birth spoke to his mother, saying: "I will put to an end the sufferings and sorrows of the world." As these words were uttered a mystical light surrounded the infant Messiah. During his earthly pilgrimage the Buddha was tempted by Mara, the evil One, but he heeded not the devil, saying, "Be gone; hinder me not." In the words of Graves: "He believed and taught his followers that all sin is inevitably punished, either in this or the future life; and so great were his sympathy and tenderness, that he condescended to suffer that punishment himself, by an Ignominious death on the cross after which he descended into Hades (Hell) to suffer for a time, (three days) for the inmates of that dreadful and horrible prison, that he might show he sympathized with them. After his ascension to heaven, as well as during his earthly sojourn, he imparted to the world some beautiful, lofty, and soul elevating precepts" [The Worlds Sixteen Crucified Saviors, p. 116].

Anyone interested in the life of Buddha should consult Sir Edwin Arnold's *The Light of Asia*, a biography of Gautama Buddha written as poetry. To give an example, when Buddha went out into the world to teach his doctrine, he found himself confronted with much evil: "About the painted temple peacocks flew, the blue doves cooed from every well, far off the village drums beat for some marriage feast; all things spoke peace and plenty and the prince saw and rejoiced. But, looking deep he saw the thorns which grow upon the rose of life: How the swarthy peasant sweated for his wage, toiling for leave to live; and how he urged the great-eyed oxen through the flaming hours, goading their velvet flanks; then marked he, how lizard fed on ant, and snake on him, and kite on both; and how the fish-hawk robbed the fish-tiger of that which it had seized; the shrike chasing the bulbul, which did chase the jewelled butterflies; till everywhere each slew a slayer and in turn was slain, life living upon death. So the fair show veiled one vast, savage, grim conspiracy of mutual murder, from the worm to man, who himself kills his fellow" [*The Light of Asia*, pp. 28-29].

Gautama the Buddha met a mother who was grieving the death of her infant son. The sorrowing mother requested the Master to bring her child back to life, and he answered: "They who seek physicians bring to them what is ordained. Therefore, I pray thee, find black mustard seed, a tola; only mark thou take it not from any hand or house where father, mother, child or slave hath died; it shall be well if thou canst find such seed.

The mother went away, then later returned and addressed Buddha: "I went, Lord, clasping to my breast the babe, grown colder, asking at each hut—here in the jungle, and towards the town—I pray you, give me a mustard of your grace, a tola—black; and each who had it gave, for all the poor; but when I asked, 'In my friend's household here hath any peradventure ever died—husband, or wife, or child, or slave'? They said: 'O Sister! What is this you asked? The dead are very many, and the living few!' So with sad thanks I gave the mustard back, and prayed of others, but the others said, 'Here is the seed, but we have lost our slave!' 'Here is the seed, but our good man is dead!' 'Here is some seed, but he that sowed it died, between the rain-time and the harvesting! oh, sir! I could not, find a single house where there was a mustard seed and none had died!

'My sister! Thou hast found,' the master said, 'Searching for what none finds—that better balm I had to give thee. He thou lovedst slept dead on thy bosom yesterday: today thou knowst the whole wide world weeps with thy woe: the grief which all hearts share grows less for one. Lo! I would pour my blood if it could stay thy tears and win the secret of that curse which makes sweet love our anguish, and which drives o'er flowers and pastures ot the sacrifice—as these dumb beasts are driven—men their lords. I seek that secret: bury thou they child!'" [*The Light of Asia*, pp. 127-129].

On the extensive parallels between the careers of Gautama Buddha and Jesus Christ, the reader might consult, with profit, chapter XXIX of *Bible Myths* by T.W. Doane.

Review Essay

ANCIENT KUSHITE ROOTS IN INDIA:
A SURVEY OF THE WORKS OF GODFREY HIGGINS

Reviewed by Gershom Williams

Within the long line of the many European scholars and writers on Africa, there have only been a few who have been bold or courageous enough to come forward with real truths concerning the African's ancient history and cultural heritage. This small minority of scholars represents an enduring challenge to the present ranks of Eurocentric scholarship and intellect. As Afrocentric historians, we should indeed be grateful to C.F. Volney, Gerald Massey, Albert Churchward, Godfrey Higgins, and others who have boldly proclaimed to the world the African origins and contributions to world civilization.

A brilliant critical study has already been done by Charles S. Finch on the works of Gerald Massey. In this essay Finch states, "Massey, through typology, plumbed to depths that revealed to him a record of human development hidden to all else."[1] But as Finch reminds us, "One exception to this statement is the work of Godrey Higgins, *Anacalypsis* . . . published almost 50 years before [Massey's] *Book of Beginnings*. The massive scholarship and penetrating understanding evident in this stupendous book seemed to prefigure Massey."[2]

Anacalypsis, a monument of erudition, is truly an extraordinary work written by an equally exceptional author. Higgins was writing at a time when it was unpopular, and even dangerous, to publish this kind of information about people of African descent, and there were major myths about African people being propagated by scholars and laymen alike during the period. The racist myth of inherent Black inferiority, and the myth that Africans had not made any worthwhile contributions to world civilization, were widespread.

Godfrey Higgins, humanist, social reformer, archaeologist, author, and historian, was one of the most remarkable men of his time. Born on January 30, 1772, the only son of Godfrey Higgins of Skellow Grange, near Doncaster England in the West Riding of Yorkshire, Higgins came from an old and respected family in Yorkshire.[3] After attending school at nearby Hemsworth, Higgins was admitted as a pensioner to Cambridge University where he matriculated in 1790. He studied law at London's Trinity Hall at the Inner Temple Center of Education, but due to the limitation of family funds, never took the legal degree. He also, interestingly enough, became a Freemason. When England was threatened by the invasion of Napoleon, Higgins joined the West York militia. Due to poor health, however, he was forced to resign his commission with the military and return home. It was this illness that induced him to turn his attention to more serious matters. He became determind to enter into a careful investigation of the evidence upon which our religions were founded. To quote Higgins:

> This at last led me to extend my inquiry into the origins of nations and languages; and ultimately I came to six hours a day to this pursuit for ten years. Instead of six hours a day for ten years, I believe I have, upon the average, applied myself to it for nearly ten hours daily for almost twenty years.

Higgins was about forty when he began his vast research on the antiquities of nations and religions. Early in his labors, he decided that he would apply himself to at least one ancient language and selected Hebrew as the closest to his immediate need. He further dedicated all his *spare* time to the study of history, archaeology and religion. He became a member of the Royal Asiatic Society, the Society of the Arts, the British Association for the Advancement of Science, and other learned bodies. In gathering material while conducting his research, Higgins made two journeys, one to Rome and the other to Naples. He made plans to visit the middle east where he believed he could make discoveries of profound significance. Even in his later years, and his health failing, he was hopeful that he might reach Egypt.

In 1826 Higgins published a slender volume entitled *Horae Sabbaticae; or, An Attempt to Correct Certain Superstitions and Vulgar Errors Respecting the Sabbath*. Within this volume, Higgins reaches the conclusion that there is Biblical or other justification for the popular sacredness of Sunday.

Higgins' next work appeared in 1827 and was the first real fruit of his long researches into history and religion. This important work was called *The Celtic Druids; or An Attempt to Show That the Druids were the Priests of Oriental Colonies Who Emigrated from India, and were the Introducers of the First or Cadmean System of Letters, and the Builders of Stonehenge, of Carnac, and of other Cyclopean Works, in Asia and Europe.*[5] Higgins explains that a great deal of his research in preparing the *Celtic Druids* was spent in the British Museum; another parallel to the work of Gerald Massey. Cited below is one of the many interesting and significant passages found within the volume's contents:

> Mr. Maurice labours hard to prove, that a great nation of Cuthites or Cushites overran Asia. By Cushites are always meant Blacks or Ethiopians. Sir W. Jones was also of this opinion, and thought the seat of their empire was Sidon. In the first part of their opinion I quite agree with these gentlemen, but I think the situation of the capital of their empire may be doubtful. The influx of Scythians mentioned in Ezekiel and alluded to by Mr. O'Connor, is of much more recent date. The empire alluded to by Sir William Jones, I take to have been the empire of the Asiatic Ethiopian Memnon, the Negro, whose colossal busts we have in the British Museum. These people were known probably from ancient tradition to Homer, and by a very allow-

Women of Orissa. Northeast India (1962 photo).

able liberty he brings this Memnon, though evidently of a date far earlier than the Trojan War, to his siege of Troy. The profound philosophers who take their history from epic poems, are of course obliged to make two Memnons. And this in our museum they call the younger. This eruption of Negroes, of the country men of the flat-faced, curly-headed Buddha, from upper India, were perhaps the first people who settled and inhabited Africa, built the pyramids, and made the colossal bust of Memnon, etc.[6]

Next among Higgins' writings, mention may be made of a text which was to prove even more disturbing to religious orthodoxy than *Celtic Druids*. This being a small book entitled *An Apology for the Life and Character of the Celebrated Prophet of Arabia called Mohamed or the Illustrious*, published in 1829.

Higgins last and best known manuscript was indeed his greatest. *Anacalypsis, and Attempt to draw Aside the Veil of the Saitic Isis; or an Inquiry into the Origins of Languages, Nations and Religions*, was published in 1836. The word anacalypsis itself is a rare one, deriving from the Greek, and meaning an uncovering or a revealing. According to Plutarch, the true devotee of the goddess Isis is he who ponders over sacred matters and seeks therein for hidden truth. It was Plutarch who described the veiled Isis in front of her temple at Sais with the famous inscription, "I Isis, am all that has been, all that is, or shall be; and no mortal man hath ever unveiled me." *Anacalypsis* will forever stand as one of the boldest attempts to answer this age old enigma of historical beginnings and religious origins.

Buddha. South-East Asia, 10th century AD.

Anacalypsis is a very complex work, containing a virtually inexhaustible mine of information, and it is very difficult to provide a critical discussion in such a short space. A brief overview, however, is possible. Higgins discusses the origins of the ideas of God, and shows the universality of basic religious concepts.

He examines the myths and beliefs relating to the deluge and other cataclysms of prehistory and gives his own elucidation of the vast cycles of time in the Mahayugas and Kalpas of Hindu religious chronology. He traces the spread of religions throughout the ancient world, and the relationships of languages and systems of writing to religious ideas in the migrations of races. In these discussions Higgins considers also the temples, monuments and ceremonies of former times. There also is a detailed examination of the sacred scriptures of different peoples and the impact of Christianity and its doctrines on earlier religions. Higgins repeatedly stressed the persistence of an esoteric knowledge, a "secret doctrine" of the leading world religions, which co-existed within the formalities and rituals of the priesthood.

The author traces the Black or Ethiopian presence in the middle east and India, which asserts is the source of all language, mythology, writing, and religious symbolism. The book also contains an extensive examination of the various ancient forms of male and female symbolism and the struggle all over the world between the adherents of the masculine principle and the femine principle for supremacy.

There are several basic and unifying themes that are present throughout *Anacalypsis*. Among the most prominent are: that there were ancient black civilizations that had achieved superior religious knowledge, much of which has been lost; that there is a universal basis to all religions; that all the mythologies of the ancient world, which however varied and corrupted in recent times, were originally one, and that that one religion is founded on principles sublime, beautiful and true. These ideas constitute the core of *Anacalypsis*. A brief summary of the author's intentions for the whole work may be found in the following passage:

> I shall, in the course of this work, produce a number of extraordinary facts, which will be quite sufficient to prove that a black race in very early times, had more influence over the affairs of the world than has been lately suspected. And I think I shall show, by some very striking circumstances yet existing, that the effects of this influence have not entirely passed away.[8]

In this same remarkable chapter Higgins discusses the existence of two ancient Ethiopia the black Buddha of India, and the Arabian Cushites. On the black Buddha of India, cites Higgins:

> The religion of Buddha, of India, is well known to have been very ancient. In the most ancient temples scattered throughout Asia, where his worship is yet continued, he is found black as jet, with the flat face, thick lips and curly hair of the Negro. Several statues of him may be met within the museum of the East India Company.

Concerning ancient Ethiopia, Homer also stated that there were two separate Ethiopian nations, one in Asia and the other in Africa. Furthermore they wrote that the inhabitants of several major regions, including the Sudan, Egypt, Arabia,

Buddha. 12 century AD.

Palestine and western Asia, and India, were Ethiopians. According to these eyewitnesses, the only physical was in the texture of hair.

Following is a typical example of Higgins' view of the remote antiquity of Ethiopia:

> There were two Ethiopias, one to the east of the Red Sea, and the other to the west of it; and a very great nation of Blacks from India, did rule over almost

all Asia in a very remote era, in fact beyond the reach of history or any of our records.[10]

There are numerous examples of Black religious and cultural influences in the ancient world given by Higgins in *Anacalypsis*. There are chapters devoted to discussions on the Black Madonnas, the Black Christ, crucified saviors, Black gods and messiahs, Black Egypt, and the Black Jews of India.

> We have found the black complexion or something relating to it whenever we have approached the origin of nations. The Alma Mater, the goddess Multimammia, the founders of oracles, the Memnons or first idols, were always black. Venus, Juno, Jupiter, Apollo, Bacchus, Hercules, Asteroth, Adonis, Horus, Apis, Osiris, Ammon, in short all the wood and stone deities were black. The images remain as they were first made in very remote times.[11]

Summary and Conclusion

Anacalypsis is the record of Higgins' search for the secret wisdom of the ancients, and of his firm belief in the underlying unity of all religions. In searching for the truth, he was led to make individual assessments of the contributions of archaeology, astronomy, philology, history, and other sciences as a basis for understanding religious beliefs. He was the first scholar to draw on so many sources and compile them together into one vast system. Two noted Black historians who have quoted extensively from *Anacalypsis* in their writings are Joel A. Rogers and John G. Jackson.[12]

The London Athenaeum, on August 2, 1956, describes a visit to the British Museum, which contains a reference to Higgins.

> Never was there more wildness of speculation than in this attempt to lift the veil of Isis. But thousands of statements, cited from all quarters, and very well indexed, apparently brought the book into such a demand as made it convenient that it should be in the reading room itself.[13]

Indeed, *Anacalypsis* is a book which deserves to occupy a place in any library. Historians and scholars of future generations will surely recognize and appreciate the extraordinary labors and monumental contributions.

Notes

1. Charles S. Finch, "The Works of Gerald Massey," *Journal of African Civilizations*, Vol. 4, No. 2, pp. 53-64.
2. Finch.

3. The useful biography of Godfrey Higgins in the *Dictionary of National Biography*, Vol. 26, pp. 368-369, gives the date of his birth as May 1, 1773. Other reference works give dates varying between 1771 and 1773. The date of January 30, 1772 is taken from a tablet on the cast wall of the south chapel of Wadworth Church, Doncaster where Higgins was buried. Also, for the information stated here, acknowledgement must go to Leslie Shepard and Manly P. Hall.

4. This is now known to be a false assumption made by not only Higgins, but other early scholars. The source of western culture (i.e. Greek philosophy, science, Judaism and Christianity) is not found in Asia, but in Africa among the ancient Nile Valley civilizations. See Bruce Williams, "Lost Pharaohs of Nubia," *Archaeology*, Vol. 33, No. 5, pp. 12-21. Because of the overwhelming African presence found in the region's of Arabia, Mesopotamia, Babylon, Sumer, Elam, China, India, etc., many early scholars were led to assume that Asia was the birthplace, not only of the Black race, but the cradle of civilization and the original home of man itself.

5. The *Celtic Druids*, one of the more pretentious literary undertakings of Godfrey Higgins, was long out of print but in 1977 was reprinted in limited numbers by the Philosophical Research Society Inc. of Los Angeles, California.

6. *Celtic Druids*, pp. 160-162.

7. The first volume *Anacalypsis* was completed in 1833, but the title page for the sake of uniformity, bears the date of 1836. This was three years after the author's death. The second volume of the work was unfinished (only four pages were completed) but was finally brought to printed form by the deceased author's only son. *Anacalypsis* was last reprinted by Health Research, Mokelumne Hill, 1972.

8. *Anacalypsis*, Vol. 1, bk. 1, ch. 4; Section 1, p. 51.

9. *Anacalypsis*.

10. *Anacalypsis*, Bk. 1, ch. 4, Section, 10, p. 59.

11. *Anacalypsis*, Bk. 5, ch. 13, Section 2, pp. 284-286.

12. J.A. Rogers, *Sex and Race* (Helga M. Rogers: New York, 1967); John G. Jackson, *Introduction to African Civilizations* (Citadel Press; Secaucus, 1974); see also John G. Jackson, *Man, God & Civilization* (Citadel Press: Secaucus, 1972).

13. *Anacalypsis*, p. 458.

AFRICAN PRESENCE IN EARLY CHINA

James Brunson

*The inhabitants of China are of the yellow race type, but
no doubt build upon a black foundation. The ethnologist
found there the evidence of a remote pygmy or Negroid
population.*[1]

To the Western mind, the Far East conjures images of glistening porcelain,
precious jade objects, colorful silk garments, and infinitely wise sages. Ancient
China is given priority as the most enduring culture in the Orient. It is generally
accepted that its modern inhabitants are primarily responsible for the creation of
Chinese civilization. However, the evidence indicates a "non-Chinese" or African element as seminal in propelling China toward civilization. The aim of this
article is to identify that element.

Anthropological finds dating from the Upper Paleolithic through the
Mesolithic periods (20,000 B.C.–8,000 B.C.) substantiate the existence of
"Negroid" types in China. At Chou-Koutien, in a cave near Peking, skeletal
remains of an old man (Negroid Neanderthal), a woman (Eskimo or Mongolian), and a young female (Modern day Melanesian), were found.[2] The
anthropologist, Carleton Coon, considered the Eskimo a Caucasoid type.
These skeletal remains are incredible, in view of the evolutionary theories
pertaining to man. Because of the ethnic features of many yellow peoples (full
lips, platyrrhinia, and prognathism), Diop has suggested the possibility of the
Mongolian types originating from a mixture of Blacks and Whites:

> The yellow race as well was probably the result of crossbreeding between
> Blacks and Whites at a very ancient time in the history of mankind. In fact,
> the yellow peoples have the pigmentation of mixed breeds so much so that
> comparative biochemical analysis would be unable to reveal any great differ-
> ence in the quality of melanin . . . and it has been observed that wherever
> there are yellow-skinned peoples, one still finds pockets of Black and Whites
> who seem to be the residual elements of that race.[3]

Even earlier fossil remains of the Negroid type have been found in the Upper
Pleistocene period (50,000 B.C.–10,000 B.C.). From southern China, the
provinces of Szechwan and Kiangsi, two human skulls, the Tzu-yang Man
(Mongoloid) and Liu-chiang (Negroid type) man, have been unearthed:

> On the basis of the two skulls, one might be tempted to suggest that the
> population of southern China . . . represents an early form of Homo Sapiens
> which later differentiated into some of the constituent elements of modern
> Mongoloid and the Oceanic Negroid populations.[4]

It may be emphasized that the Mongoloid type from these periods, has been recognized as a "primitive" form of Mongol. A. Keith noted: "Mongolian humanity seems to have evolved from a darker prototype".[5]

The missing element to this puzzle may be found in ancient Chinese legends. They describe in their annals, a primitive, "hairy" race of people, whom scholars now identify as the Ainu. These Ainu, who live predominately in Japan (some still live in the mountains of China) show signs of Negroid and Mongolian admixture. Some anthropologists consider them Caucasoid. However a leading authority remarked:

> Their noses too, are flattish and thick. Their hair which is long and thick is coarse . . .[5]

Resembling Mongolian peoples in few ways the closest relative to the Ainu are the Negroid Maori peoples. A final note of interest is the recording of the Anu (Ainu?) in ancient Egypt and Mesopotamia. Churchward emphatically noted that the Ainu came out of Egypt and settled in Persia, India, China, and Asia. They are described as "Children of the Bear", and evidence shows a Bear cult in prehistoric China. In Egypt and Mesopotamia, we come across references to the "Striking Down of the Anu", perhaps some legend of their expulsion from these areas.[6]

South of the Yangtze river, the earliest Neolithic sites (6000 B.C. - 4360 B.C.) are to be found in the provinces of Szechwan, Kwangsi, Yunnan and the western parts of the Kwangtung as far as the Pearl River. Other sites, central Shensi, southwestern Shansi, and western Honan, all show evidence of Negroid skeletal remains, that are associated with stone implements.[7] As late as the Chin Dynasty (221 B.C. - 206 B.C.), a continuous occupation of this region by Black types existed:

> Negritos whom the Chinese call "Black Dwarfs" are reported in the mountainous districts south of Yangtze; after the third century of our era, however, they are not mentioned. Some emigrated, but others remained and were assimilated by the dominant southern Mongolian stock, as witness to kinky hair and swarthy skin noticeable among a few southern Chinese.[8]

The Negritos in question appear to have been the ancestors of the Australian aborigine stock and Papuan people, known as Melanesians.[9] During the Neolithic period, the Australian Negroids maintained a "shoulder axe" (shoulder celt) culture that extended from its base in Szechwan and Yunnan towards India in the west, and from Nanking to Tonking, and Yunnan to Fukien as far as the coasts of Korea and Japan. These Austroasiatics, who are also known as the Black Pottery people (or Eastern I culture), would later be called the "Squatting Barbarians." On the East coast, stretching north to far south was an oval axe culture of the Papuan peoples. Quatrefages described the earliest inhabitants of

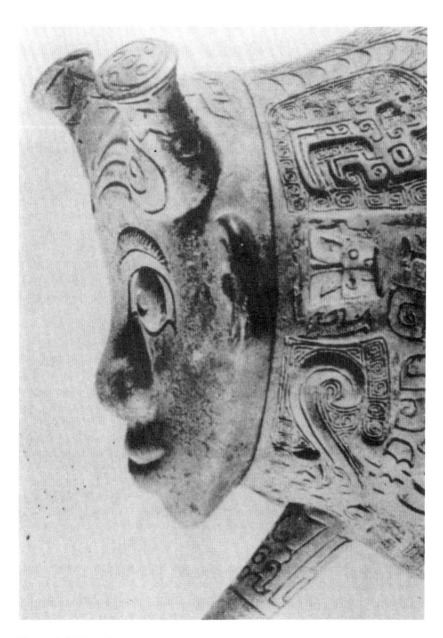

Figure 1. Melanesian type.

China as having straight and wooly hair; jet black and glossy skin; thick lips, flat nose, and protruding bellies. He further remarked:

> The Negro type was originally characterized in southern Asia, of which, no doubt, it was the sole occupant for an infinite period of the time. From there, the various representations of the type migrated into various directions. . . . Invasions or infiltrations of various yellow and white races have separated the Negro populations which formerly occupied a continuous area. . . . The Negrito subtype is one of the oldest of the race, and was at least predominant in India and Indo-China when the racial crossing began.[10]

Central China's Huangho Basin provided the impetus for its fermenting new civilization. Of its three major cultures, Yang-shao, Hsiao-t'un, and Ta-p'en-k'eng, two are of special attention. The Hsiao-t'un culture, which can be associated with the Austroasiatics and Papuans, is considered an indigenous phenomenon. It is believed that the Yang-shao culture may be identified with immigrants from Western Asia.[11] These people, who had painted pottery, influenced western Honan, western Hopei, and eastern Szechwan. At any rate, three things are apparent after 3200 B.C.: (1) The human skeletal remains were primarily non-Chinese or Proto-Chinese,[12] (2) The cultural transformation that emerged from this basin was the Lungshanoid culture (Black Pottery), and (3) The first three Chinese Dynasties grew out of this cradle—Hsia, Shang (Chiang), and Chou.

Early Chinese legends relate traditions of divine dynasties, one being the Epoch of the Five Emperors. The first Emperor, known as Fu-Hsi/Fu-hi (2953 B.C. - 2838 B.C.), is described as being a wooly-haired Negro.[13] He is credited with establishing government, originating social institutions and cultural inventions. Similar to the Egyptian god Thoth, he ''taught his people to fish with nets and rear domestic animals . . . [and] devised cultural inventions.''[14] Fu-Hsi was the first to develop writing, organize sacrifices and taught the worship of spirits. The second emperor Shen-nung (2838 B.C. - 2806 B.C.) is associated with the introduction of agriculture:

> During the age of Shen-nung, people rested at ease and acted with vigor. They cared for their mothers and not their fathers. They lived among deer. they ate what they cultivated and wore what they wove. They did not think of harming one another.[15]

Diop's Two Cradle Theory becomes intriguing when equated with the matrilinear and agrarian institutions of the earlier dynasties. At this juncture, an appraisal of pre-patriarchal China seems in order. In the pre-historic periods, the status of women was one of dominance.[16] Among the more primitive Ainu people, the ''wives dictate to their husbands and make them fetch and carry''.[17] The Tungus (ancient Manchus) and the Tartars (Mongols) also exhibit remnants of

Figure 2. Melanesian type, known as the "Squatting Barbarian."

the matriarchal state. One ancient writer remarked that, ''the custom of counting geneologies [is derived] from the female side.'' Incidentally, the ancient Tartars were an aboriginal, platyrhinne-nosed, black-skinned people. This Veddic people (Australoid type), are described in Oxford's Dictionary as the *Dasyus*. They were considered outcasts of the tribes of Brahma.[18] Tartar women were not only equal with their men, but fought alongside of them. However, Diop has emphasized distinct cultural phenomena for matriarchy and the emergence of the Amazonian spirit. Among ancient Chinese, it was the privilege for men to have as their great wife a Tartar.[19] Summarizing, Fu-Hsi considered himself born of mother, and knew no father. However, ''the Chinese state that marriage was instituted by Fu-Hsi, sexual relations having been previously unrestricted.''[20] Based upon the recommendations of his sister and wife, Niu-Kua, this allowed Fu-Hsi to penetrate into ''the mystery of the maternity of primary matter (Yin-Yang or Male/Female Principle).'' He was eventually succeeded by his sister-wife, who reigned for 130 years.[21] All the early dynasties trace their descent from women alone: the Shang Dynasty descended from Princess Kien-Tsi, the Chou Dynasty from Princess Kiang Yun, and the Ts'u Dynasty from Niu Sheou. Matrilinear societies still exist in southern China, and to some extent, women work while men care for the children and the home.[22]

   Following the divine dynasties, the Epoch of the Three Dynasties included Hsia, Shang, and Chou. The earliest Yang-shao sites are found in central Shensi, southwestern Shansi and western Honan. This region of southwestern China, according to ancient traditions, was the domain of the Hsia Dynasty (2205-1766 B.C.). During this semi-historical period, hostilities were beginning to grow between the north and south, forcing the southerners to continuously build walls to keep out their antagonistic neighbors. The founder of the dynasty, Yu-Hsia, was recognized as a great hydraulic engineer. Prehistoric hydraulics are often associated with agriculture, and again tradition locates its cradle in the southern Shensi.[23] Though archaeological evidence on this dynasty has not been forthcoming tradition divides it into nine great divisions. One of these divisions was known as the Li-Chiang. The Chiang, who may have originally come from the west,[24] were black. A present-day people, known as the Nakhi/Nasi consider themselves descendants of the Chiang.[25] The name Nahki was apparently given to the Chiang by the Moso people, due to their darker complexion. Nahki means black man (Na=black; Khi=Man).[26] The Moso were also dark, but not as dark as the Nahki. These people currently live in the Tibetan mountains. Southwestern Shansi, the stronghold of the Hsia Dynasty, and the southern province Shensi were occupied by the Chiang.[27]

   If the Hsia Dynasty cannot be established archaeologically, evidence of contact with the west during the second millenium is evident. In a tomb from Hsiao-t'un, was found a decorative motif of intertwining animal forms, of Egyptian/Mesopotamian origins. This was evidently a degenerated version of the fam-

Figure 3. Melanesian or Africoid type, Shang Period.

ous Hero and Beast motif, which also originated in Mesopotamia and Egypt.[28] Also, a jar cover, with a phallic-shaped handle (also from Hsiao-t'un) which is similar to types found at Mohenjo-Daro and Jemdet Nasr. Based upon the evidence, A.C. Haddon concluded that, "the conventionalized pottery (of China) bears a close resemblence to that of Pre-Sumerian Babylonia, the eastern borders of Persia (Susa), Anau I, and Asia Minor.[29] This period (3,000 - 2,500 B.C.), corresponds roughly with our concerns, and, as is known, Blacks or Negroid types resided in these areas.

The Shang [Chiang or Chi'ang] (1766 - 1100 B.C.), is recognized as putting China on its history proper. This royal house is considered an off-shoot of the Neolithic Lungshanoid culture, giving it a long unbroken tradition. Many Chinese archaeologists are convinced that the Shang settlement at Erh-li-tou (in southern Shansi, and northwestern Honan), is the earliest evidence of their existence. Traditionally, the territory of the Hsia dynasty, Erh-li-tou, is believed to be the site of Po, capital of King T'ang or Ta, founder of the Shang Dynasty. As mentioned, these people were initially matrilinear in culture, worshipping a mother goddess, and practicing agriculture. They had a priesthood, and practiced religious ceremonies that included a form of *sati* burial (ritual sacrifice). Acquainted with metal-working in bronze, the making of a form of porcelain ware, and silk-weaving (an invention of southern China), the Shang people are credited with bringing together the elements of China's earliest known civilization.

Two distinct racial types seemed to have co-existed in China, one Mongoloid, and the other Negroid. The Shang were a diminutive Black race. Those that migrated from the west amalgamated, perhaps, into the indigenous population, and infused new cultural ideas. However when the Chou conquered and usurped the political power of the Shang Dynasty, they described the inhabitants of the area as having "black and oily skin".[31] The patrilinear Chou clans, after taking the Shang capital, Anyang, integrated fully with the matrilinear Shang population. Before the demise of the Shang Dynasty, one can witness vestiges of the patrilinear culture emerging. Inheritance through the female began to play a decreasing role, until the cultural element finally disappeared.[32] This process of infiltration or amalgamation with a dominant culture has been seen in Egypt and Western Asia (Sumer).

In a limited crania study from Anyang, one anthropologist observed two dominant groups, one classical Monogloid and the other, an Oceanic Negroid type.[33] Another study of this Bronze Age culture complemented earlier results, with similar finds:

> Many [Skulls] were classically Mongoloid, but others strongly recalled other racial forms: skulls selected from the series were almost duplicates of Chukchi (Buriat), Melanesian, Eskimo or Caucasoid (or perhaps Plains Indian).[34]

Figure 4. Melanesian type, Shang period. Bronze pottery vessel believed to have been used as a wine libation container.

The preceding study considered all but the Melanesian type to be Mongoloid. In remarking upon a certain Chinese letter symbol and its origins, one archaeologist noted:

> The Tsung-jen character is formed by a group of three men usually placed under a sun, signifying that they are working on the farm in the sun. In later periods, the common people were called li-min, literally the brown people . . .[35]

This was considered a "tanning" of the skin, while working in the fields. However, nothing about this symbol indicates agriculture. One historian has suggested that when the Chou saw the Shang, they designated them the "black-haired people". This is also perplexing, in that the Chou, considered Mongoloids, should have had black hair as well. The Shang depicted human types in thousands of their figurines:

> Most of them [sculptural figurines] were so realistically portrayed that two distinct racial groups may be recognized. One is characterized by a broad face, low forehead, wide open eyes, broad nose, a wide mouth and a short chin. Figures of this type . . . Li Chi calls Melanesian. . . .[36]

Of the many sculptured figurines I discovered, while researching this paper, a surprising number fit into the above mentioned category. From the Shang's last capital, Anyang, many Negroid images in stone, metal, and jade have been found. A stone figure from the site of Ssu-p'an-mo, and a jade figure from Henan, offer intriguing contrast and possibly emphasize the transitional period between dynasties. Semi-reclining figures are associated with the Austroasiatics and Papuans. This pose is associated with the "Squatting Barbarians" mentioned earlier. A kneeling figurine of jade, from Lady Fu-Hao's tomb (14th century B.C.), displays the sitting habit or pose of royalty, later known by the Japanese as Seiza.[37] "Whether they (Shang) learned this from the Egyptian scribes or developed it independently remains to be investigated."[38] Lady Fu-Hao was a royal consort and female general who led military expeditions on behalf of her emperor:[39] The Tartar and Mongol women of central Asia have long been noted as active and warlike viragoes. Their horsemanship surpasses that of men in most countries, and their bows and arrows, are the rings and jewels . . . They accompany their husbands in the wars, and many times charge with them into the very midst of the enemy's battalion.[40]

> One cannot help reflect upon the royalty and strong leadership ability of the Egyptian and Ethiopian Queens Tetisheri, Hatshepsut, Tiy, and the Candaces. At any rate, this statuette was a perforated amulet meant to be worn or attached to wood for ritual ceremonies and worship. Another miniature jade figurine from Hsiao-t'un, and Hou-chia-chuang suggest "Negroid" features:

Figure 5. Africoid type, Shang Art (jade).

"flattened" nose, prominent chins and foreheads, and a lack of the epican-
thus fold that Mongoloids possess. A sudden burst of animal and human
representation in art seems to coincide with the historical Shang-Dynasty,
and apparently because of their skill, artisans were identified with the aristocracy.[41]
    Though subdued by the Chou, the Shang culture was basically assimi-
lated. Curiously, some historians suggest an ethnic affinity between the
Shang and the Chou. The Shang, who placed their beginning before the Hsia
Dynasty, allege that a mythological Queen swallowed an egg of a Black
bird, giving birth to Chi', Lord of Shang.[42] The Chou Dynasty (1100 - 225
B.C.) utilized the organized priesthood of the Shang to teach their royalty
and perform religious ceremonies. Shang women served as priestesses in
rituals of worship and sacrifice also. Chou kings imitated the Shang in bury-
ing their kings in large, subterranean, cross-shaped tombs outside the city.
They were lavishly buried. Human sacrifice however, was abolished. The
Shang priesthood became "scholars" for the Chou Dynasty and formed an
independent, though nonroyal class. After a major Shang revolt, a large part
of the population was transferred from Anyang to its twin capital Loyang.

    Dr. Joseph Rock's study of the Black kingdom, known as Nahki, has been in-
strumental in shedding light upon the existence of Africans on the Asian continent. During the Shang and Chou periods, those members of the Chiang clan
living southwest of Honan province were called Hsi-nani or barbarians. They
(the so-called barbarians) were always at war with both dynasties. The Shang apparently frowned upon them even as the imperial Romans frowned on their colo-
nials or those outsiders with a different way of life. As a result a name later
applied to blacks in general was Wu-man (Tien-hsi), a derogatory term meaning
"Black savages".[43] The chronicles of the Han and Tang Dynasties speak of these
Black kingdoms in southwest China.
    The emergence of the Buddha cult in Chinese culture witnesses the revival of
African religious concepts. Under various appelations, Sak-hae, Sukhyamani,
Sut-Nasi, or Sacya, Buddha's cult was brought into China from India. One tradition holds that Buddha was an Egyptian priest, fleeing the persecution of Cam-
byses.[44] Higgins emphasized that the most ancient people throughout Asia preserve his features as black-faced, with thick lips, and the curly hair of the
Negro.[45] Though known in China at an earlier date, the Buddhist cult was officially recognized during the Han Dynasty. Around 100 B.C., an emissary known
as Chang Chien was sent to a country west of China known as "Tien Chou"
(India). It is further related that, of the thirty apostles sent to China, ten were
yellow, ten brown, and ten black.[46] This is a curious statement, in that initially,
only those from the "Western Regions" or India could become monks.[47] By 518
A.D., more than 30,000 monasteries were built in China:

    The doctrine of the Buddha extends throughout China and its tributary na-
    tions; over the great empires and states of Cochin-China, Cambodia, Siam,
    Pegu, Ava, Assam, Tibet, and Budtan . . .[48]

Images of Buddha in stone and metal were made, and cave temples dedicated to the cult were widespread. Noted historian J.A. Rogers has emphasized the tendency to deny any Negroid origin for Buddha, despite his hair texture and features. In analyzing the coiffure on the statuettes, the earliest have wooly hair and through the centuries, there is a change towards grecian ideals of beauty. Gerald Massey noted:

> It is certain that the Black Buddha of India was imagined in the Negroid type. In the Black Negro God, whether called Buddha or Sut-Nashi, we have a datum. The people who first fashioned the divine image in the Negroid mould of humanity must according to all knowledge of human nature, have been Negroes themselves.[49]

Postscript

It can be safely estimated that an African presence existed in China from a most remote period, and an evolution of this physical type is an indigenous phenomenon. Ethnically, through climate and other environmental factors, the Negroid type appears to have differentiated into the "Mongolian" or modern Chinese type. The Negrito or pygmy (in which category the Bushman is included) were perhaps the earliest homo-sapiens to occupy a region extending from the Himalayas in the west, to the eastern China seaboard. From about 30,000 B.C. - 1100 B.C., this diminutive Black people played a dominant role in the civilization of Central Asia. Kephart calls the pygmies an "early branch of the Turanian race," with whom he associated the Bushman type. They are "a dirty yellow color, with slightly slanting eyes and prominent cheekbones . . . a primitive . . . handsome, dolichocephalic people.[50]

There appears to be diverse opinion regarding the area of dispersal for the inhabitants of Central Asia. However, many scholars and historians point to the west, particularly India and Indo-China as the "center of dispersion":

> . . .the earliest Chinese we know of are the northernmost fringes of a racial and cultural group whose western representations are the Tibeto-Burman peoples of Tibet, Szechwan, Yunnan, and Burma, and whose southern representations are the tribes which survive in the hills of Central and South China and in Indo-China.[51]

Scientists largely agree that this modern man was, "well built, dolichocephalous, dark complexioned, with dark hair and eyes. His facial features, tended to be Negroid [i.e. prognathic and platyrrhinal].[52] A name associated with these early people was "Min"[53] and the original site of their occupation appears in the fertile crescent of Szechwan and the Upper Yangtze river. These people would later be identified with the "primitive Manchus." The term "Mongol" originates with the Tartars, also called Tungus or Tung'hu in ancient China.[54] These Tartar or "Turks" (Veddas or Australian type) no doubt integrated with the Min clan. During the Neolithic period, these Tartar were the most advanced group in central Asia, who, no doubt, built upon a Min foundation. The ancient Tartary kingdom centered in the Tarim Basin, but included part of Tibet, and Manchuria. Extensions of the Negrito still remain, however, and the durability of this type is still evident: in Ceylon with the Veddas; in the Himalayas and India with the Yeruba and Chuang; in the Malay peninsula with the Senol; in Eastern Sumatra with the Kuba; in Borneo with the Ulaaja; in the Celebes with the Toais; in southern China with the Miao-tse or Miao; in Cambodia with the Hieng.[55] The Semangs, Andamese, Papuans, Melanesians, and Ainu even possess pygmy-Veddic affinities.

As previously mentioned, Lady Fu Hao's tomb, at Anyang, has offered many priceless relics, including evidence of African participation in royalty. Sati burial, which we have found in Nubia, Egypt, and Mesopotamia, thousands of cowrie shells used for money, and over five hundred jade objects, have been found in her tomb. Lady Fu Hao, who was probably a Tartar warrior-priestess, served as principal consort and general to the Shang king, Wu Ding.[56] Oracle-bone inscriptions describe how Fu Hao led an army of 13,000 against Tu Fang, a tribal state in the northwest; "The king has mastered his troops and is going to conduct a military campaign with Fu Hao as its commander against the Tu-Fang this year. Will he be protected?"[57] As a warrior-priestess, she presided over ceremonial sacrifices of cattle, slaves and war prisoners. Offerings of wine were also given by her to the ancestors . . .

Scholars readily admit that the southern Mongolian element has integrated with a Negroid substratum.[58] These Mongolians drove out many of the indigenous Negroid and Indonesian inhabitants, sending them into southeastern Asia. It seems probable that many left southern China to join their kinfolk in the south. During prehistoric times, Black peoples drifted to Cambodia, and developed the Funanese culture. By 300 A.D., Funan became a powerful nation, invading and conquering surrounding nations. This culture was of native stock, who later came under "strong Indian influence".[59] Around 550 A.D., this people was absorbed by a people known as the Khmers.[60] Physically similar to the dark-skinned Funese, and Annamites of Indo-China (later known as the Vietnamese), the Khmer was classified as:

> darker than the Vietnamese. He averages four feet four inches . . . and has a somewhat flatter nose than either the Vietnamese or the Thai. His eyes are oval and free from the Mongolian fold, which led to an early belief, no longer held, that Khmer originated in India.[61]

Originally, the Khmers shared Indo-China with the Funanese and Khams. The Khmer kingdom of Tchen-la existed in the northern half of Cambodia, while the Khams resided in Khampa, a southern portion of Vietnam. Presently, the

Funanese occupy the Mekong River Delta area of south Vietnam. One Khmer legend remarks how Kambu Svayambhuva, led the Kambujadesa or "sons of Kambu" in victory over the Funanese. Kambujadesa, which replaced Khmer (whose name has lost its meaning), became the westernized term Cambodia.[62] The Khmers, who came to Cambodia, around 300 A.D., brought with them the worship of Shiva. This dynamic people built the Cyclopean city of Anghor, with its stone temples. An ancient Chinese traveller of the third century A.D., remarked that, "The men are all dark. Their hair is curly. They go about naked and barefoot."[63]

This paper merely scratches the surface of the African role in ancient China, or for that matter, the Far East. Chancellor Williams' reflection on the Black populations in southern China, "powerful enough to form a kingdom of their own"[64] demands further reflection and research. More work needs to be done. The Hsia, Shang, and Chou Dynasties should be studied fully to gain more insight into the African role in Chinese history. These early dynasties, as well as China's earliest history, need to be demystified. For example, some scholars and historians consider the racial composition of the Shang as unknown in spite of obvious evidence. One historian curiously calls the Shang the "black haired" people, as if all other Orientals had some other hair color. As in other cultures where the evidence of the black type exist, references to him are changed to hair color, clothing, or any other nonsense to avoid an open acknowledgement of the obvious. The habitat of the Negroid types are largely known. But we must seek beneath the obscuring veil of ancient name-designations in order to find them.

Notes

1. Means, Sterling, *Ethiopia and the Missing Link in African History*. Originally published by the Atlantis Publishing Company, Harrisburg, Penn., 1980, copyright by D. Hakim, p. 58.
2. Te-K'un, Cheng, *Prehistoric China Vol. 1* [Archaeology in China], Cambridge, W. Heffer and Sons, Ltd., 1960, p. 35.
3. Diop, C.A., *The African Origin of Civilization*, Lawrence and Hill Co., 1974, p. 280-1.
4. Chang, Kwang-chih, *The Archaeology of Ancient China*, Yale University Press, London, 1968, p. 64.
5. Rogers, J.A., *Sex and Race Vol. 1*, Helga Rogers, N.Y., 1967, p. 70.
6. Heras, H., *Studies in Proto-Indo-Mediterranean Culture, Vol. 1*, Indian Historical Research Institute, Bombay, 1953. Portraits of a Negroid type from Egypt during the Prehistoric Epoch, and Agade (2700 B.C. ?), bear similar physiognomy in head structure (dolichocephalic), and line from nose to mouth. Diop offers evidence of an Anu chieftain, Tera Neter from Abydos, portraying Negroid characteristics. According to Diop, these Anu resided in southern Egypt, Nubia, Sipai, and Libya (Peopling of Ancient Egypt, p. 77, UNESCO, 1978). A portrait in relief of a Negroid "Tribute Bearer of Agade", offers striking similarities. At Heliopolis (Annu), one of their cities, skulls have been found and considered Negroid by G. Childe, "the Heliopolis Skulls display distinct prognathism". (Childe, Gordon, *New Light on the Most Ancient East*, Norton and Co., N.Y., p. 75). Even before Diop, Albert Churchward saw the Ainu (Anu) as originating in Egypt. He believed that the Ainu migrated from their original home, known as the "Haunch," opposite the city of Annu.

Situated near old Memphis, the "Haunch" was known as the Great Bear. This bear which was an early totem of the Ainu/Anu, was based upon the bear star constellation. As is known the early recognition of the bear continued in the Hsia and Shang periods. The Ainu still rever the bear (Churchward, A. Signs and Symbols of Primordial Man P. 218, Greenwood Press, Westport, Connecticut). As an evolutive type, the primitive Ainu/Anu may be a representative type; the decline of worship of Anu at Uruk (study of the stars), in Sumer, and the so-called legends of the "Striking Down of the Anu" in Egypt, and Sumer may suggest the replacement of an older population by a new and vigorous physical type. This may have been a Nilotic type.

7. Chang, Kwang Chih, *The Archaeology of Ancient China*, Yale University Press, London, 1977, p. 76.

8. Goodrich, Carrington C. *A Short History of the Chinese People*, George Allen and Unwin Ltd., London, 1957, p. 86.

9. Eberhard, Wolfram, *A History of China*, University of California Press, Berkley and Los Angeles, 1960, p. 10.

10. Quatrefages, Armand De, *The Pygmies*, D. Appleton and Co., New York, 1885, p. 51.

11. Chang, op. cit., p. 8.

12. Eberhard, p. 8.

13. Rogers, p. 266.

14. LaTourette, Kenneth S. *The Chinese*, MacMillan Co., N.Y., 1942, p. 38.

15. Chang, p. 80-1.

16. Briffault, Robert, *The Mothers, Vols. I-III*. MacMillan Co., N.Y., 1931, p. 326-7.

17. Ibid., p. 366-7.

18. *Oxford English Dictionary*, Oxford University Press, N.Y., p. 477.

19. Briffault, p. 312.

20. Ibid., p. 522.

21. Ibid., p. 366.

22. Rock, Joseph S. *The Ancient Nakhi Kingdom of Southwest China, Vol. 1*, Harvard University Press, Cambridge, Mass., 1947, Plate 75.

23. Chi, Li, *Anyang*, University of Washington Press, p. 161-2, Seattle, 1977.

24. Chang, p. 80-1.

25. Rock, p. 4.

26. Ibid., p. 65.

27. Eberhard, p. 16.

28. Chi, Li, *The Beginnings of Chinese Civilization*, University of Washington Press, Seattle, 1957, p. 27.

29. Haddon, A.C., *Races of Man*, p. 113, MacMillan Co., 1925.

30. Chang, p. 259.

31. Rogers, p. 67.

32. Eberhard, p. 24.

33. Chang, p. 334.

34. Keightly, David, *The Origin of Chinese Civilization*, University of California Press, Berkley, 1983, p. 305.

35. Te-K'un, Cheng, *Sheng Civilization Vol. II*, Archaeology in China, Cambridge, W. Heffer and Sons Ltd., 1960, p. 214.

36. Ibid., p. 233.

37. Chi, Li, *The Beginnings of Chinese Civilization, p. 21*.

38. *Ibid.*

39. *Juliano, Annette, Treasures of China*, Richard Marek Publishers, N.Y., p. 162, 1981.

40. Briffault, p. 455.

41. Chang, p. 286.

42. Te-K'un, p. XXV.

43. Rock, p. 65.
44. Diop, p. 287.
45. Higgins, Geoffrey, *Anacalypsis, Vol. 1*, London, 1836, p. 52.
46. DuBois, W.E.B., *The World and Africa*, International Publishers, New York, 1947, p. 178.
47. I-Fan, Yang, *Buddhism in China*, Union Research Institute, Knowlon, Hong Kong Union Press Ltd., 1959, p. 4.
48. Higgins, p. 161.
49. DuBois, p. 177-8.
50. Kephart, Calvin, *Races of Mankind*, Philosophical Library Inc., N.Y., p. 91.
51. LaTourette, p. 33.
52. Kephart, p. 64.
53. Ibid., p. 91.
54. Haddon, p. 34.
55. Ibid., p. 17-18.
56. Hao, Qian, *Out of China's Earth*, Harry Abrams, Inc., N.Y., 1981, p. 24.
57. Ibid.
58. Kephart, P. 161.
59. Jackson, John G., *Introduction to African Civilization*, The Citadel Press, Secaucus, N.J., 1980, p. 278.
60. Edmonds, I.G., *The Khmers of Cambodia*, Bobbs-Merrill, Inc., 1970, p. 24.
61. Ibid., p. 25.
62. Op. cit., p. 23.
63. Jackson, p. 278.
64. Williams, Chancellor, *Destruction of Black Civilization*, Third World Press, 1974, p. 44. One underlying element that represents the cultures of Crete, early Egypt, early Mesopotamia, and China is the use of human sacrifices in royal burials. This practice seems closely related to Nilotic African types. In postulating a Nilotic origin for this, let us cite I. L. Wooley: "There is nothing in Sumerian literature to prepare us for human sacrifice on this or any other occasion, but parallels were easy to find; there is Herodotus' well-known description of the funeral rites of the Scythic kings, lately illustrated by archaeological discoveries in South Russia, there are the first dynasty graves of Ethiopian kings or Egyptian nobles in Nubia and the Sudan . . . " (*Ur Excavations*, vol. 1, I.L. Wooley, Carnegie Corporation, 1934, p 38). As mentioned, the Dasyus were considered outcasts of the tribes of Brahma; Higgins called these black-skinned curly haired aborigines by their tribal names: Celtae, Scythians, Sacae, and Tartar/Tatar (Higgins, vol. 2, p. 203). Higgins asserted that they existed "in Eastern Scythia or Northern India" (Ibid., p. 262). At any rate, whatever race the Scythians later became, the royalty was a black-skinned folk. In this light, we may perhaps find the answer regarding satai burial during the Shang Dynasty. The legend pertaining to Sesostris I (1971–1928 B.C.) and his subjugation of Asia, in particular Southern Russia, is intriguing. From such a standpoint, we may note walled cities in this area. Also, the mention of the Sarmato-Scythiana, who penetrated Central Asia, described as "reddish-brown" and differing from other Scythians. Furthermore, "the early skulls in Scythic tombs are mostly long but brachecephalic during the Scythic Period" (Scythians and Greeks, Ellis H. Minns, part I, Biblo and Tannen, 1965, p. 45–7.

COMMENTARY:
BLACK BONDAGE IN ASIA

Runoko Rashidi

The story of the African presence in early Asia would be incomplete without an expose of the black role as servant and slave. The subject of black enslavement anywhere is clearly the most sensitive and delicate of historical issues, and all too often it is asserted that the great international movements of blacks occurred only under the guise of slavery. Obviously, as we have seen, this has not been the case. In order to develop a comprehensive understanding of the story of Africans in early Asia, the aspect of servitude must be objectively examined, however painful it might be. What is important to accentuate in this context then is that the period of black bondage in Asian lands is only one part of a much wider story. The period of bondage is in fact dwarfed by the ages of black glory and splendor in Asia's past, and even under the guise of slaves and freedmen the blacks of Asia distinguished themselves time and again in a number of roles.

The issue of black servitude in Asia is intimately connected with the early spread of Islam in the continent's western and southern regions when, with the success of the Islamic jihads, large numbers of the conquered "non-believers" of all races fell into Muslim hands and were dispersed throughout the lands they dominated. While slavery was not at all confined exclusively to the blacks, increasing numbers of black slaves in Muslim lands became so disproportionate that in time the Arabic word *abd*, meaning slave, became applicable to the blacks only.

Of all the territories of western Asia it was perhaps in Mesopotamia, or Iraq, that the black presence, albeit in the capacity of slave and slave descendant, manifests itself most prominently. An example of this is Dhu'l-Nun al-Misri, who was actually born in Upper Egypt around 796 A.D. Dhu'l-Nun was known as the head of the Sufis and is regarded as a founder of the Sufi doctrine of Islamic mysticism. He is said to have been the initial enunciator of the Sufi concepts of ecstatic states and the mystic ways towards a true knowledge of god.

Abu 'Uthman 'Amr Ibn Bahr Al-Jahiz, 776–868, the multi-talented scholar of the ninth century Islamic world was, like Dhu' l-Nun before him, a black resident of early Baghdad. Al-Jahiz was a theologian, anthropologist, naturalist, zoologist, philosopher and philologist. He studied under the most brilliant scholars of his time, and was a prolific writer who lived during a time when racial ostracism for blacks emerged as an overt reality in Muslim lands. The greatest and most significant literary work of Al-Jahiz then was the controversial *Book of the Glory of the Blacks over the Whites (Kitab Fakhr As-Sudan 'Ala Al-Bidan)* where in order to help stem the rising tide of racism confronting the Blacks, the author extolls what he regarded as the many virtues of the blacks over the whites, both biologically and culturally.

It was also in Iraq where the largest African slave rebellions occurred. Here were gathered tens of thousands of East African slave laborers called Zanj who worked in the humid salt marshes in conditions of extreme misery. Conscious of their large numbers and oppressive working conditions the Zanj rebelled on at least three occasions from the seventh through the ninth centuries. The largest of the rebellions lasted for fifteen years, from 868 to 883, during which time the blacks inflicted defeat after defeat upon the Arab armies sent to suppress their revolt. It is interesting to note that the Zanj forces were rapidly augmented by large-scale defections of black soldiers under the employ of the Abbassid Caliphate at Bagdad. The rebels themselves, hardened by years of brutal treatment repayed their former masters in kind, and were responsible for great slaughters in the cities and towns that came under their sway.

At its height the Zanj rebellion spread to Susiana in Iran and advanced to within seventy miles of Baghdad itself. The Zanj even built their own capital, called Moktara (the Elect City) which covered a large area and flourished for several years. The Zanj rebellion was only suppressed with the intervention of large armies of Arabs withdrawn from points throughout West Asia, and the lucrative offer of amnesty and rewards to any blacks who might choose to surrender.

India also received its share of African bondsmen, of whom the most famous was the celebrated Malik Ambar who, like a number of other former African slaves, elevated himself to positions of great authority and even rulership. In a collective form however, and in respect to long term influence, the African sailors called the Siddis stand out. Indeed, Siddi kingdoms were established in western India in Janjira and Jaffrabad as early as 1100 A.D. After their conversion to Islam the African freedmen of India, originally called Habshi from the Arabic, called themselves Sayyad, descendants of Muhammad, and were consequently known as Siddis.

The Siddis were a tightly knit group, highly aggressive, and even ferocious in battle. They were employed largely as security forces for Muslim fleets in West India, a position they maintained for centuries. The Siddi commanders were titled Admirals of the Mughal Empire and received an annual salary of 300,000 rupees. According to Ibn Battuta, 1304-1377, the noted Muslim writer who journeyed through both Africa and Asia, the Siddis ''are the guarantors of safety on the Indian Ocean; let there be but one of them on a ship and it will be avoided by the Indian pirates and idolaters.''

It should be pointed out in closing that the black slaves of Asia were not exclusively from Africa. During the fourteenth and fifteen centuries, for example, the Muslim Indonesian sultanate of Tidore was a heavy slave raider of the coasts of New Guinea, transporting their black captives to the slave markets of China, Turkey and Iraq. It was apparently during this period that the Malay term *Papuan* (literally ''kinky-haired'') became synonymous with slave.

AFRICAN BONDAGE IN ASIAN LANDS

Graham W. Irwin

There has always been a considerable population in Arabia of African origin. Perhaps the most famous of these people was Antara. He had an Arab father and an Ethiopian mother and became in time the national hero of the Arabs. That's not too strong a statement. There was nobody to equal the valor and strength of Antara. He's rather like King Arthur in the English tradition but, in fact, more important, because he was a more historical figure.

The Muslim societies of the Middle East, India and central Asia, throughout their history, adopted the practice of using people from other lands. These people were slaves, but the essential thing about them was that they were people from other lands, who were employed in preference to local people, in certain specialized occupations. Of these, there were three main kinds. First there was the military profession: slave soldiers, slave body guards, slave garrison forces, slave commanders, slave generals. This was quite common in the Middle Eastern world. The second role was bureaucratic. You find slave officials right up to the rank of prime minister. The third was the most obvious one, the domestic role: the house servants, concubines, eunuchs, and so on.

Now why slaves? Basically because if you have a slave that comes from somewhere else, and you put him in a position of authority, he does not have kinship ties with the local people. That means that he tends to be loyal rather than disloyal. That means that he is unlikely, other things being equal, to head a coup d'état. Because how can he rely on local support? You see, it's not because he is a slave. It's because he comes from somewhere else. He's an alien. He's a foreigner. Why not enslave the local people? Because it was unlawful under Islam to enslave a Muslim. It is true that Muslims were sometimes enslaved by other Muslims, but because they were regarded as heretics. It is against Muslim law to enslave a true believer.

It was possible for an African, in the Middle East and India, to reach to the very top of the social and political ladder. How would he do this? You are familiar, of course, with Bilal, the first muezzin, the first crier of the call to prayer under Islam, who was African and the immediate associate of the prophet. What is not so well known is that at various times people of African descent held the highest positions that one could hold in the holy cities of Islam. There was a mufti at Mecca who was African. There was an Imam at Medina who was African. So religion is one of the ways in which distinction was achieved.

Excellence as musicians, according to the records we have, seems to have been another quite common way up. Biographies written in Arabic say that such

Plate 1. Black dignitary in 14th-century China. Courtesy of the Asian Art Museum of San Francisco.

and such a musician was the greatest musician of his time, and, reading on, you find that he was African.

Africans and persons of African descent were prominent in government. They were provincial governors, army commanders. Several of the Abbasid Caliphs of Baghdad, in what is now Iraq, were African. They were the sons, in many cases, of Ethiopian women by former rulers and the brothers of former rulers. And many of them, and this is quite dispassionately recorded in the accounts, are stated to be "very black." This is not a derogatory statement. It is simply an ethnographic remark.

Another success story is that of an African palace guard commander in the state of Bengal in the late fifteenth century. Bengal is just south of where Bangladesh is today. This African made himself ruler of that state. He was able to do this because of dissatisfaction on the part of the people with the previous government. It was not a very stable state, I am bound to say. African rule only lasted seven years, and then there was a rebellion and the Africans got thrown out. But still, there was an African ruling line in an East Indian state for seven years at the end of the fifteenth century.

And of course, the most famous of all the African rulers in India was Malik Ambar, "king" Ambar, who ruled the Indian Muslim state of Ahmadnagar—that's on the western coast of India—from 1607 to 1626. About 1575 he was brought to India, having already been a slave in the Middle East. He was born in Ethiopia. After his arrival in India he had an opportunity to trade, to make money. He recruited followers. He formed his own army, and then he was able, because he had the largest army and the largest number of supporters, to impose himself on the state of Ahmadnagar. He did not make himself the king. There was a little puppet king: a boy, who did what Malik Ambar told him to do. Ambar was maybe not the legitimate king, but he had the power.

As military commander Ambar invented guerrilla warfare tactics which were commented on by the historians of the day as being remarkable and innovative. He was a brilliant diplomatist and administrator. He sent an ambassador from India to Persia who happened also to be an African. He encouraged manufactures. He built canals. He gave pensions to poets and scholars. He built mosques. He established a postal service. All in all he was one of the most famous men in seventeenth century Indian history.

Another example of African achievement in India is provided by the story of the sailors known as the Siddis. They had a base on an island off the Indian coast. Late in the seventeenth century, which was the peak of their power, there were thousands of them with many ships. They can be said to have dominated the northwest coast of India at that time. They were all Africans. We don't know where they came from. Some probably came from the East African coast, and some from the Red Sea area. Their commander was appointed admiral for the Indian ocean by the Mughul emperor of India, and he was known as the "Mughul's Admiral."

The Mughuls—they're the same people as the Mongols who ruled China—were nomads who came down into India from Central Asia. They didn't know anything about the sea. In fact they are said to have gotten sea sick crossing rivers. They didn't like the sea at all. None of their people could handle ships and shipping. So when they established their empire in India, they needed people who could control the sea for them. The African Siddis filled this particular role. The Siddis became mercenary sailors working for the Mughuls. They protected the ships that were taking Muslim pilgrims to the holy cities of Islam in Arabia. They dominated the northern Indian Ocean from the seventeenth century to about half way through the eighteenth. Then the British replaced them as the policemen of the seas in that area. But the descendants of the Siddi sailors still live on the island that was their naval base, Janjira, and also in certain places in the state of Gujarat. These modern Siddis remember their ancestors and know about their African origin.

So much for the famous Africans in the Middle East and India in historic times. But what about others? What about the masses? What did they do? Well, they were the servants, wives and concubines, eunuchs, traders, artisans, agricultural laborers, pearl divers, stevedores, sailors, fishermen, miners. People often wonder if there was any equivalent in Asia to the plantation slavery of the New World. There was one, and it led to the revolt of the Zanj in Basra. Basra is a port-city in the Persian Gulf area, and Zanj is the word that was applied by the Arabs to the East African coast. It still survives in the name, Zanzibar. The Arabs called the Africans who came from the East African coast, the Zanj.

Now it appears that large numbers of Zanj were imported to do a special job, which was to dig the salt marshes around Basra as part of the manufacture of saltpeter. They worked in gangs under task masters. They were oppressed. They were undernourished. And they rebelled. This is a familiar pattern in New World history, but in the Old World, full-scale revolts by plantation slaves are not common. In fact, the Zanj of the Basra salt marshes rebelled at least three times between the seventh and ninth centuries. The last and greatest of their revolts lasted fifteen years, from 868 to 883. This incident is called, in the histories of the Middle East, the Revolt of the Zanj. The threat posed by the Zanj to the Abbasid establishment was so great that armies that were being used to put down another revolt had to be withdrawn and devoted to the defense of the Caliphate against black slaves. The Zanj rebellion was eventually put down, but not before many thousands had been killed on both sides. In the Middle East from this time onwards no ruler allowed large concentrations of slaves to develop in one area. Africans were dispersed throughout the region. The only exceptions were the armies, including black regiments, that were maintained by some Middle Eastern states.

The revolt of the Zanj was a special case, a frenzied reaction to cruel oppression. Otherwise how were Blacks in the Middle East and India treated? What sort of a life did they have? By and large, one can say, it was better than in the

Americas, and there are two reasons why this was so. The first is that a slave in Asia was valuable. It didn't matter whether he came from Europe or whether he came from Africa, whether he was white or black. He was valuable and he was relatively expensive. Secondly, there was not the identification of slavery with Africa because of the fact of white slaves working alongside black ones. After all, the word slave comes from Slav because so many slaves originated in the Slavic part of the world. There was, however, discrimination based on color in the Muslim world.

Many people are perhaps not aware that Africans went to China, and were taken to China against their will, beginning as long ago as the third century A.D. Maybe the migration began before that, but there isn't any record of it that I know of. The Africans were taken by sea from Africa itself, from the Middle East and from the Red Sea area. The trans-shipping was done by Arabs. The Arabs were the greatest international sailors of those days. Africans were also brought overland to East Asia along the caravan routes from the Middle East.

Mostly these Africans were domestic servants. That seems to be clear. Typically, they were doorkeepers. In China there was a fashion during the T'ang and as recently as the Ming Dynasty, for African doorkeepers. But Africans in China also seem to have had a specialized activity which was curious: they were able to caulk the seams of ships while those ships were still lying in the water. They could keep their eyes open under water. According to Chinese accounts, Africans were famous for this skill and they were valued for it. Perhaps this particular skill arose because Africans were well known as proficient divers for pearls. That's just a guess on my part, but certainly there were African pearl divers throughout the Middle East. When they were brought to China, maybe that particular expertise was capitalized on.

Also we find in the Chinese records many stories about Africans with supernatural strength, and great resourcefulness. In Chinese folklore this seems to have been the role that Africans came to fill. If you were a Chinese provincial governor, say, and you couldn't get at some treasure because it was being guarded by a dragon, you sent for an African. Africans were supposed to be able to lull dragons to sleep and then take the jewels away from between their paws. Africans could dive to a depth of at least two hundred and fifty feet. If your discarded mistress had angrily thrown away the presents you'd given her—such as rings and precious stones—an African was just the person to recover them for you. Africans in China were called Kun-lun.

In a short talk like this, I've been able only to outline my topic. A great deal still needs to be found out. There are, for example, the records of the Ottoman Empire. Nobody to my knowledge has as yet systematically searched through them for information about African immigration to the Middle East. Indian records need to be further examined, as do those of East and Southeast Asia.

I want to end by saying that if one studies the history of past centuries, Africans can be found all over the world. But nobody has as yet gone to the trouble to search the records to find the evidence. The work is difficult. It is often a matter of chance discoveries of information in books that were written for entirely different purposes. We know, for instance, that soldiers from what is now Ghana served in what is now Indonesia in the nineteenth century. This has not really been written up. We know that there were Africans in Georgia: not Georgia in the United States, but Georgia, southern Russia. There were many Africans in Iran. Very little is known about them, but significant place names survive. One of them is "Town of the Africans." Another place name in Iran is "Castle of Africans." Africans apparently built, or at least inhabited, a castle in Iran at some time. More needs to be found out about these scraps of evidence.

One of the sad things one has to note about Asian history is that, where there was prejudice, the racial origin of a person will be mentioned. But where there was no prejudice, the ethnic origin of individuals may not be mentioned at all. One of the regrettable facts, therefore, about African diaspora research is that only where discrimination existed is it possible to reconstruct Black history. In areas and at periods when people of African origin were *not* discriminated against, attention is not drawn to the fact that they were Black. Often one has to guess. Often it is only a name that gives a clue. Such and such an official in India, for example, is listed as Habashi so-and-so. With a name like that he was certainly of African origin, because *habashi* is Arabic for Ethiopian.

Research on the history of Africans in Asia can, therefore, be very arduous. But I hope I've said enough to indicate that it is possible. What we need now is a lot more systematic work on the subject. The fascinating story of the African diaspora in Asia can be recovered.

MALIK AMBAR: AFRICAN REGENT-MINISTER IN INDIA

Joseph E. Harris

The most dramatic assertion of power by a single African in Indian history was made by Malik Ambar, one of the great men of the Deccan, at a time when the Mughuls were extending their authority into central India. Ambar, whose original name was Shambu, was born around 1550 in Harar, a province of Ethiopia. Almost nothing is known of his life in Ethiopia, except that he was sold into slavery. The circumstances of that sale are unknown, but it is clear that before he finally reached India he was sold several times in the Arab world—in the Hejaz, Mocha, and Baghdad, among other places.

Ambar's Rise to Power

His master at Mocha, Kazi Hussein, recognizing that Shambu possessed intellectual qualities, thus educated him in administration and finance. It was during this period that Shambu became a Muslim and was named Ambar by Hussein.[1] When Hussein died, Ambar was sold to a slave dealer, who took him to India. Around 1575 he was purchased by Chingiz Khan, the prime minister to Nizam mul-Mulk Bani, king of Ahmadnagar. Chingiz Khan was himself of African origin and may well have been a descendant of African mercenaries who served as far back as the thirteenth century in many parts of India, especially in Gujarat, where Ahmadnagar is located. At any rate, in the late sixteenth century, Chingiz Khan was one of several prominent Habshis in the area. When Khwanze Humayun, the queen of Ahmadnagar, sought to consolidate her power after her husband's death, her son Murtaza I led several Habshis in a successful revolt in which the queen was imprisoned. Chingiz Khan continued as prime minister.[2]

Chingiz Khan was impressed by Ambar's knowledge of Arabic, his loyalty, and his general intelligence. It is likely that those qualities also won Ambar the respect of other Habshi slaves. For that reason the prime minister, hoping to solidify his control of the African slave-soldiers, promoted Ambar to a position of military and administrative responsibility. With the death of the prime minister, however, Ahmadnagar became the scene of civil strife. Ambar was sold to the shah of Golconda and later to the king of Bijapur (both of these kingdoms were in the Deccan). Because of the training he had received from Kazi Hussein and Chingiz Khan, Ambar made a good impression on the king of Bijapur, who gave

This article originally appeared in *The African Presence in Asia* (Evanston, Ill.: Northwestern University Press). Copyright 1971 by Northwestern University Press. Reprinted with permission.

Plate 1. Portrait of Malik Ambar (Mughul, c. 1620-1630). Courtesy of the Museum of Fine Arts, Boston).

him the title of Malik ("like a king"). At Bijapur he became a military commander and was well respected by the Arab troops he commanded. In fact, he made it
a practice to appoint Arabs to positions of command. In about 1590, when the
king refused to grant him additional funds for Arab trainees, he deserted and took
several Arabs with him.[3]

Malik Ambar and his Arab supporter attracted other men, both African and
Deccani, and eventually built up an independent army of over 1,500 cavalrymen
and infantrymen who fought as mercenaries for various kings. Thus, when the
king of Ahmadnagar organized a Habshi army in 1595, the prime minister,
Abhangar Khan, another Habshi, invited Ambar and his men to join him.[4] This
return to Ahmadnagar provided the opportunity for Ambar to become a great
champion of the Deccanis against the Mughuls. Ambar and a Deccani, Mian
Raju Dakhani, combined their military efforts on several occasions to repel attacks by the Mughuls. Although they eventually became political and military rivals, Raju and Ambar fought together gallantly to defend their province.[5]

Ambar and Raju were able and popular rivals; they were also ambitious, and
each sought to gain control over King Murtaza II. In 1602 Ambar imprisoned
Murtaza and named himself regent-minister. He resisted several Mughul attacks
and prevented the Great Mughul, Emperor Akbar, from fulfilling his aim of conquering the Deccan. By the time Jahangir succeeded Akbar in 1605, Ambar had
founded a capital at Kirkee and had become well entrenched in the Deccan. He
continued to fight off his rival, Raju; in 1607 he captured him and had him executed. Ambar thus stood supreme in Ahmadnagar.[6]

Ambar organized an estimated 60,000-horse army. His light cavalry was very
effective as a mobile unit; he also employed artillery obtained from the British.
Ambar also enlisted the naval support of the Siddis of Janjira in 1616 in order to
cut Mughul supply lines and in general to conduct harassing missions.[7] His guerrilla tactics were particularly successful. On one occasion Emperor Jahangir observed:

> Ambar the black-faced, who had himself in command of the enemy, con-
> tinually brought up reinforcements till he assembled a large force. . . . It was
> deemed expedient to retreat and prepare for a new campaign.[8]

This was only one of several times the Mughuls were forced to retreat. While
Ambar probably benefited from disputes between Jahangir and his son, which
ultimately let to revolt, Ambar, too, frequently fought rivals in order to
strengthen his position in the Deccan.[9]

Ambar built his greatest fortifications at Daulatabad to protect his kingdom
from Prince Shah Jahan, who later became a great Mughul emperor. In 1621
Shah Jahan's forces launched an attack against Daulatabad in which they suffered
heavy losses. Despite this initial victory, however, Ambar was aware that he
could not withstand the Mughuls without allies. He therefore continued to seek

the cooperation of the Deccanis; to secure the support of Ibrahim Adil Shah II, Ambar had his daughter marry the shah's favorite courtier. His long and distinguished service in Golconda and Bijapur brought support from those southern kingdoms, for they realized that Ambar served as a buffer between them and the Mughuls.

By the 1620s, however, Ambar was having difficulty in maintaining the loyalty of his officers. Almost continuous warfare for about twenty years had demoralized many Deccanis and had drained much from the economy of the kingdom. Although Ambar was never conquered, he had suffered several defeats. Thus, when he died in 1626 at close to eighty years of age, friction and enmity were just beneath the surface. His son, Fettah Khan, succeeded him as regent-minister of the kingdom; but in 1629 the nizam reduced Fettah's status to that of an officer and later imprisoned him for insubordination. Thus ended the short but influential role of Africans in the Deccan.[10]

Ambar's Achievements

Several Indian writers have favorably assessed Malik Ambar's reign. With regard to administration, his early training by Kazi Hussein and Chingiz Khan proved invaluable. He improved the communication system within his kingdom by developing a postal service with messengers dispatched throughout the region. He recognized that the Deccan was inhabited by several minority groups whose loyalty he would receive only if they had a stake in the kingdom. He particularly encouraged the enlistment of Habshis in his army and gave them a Koranic education. Some of them became businessmen, but the largest number were enlisted in his private guard. He reportedly purchased 1,000 Habshi slaves for this guard, which became a strong corps of shock troops.[11] Ambar granted land to Hindu residents and appointed Brahmins as his principal financial officials and tax collectors. Marathas were also prominent as clerks in the military and civil service. Arabs and Habshis were appointed to key military posts; they also, along with Persians, were the core of small business. Arabs and Persians monopolized the foreign trade, principally between the Deccan and the Persian Gulf. During Ambar's reign a great amount of silk and paper were manufactured; arms—swords, axes, and guns—were also made. Those items provided a solid base for trade with various parts of India, Persia, and Arabia, and trade was also developed with the Portuguese and the English.[12]

Ambar's land policy deserves special mention. Both communal and private ownership of property were practiced. Communal property, prevalent in rural or village areas, was regarded as joint property of the people. Canals and irrigation schemes were fostered to improve trade and agriculture, and taxes levied on the use of those facilities were paid in kind to the central treasury. Lower rates of taxation were applied to the poorer areas of the kingdom and even to the richer districts when there were crop failures. Private land ownership was fostered in the

more prosperous districts in order to encourage greater production through competition. This system, according to oral and written accounts, continued in the
area until about 1822.[13]

Asad Beg, a Mughul envoy who was sent to win Ambar's favor with gifts, observed that the Habshi

> was a fairly cultured man loving the society of the learned and the pious. He
> was also very punctilious in the observance of the routine of religion. . . . He
> became the nucleus of the revival of the cultural traditions of Ahmadnagar.[14]

An Arab historian, Shili Trimi, has written that Ambar attracted poets and scholars, mostly Arab and Persian, to the royal court and rewarded them, sometimes
appointing them royal advisers. The official language of the court was Persian,
though Arabic and Marathi were common languages among the general public.
Ambar also patronized Hindu men of learning, and at Kirkee he built a place
"where Hindus and other pundits gathered." Schools were started, and free education was available, though their extent is not known.[15] All of these cultural
achievements were part of the tradition of Islam and contributed to the praise
Ambar received from both Arabs and Persians: "In the service of the Prophet of
God there was Bilal; after a thousand years came another, Malik Ambar."[16]

Ambar's reign is also noted for architectural developments. Long, wide roads
were laid, canals and drains were built, public gardens were laid out, and several
mosques and public buildings were constructed in and around Kirkee. The most
renowned buildings are the Kalachabutra ("black stadium," in which elephant
games were played), the Kalamajid ("black mosque"), the Bhadkal Darwaza,
and the Nakhuda Mhala (royal public buildings).[17] An interesting discussion
centers on the fact that Ambar's public buildings and his tomb are made of black
stone. One groups maintains that this was coincidental, that black stone was
available in the region and would probably have been used as building material
by any sovereign interested in architecture. (The fact remains, however, that
other stones were available in the region, but Malik Ambar limited his buildings
to the black stone.) A second group proposes that Ambar constructed the public
buildings of black stone because he was sensitive about his African heritage and
color. It is reported that on several occasions derogatory comments were made
about his blackness. The Mughul emperor, Jahangir, associated Ambar's color
with degradation and, according to some historians, seldom mentioned Ambar in
his *Memoirs* without abuse.[18] While this may not have reflected racism or even a
sense of cultural superiority on his part, Jahangir's comments do at least reveal a
sensitivity to color which could very well have carried value judgments. One
could reasonably conclude, therefore, that Ambar's desire to dignify his color,
together with the availability of black stone, encouraged him to construct impressive black buildings around Kirkee.

Malik Ambar's achievements in the Deccan would have been impressive even if he had been a member of the native majority; but as a member of an immigrant minority group, which on occasion was the object of degrading epithets, Ambar's place in Deccani history must be regarded as a mark of greatness. A few historians have accorded him that honor. Elliot and Dowson wrote:

> Ambar was a slave, but an able man. In warfare, in command, in sound judgments and in administration, he had no rival or equal. . . . History records no other instance of an Abyssinian slave arriving at such eminence.[19]

Ferista, a contemporary Arab historian, regarded Ambar as one ''who had risen from the condition of a slave to great influence.'' Ferista continues in most generous praise of the African:

> The justice and wisdom of the government of Mullik Ambar have become proverbial in the Deccan. He appears to have been the most enlightened financier of whom we read in Indian history.[20]

D.R. Seth notes that Jahangir, the great Mughul emperor who had failed to conquer Ambar and had called him despicable names, nonetheless admired the Habshi's record. In his *Memoirs* Jahangir wrote: ''In the art of soldiering Ambar was unique in his age.''[21] Mirza Muhammad Hadi, who continued Jahangir's *Memoirs*, wrote:

> Ambar, whether as a commander or strategist was without an equal in military art. He kept the rabble of that country [the Deccan] in perfect order and to the end of his days lived in honour. There is no record elsewhere in history of an African slave attaining to such a position as was held by him.[22]

Seth gave Ambar highest praise when he wrote:

> Malik Ambar was one of the greatest men who played their parts on the stage of Deccan history. The Moghuls succeeded in conquering the Deccan only after his death.[23]

The noted historian of Gujarat, Radhey Shyam, characterized the twenty years of Ambar's rule: ''The history of the next twenty years of the Nizam Shahi kingdom [Ahmadnagar] may be said to be a record of heroic activities of one individual [Ambar].''[24]

According to oral testimonies in Hyderabad in 1968, Malik Ambar is still regarded as a great figure in Deccani history, best remembered and most revered by the Muslims. His accomplishments unquestionably established him as an outstanding figure in Indian history. The example of Malik Ambar substantiates two important points: Africans played significant roles in Indian history, and they managed to win and maintain the support and respect of numerous Indians, primarily Muslims. The conclusion must be that Islam provided a common denominator for cultural identification and was a means of facilitating political and military success for Africans in the Deccan.

Notes

1. Sheikh Chand, *Malik Ambar* (Hyderabad, 1931), pp. 1-2, translated from Urdu for the author by Marzeur Rahman, Assistant, University of Bombay Library: and D.R. Seth, "The Life and Times of Malik Ambar," *Islamic Culture: An English Quarterly*, XXXI (Hyderabad, January, 1957), 142.

2. Bena Rasi Prasad Saksena, "Malik Ambar," *Hindustani Academy*, no. 4 (October, 1933), p. 343, translated from Hindi for the author by Shri Parnlakar, Senior Assistant, University of Bombay Library; and Chand, *Malik Ambar*, p. 5.

3. Chand, *Malik Ambar*, pp. 8-12, 14.

4. Ibid., pp. 15-17; Saksena, "Malik Ambar," pp. 342-48.

5. Bombay, *Gazetteer of the Bombay Presidency, Ahmadnagar* (Bombay, 1884), XVII, 389.

6. Seth, "Life and Times," pp. 145, 146, 147; and Bombay, *Gazetteer, Ahmadnagar*, p. 390. According to one source, Kirkee "was not only the best city in the Deccan, but the like of it was not found even in Hindustan" (*Lalit Kala: A Journal of Oriental Art, Chiefly Indian*, nos. 1, 2 [April, 1955-March, 1956], p. 24.

7. See pp. 82-83 above.

8. Quoted in J.D.B. Gribble, *A History of the Deccan* (London, 1896), I, 253-54.

9. Ibid., pp. 251,252; and Saksena, "Malik Ambar," p. 341.

10. Bombay, *Gazetteer, Ahmadnagar*, p. 395; and Seth, "Life and Times," p. 150.

11. Seth, "Life and Times," p. 155; and Chand, *Malik Ambar*, pp. 123-24.

12. Radhey Shyam, *The Kingdom of Ahmadnagar* (New Delhi, 1966), p. 280; Bombay, *Gazetteer, Ahmadnagar*, pp. 393-95; and Chand, *Malik Ambar*, pp. 123-29, 185-87, 190-91, 195.

13. Bombay, Gazetteer, Ahmadnagar, pp. 323-24, 393-95; and Chand, *Malik Ambar*, pp. 127, 154-58.

14. Quoted in Saksena, "Malik Ambar," p. 603.

15. Seth, "Life and Times," p. 154; Chand, *Malik Ambar*, pp. 148, 194-96; and Shyam, *Ahmadnagar*, pp. 284-85.

16. Chand, *Malik Ambar*, p. 195. Bilal, an Ethiopian, was Prophet Mohammed's muezzin (caller for the Muslim prayer services).

17. See Chand, *Malik Ambar*, pp. 163-76; Shyam, *Ahmadnagar*, p. 287; Seth, "Life and Times," p. 154; Gulam Ahmad Khan, "History of the City of Aurangabad," in *Transactions of the Indian History Congress* (Hyderabad, 1941), pp. 604-5; and Bombay, *Gazetteer of the Bombay Presidency, Aurangabad* (Bombay, 1884), p. 172.

18. Gribble, *Deccan*, p. 252; Saksena, "Malik Ambar," p. 341; and *Lalit Kala*, p. 24.

19. H.M. Elliot and J. Dowson, *History of India As Told by Its Own Historians* (London, 1867), VI, 414-15. See also Gribble, *Deccan*, I 256.

20. Quoted in Elliot and Dowson, *History of India*, p. 320.

21. Quoted in Seth, "Life and Times," p. 155.

22. Quoted in *Lalit Kala*, p. 24.

23. Seth, "Life and Times," p. 142.

24. Shyam, *Ahmadnagar*, p. 329.

RESEARCH NOTE:
THE CASE OF THE HABASHIS OF THE DAKAN

By Omar Khalidi

There is no substantial evidence to show that there was great demand for African slaves in India. In a land teeming with surplus labour it could hardly be expected that there would be great need for foreign slaves. Despite their small numbers, the Habashis played significant roles in medieval and modern Dakani history. Numerous individual Habashis achieved political and military successes in different parts of India, particularly in the Dakan. Habashi chiefs and nobles built mosques and monuments, struck coins in their own names, and patronized arts and letters. Islam and the Muslim community provided Africans of diverse origins and backgrounds with a common denominator for cultural identification in a region known for its diversity. Most Habashi nobles were so steeped in Indian Islamic political culture that Persian chroniclers do not always distinguish between Habashi nobles and those belonging to other ethnic affiliations. Therefore it is not always possible to identify an achievement or failure in strictly ethnic African terms. In the 16th century we have the example of Malik 'Anbar and his son who gained political power and used it wisely. In the 17th century, numerous Habashi officers were prominent in the Muslim courts of the Dakan and the Mughal empire in North India. Beginning in the 18th century the Siddi chiefs of Janjira ruled an island fortress on the strategic west coast of India until the late 19th century. A Habashi named Siddi 'Anbar was the trusted *khān-i sāmān* (steward) of Nawwāb Mukhtār al-Mulk, known as Salar Jang I, who was the vizir of the Hyderabad State during 1853–88. Although Siddi 'Anbar's designation was humble, he exercised great powers—granting access to the *divan*, recommending appointments and so forth. He was evidently richly rewarded for his services and died a wealthy man, having owned commercial real estate property in the heart of Hyderabad city. A retail centre known as Siddi 'Anbar Bazar is named after him. In the 20th century, we have the example of Nāsir ibn Miftāh, who won the confidence of the last Nizam, Mir Osman Ali Khan, after his deposition from power by the Indian army. As a *khānahzād*, he was raised in the King Kothi palace, where he eventually acquired charge of the palace, the huge kitchen, and other matters relating to the *khānahzāds*. Ibn Miftāh owned sizeable rental property and a poultry farm, which his son inherited upon his death in 1974.

The present position of the Habashi communities is one of marginal existence. Considering large scale inter-marriages, spread of education, and efforts toward greater conformity to the norms of the larger Muslim community among the Habashis, it is safe to predict that most Habashis may soon get assimilated into the local Muslim communities in the states of Gujarat, Andhra Pradesh, Karnataka, and Maharashtra.

AFRICAN DYNASTIES IN INDIA: A SELECTED BIBLIOGRAPHY OF THE SIDDIS

Compiled by Runoko Rashidi

"African Races to Bring Glory to India." *Dalit Voice* 10, No. 18 (1–15 Aug 1991): 10.

Banaji, D.R. *Bombay and the Siddis.* Bombay: Macmillan, 1932.

Chandrashekharaiah, B.M. "Siddis: A Negroid People of Karnataka." *Vanyajati* 13, No. 1 (1965): 9–14.

Chandrashekharaiah, B.M. "Life Organization of the Siddhis." *Journal of the Indian Studies in Social Sciences* 1, No. 1 (1967): 55–57.

Harris, Joseph E. *The African Presence in Asia: Consequences of the East African Slave Trade.* Evanston, IL: Northwestern University Press, 1971.

Harris, Joseph E. "Malik Ambar: African Regent-Minister in India." *African Presence in Early Asia.* Edited by Runoko Rashidi and Ivan Van Sertima. New Brunswick: Journal of African Civilizations, 1988: 152–58.

Hunwick, John O. "Black Africans in the Islamic World: An Understudied Dimension of the Black Diaspora." *Tarikh* 5, No. 4 (1978): 20–40.

Irwin, Graham W., ed. *Africans Abroad: A Documentary History of the Black Diaspora in Asia, Latin America, and the Caribbean During the Age of Slavery.* New York: Columbia University Press, 1977.

Irwin, Graham W. "African Bondage in Asian Lands." *African Presence in Early Asia.* Edited by Runoko Rashidi and Ivan Van Sertima. New Brunswick: Journal of African Civilizations, 1988: 146–51.

Khalidi, Omar. "African Diaspora in India: The Case of the Habashis of the Dakan." *Islamic Culture* 53, Nos. 1–2 (1989): 85–107.

Parkhurst, Richard. "The Habshis of India." Appendix to his *An Introduction to the Economic History of Ethiopia.* London, 1961: 409–22.

Prasad, Kiran Kamal. *Siddis in Karnataka: A Report Making Out A Case That They be Included in the List of Scheduled Tribes.* Bangalore: Prasad, 1984.

Rao, Vasant D. "The Habshis: India's Unknown Africans." *Africa Report* 18, No. 5 (Sep–Oct 1973): 35–38.

Rao, Vasant D. "Siddis: African Dynasty in India." *Black World* (Aug 1975): 78–80.

Rao, Vasant D. "Unknown African Dynasty in India." *India News,* 24 Apr 1978: 6.

Rashidi, Runoko. "Black Bondage in Asia." *African Presence in Early Asia.* Edited by Runoko Rashidi and Ivan Van Sertima. New Brunswick: Journal of African Civilizations, 1988: 144–45.

Rogers, Joel A. "Malik Ambar." Chap. in *World's Great Men of Color,* Vol. 1. New York: Collier-Macmillan, 1972: 172–76.

Rogers, Joel A. "Malik Andeel." Chap. in *World's Great Men of Color,* Vol. 1. New York: Collier-Macmillan, 1972: 177–78.

Seth, D.R. "The Life and Times of Malik Ambar." *Islamic Culture: The Hyderabad Quarterly Review* 31, No. 2 (Apr 1957): 142–55.

Talib, Y., based on a contribution by F. Samil. "The African Diaspora in Asia." *UNESCO General History of Africa. Vol. 3. Africa from the Seventh to the Eleventh Century.* Edited by M. El Fasi. Berkeley: University of California Press, 1988: 704–33.

Tamaskar, B.G. "An Estimate of Malik Ambar." *Quarterly Review of Historical Studies* 8 (Calcutta, 1968–69): 247–50.

"Warrior Tribe of African Descent in Gujarat Struggling to Keep Alive." *India Tribune-Chicago Edition,* 17 Sep 1994: 4.

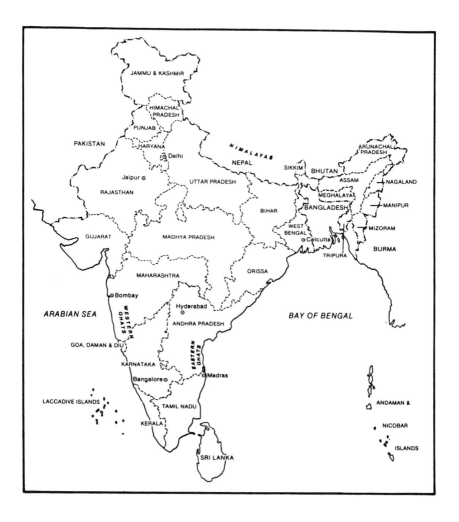

A general map of India

PEOPLE OF THE FIRST WORLD:
SMALL BLACKS IN AFRICA AND ASIA

Runoko Rashidi and James E. Brunson

By *Small Blacks*, we are referring to the extremely important (and much romanticized) family of Black people phenotypically characterized by: unusually short statures: skin-complexions that range from yellowish to dark brown; tightly curled hair; and, in frequent cases (like many other Blacks), steatopygia. They are probably more familiar to us by such perjorative terms as *"Pygmies," "Negritos"* and *"Negrillos."* Noted scholars Dr. Yosef Ben-Jochannan and Basil Davidson, among others, respectfully refer to them as "Twa." Dr. Alfred M. Ligon, Richard D. King, M.D. and Dadisi Sanyika refer to them as "Seed People." Albert Churchward referred to them as "Little Red Men." Similar peoples who live today in Southern Africa have been titled "Bushmen" and "Hottentots." More accurate names for these latter, gentle and highly civilized Black folk are *San* (translated as "original inhabitants") and *Khoikhoi*.

The *Small Blacks* are particularly important to us because they are very closely related both physically and culturally to the world's earliest human inhabitants. Moving slowly from their birthplace in Mother Africa, they eventually scattered around the earth. Although they currently exist in only limited numbers and are generally found in terrains heavily forested, barren, isolated, etc., the *Small Blacks* were at one time the true lords of the earth. It is indeed unfortunate that the histories of these small black people and their basic and essential contributions to high-cultures characterized by urbanization, mining and metallurgy, agricultural science and advanced scripts are so little understood and appreciated.

Complementing the works of a number of early scholars who viewed the Small Blacks as major contributors to human advancement (including Armand De Quatrefages, Gerald Massey and Albert Churchward) are an entire series of recent scientific studies. After a meticulous analysis of nuclear DNA polymorphisms, a significant group of Oxford University based scholars, for example, provided the following summary of its labors:

> The earliest fossils of anatomically modern man (Homo sapiens sapiens) have been found in Africa at Omo in Ethiopia, Border Cave [Ingwavuma] in South Africa and at Klasies River Mouth in South Africa. The data from the last site suggests that Homo sapiens sapiens was present in South Africa more than 100,000 years ago, and an adult mandible from Border

Cave has been dated to about 90,000 years Before Present. Hence, it has been argued that the evolution of modern man took place in Africa. Our data are consistent with such a scheme, in which a founder population [Small Blacks] migrated from Africa and subsequently gave rise to all non-African populations.[1]

Less than a year after the publication of this virtually revolutionary data assessment, Oxford's Jim Wainscoat, apparently the leader and most actively involved of the scientists engaged in these studies, was even more convinced of their validity. In a more specific report Wainscoat elaborated on what is being labeled "the Out of Africa hypothesis." According to Wainscoat, "It seems likely that modern man emerged in Africa and . . . that subsequently a founder population left Africa and spread throughout Europe, Asia and the Americas."[2]

In a related and corroborative report based on the calculation of the slow changes that have occurred in human DNA over the millennia, a team of scientists at the University of California at Berkeley "indicate that everyone alive today may be a descendant of a single female ancestor who lived in Africa 140,000 to 280,000 years ago."[3]

That these early ancestors were "phenotypically Black," as well as native African, is clear. As C.A. Diop noted, "The man born in Africa was necessarily dark-skinned due to the considerable force of ultraviolet radiation in the equatorial belt."[4] Dr. Douglas Wallace, who has been engaged in highly detailed studies in this area of research, adds that "The scientist's Eve—subject of one of the most provocative theories in a decade—was more likely a dark-haired, black-skinned woman, roaming a hot savanna in search of food."[5] Any

AFRICA

Regional Locations:	*Names and Designations:*
Central Africa	Negrillos, Negritos, Pygmies, Twa
Southern Africa	Bushmen, Hottentots, Khoikhoi, San

ASIA

Regional Locations:	*Names and Designations:*
Andaman Islands	Great Andamanese, Jarawas, Onges, Sentinelese
Burma	Seng-Ch'i
Cambodia	Chong, Kui, Porr, Samrae, Saoch
Southern China	Black Dwarfs, Haio, Ho-Nhi, Tiao-Hao
Malaysia	Menik, Orang Asli, Pangan, Sekai, Semang, Than
Pakistan	Khyeng
Philippine Islands:	
Luzon, Mindanao, Panay, Zambales	Aeta, Agta, Ata, Igorotes
Taiwan	Little Black Man
Thailand	Chonga, Hami, Kensiu, Kintak, Jahai, Mos,
	Ngok, Porr, Suku, Tonga,
Vietnam	Cuci, May, Ruo

fundamental alterations of this "Africoid phenotype" (occurring sometimes after distant migrations from their original African bases with the resulting necessary adaptations to different environments) could have ensued only very gradually after extensive passages of time.

Traces of the presence of *Small Blacks* have been identified in the most remote periods of Asian history. A recent report carried by the Associated Press, for example, informs us that, "The oldest Stone Age hut in Japan has been unearthed near Osaka . . . Archeologists date the hut to about 22,000 years ago and say it resembles the dugouts of African bushmen . . . "[6]

Notes

1. Wainscoat, J.S., et al. "Evolutionary Relationships Of Human Populations From An Analysis Of Nuclear DNA Polymorphisms." *Nature*, February 6, 1986.
2. Wainscoat, J.S. "Out of The Garden of Eden." *Nature*, January 1, 1987.
3. "DNA Researchers Trace All Humans To Single Woman In Ancient Africa." *New York Times*, March 30, 1986.
4. Diop, Cheikh Anta. *Great African Thinkers Vol. 1: Cheikh Anta Diop.*, eds. Ivan Van Sertima and Larry Williams New Brunswick: Transaction Books, 1986.
5. Wallace, Douglas. "The Search For Adam and Eve." *Newsweek*, January 11, 1988, p. 46.
6. "African-Like Stone Age Hut Is Unearthed In Japan." *Associated Press*, February 15, 1986.

Bibliography

"African-Like Stone Age Hut Is Unearthed In Japan." *Associated Press*, February 15, 1986.
Brunson, James E. *Black Jade: African Presence In The Ancient East.* Chicago: KARA Pub., 1985.
Diop, Cheikh Anta. *Great African Thinkers Vol. 1: Cheikh Anta Diop.* eds. Ivan Van Sertima and Larry Williams. New Brunswick: Transaction Books, 1986.
"DNA Researchers Trace All Humans To Single Woman In Ancient Africa." *New York Times*, March 30, 1986.
Churchward, Albert. *Signs And Symbols of Primordial Man.* 1913 rpt. Westport: Greenwood Press, 1978.
Evans, Ivor H.N. *The Negritos of Malaya.* London: Cambridge University Press, 1937.
Finch, Charles S., III. "Race and Evolution in Prehistory." *African Presence In Early Europe.* ed. Ivan Van Sertima. New Brunswick: Transaction Books, 1985.
Griffin, P. Bion and Anges Estioko-Griffin. *The Agta of Northeastern Luzon.* San Carlos Publications: Cebu City, Philippines, 1985.
Journal Of The Siam Society. January, July, 1965. Bangkok, Thailand.
Levin, Roger. "Africa: Cradle of Modern Humans." *Science*, Vol. 237 (September 11, 1987), pp. 1292-1295.
Luce, G.H. *Phases of Pre-Pagan Burma.* London: Oxford University Press, 1985.
Massey, Gerald. *Ancient Egypt*, 2 Vols., 1907 rpt. New York: Weiser, 1970.
Mutunhu, Tendai. "Africa: The Birthplace of Iron Mining." *Negro History Bulletin.* Vol. 44, No. 1, 1981.
Orang Asli Studies Newsletter. Department of Anthropology, Dartmouth College, Hanover, New Hampshire.
Quatrefages, Armand De. *The Pygmies.* New York: D. Appleton & Co., 1885.
Rouse, Irving. *Migrations In Prehistory.* New Haven & London: Yale University Press, 1986.

Sarawak Museum Journal, Vol. 8, No. 10, 1957. Kuching, Sarawak, Malaysia.

"The Search For Adam & Eve." *Newsweek*. January 11, 1988, pp. 46-52.

URAEUS: The Journal of Unconscious Life. Los Angeles, California.

Wainscoat, J.S., et al. "Evolutionary Relationships Of Human Populations From An Analysis Of Nuclear DNA Polymorphisms." *Nature*, February 6, 1986.

Wainscoat, J.S. "Out of The Garden of Eden." *Nature*, January 1, 1987.

Warren, Charles P. "Minority Student Response to the Anthropology of Asian Black Populations." *Department of Anthropology, University of Illinois at Chicago*, 1982.

MORE LIGHT ON SUMER, ELAM AND INDIA

Runoko Rashidi

*Since Egyptian history, according to the most moderate esti-
mates, starts in 3200 B.C., it becomes indispensable, 'out of
solidarity,' to make Mesopotamian history begin at about
the same time, even if all the known historical facts about
that region can fit into a much shorter period.*[1]
*Egypt was the first to emerge, all ideology put aside. It is not
possible—it clashes with chronology—to establish a parallel between Mesopotamia and Egypt, even though the first
Mesopotamian civilizations were black. It was much later,
compared to Egyptian history, that this region, that this
black world, was also to emerge to civilization.*[2]

Until just over a century ago the existence of a Sumerian civilization or a
Sumerian people was largely unsuspected. The first known modern mention
of Sumer was made in 1869 by French philologist Jules Oppert. After carefully
examining cuneiform inscriptions on clay tablets recently exhumed from
southern Mesopotamia (modern Iraq), Oppert, who along with Henry
Creswicke Rawlinson and Edward Hincks formed cuneiform's "holy triad,"
correctly argued that the Sumerians (c. 3000 B.C. to 1750 B.C.) were the non-
Semitic founders and guardians of West Asia's oldest known civilization.

Although our general knowledge of Sumer has grown tremendously since
1869, persisting still is what has been labelled the "problem of Sumerian
origins." Problems numerous and complex seem to inevitably arise within the
ranks of western scholars and academicians when confronted with the origins
and ethnicity of civilizations, such as Sumer, that are admittedly "neither
Semitic nor Indo-European."

Independent and objective studies of the available data however, reveals the
very real question of whether the so-called "problem of Sumerian origins" is
actual or artificial. The Sumerians did, after all, call themselves the black-
headed people, and their most powerful and pious leaders, such as Gudea of
Lagash, consistently chose very dark, and preferably black, stone for their
statuary representations. There is also no doubt that the oldest and most
exalted Sumerian deity was Anu, a name that loudly recalls the thriving and
widely-spread black civilizers found at history's dawn in Africa, Asia and even
Europe.

Physical Anthropology as Evidence of Racial Grouping

The evidence of physical anthropology should be highly considered in the
determination of Sumerian origins and ethnic composition. Although they

were politically and socially dominant, the blackheads of Sumer were probably never numerically substantial. Their arrival from any considerable distance would suggest that they probably did not come in large numbers, and the blackheads need not have pervaded the entire strata of the regional population. Although their impact on West Asia was huge, the total number of Sumerian blackheads was in all likelihood very small.

Of the physical anthropologists who have examined actual Sumerian remains and published the results, the works of Henry Field, T.K. Penniman, L.H.D. Buxton, Arthur Keith and Mario Cappieri stand out. Of these distinguished scholars, Field's studies are probably the most comprehensive. Cappieri's are the most recent. The reader should be aware however, that *none of these eminent scientists possessed enough honesty to call a black a black.* They instead resorted to the use of ridiculous ethnic euphemisms, and for Sumerian physical types presented us with "Proto-Mediterraneans, Mediterraneans, and members of the Brown race." If their reports are read with care and objectivity though, it becomes clear that at least the elites of Sumer were Africoid peoples.[3]

In reference to a skull from the Kish Excavations, Buxton wrote that: "It undoubtedly belongs to the same type as that which Elliot Smith has called the Brown race and which Sergi has termed Mediterranean. This type is widely spread throughout the whole region and extends from the Mediterranean to India. It formed the main bulk of the ancient inhabitants of Egypt and has been called the Proto-Egyptian type."[4] Cappieri summarized the physical remains from Jemdet Nasr, Asshur, Tepe Gawra, Al-Ubaid, Ur of the Chaldees and Kish, and expressed that "the Ur, al'Ubaid, Kish and Tepe Gawra inhabitants were of the same stock as all the dwellers of the other settlements. In addition, I point out that Keith, who examined the skeletal remains, considered them—together with Buxton—to belong to the Mediterranean Race."[5] Of the Jemdet Nasr [northeast of Kish] remains: "These remains were studied by Field who judged all the crania to be Proto-Mediterranean. During later excavations (1948) a female skull dated 4500-4000 B.C. was found; it was examined and measured by Krogman, who judged it of Mediterranean type."[6]

Of the "Group B Crania" from Kish, Cappieri says that, "The series appear dolichocephalic, very homogeneous, showing a Proto-Mediterranean typology. This is also Buxton's opinion when he compares this group with the prehistoric Egyptian skulls."[7] Arthur Keith, on crania from Ur and other sites, stated that the "early dwellers in the valley of the Nile were certainly near akin to the people of Ur, whose remains are described here [al'Ubaid] . . ."[8]

Sumerian Gods and Founders

Anu: Sumer's Oldest God

Anu was early recognized as the highest power in the universe and the sovereign of all the gods. Anu was "older than all the other gods and the source of all existence." As God par excellence Anu occupied an independent position, and well before the time of Gudea, the pious priest-king of Lagash (c. 2060-2042 B.C.), he became supreme. Anu was ultimately superseded in his capacity of most exalted god first by Enlil, the "strong man of Sumer," and secondly by Marduk, the tutelary deity of Babylon.

Nimrod the Brave

Nimrod, whose name means "the brave," was the Biblical son of Kush (Ethiopia). He was a world-renowned militarist, city-builder, and the national founder of Sumer (Biblical Shinar). First century Jewish historian Flavius Josephus wrote that "Nimrod was the grandson of Ham, the son of Noah, a bold man, and of great strength of hand."[9] Josephus says also that Nimrod instituted the construction of the stupendous "Tower (ziggurat) of Babel," which was destroyed by Alexander, the son of Philip of Macedon.[10]

According to the Talmud, Nimrod was the king of Babylon and the persecutor of Abraham. Moses of Chorene, the great eighth century Armenian historian, identified Belus, King of Babylon, with Nimrod, and genealogically recorded Nimrod as the grandson of Kush and the son of Mizraim (Egypt). He thus exposed the intimate connections between Sumer, Babylonia, Egypt and Ethiopia. As one writer expressed it: "It seems most probable that the race designated in Scripture by the hero-founder Nimrod, and among the Greeks by the eponym Belus, passed from East Africa, by was of Arabia, to the valley of the Euphrates, shortly before the opening of the historical period."[11]

Oannes: God of Great Gifts

"Berossus, who lived in the age of Alexander, the son of Philip of Macedon, informs us that in the first year there appeared, from that part of the Erythraeaen (Red) Sea which borders upon Sumer, Oannes.

This Being was accustomed to pass the day among men; but took no food at that season; and he gave them an insight into letters and sciences, and arts of every kind. He taught them to construct cities, to found temples, to compile laws, and explained to them the principles of geometrical knowledge. He made them distinguish the seeds of the earth, and showed them how to collect the fruits; in short, he instructed them in every thing which could tend to soften manners and humanize their lives. From that time, nothing material has been added by way of improvement to his instructions."[12]

Lord Enki

Enki, whose name means Lord of the Earth, was one of the most important and most interesting figures in the Sumerian pantheon. Enki began his career as the local deity of the city of Eridu, and like Oannes, to whom he is very similar, became the personification of the watery element in general. Because the Persian Gulf, near which Eridu was located, was the largest body of water known to the blackheads, Enki was the "father" of all the waters. The oldest settlements of the Euphrates Valley, we should note, are those nearest the Persian Gulf. This is a vital point in tracing Sumerian origins. The part that water plays in the life of mankind and in the development of human cultures is quite sufficient to account for the hallowed position acquired by Enki in the Sumerian pantheon as the protector of humanity. He is the teacher also who instructs humankind in the various sciences. It is Enki who endowed the Sumerian rulers with direction and intelligence, as it is Enki, too, who presides over the fine arts; instructing men in architecture, in working precious metals and stone, and in all the expressions of man's intellectual activities. Thus Enki may briefly be defined as the god of Supreme Wisdom and Civilization itself.

One of the regions most cherished by Enki was Meluhha, a land of mariners, whose prized exports included timber and wooden furniture, copper, gold dust, lapis lazuli and carnelian. There was clearly a close relationship between Meluhha, which was known as "the Black land," and Sumer itself—the land of the "blackheads." After initially fashioning the blackheaded people themselves, Enki is said to have immediately journeyed to Meluhha to profusely bless it.[13] In post-Sumerian times Meluhha is mentioned repeatedly as a place of "black men," and from the first millennium B.C. comes the expression "Black Meluhhaites."

Meluhha's precise geographic location has frequently been attached by modern scholars to either the African Ethiopia, or the Indus Valley (Harappan) region of Pakistan and western India. Both regions were lands of black men, but Harappa, whose civilization was larger in area than ancient Mesopotamia and Egypt combined, was much closer to Sumer than African Ethiopia. Harappa and its Dravidian descendant kingdoms are also known for their extensive long-distance commercial activities and mastery of the seas.

The major center of Enki's cult was the southern Sumerian city of Eridu. Originally settled about 3000 B.C., Eridu was traditionally the first Sumerian site of kingship before the great Flood. By the end of the third millennium B.C. desiccation had let to its gradual isolation and general decline. Although the city and its famous school sank into gradual oblivion towards the fall of Sumer, Lord Enki, the Sumerian god of wisdom and philosophy, of atonement and consecration, continued to hold his place of almost supreme importance in religion, poetry and tradition. So necessary was his cult to the practice of religion that every Sumerian city possessed and dedicated a temple or chapel to Enki specifically. The city of Eridu eventually lost its position in the political and social history of Sumer, but without real detriment to the stature of Lord Enki himself.

Kish: The Sumerian City Supreme

> It was formerly thought that Kush or Cush and their derivations were of
> Egyptian or Hebrew origin, but the discovery of their counterparts in an
> Ethiopian record seem to indicate that the words were indigenous to the
> country and peoples to which they were generally applied.[14]

The important archaeological site of Kish lies about twenty miles due east
of ancient Babylon (the "Gate of God") in central Iraq.[15] The name "Kish" is
used as a short-hand description for many closely related settlements extending far back into prehistory, and existing up to the period of Mongol invasions
about 1250 A.D. Serious archaeological and related researches on the Kish of
the Sumerian blackheads began in 1923. These efforts were jointly sponsored
by the Field Museum of Chicago and Oxford University, and directed by
Stephen H. Langdon, Professor of Assyriology at Oxford. Ernest Mackay, a
Flinders Petrie trained archaeologist who later achieved wide acclaim for his
Indus Valley researches, was field director at Kish until 1926. From 1927 until
1933, the last year of the expedition, Louis-Charles Watelin, a French engineer
who had previously dug at Susa, served as field director. Among the physical
anthropologists involved in the digs at Kish were L.H.D. Buxton, Henry Field
and T.K. Penniman. The published field reports of the 1923-1933 Kish Excavations have long been available and should have all by themselves resolved
the "problem of Sumerian origins." The real problem is mostly in the arrogant
attitudes of European academicians.

According to the Sumerian kinglist Kish was the seat of kingship after the
Flood. It is not mentioned as a pre-Flood city, and never again held the
powerful stature which it had during this very early period in Sumerian history. The emergence of Kish as an influential Mesopotamian city-state began
in the early third millennium B.C. A monumental building at Kish, dated to
2800 B.C., was likely the palace of an earthly ruler, rather than a priestly
temple. This palace had hundreds of rooms and was considerably larger than
the French palace at Versailles thousands of years later. In spite of her general
decline Kish for a long time possessed such prestige that Mesopotamian political leaders continued to claim overlordship of the city.

Perhaps the most remarkable single figure in the history of Kish in the Early
Dynastic period is recorded in the King List as the "barmaid" ("woman of
wine"). Her name was Ku-Baba, and she is said to have "consolidated the
foundation of Kish." According to a later account she seized power over Kish
from the city of Akshak. Ku-Baba reigned one-hundred years, and after her
passing Kish played an increasingly minor role in Sumerian affairs.

Uruk: The House of Anu

The modern name for Uruk is Warka. The Old Testament name is Erech, or
"Healthy." To the Sumerians this extremely ancient city was known as Eanna,

the House of Anu. Uruk was dedicated to both Anu and Inanna, the Sumerian goddess supreme. One of Uruk's very earliest structures was the White Temple of Anu, the construction of which may be placed in the latter part of the fourth millennium B.C. According to the Sumerian kinglist, after the Flood Uruk assumed power from Kish, only to then lose it to Ur, although the dynasties of all three cities apparently overlapped.

Uruk was also the city of the heroic semi-legendary king Gilgamesh. The Epic says of Gilgamesh that "In Uruk he built walls, a great rampart and the temple of blessed Eanna for the god of the firmament Anu, and for Inanna, the goddess of love."[16]

Nippur: Sumer's Religious Capital

Nippur, presently known as Tell Niffer, was located towards Sumer's northern borders. In historic times Nippur became the supreme religious center of Sumer. Nippur was also the chief seat of Enlil, who was initially the executive of Anu, and eventually Anu's actual successor. Enlil, sometimes called "Nippur's young man," was later identified with the powerful Babylonian deity called Bel (Lord). Tummal was the name of the district in Nippur consecrated to Ninlil, the wife of Enlil.

Extensive excavations were conducted at Tell Niffer between 1889 and 1900 by the University of Pennsylvania in four campaigns which resulted in the recovery of thirty thousand tablets and fragments. Much of our current knowledge of Sumer is derived from these documents. Some of the results of these digs were published as early as 1893.

Adab: Sumerian City of Mother Worship

Adab, about twenty-five miles south of Nippur, was supplied by a broad canal which branched from the river Euphrates eastward and passed through the city itself after having fed the adjoining regions along the way. In the centre of Adab the canal divided to form an island on which stood the prehistoric temple of the mother-goddess Aruru. It was known as Emakh, a name common to all the temples of the goddess of birth. The goddess herself had the name Makh, "the far-famed," at Adab. The cult of Adab was devoted entirely to the worship of the mothers-goddess. The stage-tower or ziggurat of Adab is one of the oldest in Sumer.

Ur: The Heart of Sumer

Ur's collapse at the end of the Third Dynasty is a major turning point in Sumerian history. Ur was probably the most powerful Sumerian city of its era. After the fall of Ur the Sumerians as a nation would rule no more. The

Semites, who were really fundamental in the destruction of Ur, became the new masters of the land. What of the Sumerians themselves? The ancient records state that the "teeming blackheaded people were put to the mace."

British archaeologist Leonard Woolley, who from 1907 to 1949 directed major excavations in Egypt, Nubia, Syria, and Iraq, was almost personally responsible for focusing modern world attention on ancient Ur. In 1907, before his work at Ur, Woolley excavated in Nubia in partnership with Randall MacIver. At Karanog he dug the first big Meroitic cemetery on record, but in spite of the rich finds that were recovered, Woolley concluded, "in a manner typically subjective and marked by personal bias," that "the whole Meroitic civilization was but a backwater, remarkable as an isolated phenomenon in African history, but contributing nothing to the general stream of culture and of art."[17]

From 1922 to 1934 Woolley directed extensive excavations at Ur on behalf of the joint expedition of the British Museum and the University of Pennsylvania. The best-known artifacts form these excavations are those removed from the so-called "royal cemetery" of Ur's first dynastic period (c. 2600–2500 B.C.). Among the several written works to his credit are Ur of the Chaldees in 1929 and Excavations at Ur in 1954. These works were particularly designed to appeal to popular consumption, and helped establish the narrow-minded, Oxford University trained Woolley as one of the world's most famous archaeologists.

The Semitic Ascendancy

The ascension to rulership of Sargon of Akkad (c. 2350 B.C.) began the first clear phase of Semitic dominance in Mesopotamia. Sargon was West Asia's first empire builder and established a Semitic dynasty which endured about 150 years. He is first identified in the service of Ur-Zababa, the king of Kish. Rising to power swiftly, he outgeneraled and successively defeated the forces of Uruk, Ur, Mari and Lagash. Encountering little opposition from the other city-states, Sargon's armies rather easily subjugated all of Sumer, and shortly thereafter the whole of Mesopotamia. In the Chronicles Concerning Sargon, King of Agade, the bold victor boasts with arrogance that "The blackheaded peoples I ruled."[18] To symbolize his conquests Sargon rinsed his sword in the Persian Gulf, and took the still prestigious title of "King of Kish."

In governing the Sumerian cities of the empire, Sargon appointed only Akkadians to the higher administrative posts, and utilized all-Akkadian garrisons to maintain authority. Later Assyrian rulers of power possessed knowledge of Sargon and his exploits, and were impressed enough to take his name as their own.

The Akkadians, who culturally only imitated their Sumerian teachers, were ultimately altogether expelled by the onrushing hordes of Guti, nomadic mountain tribes from the Zagros. The Gutian invasion brought down the Sargonic dynasty of Akkad about 2200 B.C., and ushered in an ear of extreme anarchy. Their only real historical significance is the ruination of the Sargonic line. Of the Guti, Sumerologist C.J. Gadd pointed out that:

> They were doubtless mere destroyers and harpies of the wealth of the country . . . Nothing was recalled concerning this period, ever afterwards held in humiliating memory by the Babylonians [Sumerians], except its end, a glorious deliverance hailed no less fervently and followed by no less vigorous a reaction, than the expulsion of the Hyksos from Egypt.[19]

The Dynasty of Isin constitutes the last official dynasty in the Sumerian king-list. Isin was governed for a short time by a certain Zambia (1836-1834 B.C.), after which time Ishbi-Erra established an Isin dynasty which lasted over 200 years.

In official inscriptions from Isin the Sumerian language is used exclusively. It must also be emphasized that practically all the great pieces of Sumerian literature found in the famous 'library' of Nippur were composed or carefully copied during the Isin period of dominance at the request of Semitic monarchs craving for Sumerian culture.

Elam/Susa

In its largest extention Elam included a vital lowland component (Khuzistan) that often had very close relationships with the Sumerian city-states. Greater Elam also included an array of highlands and valleys to the north and east of Khuzistan. These valleys, linked by few routes of easy communication, were accessible to the Sumerian cities, but seldom the clear targets of Sumerian aggression. They were more than capable of independent political actions and established foreign policies according to their own best interests. These Elamites were sometimes even strong enough to dominate Khuzistan and remove it from the Sumerian political sphere.

In the second half of the nineteenth century B.C. appeared a new and dynamic Elamite ruling family. Its founder was named Eparti, and took the title King of Susa and Anshan. His son and successor, Shilkhakha, was succeeded upon his death, around 1850 B.C., by his sister as supreme ruler of Susa. We do not even know her name, but as "Shilkhakha's sister" she attained the status of ancestral mother to the dynasty. Of the later Eparti kings, only those descended from Shilkhakha's sister were considered truly entitled to the throne.[20]

The politically significant and far-famed city of Susa was a boundary phenomenon in the histories of both Elam and Sumer, and at least for the present, the history of Elam itself is largely the history of Susa and its environs. Susa was generally thought by the ancients to be the residence of the legendary black warrior-king, Memnon. The story of Memnon was one of the most widely circulated of the non-Hellenic heroes of antiquity. He is mentioned in the works of Hesiod, Virgil, Ovid, Pindar, Diodorus Siculus, Aeschylus, Pausanias, Strabo and Apollonius of Tyana among others. Arctinus of Miletus composed an epic poem, *Ethiopia*, in which Memnon was the leading figure.

When after many years of hard and intense fighting the Assyrians finally took Susa, they savaged it with a ferocity rarely equaled in human history. Ashrubanipal's own texts recall in horribly triumphant detail the looting and razing of temples, the destruction of sacred groves, the desecration of royal tombs, the seizure of Elamite gods, the removal of royal memorials, the sowing of ruined ground with salt, and the deportation of people, livestock, and even rubble from the devastated city. The style of the report suggests that the destruction of Susa was a sweepingly calculated effort designed to shock the entire world and proclaim Susa's total earthly eradication.

India, A Continuation of Egypt and Ethiopia

Exceptionally valuable writings expressing intimate connections between early India, Egypt and Ethiopia have existed for more than two thousand years. In the first century B.C., for example, the famous Greek historian Diodorus Siculus penned that, "From Ethiopia he (Osiris) passed through Arabia, bordering upon the Red Sea as far as to India . . . he built many cities in India, one of which he called Nysa, willing to have remembrance of that (Nysa) in Egypt where he was brought up."[21] Apollonius of Tyana, who is said to have visited India near the close of the first century A.D., was convinced that, "The Ethiopians are colonists sent from India, who follow their forefathers in matters of wisdom."[22]

The Christian writer Eusebius, born in Palestine in A.D. 264 and appointed Bishop of Nicaea in A.D. 325, has been called the "Father of Church History." The basis for this reputation is his *Historia Ecclesiastica*. Eusebius' work is particularly important to us because of its preservation of the tradition that, "In the reign of Amenophis III, a body of Ethiopians migrated from the country about the Indus, and settled in the valley of the Nile."[23] Also important is *The Itinerarium Alexandri*, a Latin work written about A.D. 345 for the Roman emperor Constantius. *The Itinerarium Alexandri*, 110 says that, "India, taken as a whole, beginning from the north and embracing what of it is subject to Persia, is a continuation of Egypt and the Ethiopians."[24]

Notes

1. Cheikh Anta Diop. *African Origin of Civilization*, trans. Mercer Cook. (Westport: Lawrence Hill & Co., 1974), p. 105.

2. Cheikh Anta Diop. *Great African Thinkers Vol. 1: Cheikh Anta Diop*, eds. Ivan Van Sertima and Larry Williams (New Brunswick: Transaction Books, 1986), p. 235.

3. "A racial classification is given to a group of individuals who share a certain number of anthropological traits, which is necessary so that they not be confused with others. There are two aspects which must be distinguished, the phenotypical and the genotypical. I have frequently elaborated on these two aspects.

If we speak only of the genotype, I can find a black who, at the level of his chromosomes, is closer to a Swede than Peter Botha is. But what counts in reality is the phenotype. It is the physical appearance which counts. This black, even if on the level of his cells he is closer to a Swede than Peter Botha, when he is in South Africa he will live in Soweto. Throughout history, it has always been the phenotype which has been at issue; we must not lose sight of this fact. The phenotype is a reality, physical appearance is a reality.

Now, every time these relationships are not favorable to western cultures, an effort is made to undermine the cultural consciousness of Africans by telling them, 'We don't even know what a race is.' What that means is that they don't know what a black man is; they do know what a white man is, they do know what a yellow man is. Despite the fact that the white race and the yellow race are derivatives of the black which, itself, was the first to exist as a human race, now we do not know want to know what that is. If Africans fall into that trap, they'll be going around in circles. They must understand the trap, understand the stakes." Cheikh Anta Diop, pp. 235-236.

4. Stephen Langdon. *Executives At Kish, Vol. 1*. (Paris: Paul Geuthner, 1924), pp. 58-59.

5. Mario Cappieri. *The Mesopotamians of the Chalcolithic and Bronze Ages*, ed. Henry Field. (Coconut Grove, Miami: Field Research Projects, 1970), p. 5.

6. p. 11.

7. p. 19.

8. p. 6.

9. Flavius Josephus, *The Works of Flavius Josephus* (Philadelphia: John C. Winston Co., n.d.), p. 37.

10. p. 37.

11. George Rawlinson. *Ancient Monarchies, Vol. 1*, (New York: Dodd, Mead & Co., 1881), pp. 54-55.

12. Berossus. In, *Ancient Fragments*, ed. Isaac P. Cory; (Minneapolis: Wizards Bookshelf, 1975), pp. 18-19.

13. "Enki, the king of the Abzu, [decrees] (its) fate: 'Black land, may your trees be large trees . . .'" Samuel N. Kramer. *The Sumerians*. (Chicago: University of Chicago Press, 1963), p. 178.

14. William Leo Hansberry. *Africa & Africans As Seen By Classical Writers.*, ed. Joseph E. Harris. (Washington, D.C.: Howard University Press, 1981), p. 9.

15. "In 1894 an Amorite chief named Sumuabum chose for his capital a site a few miles west of Kish. Sumerian, KA.DINGIR.RA, Akkadian, Babilim, which both mean 'Gate of God.' The Greeks called it Babylon." George Roux. *Ancient Iraq*. (Penguin, 1966), p. 169.

16. *Epic of Gilgamesh.*, ed. B. Radice. (New York: Penguin Books, 1972)

17. M.E.L. Mallowan. *Expedition*. (Fall, 1960), pp. 25-28.

18. William H. McNeill, ed. *The Origins of Civilization*. (London: Oxford University Press, 1968), p. 54.

19. C.J. Gadd, *The Dynasty Of Agade And The Gutian Invasion*. (Cambridge: Cambridge University Press, 1963), p. 44.

20. Walther Hinz. *Persia: c. 1800-1550 B.C.* (Cambridge: Cambridge University Press, 1964), pp. 7-8.

21. *Diodorus Siculus*. Bk 1: 11, 12.

22. Flavius Philostratus. *The Life of Apollonius of Tyana, Book VI*.

23. Eusebius. Quoted by George Rawlinson in *Ancient Monarchies, V. 1*, p. 49.

24. *The Itinerarium Alexandri*, 110.

THE BLACKHEADS OF SUMER: A BIBLIOGRAPHY

Runoko Rashidi

Anthropology

Cappieri, Mario. *The Mesopotamians of the Chalcolithic and Bronze Ages.*, ed. H. Field. Field Research Projects. Coconut Grove, Miami, 1970.

Field, Henry. "Human Remains From Jemdat Nasr, Mesopotamia." *Journal of the Royal Asiatic Society.* October, 1932.

Field, Henry, *Ancient and Modern Man in Southwestern Asia: I.* University of Miami Press. Coral Cables, Florida, 1956.

Field, Henry. *Ancient and Modern Man in Southwestern Asia: II.* University of Miami. Coral Gables, Florida, 1963.

Keith, Arthur. "Report on the Human Remains." In H.R. Hall and Leonard Woolley, *Ur Excavations, al' Ubaid Cemetery.* Oxford, 1927.

Keith, Arthur. "Report on Human Remains." In H.R. Hall and Leonard Woolley, *Ur Excavations, The Royal Cemetery, Vol. 2.* British Museum. London, 1934.

Swindler, Daris R. *A Study of the Cranial and Skeletal Materials Excavated at Nippur.* Philadelphia, 1956.

Art

Johansen, Flemming., trans. J. Manzello. *Statues of Gudea: Ancient and Modern.* Akademisk Forlag. Copenhagen, 1978.

Lloyd, Seton. *The Art of the Ancient Near East.* Oxford University Press. New York, 1961.

Moorey, P.R.S. *Materials and Manufacture in Ancient Mesopotamia: The Evidence of Archaeology and Art.* BAR International Series 237. Oxford, 1985.

Dilmun

Bibby, Geoffrey. *Looking For Dilmun.* New American Library. New York, 1969.

Lamberg-Karlovsky, C.C. "Dilum: Gateway to Immortality." *Journal of Near Eastern Studies.* Vol. 41, No. 1 (1982) 45-49.

Kramer, Samuel N. "Dilmun: Quest for Paradise." *Antiquity.* Vol. 37 (1963) 111-115.

Kramer, Samuel N. "The Indus Civilization and Dilmun: The Sumerian Paradise Land." *Expedition,* Vol. 6, No. 3 (1964) 44-52.

Eastern Ethiopia

Baldwin, John D. *Pre-Historic Nations.* Harper & Brothers. New York, 1872.

Brunson, James E. *The African Presence in Ancient Mesopotamian Art.* MS. 1984.

Copher, Charles B. "Blacks and Jews in Historical Interaction: The Biblical/African Experience." *Journal of the I.T.C.* Vol. 3, No. 1 (1975) 9-16.

Cox, George O. *African Empires and Civilizations.* African Heritage Studies, 1974.

Diop, Cheikh Anta. *African Origin of Civilization.* trans. Mercer Cook. Lawrence Hill & Co. Westport, 1974.

Diop, Cheikh Anta. *Cultural Unity of Black Africa.* Third World Press. Chicago, 1978.

Forlong, J.G.R. *Rivers of Life.* Bernard Quarith, London, 1883.

Hansberry, William Leo. *Africa & Africans As Seen By Classical Writers.*, ed. Joseph E. Harris. Howard University Press. Washington, D.C., 1981.
Higgins, Godfrey. *Celtic Druids.* 1829; rpt. Philosophical Research Society. Los Angeles, 1977.
Higgins, Godfrey. *Anacalypsis.* 1836; rpt. Health Research. Mokelume Hills, California, 1972.
Houston, Drusilla Dunjee. *Wonderful Ethiopians of the Ancient Cushite Empire.* 1926; rpt. Black Classic Press. Baltimore, 1985.
Jackson, John G. *Ethiopia and the Origin of Civilization.* 1939; rpt. Black Classic Press. Baltimore, 1985.
Jackson, John G. *Man, God and Civilization.* University Books. New Hyde Park, 1972.
Jackson, John G. *Introduction to African Civilizations.* Citadel Press. Secaucus, New Jersey, 1974.
Lenormant, Francois. *Ancient History of the East.* Asher & Co. London, 1869.
Massey, Gerald. *Book of Beginnings*, Vol. 2. University Books, Inc., 1881; rpt. 1974.
Massey, Gerald. *Ancient Egypt.* Samuel Weiser. New York, 1970.
Means, Sterling. *Ethiopia & The Missing Link in African History.* Atlantis Publishing Co. Harrisburg, Pennsylvania, 1945; rpt. 1980.
Norris, John William. *The Ethiopian's Place in History.* Baltimore, 1916.
Perry, Rufus L. *The Cushite.* The Literary Union. New York, 1887.
Rashidi, Runoko. "African Presence in Sumer and Elam." *Egypt Revisited.*, ed. Ivan Van Sertima. *Journal of African Civilizations.* New Brunswick, New Jersey (1982) 137-147.
Rashidi, Runoko. *Kushite Case-Studies.* Los Angeles, California, 1983.
Rashidi, Runoko. "Kushite Origins of Sumer and Elam." *UFAHAMU*, Vol. 12, No. 3 (1983) 215-233.
Rashidi, Runoko. "Nile Valley Presence in Asian Antiquity." *Nile Valley Civilizations.*, ed. Ivan Van Sertima. *Journal of African Civilizations.* New Brunswick, New Jersey (1984) 201-220.
Rashidi, Runoko. "Dr. Diop on Asia: Highlights and Insights." *Great African Thinkers, Vol. 1: Cheikh Anta Diop.*, eds. Ivan Van Sertima & Larry Williams. *Journal of African Civilizations.* New Brunswick, New Jersey (1986).
Rawlinson, George. *History of Herodotus, Vol. 1.* John Murray. London, 1858.
Rawlinson, George. *Ancient Monarchies, Vol. 1.* Dodd, Mead & Co. New York, 1881.
Rawlinson, George. *Origin of Nations.* Scribner's. New York, 1912.
Rogers, Joel Augustus. *Sex and Race, Vol. 1.* Helga M. Rogers. New York, 1967.
Rogers, Joel Augustus. *One-Hundred Amazing Facts About the Negro.* Helga M. Rogers. New York, 1970.
Van Sertima, Ivan, & Runoko Rashidi, eds. *African Presence in Early Asia. Journal of African Civilizations.* New Brunswick, New Jersey, 1985.
Windsor, Rudolf. *From Babylon to Timbuktu.* Exposition Press. New York, 1969.
Winters, Clyde Ahmad. *Lectures in Africana: Kushite Diaspora.* Chicago, 1982.

Elam/Susa

Amiet, Pierre. "Archaeological Discontinuity and Ethnic Duality in Elam." *Antiquity.* LIII (1979) 196-204
Cameron, George C. *History of Early Iran.* Greenwood Press. New York, 1976.
Carter, E. & Matthew W. Stolper. *Elam: Surveys of Political History and Archaeology.* University of California Press. Berkeley, 1984.
Dieulafoy, Marcel A. *L'Acropole de Susa.* Hachette. Paris, 1892.
De Mecquenem, R. "Excavations at Susa (Persia), 1930-1931." Antiquity. Sept. (1931) 330-343.
English, Patrick T. "Cushites, Colchians, And Khazars."*Journal of Near Eastern Studies.* (1959)
Field, Henry. *Contributions to the Anthropology of Iran.* Anthropological Series, Field Museum of Natural History Vol. 29, No. 1 Chicago, 1939
Ghirshman, R. *Iran.* Penguin Books. Baltimore, 1954.
Hansman, John. "Elamites, Achaemenians and Anshan." *Iran* Vol. 10 (1972) 101-123.
Hinz, Walther. *Persia: c. 1800-1550 B.C.* Cambridge University Press. Cambridge, 1964.

Hinz, Walther. *The Lost World of Elam.* trans. J. Barnes. New York University Press. New York, 1973.

Lamberg-Karlovsky, C.C. "The Proto-Elamites on the Iranian Plateau." *Antiquity.* LII (1978) 114-120

Le Breton, L. "The Early Period at Susa, Mesopotamian Relations." *Iraq* Vol. 19, Pt. 2 (1957) 79-124

McAlpin, David W. "Dravidian and Elamite—a Real Breakthrough?" *Journal of the American Oriental Society,* Vol. 93, No. 3:384-85, 1974.

McAlpin, David W. "Towards Proto-Elamo-Dravidian." *Language,* Vol. 50, No. 1:89-101, 1974.

McAlpin, David W. "Elamite and Dravidian: Further Evidence of Relationship." *Current Anthropology,* Vol. 16, No. 1:105-115, 1975.

Mecquenem, R. de. "Excavations at Susa." *Antiquity,* Vol. 5, 1931, 330-344.

Olmstead, A.T. *History of the Persian Empire.* University of Chicago Press. Chicago, 1948.

Sykes, Percy. *A History of Persia.* Macmillan & Co. London, 1930.

Weiss, H., and T.C. Young, Jr. "The Merchants of Susa: Godin V and Plateau-Lowland Relations in the Late Fourth Millennium B.C. *Iran* (1975) 1-18.

Excavations

Langdon, S. *Excavations at Kish, Vol. 1.* Paul Geuthner. Paris, 1924.

Lloyd, Seton. *The Archaeology of Mesopotamia.* Thames & Hudson. London, 1984.

Mackay, E.J.H. *Report on the Excavations of the 'A' Cemetery at Kish, Mesopotamia. Pts. 1 and 2.* Field Museum of Natural History, Chicago, 1925.

Mackay, E.J.H. *A Sumerian Palace and the 'A' Cemetery at Kish, Mesopotamia. Anthropology Memoirs, Vol. 1, No. 2,* Field Museum of Natural History, 1929.

Moorey, P.R.S. *Kish Excavations 1923-1933.* Clarendon Press. Oxford, 1978.

Watelin, L. Ch., & S. Langdon. *Excavations at Kish, Vol. 4 1925-1930.* Paul Geuthner. Paris, 1934.

Woolley, Leonard. *Excavations at Ur.* Crowell. New York, 1954.

Zettler, Richard L. "Woolley's Ur Revisited." *Biblical Archaeology Review,* Sept./Oct. (1984) 58-61

General

Frankfort, Henri. *Birth of Civilization in the Near East.* Doubleday Anchor. New York, 1956.

Gadd, C.J. *History and Monuments of Ur.* Chatto & Windus. London, 1929.

Gadd, C.J. *The Cities of Babylonia.* Cambridge University Press. Cambridge, 1962.

Gadd, C.J. *The Dynasty of Agade and the Gutian Invasion.* Cambridge University Press. Cambridge, 1963.

Jastrow, Morris. *Civilization of Babylonia and Assyria.* J.B. Lippincott Co. Philadelphia, 1915.

Jones, Tom., ed. *The Sumerian Problem.* John Wiley & Sons. New York, 1969.

Kramer, Samuel N. *The Sumerians.* University of Chicago Press. Chicago, 1963

Lamberg-Karlovsky, C.C., & Jeremy A. Sabloff. *Ancient Civilizations.* Benjamin/Cummings Pub. Co. Menlo Park, California, 1979.

Landsberger, Benno. *Three Essays on the Sumerians.* trans. M.D. Ellis. Undena Publications. Los Angeles, 1974.

Macnaughton, Duncan. *A Scheme of Babylonian Chronology.* Luzac & Co. London, 1930.

Oppenheim, A. Leo. *Letters From Mesopotamia.* University of Chicago Press. Chicago, 1967

Oppenheim, A. Leo. *Ancient Mesopotamia.* University of Chicago Press. Chicago, 1977.

Roux, George. *Ancient Iraq.* Penguin. 1966.

Sayce, A.H. *Ancient Empires of the East.* Charles Scribner's Sons, 1898

Indus And India

Allchin, B. *The Rise of Civilization in India and Pakistan.* Cambridge, 1982.

Fairservis, Walter A. *The Roots of Ancient India,* 2nd ed. London, 1971.

Possehl, Gregory L. *Cities Of The Indus.* New Delhi, 1979.

Possehl, Gregory, L. *Harappan Civilization*
Tambimuttu, E.L. *Dravida*. Madras, 1945.
Winters, Clyde Ahmad. "The African Influence on Indian Agriculture." Editor, Ivan Van Sertima. *Journal of African Civilizations*. Vol. 3, No. 1, April 1981, New Brunswick: Transaction Books, pp. 100-110.
Winters, Clyde Ahmad. "African Origins of Glorious Dalits," Editor, V.T. Rajshekar. *Dalit Voice*, April 16, 1986. Bangalore.

International Relations

Bibby, Geoffrey. *Looking For Dilmun*. New American Library. New York, 1969.
Blackman, Aylward M. "The Rite of Opening the Mouth in Ancient Egypt and Babylonia." *Journal of Egyptian Archaeology* Vol. 10, April-July (1924) 47-59
Buccellati, Giorgia & Marilyn Kelly-Buccellati. "The Glory of Ancient Syria." *Terra* Vol. 24, No. 4 (1986) 6-14.
Buccellati, Giorgia & Marilyn Kelly-Buccellati. "The Glory of Ancient Syria—Ebla to Damascus, Pt. 2." *Terra* Vol. 24, No. 5 (1986) 22-29.
Buchanan, Briggs "A Dated Seal Impression Connecting Babylonia and Ancient India." *Ancient Cities of the Indus*, ed. G.L. Possehl. New Delhi, 1979.
During-Caspers, Elisabeth C.L. "Further Evidence For Cultural Relations between India, Baluchistan, and Iran and Mesopotamia in Early Dynastic Times." *Journal of Near Eastern Studies*. Vol. 24, Nos. 1 & 2 (1965) 53-56.
During-Caspers, Elisabeth C.L. "Sumer, Coastal Arabia and the Indus Valley in Protoliterate and Early Dynastic Eras. Supporting Evidence For a Cultural Linkage." *Journal of the Economic and Social History of the Orient*. Vol. 22, No. 2 (1977) 121-135.
Hayes, William C., & M.B. Rowton. *Chronology: Egypt; Western Asia; Aegean Bronze Age*. Cambridge University Press. Cambridge, 1962.
Jairazbhoy, Rafique A. *The Spread of Ancient Civilizations*. Ra Publications. Middlesex, 1982.
Kohl, Philip L. "The Balance of Trade in Southwestern Asia in the Mid-Third Millennium B.C." *Current Anthropology* Vol. 19, No. 3 (1978): 463-492
Langdon, S. "The Early Chronology of Sumer and Egypt and the Similarities in Their Culture." *Journal of Egyptian Archaeology* Vol. 7, Oct. (1921) 133-153.
Mackay, E.J.H. "Sumerian Connections with Ancient India." *Journal of the Royal Asiatic Society of Great Britain and Ireland*, 1925, 697-701.
Mackay, E.J.H. "Further Links Between Ancient Sind, Sumer and Elsewhere." *Antiquity*, Vol. 5:459-473, 1931.
Oates, J. "Seafaring Merchants of Ur?" *Antiquity*. Vol. LI (1977) 221-234.
Oppenheim, A.L. "The Seafaring Merchants of Ur." *Journal of the American Oriental Society* (1974) 6-17.
Rao, S.R. "A Persian Gulf Seal from Lothal." *Antiquity*, Vol. 37, 1963, 96-99.
Smith, G. Elliot. *The Influence of Ancient Egyptian Civilization in the East and in America*. 1916.
Smith, G. Elliot. *Human History*. Norton & Co. New York, 1929.

Literature

Berossus. In, *Ancient Fragments*, ed. Isaac P. Cory; Wizards Bookshelf. Minneapolis, 1975.
Epic of Gilgamesh., ed. B. Radice. Penguin. New York, 1972.
Kramer, Samuel N. "The Weeping Goddess: Sumerian Prototypes of the Mater Dolorosa." *Biblical Archaeologist*, Vol. 46, No. 2 (1983) 69-80
McNeill, William H., ed. *The Origins of Civilization*. Oxford University Press. London, 1968.
Pritchard, James B., ed. *The Ancient Near East*. Princeton University Press. Princeton, 1958.
Wolkstein, Diane, & Samuel N. Kramer. *Inanna: Queen of Heaven and Earth*. Harper & Row. New York, 1983.

Magan and Meluhha

Peake, Harold. "The Copper Mountain of Magan." *Antiquity*
Potts, D. "The Road to Meluhha." *Journal of Near Eastern Studies*, Oct. (1982) 279-288
Prehistory:
Mellaart, James. *Earliest Civilizations of the Near East*. McGraw-Hill. New York, 1965.

Nimrod/Belus

Hislop, Alexander. *The Two Babylons*. Loizeaux Brothers, 1969.
Josephus, Flavius. *The Works of Flavius Josephus*
Rawlinson, George. *Egypt And Babylon*. Lovell. New York, n.d.
The Talmud.

Religion

James. E.O. *The Ancient Gods*. Capricorn Books. New York, 1964
Parrot, Andre. *Babylon And The Old Testament*. Philosophical Library. New York, 1958.
Hoberman, Barry. "George Smith: Pioneer Assyriologist." *Biblical Archaeologist*, Winter (1983)
    41-42

BLACKS AND JEWS IN HISTORICAL INTERACTION: THE BIBLICAL/AFRICAN EXPERIENCE

Charles B. Copher

The subject before us for consideration is part of a larger one, in the light of which it must be studied and only in the light of which it can be understood. That larger subject is: "Blacks and Jews in Historical Interaction: The Biblical/Black Experience." But having stated the larger subject of which the immediate one is only a part takes us short distance in dealing with it. Before real treatment can be given it is necessary first of all to establish a foundation upon which a superstructure can be erected. The foundation consists in confirming the existence of Black peoples in the Biblical world with whom Jews could have interacted; it cannot be taken for granted that there were. Once such a confirmation is made, then and then only may the presentation proceed. For this reason the paper consists of two parts, the foundation and the superstructure.

The existence of black peoples in the Biblical world, especially of so-called Negroes, with whom ancient Jews could have interacted, is a matter of great interest, discussion, debate, and of confusing, contradictory opinions. Within modern times, in Western civilizations, two diametrically opposed views have developed, with several sub-views between two extreme positions. From the introduction of Blacks, especially those who came to be called Negroes, into the consciousness of Western Europeans around 1450 C.E. until roughly 1800 C.E. there was one view rather commonly held in both the popular and scholarly mind. This view was that the Hamites referred to in the Bible were peoples black in color, and generally regarded as what were called Negroes. It may be called the old, traditional Hamite view; and what was based upon the Genesis account of Noah's sons,[1] particularly Ham-Canaan, and upon the so-called Table of Nations in Genesis 10 and I Chronicles 1, which lists Ham and his descendants. At times the view was associated with Noah's curse of Canaan, interpreted more frequently to be a curse of Ham and his descendants, at times not, on the basis of which curse the Hamites were destined to be slaves of the families of Shem and Japheth, and to be black in color—despite the fact that in the Biblical accounts Ham is not cursed, nor is color mentioned or even implied unless of course the word Ham in Hebrew meant black at the times the stories and the Table originated.

This article originally was presented as a paper at the National Consultation on Black-Jewish Relations held at Fisk University, June 9-12, 1974. It was initially printed in the *Journal of the Interdenominational Theological Center*, Vol. III, Number 1, Fall, 1975, pp. 9-16.

Additionally, although a rival view came into existence around 1800 C.E., this traditional Hamite view continued to be held; and associating Hamites with Blacks/Negroes especially, and further associating these peoples with Noah's curse of (Ham)-Canaan, it was employed to justify the enslavement of black Africans. This use was made to the fullest between the year 1800 and the American Civil War. But the emancipation of Blacks from slavery did not terminate the usage. The practice has continued in America and elsewhere, at times receiving greater emphasis than at others, as in the United States of America during the years immediately after the 1954 Supreme Court decision in regard to segregation in education. Some traditionalist, conservative "Christians" resurrected the view and employed it as a divine justification for the continued segregation of Blacks. Twenty years later the view is still adhered to by many.

Dissociated from the curse of (Ham)-Canaan, and/or in spite of the association, the traditional Hamite view was and still is used in favor of black peoples including the so-called Negroes.[2] According to this usage which has been made by some Whites and by numerous black individuals and groups, the Biblical Hamites were Negroes and included the Hamites listed in the Biblical Table of Nations, notably: Egyptians, African Cushites (Ethiopians), and Asiatic Cushites of South Asia, Mesopotamia, Phoenicia, and Canaan. These peoples, taken to be black in color, are regarded as the founders of the great ancient civilizations of the Middle East. And, to be sure, according to the Biblical accounts, Jews were in interaction with all of them.

Over against the traditional view, whether or not associated with the curse of (Ham)-Canaan, there came into being around 1800, as has been stated, a new Hamite hypothesis or view.[3] It dissociates the so-called Negroes from the Hamites, removes color from the criteria for determining racial identity, and regards black non-Negroids to be white—Caucasoid or Europoid Blacks. It is this view or hypothesis which came to characterize the so-called sciences of anthropology, ethnology, and kindred studies, but also critical historical-literary Biblical studies. And just as anthropology and ethnology removed Negroes from the Biblical world so did critical study of the Bible remove Negroes from the Bible and Biblical history—except for an occasional Negro individual who could only have been a slave. Thus today in critical Biblical studies, as in anthropology and ethnology, the ancient Egyptians, Cushites, in fact all the Biblical Hamites, were white; so-called Negroes did not figure at all in Biblical history, and there could not have been interaction between Blacks and Jews if by Blacks is meant so-called Negroes.

He who would build the superstructure called for by the title of this paper is thus faced with the further task of choosing between Scylla and Charybdis, between two diametrically opposed views: one that allows for an interaction, one that does not.

In an endeavor to find the truth of the matter the reader undertook research which now permits of rather well supported conclusions.[4] Making use of what he regarded to be tenable supports for the traditional Hamite views; and supports supplied by adherents to the newer view, including critical Biblical scholars, he assembled several categories of evidence that testify to a Black including Negro presence in the Biblical world. This Black presence was to be found in Egypt, African Cush, Asiatic Cush, and in eastern Mediterranean lands.

For Egypt-African Cush the categories of evidence are: archaeological data, consisting of Egyptian-Cushite written records, paintings, sculptures, and skeletal remains; modern historical works; critical Biblical scholarly works; personal names and adjectives; opinions of modern travelers, archaeologists and anthropologists; ancient Greek-Roman legends and historical writings; works of early Christian commentators; and ancient Jewish writings, including the Bible, Babylonian Talmud, Midrashim, and legends. Categories of evidence for Asiatic Cush are: writings of ancient Greeks; modern historical works; archaeological data; and ancient Jewish works, the same as above. And for the Mediterranean lands, archaeological data and modern historical works are the categories.

The evidences testify that, according to American sociological definitions of Negro, the ancient Egyptians were Negroes.

***

They indicate that the African Cushites (Ethiopians) were predominantly of Negroid identity; and that Blacks, including Negroes, during Biblical times, inhabited parts of Asia from the Indus River Valley westwards into Elam-Persia, Mesopotamia, parts of Arabia, Phoenicia, Canaan, Crete and Greece. Further, the evidences indicate that, *in the main*, wherever in the Bible Hamites are referred to there were peoples who today in the Western world would be classified as Black, and Negroid. Additionally, they establish a Black element within the ancient Hebrew-Israelite Jewish population itself.

With respect to the superstructure that may now be erected, it may be done in several ways. This essay proceeds by pointing to interactions across the years of Biblical history in chronological sequence, beginning with the prehistoric period. Materials used will be mainly conditions and events of history as these are set forth in the Bible, supplemented by archaeology, and "Legends of the Jews."

First of all, it is to be noted that in prehistoric times, before the coming of the Hebrews to Canaan, and also during the time of Hebrew-Israelite-Jewish occupation, Negroid peoples lived in the land, apart from any black element in the Hebrew-Israelite-Jewish population.[5] Shortly after 2000 B.C.E., a time when even new Hamite hypothesis advocates claim the so-called Negro first appeared in history, the Patriarchal period began. At the beginning of this period, according to one Biblical tradition, the patriarch Abraham migrated from what later came to be called Chaldea, a land occupied by Cushites. Jewish legend has it that Abraham and his people suffered persecution at the hands of none other than Nimrod, the Cushite founder of Mesopotamian civilization and culture.[6] According to another tradition which is not necessarily in conflict with the other, Abraham's starting place was Haran in northwestern Mesopotamia. From this region he migrated into Canaan where he moved among Hamites and non-Hamites, remaining aloof from all, and refusing to permit intermarriage. From predominantly Hamite Canaan he moved to Egypt where despite the designs of a Hamite pharaoh upon Sarah the tribal blood remained pure. Nevertheless the patriarch himself produced a son by an Egyptian woman who herself later on obtained an Egyptian wife for the son. Under Isaac and Jacob, according to the prevailing tradition, there was no regular intermarriage with the Hamitic Canaanites. But in Canaan Esau and Judah engaged in marriage with Canaanite women;[7] and, whatever were the Hebrew tribes that migrated to and settled in Egypt during the patriarchal age, in that land occurred a significant infusion of black blood. Joseph married an Egyptian wife to whom were born two of the more important Hebrew tribes, Ephraim and Manasseh. Apart from and in addition to the interactions occasioned by such a marriage as that of Joseph, there were interactions arising from the Hebrew state of affairs during the period of Egyptian sojourn. Whether or not the Hebrew settlement was related to the Hyksos invasion and occupation of Egypt, the first years saw a favorable position. The latter years saw a state of oppression, with concomitant reactions, and it was these that the Jews best remembered. But more remains to be said about the infusion of black blood into the Hebrew tribe or tribes in Egypt, through Moses and his family, with all the implications for Black/Negro-Jewish interactions. The book of Exodus records Moses' escape from Egypt to Midian where the daughters of Jethro, on the basis of his appearance, mistakenly identified him to be an Egyptian, and where Moses married Zipporah, one of Jethro's daughters. Then the book of Numbers states that Moses had married a Cushite woman who could very well have been none other than a Cushite Zipporah herself, Cushites having been inhabitants of Arabia and adjacent regions as well as Africa. Josephus, and Jewish spinners of legends were later to say much about Moses' marriage to a Cushite woman in spite of some rabbinic explanations to the contrary.[8] Furthermore, there are good grounds for believing that the tribal family of Moses was of black Cushite origin. Support for the opinion comes in the form of Egyptian names carried by members of the family as well as by other Hebrews: Moses, Phinehas, Hophni, Merari, Pashur, etc., especially Phinehas, which means Black, Negro, Nubian, etc.[9] This last name it is to be observed was the name of a grandson of Aaron, and was carried by members of the priesthood through the period of the Babylonian exile.

Still further, indications of interactions between Black Africans and possibly Hebrew tribes in Canaan during the patriarchal period lie in the Tel-el-Amarna correspondence. According to one communication Black/Negro troops in the Egyptian army were plundering the community because they had not received their pay.[10]

During the period of the conquest and settlement of Canaan, the period of the judges, interactions between Hamites-Jews are to be seen in the several Biblical accounts that have to do with relations between Hebrews and Canaanites and between Hebrews and other Cushites. In these accounts there are directives against intermarriage and to exterminate, contrary to which there were co-existence, intermarriage, and the beginnings of amalgamation of the Canaanites. There is also the recounting of an invasion and oppression by a Mesopotamian ruler with the name Cushanrishathaim—the "Cushite of double infamy." And toward the end of the period pristine Hebrew religion was Canaanized-Africanized, and thus polluted, by fertility practices instituted by Eli's Egyptian-Cushite named priest-sons, Phinehas and Hophni.[11]

For the period of the United Monarchy interactions are to be noted in the accounts of relations between the Israelites-Judeans and Canaanites and Phoenicians; in the account of the Cushite messenger in David's army;[12] in the accounts of Solomon's dealings with the king of Egypt and marriage to an Egyptian princess; in the narrative about the Queen of Sheba; and in the accounts of Hadad's and Jeroboam's flight to protection under the King of Egypt.

References to interactions during the two hundred-year history of the two kingdoms are in the several narratives of Jeroboam's return from Egypt, Shishak's invasion of Judah-Israel, and the invasion of Zerah, the Cushite. Additionally, they appear in the narratives and oracles of the 8th century B.C.E. recorded in Kings-Chronicles and in the books of Amos and Hosea. Within the prophetic books are Amos' comparison of Yahweh's equal regard for Israelites and Cushites (Ethiopians, Negroes);[13] and Hosea's castigation of Israel for her wishy-washy trust in Assyria and Egypt instead of trust in Yahweh. Possibly also interactions are to be seen in the account of the repopulation of Israel with outsiders by the Assyrians.[14]

For the remainder of the 8th century, that is, from 721 B.C.E. to the end of the century, interactions between Blacks and Judeans may be viewed in clearest light. This period was that of the early years of the 25th Egyptian Dynasty, the Cushite or Ethiopian. In the Bible itself the view is provided by the book of Isaiah son of Amoz, with its several references to the Egyptians-Cushites.[15] In content the references range from complimentary descriptions of Cushites to warnings against trust in Egyptian-Cushite military strength, and prophecies that the Assyrians will make of the Egyptians-Cushites captives of war. Also indicative of Black-Judean interactions is the narrative of Chaldean intrigue in Judah toward the end of the century by Merodach-baladan; and the other

anti-foreigner oracles in the book. Additionally, during the period 727-700
B.C.E. both Israel and Judah were allies of Egypt-Cush.
   Interactions between Blacks and Judeans during the period 700-582-570-
B.C.E. were both internal within the Judean community, and external outside
the community. These interactions may be seen especially in the books of II
Kings and II Chronicles, and in the prophetic books of Zephaniah, Jeremiah,
and Ezekiel. Zephaniah himself is said to have been the son of one Cushi,[16]
and his family tree is traced back to a certain Hezekiah whom some Biblical
scholars identify with Hezekiah the Judean king.[17] Assuming, as do several
Biblical scholars of note, that Zephaniah was a black Judean,[18] and that his
ancestry included King Hezekiah, Blacks were among the population, and
black blood flowed in the veins of Judah's kings.
   The book of Jeremiah makes mention of a Jehudi, great-grandson of one
Cushi, who was sent by the princes of Judah to Baruch, Jeremiah's scribe, and
who read Jeremiah's oracles dictated to Baruch in the hearing of King
Jehoiakim.[19] Additionally it contains an adage with respect to the Cushite's
color as being unchangeable; narratives concerning a Cushite friend and
helper of Jeremiah, Ebed-Melech; oracles against foreign nations including
Egypt and other Hamites; and narratives about the fall of Judah to the Chaldeans and about Judean communities in exile in various parts of Egypt. It
may be noted that the references to Blacks in the book of Jeremiah indicate
that there was a Black element in the Judean population; that black Cushites
were sufficiently well known that they could furnish an analogy between
unchangeable color and behavior; and that members of the court included
black Cushites. Further, and interesting to note incidentally, is the name of
one of the places where Judean exiles settled in Egypt—Tahpanhes. "Fort of
the Negro."
   The book of Ezekiel, as does the book of Jeremiah, contains oracles against
Hamites, including Phoenicians, Egyptians, and Cushites. Like the book of
Jeremiah also, it permits a view of Judah in exile, in Chaldea, where the
Judeans lived under rather favorable circumstances. At the same time it asserts that Judah's origins were mixed, and criticizes Judah for her whoredoms
with the Assyrians, Chaldeans, and Egyptians.
   And the historical books of Kings-Chronicles narrate the fall of Judah, the
capture of Jerusalem, the destruction of the Temple—the most tragic experience for Judeans-Jews in Old Testament history, at the hands of the Chaldeans. These events made for the most hostile interactions between the
Judans-Jews and a people regarded as black—not only at the time, but for the
times to come, whenever they were remembered. In the meantime, between
609-586 B.C.E., Egypt was alternately an antagonist-protagonist with respect
to Judah.
   With the entrance of the Persians into Judean-Jewish life in 538 B.C.E., a

new era of interactions began. In the Persian-Elamite population, and in the Persian army were Blacks.[20] Relations between the two peoples were good; so good in fact that someone has remarked that only in the instance of the ancient Persians did the ancient Jews have only good to say. But the Bible, suplemented by extra-Biblical materials such as the Elephantine papyri and Jewish midrashim and legends, provides still more insights into Black-Jewish interactions during the Persian period which for Jews may be said to have lasted from 540 B.C.E. until the beginning of the Greek Period under Alexander the Great in 332 B.C.E. There are the hopes and aspirations for a going forth from Babylon back to Palestine, and the general universalism voiced by a Second Isaiah; there are the lofty universalistic passages of a Trito-Isaiah that envision a time when Assyria and Egypt will be accepted on par with Israel by Yahweh, and when Yahweh's temple shall be a house of prayer for all peoples. At the same time there are passages such as the anti-Chaldean Psalm 137, and the Trito-Isaianic passages that envision the day when Blacks and others shall serve Israel.[21] There are also the interactions revealed by the Elephantine papyri with their record of a Jewish community in Upper Egypt that has suffered at the hands of native Egyptians. Perhaps most significantly of all, there are the anti-Black traditions and legends that began to come into existence at least by the time of Ezra, around 400 B.C.E., many of which were recorded in the Babylonian Talmud and in the Midrashim. These are the "Ham" stories, and legends about the origin of black Jews whether in Palestine or in Africa. And here it is to be noted that the stock of "Ham" stories continued to grow, after the Biblical period, on beyond the time when a historical gap between East and West was created by Islamic hegemony over the Near and Middle East, and westward over parts of the Mediterranean world.[22]

Not to be excluded for insights into Black-Jewish relations during the Persian period are the numerous particularistic and universalistic passages in the prophetic books of Joel, II Zechariah, chapters 9-14 of the book, and Malachi. Generally speaking, Jewish attitudes in these books include extremes of both particularism and universalism.

Between the end of the Persian period and the writing of the latest books in the Bible interactions between Blacks and Jews are to be seen in the books of Maccabees wherein Jewish history during the Greek period is recounted; in the Gospel according to Matthew, with its narrative of the "Flight into Egypt"; in the book of Acts with its acounts of Jews present from all the world in Jerusalem on the Day of Pentecost, of Niger among the followers of Jesus at Antioch in Syria, and of Philip's conversion of the Ethiopian eunuch; and in the writings of Josephus. The books of Maccabees show Jewish relations with Egypt. Matthew depicts Egypt as still a haven for Jews persecuted in the homeland, yet tying residence in Palestine with coming out of Egypt. The book of Acts lists adherents to Judaism from countries inhabited by Blacks, and indicates that black people were among the early members of the Christian Church. And Josephus, who recounts the history of his people, including much about Moses and Cushites, goes into lengthy dissertations about the provenance of the Jews and their affinities with the Egyptians.[23] Reviewing and summarizing, there were Black-Jewish interactions during the entire course of Biblical history. These interactions may be seen in the Bible, supplemented by archaeological data, the works of Josephus, and by extra-Biblical Jewish traditions, Biblical interpretations such as appear in the Babylonian Talmud and Midrashim, and legends. In the main, except for the relatively few universalistic passages in the Bible, the reactions, which are from the Jewish side only, are negative in nature. And in the Babylonian Talmud, Midrashim, and legends the reactions are wholly anti-Black, despite the conclusion that Blacks formed a part of the ancient Hebrew-Israelite-Jewish community.

Notes

1. Genesis 9.
2. See the book *Yaradee: A Plea for Africa*, by Frederick Freeman (Philadelphia, 1836), and also histories of the Afro-Americans written by Black authors from 1840 to the present.
3. For a discussion of the new Hamite hypothesis, see Edith R. Sanders, "The Hamite Hypothesis," *Journal of African History*, X (1969), pp. 521-532.
4. See the essay by the reader entitled "The Black Man in the Biblical World," published in the Spring issue 1974 of *The Journal of the Interdenominational Theological Center*.
5. See Anati, Emmanuel, *Palestine Before the Hebrews*, page 322; and McCown, Chester C., *The Ladder of Progress in Palestine*, pages 130, 142 f., 166.
6. See, for example, *The Talmud*, by H. Polano, pages 30 ff. for one such story.
7. Genesis 36, 38.
8. Josephus, Flavius, *Antiquities of the Jews*, Book II, Chapter 10, translated by William Whiston. For a contrary view see Ginzberg, L., *Legends of the Jews*, VI, 90, as referred by Henry S. Noerdinger, *Moses and Egypt*, page 70.
9. Albright, W.F., *From the Stone Age to Christianity*, pages 193 f.; *Yahweh and the Gods of Canaan*, page 165.
10. Pritchard, James B., *Ancient Near Eastern Texts Relating to the Old Testament*, page 232.
11. I Samuel 2.
12. II Samuel 18.
13. 9:7
14. II Kings 17:24 ff.
15. Chapters 18, 19, 20, 30, and 31.
16. Zephaniah 1:1
17. A survey of Biblical *Introductions* reveals the following: E. Sellin wrote in 1923 that Zephaniah is generally held to have been a prophet of royal blood; among those who support the view are J.A. Brewer, R.K. Harrison, E.A. Leslie, R.H. Pfeiffer, and Charles L. Taylor, Jr.
18. Some who identify the prophet as a "Negro" are: Aage Bentzen, J.A. Bewer, Curt Kuhl, E. Sellin and A. Weiser, but note the contrary view of Georg Fohrer in his revision of Sellin's *Introduction*.
19. Chapter 36: 14 ff.
20. See, for example Childe, V.G., *The Most Ancient East*, page 144; Olmstead, A.T., *History of*

the Persian Empire, pages 28 ff.; M. Dieulafoy, The *Acropolis of Susa* (English title); J.A. de Gobineau; and the ancient histories of G. Maspero, and George Rawlinson.

21. Isaiah 60, 61.

22. On the dates for the *Talmud* and *Midrashim,* one may consult I. Epstein (in *The Interpreter's Dictionary of the Bible*), who gives a brief bibliography. An excellent discussion is presented in *White Over Black* by Winthrop D. Jordan; and there are numerous collections of interpretations and legends in L. Ginzberg's *Legends of the Jews,* and in books by S. Baring-Gould, H. Polano, and Samuel Rapport.

23. *Against Apion* (Whiston's translation).

AFRICA AND PALESTINE IN ANTIQUITY

Charles S. Finch III, M.D.

In the wide-ranging re-examination of Africa's place in the history of antiquity, there is an ever more perceptible focus on Africa's relation to the Semitic world. The word "Semitic" itself has varied connotations depending on the point to be proved or world-view to be re-inforced. Thus, depending on who's using it, the term can denote a race, an ethnic group, or a language, or some combination thereof. Particularly its use has tended toward the promiscuous whenever antiquarians wish to prove that Caucasians originated civilization in Western Asia. The implicit assumption is that the Semitic peoples are and were members of the Caucasian branch of humanity. The northern Semitic group especially approximates to the Caucasian type today and it it supposed that it has always been thus. As we shall see, the case was very different in antiquity.

Clarification of this matter is imperative because there is a school of thought that sees the rise of civilization in Africa as issuing from a Semitic stimulus. Largely, this has been based on the definite affinities between the languages of a number of civilized peoples of northeast Africa and the Semitic languages of Western Asia. For scholars of the Semitic school, this is proof enough that such civilization as Africa did produce was stimulated by Semitic (read: Caucasian) peoples invading Africa. To give but one example, two Ethiopian languages, Gheez—now dead—and Amharic do indeed belong to what is called the Semitic family of languages and from this it has been inferred that Caucasian Semites gave Ethiopia her civilization. However, it can now be established, based on recent linguistic, ethnographic, and cultural history, that "Semitic" does not now, nor did it ever, denote a race as such. C.A. Diop has demonstrated that—far from being a branch of the Caucasian family as generally assumed—the Semite only begins to emerge at the end of the protohistorical period as a result of a gradual amalgamation of the autochthonous Blacks of Western Asia with the in-migrating Indo-European types.[1] The "classic" Semitic type in antiquity therefore was of a much darker hue than is true today and approximated more closely to the Africoid type which formed the basic human substratum of Western Asia. Out of this substratum the Semitic world arose.

The author does not here propose to examine in detail all of the ethnographic, archeological and historical data that bear on the question of the African origin of the Semites for that has been done very competently elsewhere.[2] Instead the author proposes to focus on the internal evidence bearing on this issue with a special emphasis on the early Hebrews of Palestine. Mention must be made of the definitive short treatment of the subject by C.A. Diop entitled "Processus de Semitisation" (Process of Semitization) which is a preface to his much larger work entitled *Parente Genetique De L'Egyptien Pharaonique Et Des Langues Negre-Africaines* (The Genetic Relationship Between Pharoaonic Egyptian and the Languages of Negro Africa). To summarize, from 8,000 B.C.—the era of the Natufian Blacks of Canaan— to 3500 B.C., most of Western Asia, including Canaan, Mesopotamia, and the Arabian peninsula, was inhabited more or less exclusively by a black people. In Canaan, these were the above-mentioned Natufians. In early Sumer, the African origin of the inhabitants is betrayed by their name for themselves which was "black heads" and by the skeletal remains which show a "hyperdolicocephalic" type.[3] In addition, one of the Sumerian capitals was Kish which is the same as the Egyptian "Kesh" or Cush, an early name of Nubia. To the northeast of Sumer was the land of Elam which Dieulafoy's excavations in 1894 showed conclusively to have been a Black civilization. In Ethiopia and the adjacent southwestern corner of Arabia, the black Sabaeans succeeded in creating a brilliant "cyclopian" civilization and became renowned for their advanced astronomy and stellar mythology. The name of this civilization, "Saba," betrays a Nile Valley connection since the Egyptian word "sba" means "star,"[4] a clear indication of the Sabaeans' reputation as star-gazers. Wherever one looks for aboriginal peoples in Western Asia one finds Blacks, and it is a mulatto type that emerges as the Semite of history as a result of the fusion between the autochthones and the in-migrating Indo-Europeans.

Nile Valley civilizations exercised a cultural hegemony over all of Western Asia in antiquity. Ancient Egypt—out of its Nubian antecedents at Ta-Seti— began its dynastic history toward the end of the 5th millenium B.C. and was a mature and flourishing civilization for 4,000 continuous years. All of the civilized arts were brought to fruition there and the total weight of its influence on the nations and peoples that surrounded it is beyond calculation. For many centuries, large parts of Western Asia were either under Egypt's direct political control or in a state of vassalage to her. But beyond that, there were no peoples, no cultures, no civilizations anywhere in her far-flung orbit which were not profoundly affected by the radiations of her culture. Art, architecture, religious symbolism, social custom, and language all over the Egyptian sphere of influence in Western Asia show the effects of this hegemony. What is more, the Sudanic civilizations of Cush and Ethiopia also left an imprint on their Western Asiatic neighbors. We have already cited the examples of Sumer, Elam, and Saba and it is known that the early Mesopotamian languages betray demonstrable Cushitic affinities.[5] The geneaology of Noah reflects this kinship when it makes Nimrod (and Saba), the mythical founder of Mesopotamian civilization, the son of Cush and the grandson of Ham. The close association of the Semitic languages with the languages of northeast Africa

then becomes understandable: what became the Semitic languages arose, like
the Semitic peoples themselves, out of the northeast African group.[6] The
Ethiopian Semitic languages therefore are autochthonous—that is they derive
from the ancient indigenous language of the black Sabaeans—they do not
arise from an external Semitic conquest or in-migration. The ancient Egyptian language was also an autochthonous African language but one with affinities to Phoenician, Hebrew, and Canaanitic. It belongs to that northeast
African language group which is *ancestral* to the Semitic languages. This is
fundamental. If the Nile Valley civilizations of Egypt and Cush were the
world's oldest, if language first became codified there, if written literature first
appeared there, if Western Asian cultures were created by Nile Valley colonists to one degree or another, then there is nothing strange in the supposition
that the African languages were primary and the Semitic languages descended
from them. Nor is there anything strange in the fact that even today, there are
Black people in Africa who speak a Semitic language. All of the discussion
that follows proceeds from the aforesaid Nile Valley cultural hegemony over
Western Asia.

The Hebrew story begins around 1700 B.C. with the migration of the shepherd Abram—later Abraham—out of Chaldea, through northern Arabia and
southern Palestine, into Egypt. This is actually a *pre-Hebrew* stage of history.
Hebrewism as a religion and a way of life is predicated on receiving and
following the Law of Moses, promulgated on Mount Sinai, an episode which
did not occur until 500 years *after* Abraham. Abraham can be seen to be the
mythical founder of an entire branch of western Semites through his first son
Ishmael, the mythic ancestor of the Arabian peoples, and through his second
son Isaac who gives rise to the Edomites through Esau and the Hebrews
through Jacob-Israel. The mixed character of at least the Ishmaelite branch is
alluded to mythically in *Genesis* because Ishmael's mother is an Egyptian,
therefore a black, woman as is his wife, the mother of his descendants.

There is hardly any section of the Bible exerting more impact on Western
and Near Eastern history than the five books of Moses. The Book of Exodus
in particular represents a watershed in the history of religion but to penetrate
beyond the conventional theology bearing upon the Book requires that a
different lens be focused upon it. Gerald Massey was able to accomplish just
that in his tour-de-force chapter in *Book of Beginnings* entitled "The Egyptian
Origin of the Jews Traced From the Monuments."[7] As with any scriptural
texts purporting to be veritable history, the germ of historical incident which
may be present is so overgrown with mythic foliage that it becomes difficult to
extract it in pure form. As Massey shows, this is clearly the case with Exodus,
and what is more, with the exception of Massey, no one has been inclined to
consider what the Egyptians themselves had to say regarding such traditions.
They did indeed have something to say. There are the accounts of two Egyptian chroniclers, Apion and Manetho, who had access to ancient Egyptian

sources and whose writings have only come down to us in fragmentary fashion through the eyes of a hostile witness. They have their own version of the
Exodus story which we know primarily through the writings of the Ro-
manized Jewish apologist of the first century A.D., Flavius Josephus, who in
his essay *Against Apion* attempted to refute them.[8] To summarize Manetho
(after Josephus), there were at least two—perhaps even three—exodes out of
Egypt that took place, one involving a remnant loyal to the defeated Hyksos
that repaired to the Canaanite city of Hierosylyma (Jerusalem), and the other
a band of downtrodden Egyptian religious dissenters led by an apostate Egyptian priest of Ra named Osarsiph ("son of Osiris") into Palestine. It appears
that the later post-Exilic Hebrew chroniclers confounded the two episodes.
Manetho equates Osarsiph with the Biblical Moses and according to him, led
a group of his followers into Palestine where he instructed them in the worship
of a single, exclusive deity apparently in reaction to Egyptian "polytheism." In
Manetho's view, these followers of Moses-Osarsiph were "unclean outcasts"
whom the Egyptians were obliged to drive out. That Osarsiph and his followers may have been inspired by the monotheistic example of Akhenaten is
entirely plausible and has been investigated in some depth by Sigmund
Freud.[9] Moreover, that the Jews were originally a group of Ethiopians and
Egyptians who migrated out of the Nile Valley to settle in Palestine was firmly
articulated by Tacitus, Eusebius, and Diodorus.[10] The evolution of the Semitic world out of the African was evidently an accepted idea in classical times.

The weight of modern antiquarian opinion favors the idea that the people
who became the Hebrews of the Exodus were related to the enigmatic Hyksos
who dominated Egyptian history for at least 200 years and perhaps longer.
There is, again, a grain of truth to this but not in the way usually imagined.[11]
Manetho had this to say about the origins of the Hyksos:

> There was a king of ours, whose name was Timaus. Under him it came to
> pass, I know not how, that God was averse to us, and there came, after a
> surprising manner, *men of ignoble birth out of the eastern parts*, and had
> boldness enough to make an expedition into our country, and with ease
> subdued it by force, yet without our hazarding a battle with them.[12]

It has been assumed as a matter of course that the Hyksos were Asiatic
invaders from outside Egyptian territory but the one Egyptian authority who
had access to the Egyptian archives informs us only that the usurpers were of
"ignoble birth" and that they came "out of the eastern parts." Nowhere does
he say that they were Asiatics or came out of Asia. The Hyksos period is a very
enigmatic one because the contemporary records were ruthlessly expunged by
later generations but what does survive gives no indication of foreign rule.
From what can be seen, Egyptian culture and political organization remained
undisturbed by even a whisper of foreign influence such as foreign conquest

would impose. The only thing that changes—and this is seen in the surviving
monumental fragments as well the attestations by Manetho—is the elevation
of Set, one of Egypt's oldest gods, to the status of supreme deity. Since Manetho refers only to the "eastern parts" and *not* to Asia, it could more logically
and plausibly be assumed that he was referring to the shepherds and nomads
of Egypt's eastern desert given that the name "Hyksos" is usually translated as
"shepherd kings." The pastoral peoples living in Egypt's eastern desert were, in
effect, Egyptian nationals who clung to their traditional way of life and were a
constant source of turbulence and unrest. Set was, par excellence, the god of
the desert and desert peoples so that there is nothing strange in assuming that
during a period of social and political instability, certain of these desert chief-
tains could have seized political power in Egypt and imposed the worship of
Set over the areas of the country that they controlled. Being Egyptian nationals themselves, they would have changed nothing essential in Egyptian
cultural, social, or political life. The worship of Set (or Sutekh) was not only
very pervasive already in parts of Ethiopia and Egypt but also in Palestine, so
that during the Hyksos period, Canaanite "co-religionists" of the Hyksos may
have filtered into northern Egypt where they could exercise their religion
under Hyksos protection. It was under these circumstances that Jacob's clan,
through the good offices of their kinsman Joseph, settled in Egypt under the
pressure of famine. They were very likely worshippers of the god Aiu, the
form of Ra as the Golden Ass who was *also* a form of Set.[13] Massey informs
us, in fact, that Joseph in Egyptian is "Iu-sif" or "Iu-sep," which means "son
of Aiu."[14] According to the Old Testament, there were 70 of the clan that came
in during Joseph's time and over 600,000 that left with Moses. Though this
latter figure is way overdrawn, it does indicate that the original 70 mixed and
merged with the indigenous people so that after several generations they were
effectively submerged into the people among whom they had settled. The
group that left Egypt under Moses-Osarsiph were—in color, culture, language,
and religion—Egyptian. Joseph and his brothers were speaking a Canaanite
dialect when they arrived in Egypt but their descendants would have lost
that—and their distinct clanic identity—within a generation or two after
Joseph, as is universally the case when a tiny, marginal group settles among a
dominant civilized people. Hebrew did not become a codified language until
three centuries *after* the Exodus so it did not even exist as a language during
the Egyptian sojourn of the proto-Hebrews. Having mixed with Egyptians for
centuries, if the descendants of Jacob weren't black when they arrived in
Egypt—which they may have been—they were certainly black when they left.
To the extent that there were any educated persons among them, they would
have read and written in Egyptian. Their religion, for which they underwent
proscription, could only have been Egyptian. Their religious proscription was
due to the profound antipathy of the orthodox worshippers of Osiris and
Amen to Set, their version of the "anti-christ," and when they regained power

under the energetic leadership of a dynasty of Amen-worshipping Theban princes, they systematically destroyed all traces of the former hateful regime of Set. The Hyksos and their allies in Egypt were anathemized by the victors as "unclean" and "outcasts" not on the basis of their national foreignness but because of their cultic allegience to Set. The Sethians were hated as remorselessly as any foreigner, as much as the Albigensian heretics of southern France were hated by orthodox Catholics in Medieval times.

We now have some good ground for examining in a novel way the nature of early Hebrewism from the perspective of Old Testament linguistic analysis using as our prism the ancient Egyptian language. The method to be employed was introduced to the author by C.A. Diop and is grounded on the facts elucidated above. In the interests of scholarly rigor, we will utilize transliterations of Old Testament names that come directly from Hebrew. The relationship in form, sound, and meaning between Biblical names and corresponding Egyptian words is really quite astounding; indeed the Egyptian permits us to uncover meanings and connections heretofore completely hidden from us. This etymology therefore unlayers a whole hidden history that conventional philology and theology seems utterly oblivious of. The results are sure to surprise and outrage.

The Hebrew Adam is the first man in the image of God, the father of mankind, and the completion of creation.[15] The Egyptian Atem is the first god in the image of Man and the father of mankind through a self-creative act. The root "tem" in Atem means both "completion" and "mankind." The word "at" is an Egyptian name for "father." Moreover we know that Adam was the first namer of created things; the Egyptian "dem" means "to name." Clearly there is an Egyptian parentage for Adam and he is to be equated to Atem. Adam's consort is Even whose Hebrew name is "(C)Havvah" and who, in the *Genesis* story, is seduced by the Serpent. The name Havvah corresponds to the Egyptian "Hefa" who is the Great Mother Serpent of the world. There are several layers of meaning to be peeled back here: Eve-Havvah as Hefa *is* the Serpent of *Genesis* in its form as Great Mother but Adam-Atem is *also* the Serpent because one of the forms of Atem is as the Great Serpent. The Serpent of Genesis, then, is indubitably Eve in one aspect but also Adam in another. The Great Serpent—along with the Tree—was originally a maternal symbol which later took on a masculine aspect; thus Adam and Eve are both humanized forms of the great Cosmic Serpent of creation that is found in all the cosmogonies of the world but which was elaborated first in the Kamite cosmogony perfected in ancient Egypt. Continuing in the Old Testament, Adam and Eve give birth to Cain, "Qayin" in Hebrew, who struck down his brother Abel in an act of murder. In Egyptian, "qen" means "to beat, to strike down, to murder," so Cain's name derives from the salient deed of his life.

In the Old Testament, the figure of Noah is seen in many guises: he is the survivor of the Flood, he is the first cultivator of the vine through which he succumbs to drunkenness, and he is also "the gardener, the husbandman, the cultivator." In Hebrew, Noah is "Nuach" (the "ch" being pronounced like a near-silent "k"). In Egyptian, "Nu" is the personification of the waters, the embodiment of the Great Flood of both heaven and earth. The Nile flood, which so completely dominated and characterized Egyptian life, is *the* arch-etypal Flood, and therefore a personification of Nu. The Egyptian word "akh" means "fertile field, garden, irrigated lands," thus the Egyptian "Nu-akh" indicates the flood of the land and fields; the flood that provides the fields with the waters of irrigation. Thus Noah-Nuach as Nu-akh is in reality the flood waters that irrigate and fertilize the cultivated lands which is in perfect keeping with Noah's double personification as the Man of the Flood *and* the Gardener or Husbandman. The ark of Noah is a replica of the boats the Egyptians used to move about during flood season as well as of the ark of the sun that floats across the heavenly waters of Nu (or Nun). Additionally, Noah-Nuach is identical to the Egyptian "nuch" which means "drunkenness," a clear reference to the drunken episode of Noah the wine-maker which led to the curse of Canaan. Since the intoxicated state was once likened to the spiritual state, the drinking of spiritous beverages like wine was reserved for the religious ceremonials of the priests. It is only when the drinking of alcoholic beverages came into common use that drunkenness became a vice. C.A. Diop has pointed out that the curse of Canaan—clearly a later interpolation into the myth—represents an anachronistic justification of later Hebrew writers for the conquest of Canaan by the Hebrews. Canaan, in fact, is identified in *Genesis* as belonging to the Black race, since, like the other eponymous ancestors of Black peoples Cush, Misraim (Egypt), and Phut (Punt?), he is the son of Noah's son Ham. The name "Ham" is derived from the Egyptian "kam" which is the strongest word in the language for "black" or "blackness." Noah's second son Shem or Sem is of course the eponymous ancestor of the Semitic peoples whom the Egyptians first encounter as nomads. Fittingly, the Egyptian "sem" means "wanderer or traveler."

The first of the patriarchs who is considered ancestral to the Hebrews—though not exclusively so—is Abram—later Abraham—the Chaldean shepherd who established his covenant with God through circumcision which provided the occasion of his name change. As Abram, his name can be analyzed in Egyptian as follows: "ab" means father in Egyptian and "rem" means "the people" giving "ab-rem" meaning literally, "the father of the people." This is perfectly consistent with Abram's position as the first patriarch of two important branches of Semitic peoples, the Hebrews and Arabians. After making the covenant with God through circumcision Abram becomes Abraham and the latter name can be broken down in Egyptian as follows: "ib" is an Egyptian word for "heart, desire, wisdom," "ra" is the sun-god Ra, and "im" means "fire or light," giving "ib-ra-im" (remembering that Abraham is Ibrahima in Arabic) which means "the desire or wisdom of Ra's light or fire."

Though this we can connect Abraham to Ra and it is Ra in Egyptian mythology who first institutes the rite of circumcision. This combination of correspondences cannot possibly be co-incidental and given the fact of Abraham's sojourn in Egypt as described in *Genesis* and the cultural hegemony of Egypt over Western Asia, there is nothing surprising in this connection between Abraham and Ra which makes him a devotee, a priest, or perhaps even a personification, of Ra himself. This connection continues in the figure of Abraham's second son Isaac which in Hebrew is Ysak. In Egyptian, "ys" means "place" and "akh" means "offering by fire or burnt offering," giving "ys-akh" or "place of the burnt offering." In the Old Testament story, the outstanding event of Isaac's life is when he is about to be sacrificed to God as a burnt offering by his father Abraham, but God prevents the sacrifice from being carried out and sends a lamb as a substitute. Ysak/Ys-akh is thus connected to Ra by his relation to fire and the lamb is his sacrificial alter ego. From Isaac comes Jacob, his second son, who after "wrestling with God" changes his name to Israel. In his first manifestation as Jacob we get, in Hebrew, Yaqub, broken down in Egyptian to: "ya" a name of the moon and moon-god and "qeb" which means "circuit" giving "ya-qeb" meaning "the circuit of the moon." This refers to the nightly and monthly travels of the moon and reflects the fact that the earliest Semitic deities were identified with the moon. But the change in the name to Israel reflects the new pattern of worship, the new dispensation as it were, because Israel in Egyptian is broken down to: "ys" meaning place, "ra" which is Ra, and "ir" meaning "creation" giving "ys-ra-ir" ("l" and "r" are linguistically interchangeable in the terminal "el/ir"); thus we have "the place of Ra's creation." On the basis of these etymologies, the God of Abraham, Isaac, and Jacob-Israel must have been Ra—very likely in the form of Aiu, the Golden Ass—who was the supreme deity of the Egyptian pantheon and whose visible emblem was the sun. Later non-Jewish writers in classical times inferred that the Jews had been worshippers of an ass deity,[16] a charge which the Jews of course vehemently denied. It is evident that these writers were familiar with the remnants of a Jewish tradition which harkened back to their pre-Mosaic history when they were worshippers of Ra as Aiu, the ass-headed, who was also a form of Set.[17] With the triumph of the Theban dynasts over the Hyksos, the worship of Set fell into increasing disrepute and though the proto-Hebrews were originally Sethians, in their new Palestinian home they gradually turned away from Set worship, eventually turning him into Satan. All of the Sethian animals like the ass and the pig accrued an evil reputation which accounts for the pork ban among the Egyptians and the Hebrews and the cruel derision to which the ass was subjected to in later times. Because of the ass's association with the discredited Set, it fell into disuse as a symbol of Ra. The Jews of Josephus' time had suppressed all recollection of their association with the ass-deity Aiu.

Finally, we must consider Yahweh, the Jehovah of the Bible. It must be remembered that the proto-Hebrews knew nothing of Yahweh until Moses introduced his name at Mount Sinai. With the introduction of Yahweh and the promulgation of the Law, an amorphous congeries of Egypto-Canaanite outcasts were converted into the Hebrews of history. In Egyptian, "yah" is the Moon god and "wah" means "increasing or growing," giving "yah-wah," the "growing Moon." This admits of several interpretations: Yahweh/Yah-wah could be a lunar form of the Great Mother goddess in which the "growing" represents her in her pregnant aspect, or Yahweh could be her son, the youthful Osiris-Khonsu who represents the growth principle. Originally, the moon as Hathor-Isis was a symbol of the Great Mother deity of Egypt and Osiris and Khonsu were identified with the moon as the son(s) of the Mother. Gerald Massey tells us that before Jehovah became the exclusive Father-god of the Hebrews, he was actually a female deity.[18] We have already noted that luniolatry was a dominant feature of ancient Semitic religion whose remains today are seen in the seven-day week. Another clue to the ancient Hebrew lunar mythos comes from the word "Jew" itself which in Hebrew is "Yahudy." This is nearly identical to the Egyptian "Jehudy" which is the name of the most important of the Egyptian lunar deities, Thoth. In his original aspect, Yahweh could have been one or all of the deities listed above—Isis-Hathor, Khonsu, Osiris, or Thoth—but after Sinai, he became the sole, exclusive *male* God of Moses from which are derived the theologies of the three major Western religions.

In the transcendental sense, the ancient Egyptians believed in the one God which was the source of all existence, but at the level of myth, the God of Abraham and the God of Moses, though manifestations of the One and therefore intimately related, were not the same. It may seem contradictory that Osarsiph, "the son of Osiris," would be the leader of a group of Sethians whose god was the veritable Archenemy of Isiris. But the Egyptians understood the interrelated nature of opposites and how a whole was comprised of a union of opposites. Thus a clue to the resolution of the paradox of Osarsiph is to be found in Egyptian eschatology. One of the most important ministers to the souls of the dead in the Book of the Dead is Babai who is a form of Set. Babai was also "the son of Osiris," Osarsiph in effect.[19] It is tempting to speculate that the Egyptians of the 18th dynasty considered the Set-worshipping outcasts who followed Moses-Osarsiph into the wilderness of Sinai ritually "dead" by virtue of their apostasy. Therefore it would be supremely fitting that they should be led by the "son of Osiris," who as Babai-Set was the "eater of the dead." The Jews of a later time read the "rite of the dead" over the names of those who had departed from orthodox teaching and thus had to be driven from the fold. At the beginning of their history as Jews, something similar may have been done to them.

Behind the development in the history of religious ideas that encompassed Egypt, Ethiopia, and the adjacent lands of Western Asia hovers the shadow of

Set. He is the oldest of the male deities in the Kamite world and only through a careful unraveling of the conundrum that he presents can the development of religion be made intelligible. He is the connection between the Great Mother cult of the Old Dark Land (Massey's rather poetic name for Africa) and the newer patriarchal dispensation which began with Ra (actually Atum, an earlier form of Ra) and which ramified into the three great Western religions. As Satan, Set has become Evil incarnate but he was not always thus. Not only was he at one time a benevolent deity and supreme among the gods, but the most important attributes of the later deities that achieved supremacy emanate from him. Moreover, he can actually be considered the progenitor of the very deities who were later established in opposition to him. Western Asia especially was an important center of his worship and remained so right up to the eve of the Christian era. As we hope to have shown, any serious investigation into the connection between Africa and the Semitic world of Western Asia must look beneath the externals to properly ascertain the role and function of Set in all of this. In the context of religion and cultural development, he was decisive.

Notes

1. Diop, C.A., "Processus De Semitisation," in *Parente Genetique De Le'Egyptien Pharoaonique Et Des Langues Negro-Africaines*, Dakar: Les Nouvelles Editions Africaines, 1977, pp. xxix-xxxvii.

2. Rashidi, R., "Africans in Early Asian Civilizations: A Historical Overview," in *African Presence in Early Asia*, I. Van Sertima Y R. Rashidi, editors, New Brunswick: Transaction Books, April 1985, pp. 15-53.

3. Ibid., p. 15.

4. Budge, E.A.W., *An Egyptian Hieroglyphic Dictionary*, Vol. 2, New York: Dover Publications, Inc., 1978, p. 655.

5. See Rawlinson, G., *The Seven Great Monarchies of the Ancient World*, Vol. 1, New York: John B. Allen, 1885, pp. 28-47, for a lucid discussion of the Cushite origins of the people, culture, and language of ancient Mesopotamia.

6. See Greenburg, J.H., "African Languages," in *Peoples and Cultures of Africa*, edited by E.P. Skinner, Garden City: Natural History Press, 1973, pp. 70-80. Let the reader beware! Though Greenburg, a leading African linguist, acknowledges the origins of the Semitic languages—as part of the Afro-Asiatic family—in the northeast Africa, he insists that these were African "Caucasians" who brought these languages into Western Asia!?!

7. Massey, G., *Book of Beginnings*, Vol. 2, London: Williams and Norgate, 1881, pp. 363-441.

8. Josephus, Flavius, "Against Apion," in *Josephus: Complete Works*, trans. by William Whiston, Grand Rapids: Kregel Publications, 1981, pp. 607-36.

9. Freud, S., *Moses and Monotheism*, trans. by Katherine Jones, New York: Random House, 1967.

10. See Massey, op. cit., pp. 428-33.

11. See Massey, ibid., pp. 363-441. It was Massey who first insisted that the Hyksos were not, *sensu strictu*, foreigners in Egypt. The author's own discussion of this subject draws from this premise.

12. Josephus, op. cit., p. 610.

13. One of the meanings for the word "set" is "fire, flame, burn"—see Budge, op. cit., vol. 2, p. 628. This meaning definitely connects Set to the sun. In the early symbolism of the Kamite—that is

to say the northeast African—world, the sun, because of its hot, burning, dessicating rays was actually considered a destructive, anti-human power. Even today, Nilotic peoples like the Nuer and the Shilluk situate their "hell" in the sun. Set can therefore be equated to the sun in this aspect and is an even earlier sun-god than Ra. In effect, Ra and Set represent the dual aspect of the sun, creative and destructive. It is for this reason that the Ass can be a symbol of both.

14. See Massey, op. cit., p. 408.

15. The etymologies and derivations in this section are based on material from Budge's *Hieroglyphic Dictionary* (see note #4) and the *Interpreter's Dictionary of the Bible*, edited by G.A. Buttrick in five volumes, Nashville: Abingdon Press, 1984.

16. Diodorus Siculus and Apion are two of the commentators in antiquity who made reference to the place of the cult of the ass-god in ancient Hebrew worship. For Apion's comment see Josephus, op. cit., p. 626.

17. See note #13.

18. See Massey, op. cit., p. 380.

19. See Budge, op. cit., Vol. 1, p. 200.

SITTING AT THE FEET OF A FORERUNNER:
AN APRIL 1987 MEETING AND INTERVIEW
WITH JOHN G. JACKSON

James E. Brunson and Runoko Rashidi

John G. Jackson was born on April 1, 1907 in Aiken, South Carolina. At the age of fifteen he moved to Harlem, New York, where he entered Stuyvesant High School. During his student days Jackson began to do active research, and was soon writing short essays about African-American culture and history. These essays were so impressive that in 1925, while still a high school student, Jackson was invited to write articles for the Honorable Marcus Garvey's *Negro World*.

In addition to his growing activities as a writer, Jackson in 1930 became a lecturer at both the Ingersoll Forum and the Harlem Unitarian Church. Among his teachers and associates during this period were such immortal figures as Hubert H. Harrison, Arthur A. Schomburg, Joel A. Rogers, and Willis N. Huggins.

In 1932 Jackson became the Associate Director of the Blyden Society. Named after the great Pan-Africanist Edward Wilmot Blyden, the Blyden Society played an outstanding role as an African-American support group for Ethiopia, after Italy's brutal 1935 invasion of that country. The Blyden Society was then under the leadership of Dr. Willis Nathaniel Huggins, the organization's founder, and an absolutely brilliant scholar and Pan-Africanist. Among the very early and, as Jackson is quick to point out, most talented students to come out of the Blyden Society is the now highly respected John Henrik Clarke.

Although these were difficult years for John G. Jackson, with race-prejudice, poverty and illness his frequent companions, he continued to produce well-researched, informative and controversial works. In 1934 Jackson co-authored with Dr. Huggins *A Guide to The Study of African History*, and in 1937—also with Dr. Huggins—*Introduction to African Civilizations*. In 1939 he authored *Ethiopia And The Origin Of Civilization*, and *Pagan Origins Of The Christ Myth* in 1941. His insightful literary contributions to the *Truthseeker Magazine* continued regularly from 1930 until 1955.

Among Prof. Jackson's more recent and most comprehensive works are *Man, God And Civilization*, first published in 1972, and its companion volume, *Christianity Before Christ*, just published in 1985. In all of these works Prof. Jackson has revealed abundant and astonishing wealth of data concerning the African presence in early Asia. His numerous contributions to this rapidly expanding field of study, and many others as well, cannot be overemphasized.

John G. Jackson has taught and lectured at colleges and universities throughout the U.S. He was a Lecturer in the Black Studies Department of the Newark College of Arts and Sciences (1971-1973), a Visiting Professor at the City University of New York (1973-1977), and a Visiting Professor at Northeastern Illinois (1977-1980).

The Interview

JAC: Could you please elaborate on the presence of Blacks in Colchis, in Southern Russia?
JACKSON: Yes. The ancient Egyptians invaded that territory under a pharaoh known as Sesostris. An Egyptian army under this pharaoh established a colony there. This area has been called the 'Black Soviet' because there are so many Black people living down there. Of course they tell you in the history books that these people are the descendants of slaves that the Russians imported in the Middle Ages. But if this territory was settled by the Egyptians in ancient times, then these people are probably their descendants.
JAC: Do you still stick with the chronology for Egypt that you used in *Man, God and Civilization*?
JACKSON: I stick with my chronology. The one I used in the book was from a Scotch Egyptologist named Duncan MacNaughton. But I've consulted Petrie and a Frenchman named Andre Pochan. They both go along with Manetho, the ancient Egyptian chronologist. The one that most of them follow is by a German Egyptologist named Meyer. James Henry Breasted was one of his disciples. The reason why they clipped two thousand years off the other chronology is in order to make Egyptian culture fit into the Bible. According to my chronology the Great Pyramid was built before the earth was created [in the biblical time-frame]. So they have to cut off two thousand years to get it into the Bible framework.
JAC: Could you comment on the Muslim writers Ibn Khaldun and Ibn Battuta?
JACKSON: They were among the important ones. Ibn Khaldun was the Karl Marx of the fourteenth century. He anticipated Marx. Ibn Battuta probably did more travelling than anybody else of his day. He travelled all over Africa and all over Asia. He went through Russia so far north until he could see the midnight sun. He wrote a book on his travels in Africa and Asia. It's been translated into English but I've never been able to find a copy.
JAC: Who exactly were the people known as the Turanians? Could you also comment on the origin of the term?
JACKSON: I don't know the origin of the term. It was probably some myth-

Figure 1. Historian John G. Jackson at home in his Chicago residence. Photo courtesy of James E. Brunson.

ical character named Turan or something like that. But these people were yellow people—Mongols. In other words, the original Africans moved into Asia and they bleached out and became brown and yellow. And then they moved into Europe. John Henrik Clarke calls Europe the world's ice-box. They bleached out white there.

JAC: Some older writers tried to make the early Sumerians, or the black-headed people, into Turanians. What are your views on this?

JACKSON: The Sumerians were the people who lived in the valley of the Tigris and Euphrates. They formed the original civilization in that area and it was pre-Semitic. The Semites got their culture from them. That's one trouble that we have with these people who call themselves Semites, because they claim that they were the world's first civilized people. Similarly, if you read the average book on the history of Egypt you will be told that the Egyptians were the first civilized people in Africa, and that they then went down and civilized Ethiopia. But we know better now, because two archaeologists from the Oriental Institute of the University of Chicago discovered an Ethiopian civilization that predated that of Egypt, so there's no argument there.

JAC: We wanted to ask you about some of the diffusionists. Could you give us some ideas on the works of Albert Churchward?

JACKSON: Well Churchward was a disciple of Gerald Massey. So he left us some outstanding books like *The Origin And Evolution Of The Human Race, The Signs And Symbols Of Primordial Man, The Origin And Evolution Of Religion, The Origin Of Freemasonry*, and so on. They're all very scholarly works.

JAC: What type of climate was Churchward writing these books in, and what kind of reaction did he receive?

JACKSON: He got a very negative reaction. Because here was a man that in 1921, in *The Origin And Evolution Of The Human Race*, said that the human race started in Africa at least two-million years ago. His fellow anthropologists laughed at him. This was in 1921. About three or four years later a fossil was uncovered in Africa that was about two-million years old. I think Churchward died in 1929, so he had a chance to laugh at his critics before he died.

JAC: How did you first hear about the works of Albert Churchward?

JACKSON: I heard about them through Dr. Hubert Harrison, who was Staff Lecturer for the Board of Education in New York. He had read *Signs And Symbols Of Primordial Man* and reviewed *The Origin And Evolution Of Religion* for Amsterdam News, and lectured about them. After Harrison died I went to the library to do research. I looked up Churchward's works and then saw where he mentioned his 'dear friend Gerald Massey.' And then I looked up Massey and found out that Massey was the master and Churchward was the disciple. That was in 1930.

JAC: What do you know about the lives and works of the Rawlinson Brothers?

JACKSON: There were two of them. The oldest was Sir Henry Rawlinson. He

made the major breakthrough in deciphering some of the important ancient languages of the Near East including Sumerian, Akkadian, Babylonian, and so on. He said that there was a common connection between these languages and Egyptian as well, and that the Ethiopian language was the foundation of all of them. His brother, George Rawlinson, was professor of ancient history at Oxford University. He was also a high official in the Church of England—Canon of Canterbury. So they called him Canon Rawlinson of Canterbury. They were both first-class scholars. Sir Henry Rawlinson was the great Orientalist. His brother was the great ancient historian.

JAC: What do think of the current linguists who have the opinion that there was a distinct difference between the early Sumerian and Ethiopian languages, and that there was no connection between them?

JACKSON: I think that they're trying to cover up something. A lot of them have taken the position that the African is the low man on the totem pole and everybody had to be ahead of him. Some of these people are just plain lying because they have to have capital in order to operate. James Henry Breasted is a fine example. He published a high school textbook in 1916 called *Ancient Times*. It had two very fine chapters on Egypt and he plainly states in there that the ancient Egyptians were not white folks, but 'a brown-skinned race.' And then he needed money to establish the Oriental Institute and to do research in Egypt. John D. Rockefeller, Jr. gave him 1.5 million dollars, and then Breasted got out a new edition of his book and the Egyptians became 'members of the great white race.' In other words, in order to get Rockefeller's money he had to switch over the Egyptians to 'the great white race.'

JAC: Could you give us a little background on W.J. Perry and G. Elliot Smith?

JACKSON: Perry was an Englishman and a disciple of Grafton Elliot Smith. Smith was a physical anthropologist, specializing mainly in anatomy, who traced most of the world's early civilizations to Egypt. He made a scholarly study of mummies in Egypt and other parts of the world. Probably his most outstanding work was a book called *Human History*. He said that the Egyptian civilization was the first, and that all the others came out of it. Smith did a credible job, but Perry was a much better man in all respects. Smith was a British imperialist.

JAC: You've referred to a scholar named Forlong in your works. Exactly, who was Forlong?

JACKSON: Major General J.G.R. Forlong was a Scottish scholar. In my book *Man, God And Civilization* I put him down as an Englishman, but I found out later that he was born in Scotland. He went to India while in the British army as an engineer to help build railroads. His great contribution was a two volume work called *Rivers Of Life*.

JAC: In one of his books Cheikh Anta Diop mentions that the worship of Buddha, or the work attributed to Buddha, was probably brought to India by Egyptian priests fleeing from the persecutions of the Persian invaders of

Egypt.

JACKSON: It could have happened that way. We do know that Diodorus Siculus, the Greek historian of the first century B.C., said that all of the astronomical knowledge of the Babylonians was brought in by a colony of Egyptian priests.

JAC: Could you talk a little bit about your relationship and interactions with J.A. Rogers?

JACKSON: Yes, that's easy. I came to New York in 1922. Rogers had been travelling through the South and he was coming back to New York. Rogers did a lecture for Dr. Hubert H. Harrison, who was my teacher and Rogers' friend. It was Harrison's forum but he let Rogers do the talking. I attended the lecture. Rogers and I became acquainted and became friends.

Later on, Rogers introduced me to Dr. Willis N. Huggins who had a B.A. from the University of Chicago, an M.A. from Columbia University, a Ph.D. from Fordham University, and he did historical research at Oxford University in England. Around 1932 Dr. Huggins established a little group to study African history at the Harlem Y.M.C.A. He called the group the Blyden Society. After Rogers introduced me, he asked me to join it. He was the Director. He made me the Associate Director. Among our students were Bayard Rustin and John Henrik Clarke. Rustin decided to pull out and join the Communists. Clarke was writing poetry. He told me that I changed his life. He said that he was wasting his time writing poetry which only a damn fool would write. Huggins and I told him that he should be a historian. He says that we put him on the right track.

JAC: Rogers makes a reference in one of his books to a General Ganges of India. Are you acquainted with this reference?

JACKSON: I saw that reference, but its probably mythology. There's a Ganges River in India, but I don't think that there was really any such person. So that's probably mythology.

JAC: Where did these early Black scholars like Rogers get the funds for their travels and research?

JACKSON: Well I can tell you about Rogers. He came from Jamaica in the West Indies. He settled in Chicago. He eventually took a job as a Pullman porter so he could visit different cities and libraries and do research. I got an interesting story about that. The story was that in a lot of large cities a lot of libraries were for whites only. Black people weren't permitted to go into them. So Rogers had to pay the Pullman conductor to go to the libraries and take out books from them. The conductor said 'Rogers, I believe you're a damn fool. But if you want to throw away your money that way, I'm willing to cooperate.' Rogers was a field anthropologist. He travelled to sixty different nations and did a lot of research and observing. He had been told when he was a child in Sunday School that God had cursed the Black Man and made him inferior. Rogers wanted to prove that the Black Man was not inferior.

Bibliography

Jackson, John G. and Willis N. Huggins. *A Guide To The Study Of African Civilizations*, 1934.
_____*Introduction To African Civilizations*, 1937.
Jackson, John G. *Introduction To African Civilizations*. New Hyde Park, New York: University Books, 1970.
_____*Man, God And Civilization*. New Hyde Park, New York: University Books, 1972.
_____Foreword. *Gerald Massey's Lectures*. New York: Samuel Weiser, Inc., 1974.
_____*The African Origin Of Christianity*. Chicago, 1981.
_____"Egypt And Christianity." *Egypt Revisited*. New Brunswick: Transaction Books, 1982.
_____*Was Jesus Christ A Negro? & The African Origin Of The Myths And Legends Of The Garden Of Eden*. Chicago: MASS, Inc., 1984.
_____*Ethiopia And The Origin Of Civilization*. Baltimore: Black Classic Press, 1984.
_____*Christianity Before Christ*. Austin, Texas: American Atheist Press, 1985.
_____*Black Reconstruction In South Carolina* Austin, Texas: American Atheist Press, 1987.
_____*The Golden Ages of Africa*. Austin, Texas: American Atheist Press, 1987.

UNEXPECTED BLACK FACES IN EARLY ASIA: A PHOTO ESSAY

James E. Brunson

In ancient times the Levant, Egypt Minor and the Sinai, served as an international road connecting Africa with Asia.[1] Towards the end of the last Ice Age, a sophisticated and stratified culture of Upper Paleolithic (Aurignacian) origins entered Asia. The Kamitic beginnings of this culture cannot be doubted. The archaic title used by the leaders of this cultural group have come down to us through time. The title, "Shaman," was derived from a proto-Turkish word for magician, priest, sorcerer, which was "Kam".[2] Evidence demonstrates that Kam meant "the land of magic or sorcery".[3] Kam, the ancient designation for Egypt, is the root word for alchemy and chemistry.[4] These are terms that Prof. John G. Jackson defines as "applied magic."

The North Asian "shamanic complex" did not exist in a void, but culminated from the cultural exchanges between agricultural Southerners and the traditions of Aurignacian hunters. Skeletal remains from Neolithic period peoples similar to Austric-Veddoid types were found at Anau (Turkestan), submerged regions along the northern Black Sea, the Caspian Sea, and the Sea of Azov.[5] These Aurignacian Blacks eventually occupied a vast area extending beyond the Ural Mountains to Lake Baikal.[6] The writers of antiquity noted three nations of blacks known to inhabit the area.[7] Successive invasions diminished these nations, which had once included the Caucasus, Afghanistan,[8] and portions of India. (fig. 1) Distinguishing features of this complex include:

1. A ritualistic communication with spirits of the unseen world.
2. The Shamanic drum, whose center of dissemination is believed to have been the Lake Baikal region.
3. A snake, serpent, or dragon mythology. The snake is not found in, nor is it indigenous to, northern Asia.
4. Distended and perforated ear-lobes.
5. A tiger, leopard, lion, or feline cult connected with initiation.
6. The ability to extract and transform ore into functional metals.
7. "Venus" figurines or statuettes connected with matriarchy.

The art of the Paleolithic period connects Europe to Asia as far as Siberia, presenting an overall "uniformity of pattern" which is an indisputable fact. A direct offshoot of a highly developed and distinctive Paleo-African tradition, steatopygous figurines bear testimony to the artistic as well as physical characteristics of their creators. (fig. 2)

Figure 1. Bust of a Black warrior. 100-200 A.D. Afghanistan.

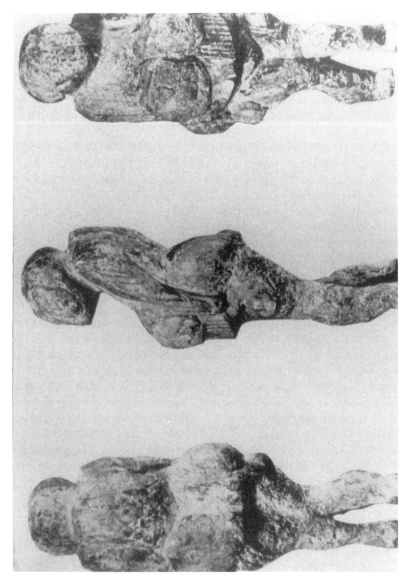

Figure 2. Female statuette. 12,890 B.C. Kostienki XIV, Paleolithic Period.

By 6,000 B.C. Asia was sufficiently differentiated into Africoid, Europoids,[9] and Mongoloid populations. It seems that an eternal battle, as indicated by written traditions, existed between nomadic and sedentary populations.

Mesopotamia

The bond between Mesopotamia and Africa existed well into modern times. While there is the consistent report of interaction between Egypt and this region, Paleo-Africans also contributed to the development of these high cultures.

In antiquity, the city-states of Mari (Syria), and Lakish (southern Palestine), occupied strategic centers of importance. Mari (2400-1350 B.C.), which sounds suspiciously similar to Ta-meri, an Egyptian goddess, was regarded as one of the outposts of the Old Sumerian culture; at one time, it held "sway over the whole of southern Mesopotamia."[10] Remnants of the Black guard still in power at that time commanded trade routes to Egypt, controlled the timber of Amanus and Lebanon, and the mines of Anatolia. Portraits from the royal palace of King Zimri-ilim (1780 B.C.), depict Black warriors (fig. 3), and royalty (fig. 4), that while obviously Africoid, were culturally aligned to Mesopotamia.[11] There is later mention of "Black Syrians" in contrast to white types. (fig. 5)

While Mari was later submerged by Semitic strains, to suggest such a fate for the city-state of Lakish, in the kingdom of Judah, would be erroneous. (fig. 6) This kingdom, which easily dates back to 1350 B.C., was sacked by the Assyrian king, Sennacherib (664 B.C.), a ruthless monarch who recorded for all posterity the ethnic features of the Judeans. (fig. 7) A Roman coin depicting Christ, a descendant of the House of David, points to a family likeness: aquiline and round noses, full lips, and wooly hair which has been described as "lamb's wool."

The earliest inhabitants of Palestine came from Egypt.[12] The skeletal remains discovered in a mass burial tomb dated to the seventh century B.C., are consistent with the earlier finds:

> The excavation uncovered a mass of human bones, which was estimated to form the remains of fifteen hundred individuals . . . Remains of 695 skulls were brought to London by the British expedition . . . Curiously, the crania indicate a close resemblance to the population of Egypt at this time . . . 'the relationships found suggest that the population of the town in 700 B.C. was entirely, or almost entirely, of Egyptian origin . . .' They show further, that the population of Lakish was probably derived from Upper Egypt . . . If so, this indeed is a conclusion of far-reaching implication.[13]

This last comment is an understatement, for such a discovery verifies what the ancient writers said all along. The Roman naturalist, Pliny, stated that Syria

Figure 3. Black warrior. Palace of King Zimri-Ilim Mari (Syria). 1786 B.C.

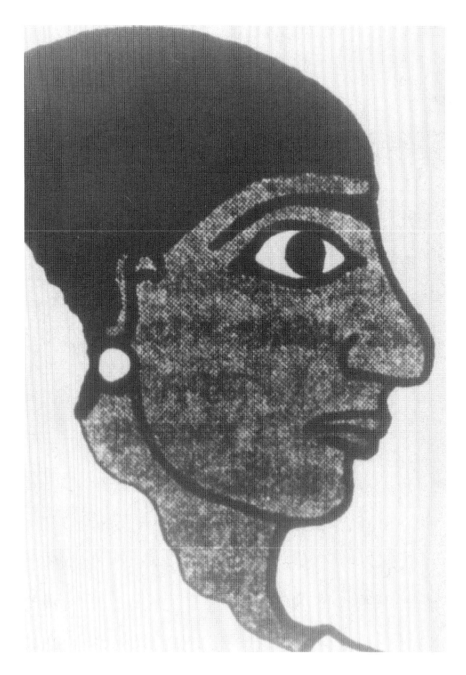

Figure 4. Black official of ancient Mari (Syria). 1786 B.C.

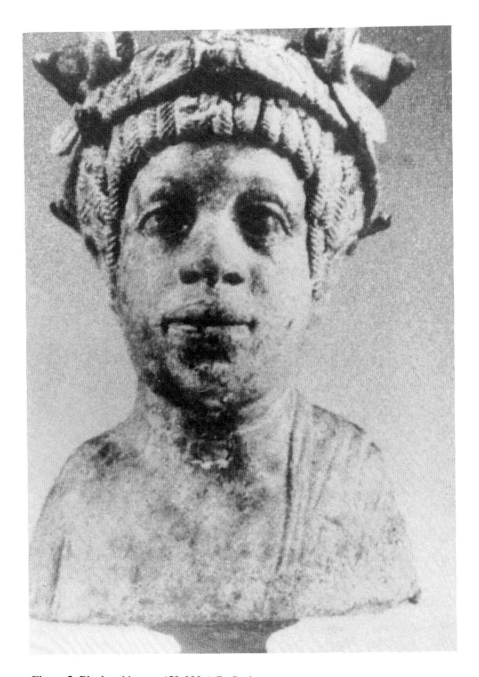

Figure 5. Black nobleman. 150-200 A.D. Syria.

Figure 6. The goddess Astarte (Isis). 1350 B.C. Palestine.

Figure 7. Jewish captives from Palestine. 660 B.C. From the Assyrian palace at Nimrud.

was at one time part of the domain of Cepheus, an Ethiopian king; Tacitus wrote that the Romans believed that the Jews originated in Ethiopia, but fled the persecutions of the king.[14] Strabo, even earlier, stressed that the people of western Judea were Africoid:

> But although the inhabitants are mixed up thus, the most accredited reports in regard to the people of Jerusalem represents the ancestors of the present Judeans, as they are called, Egyptians.[15]

In defense of their dwindling domain, which was rapidly absorbed by Indo-European invaders, Black settlers in Anatolia took the offensive. This pre-Hittite population, known as the Hatti, were physically similar to the pre-dynastic Egyptians and spoke a language akin to those in Africa.[16] One of the splinter-groups, the warrior Kashka, were not only instrumental in the downfall of the Hittites, but also had an active role along the southern part of the Black Sea; they may be connected to the legendary Colchians.[17] (fig. 8) In the *Dionysiaca*, there is reference to armed conflicts between Blacks in Egypt Minor and foreigners:

> In the morning, the god went forth to war, driving before him the violence of the black men, that he might free the neck of the Lydians and those who dwelt in Phyrgia and Ascania from the yoke of cruel tyranny . . . Now Bacchos made ready his army against the hostile troops . . . Nor did swarthy Celaineus fail to see the womanish warriors . . . [and] the heads of many men in that black-skin crowd were brought down by the womanish Thyrsus.[18] (fig. 9)

Northern and Central Asia

The Steppe regions of Asia were occupied by Indo-Europeans, but also by nomadic groups of Paleo-African and Asian origin. By the fifth century A.D., horse-riding marauders traveling as far as 90 miles a day, brought havoc and upheaval upon the Roman and Chinese empires. While this may take some readers by surprise, the historicity of this part of our heritage is supported by facts; and the facts demonstrate that well-organized confederations of Black warriors rode out of the north Asian steppes. (fig. 10) One of these groups, the Huns, initially occupied the Lake Baikal and Trans-Baikalia regions as early as the 2nd century B.C. They are conceivably related to the Kun (Kwan-lun) of Chinese history and tradition. Some scholars have noted the linguistic similarity between Kun and Hun.[19]

Modern scholars acknowledge "white Huns and other types," ignoring the contemporary testimony of the ancient writers on the subject, The Gothic writer Jordannes, described their leader Attila as having ". . .

Figure 8. Black female from Odessa (Southern Russia on the Black Sea) 300 B.C.

Figure 9. Head of an unknown Black. Anatolia. 100 B.C.-100 A.D.

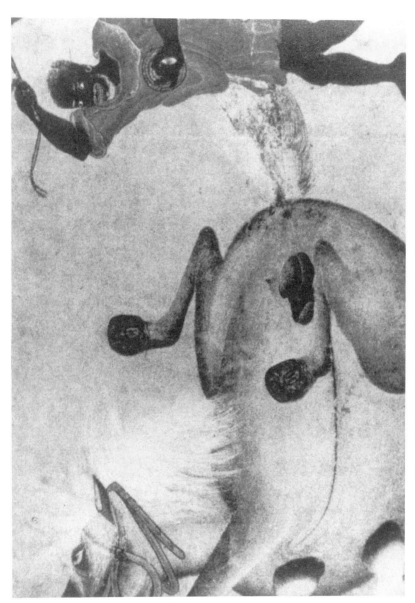

Figure 10. Black "Mongolian" horse trainer. Central Asia. 1400 A.D.

a flat nose and swarthy complexion, which showed evidences of his origin."[20] Jordannes went even farther, describing in minute detail, the type of Huns he had seen:

> The Huns . . . are of a dark complexion, almost black . . . [having] broad shoulders, flat noses and small eyes buried in their head and they were almost destitute of beards; they never enjoyed the manly graces of youth, nor the venerable aspect of age.[21] (fig. 11)

The ethnic beginning of this nation, Kun, which meant dog, is the origin of the Mongolian royal title Khan, or "Great Dog." Later, these peoples in their invasions of eastern Europe, were referred to as the "Black Tatars" or "Children of Hell"; they called themselves "Kara-Khitai" or "Black Khitans."

After the collapse of the Hunnic empire, several splinter groups developed into nations, which took possession of the steppe north of the Black Sea and around the Sea of Azov. The "Black Bulgars," who established a kingdom around the Lower Don River in 635 A.D., and the "Black Ugrians," who continued to dominate the Ural Steppe, were somehow connected to a mythological people known as the Vanir.[22] According to legend, the Vanir, before their demise, were an agricultural, matriarchal, and peace-loving nation. Their disappearance was brought on by battles with the nomadic, war-loving Aesir.[23] Recent anthropological studies confirm the existence of Veddic-Australoids and Negroid types among the ancient Bulgarians and Ugrians.[24] (fig. 12)

East Asia

> Beyond the sea to the southwest, south of the Red River [Southeast Asia], and west of the shifting sands, a man wears two green snakes on his ears and rides on two lung-dragons, and his name is K'ai the Lord of Hsia. K'ai ascended to heaven three times to have audience with [god] . . .[25]

The dragon or serpent played an important role in early Chinese mythology, and was prominent in the art of the Shang Dynasty. This dynasty, which ruled between 1766-1022 B.C., the earliest documented rule in China, had an active Black participation. Some Russian scholars point to a relatively homogenous population of Blacks not far from the Shang capital.[26] Tradition and legend point to a people known as the Kun-lun (Kwan-lun), a term later reserved for Black people. When the conquering Zhou (Chou) Dynasty emerged, they described their victory over a people possessing black and oily skin.[27] Chinese annals refer to "Dark Kings" and the Shang called themselves the "Dark-haired people." One American scholar noted that descriptions of skeletal remains uncovered from royal tombs have not been published since their

Figure 11. Black "Mongolian" horseman. Central Asia. 1369 A.D.

Figure 12. Africoid type from Southern Russia. 200 B.C.

discovery in 1935. He smugly suggested the embarrassment it would cause the Chinese people.[28]

A Chinese scholar from Harvard has noted ritual bronzes which depict priest-kings and kings. Many of these portraits have been described or classified as "Melanesian" types or Black people. The prominent role points to obvious political and economic power; bronze, at this time because of its expense, was used solely for the enhancement of the elite.[29] (fig. 13) The depiction of a king, symmetrically flanked by tigers, or dragons, was a symbol of the highest status.[30] (fig. 14) Based upon this evidence, it seems to me that, the conclusions drawn on these sculptures must have been based in part upon skeletal remains in the tombs where the bronzes were found.

Little Blacks were among the earliest occupants of Asia, coming to the region as early as 50,000 years ago. An early legendary ruler of China was Fu-Hsi, described in tradition as a little, wooly-haired black man.[31] Throughout the historic period in China, references are made to "Black Dwarfs" who resided south of the Yangtze river. Both feared and revered, these little people werer sent as royal tribute to the emperor's court. (fig. 15) This is reminescent of the Egyptian pharaoh, Pepi II, who requested a Black Dwarf from Punt. It is conjectured that these little people migrated further south, while others remained behind, giving rise to swarthy-skinned types in southern China.

The kingdoms of southeast Asia emerged as early as 200 B.C. in a region highly saturated with Blacks, and reinforced by migrants from southern China and India. These kingdoms, Khampa (figs. 16-17), Fu-nan, Kampuchea (fig. 18), Zabaj (fig. 19), and a host of other powers, alternately bidded for supremacy. Testimony from early Chinese travelers described them as black in skin color, and frizzy-haired. (fig. 20).

Awe-struck by the pride of these people, one visitor wrote, ". . . they consider black the most beautiful. In all the southern regions, it is the same."[32] These illustrious hegemonies thrived upon commerce, trading with places as far away as Africa. While Chinese people referred to the black-skinned people as Kun-lun, Arab traders confirmed their testimony. Masudi, an Arab author, called these people Zanj, a term reserved for Blacks in Asia and Africa.[33]

Among the prehistoric and proto-historic populations of Japan were Africoid types, anthropologically described as "Aoshima." The Aoshima, who appear to be the ancestors of the early Ainu, were short in stature, had long heads, broad noses, and prognathism.[34] An ancient tradition points to the conquest of Japan from the southeast by a race of warriors[35] of black or near-black origin. These invaders were probably the ancestors of the Black Samurai, and later Shogun, Sakanouye Tamuramaro. Sakanouye's father and uncle were members of the warrior class "Azumbabito" or "Men of the East."[36] The Azumbabito, who had praises sung of them in early Japanese literature, are probably the subject of that proverb, "for a samurai to be brave, he must

Figure 13. Royal Black personage from China's Shang Dynasty. Bronze, 1400 B.C.

Figure 14. Black ruler from China's Shang Dynasty. 1400 B.C.

Figure 15. Black "Dwarf" from China's Tang Dynasty. 618 A.D.

Figure 16. "Moi" woman. Vietnam.

Figure 17. Figure of a Black woman from Khampa, Southeast Asia. 650 A.D.

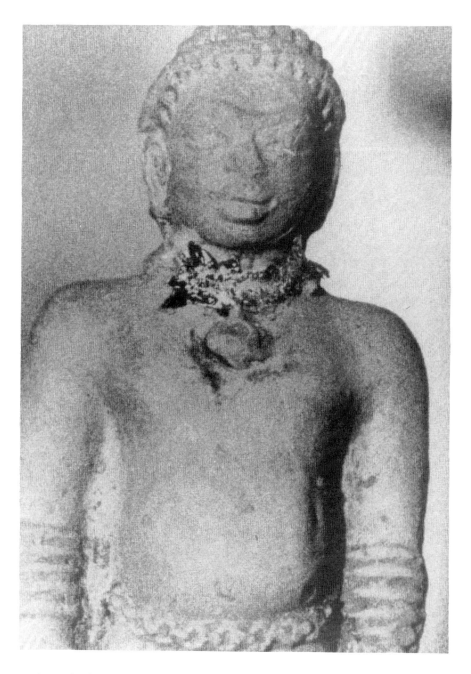

Figure 18. Figure of a Black male from Khampa, Southeast Asia. 650 A.D.

Figure 19. Figure of a Black female from Java. 1350 A.D.

Figure 20. Large stone head with prominent Africoid features. Sumatra. 100 B.C.

have a bit of black blood." Traditions point to these people as coming from southern China.[37]
In this brief summary, we have attempted to support the presence of the Africoid type in early Asia with pictoral evidence. This presence is to be noted among prehistoric and historic remains.

Notes

1. Clebert, Jean-paul *The Gypsies* Penguin Books Reprint 1970 N.Y. p. 27-8 Clebert points out that some region in the Near East, contiguous with Asia Minor, was recognized as Egypt Minor. As late as 1416 of our era, a German chronicler described migrants from this region as "Lords of Little Egypt," who were "Very black, undeveloped, and ugly. . . ." p. 106

2. Eliade, Mircea *Shamanism* transl. by W.R. Trask Pantheon Books p. 502 The Shaman is to be equated with the later Priest-Kings of historic civilizations. According to Coon, the "Shaman is descended from a long line of specialists, including priests, diagnosticians, surgeons, teachers, and scholars."

3. ibid

4. Walker, Barbara *The Woman's Encyclopedia of Myths and Secrets*, Harper and Row, San Francisco 1983 p. 18

5. Hughes, D.R. and Brotherwell, D.R. "The Earliest Populations of Man in Europe, Western Asia and North Africa" *The Cambridge Ancient History: Prologemena* Cambridge 1980 paperback p. 169.

6. Gupta, S.P. *Archaeology of Soviet Central Asia and the Indian Borderlands* Vol. II B.R. Publishing Corp. Delhi 1979 p. 185-7 These people were connected to Neolithic and Paleolithic cultures in the Urals, Siberia. Agriculture was an influence of Central Asian communities. Strategically based near metal ore sources in the foot hills of the Urals, there is evidence of copper mining and copper works.

7. Rybakov, B. *Early Centuries of Russian History* Progress Publishers, Moscow, transl. by John Weir 1965 p. 14

8. Majumdar, R.C. *Classical Accounts of India* Firma K.L. Mukhopadhyay, Calcutta 1960 p. 155 The frontiers of this people extended to the Kaukasos in the north and the eastern districts of Iran, including Arachosia and Gedrosia. (Afganistan) ". . . Shamanism was a way of life of the original people before its Brahmaryan conquest." (*Ancient India* by Megasthenes and Arrian edited by Ramchandra Jain p. XLVI)

9. Eliade, p. 497-8 Snake, serpent, and dragon symbolism emphasized rejuvenation, power and strength, wisdom, as well as the shaman's guardianship over the elements. In Chinese legends, the early kings journeyed to southeast Asia, "the land of the god," on wings of the dragon, to commune with this serpent king. The ancient royal title of these black kings was Kurung, or "Old Dragon."

10. Oklainikov, A.P. "The Temperature Zone of Continental Asia" in *Course Toward Urban Life* Aldine Publishing Chicago 1962 p. 270-1

11. Liptak, Pal *Avars and Ancient Hungarians* Akademial Kiado, Budapest 1983 p. 18-19 The Europoid according to this Hungarian anthropologist was as follows: "Light skin color is not a general feature; there are more darkly pigmented races among them. The Europoid great race was more widely spread early in the Holocene (Mesolithic) than at the beginning of our era . . . The Europoids, probably are descendants of the Veddo-Australoids." Liptak connects Proto-Mediterraneans, Western Mediterraneans (Alanto-Pontic types), and Central Mediterraneans with the Europoid.

12. De Vaux, R. "Palestine During the Neolithic and Chalcolithic Periods" *The Cambridge Ancient History: Prologomena* Cambridge University Press Cambridge 1980 paperback p. 530 The Ghassul-Beersheba culture, which came from the Nile Valley, was an agricultural, cattle, sheep, and

goat complex. They were acquainted with copper-smithing, producing it in large quantities, created pottery, leather and basketwork.

13. Ussiskhin, David *The Conquest of Lachish by Sennacherib* Tel Aviv University The Institute of Archaeology Tel Aviv 1982 p. 56-57

14. Rogers, J.A. *Sex and Race Vol. I* Helga Rogers N.Y. 1967 p. 92

15. Rogers, J.A. *Nature Knows No Color Line* Helga Rogers N.Y. 1952 p. 123

16. Lehmann, Johannes *The Hittites* The Viking Press N.Y. transl. by J.M. Brownjohn 1977 "Present indications are that Proto-Hattian, the language of the original inhabitants, was neither Indo-Germanic nor Semitic nor Caucasian. We appear to be dealing with the autochthonous Anatolian people, since their language appears to bear no relation to that of their neighbors." P.T. English even earlier pointed out that the language made use of Bantu prefixes: Aba-; Ba-; Ab- (or B-). Hence, the mention of an early African-Hattic king, Pamba, who fought the Akkadian ruler Sargon (2350 B.C.) for hegemony in Anatolia.

17. English P.T. "Cushites, Colchians, and Khazars" *JNES* Jan. 1959 University of Chicago p. 49-53

18. Nonnos *Dionysiaca* Books I-IV W.H.D. Rouse transl. Harvard University Press William Heinemann Ltd 1956 reprint lines 286-317

19. Hirth, Frederick *The Ancient History of China* Books for Libraries Press reprint 1969 N.Y. p. 194 There is a strong and old tradition for assigning the Kun-wu to northern China and connecting them with early metal production: "Perhaps we can accept . . . the hypothesis that Kun-wu was identical with Kun and Chuan ("dog"), i.e. with the so-called Hunnic tribes." (Wolfram Eberhard *Megalithic Cultures of South and East Asia* p. 70) The archaic name of Hun or Kun was Kam, according to Chinese transcriptions and it is equated with the Chinese word for priest, "Wu," hence the word Kun-wu for the early Huns in China. (Manen-chen-Helfen, J. Otto *The World of the Huns* University of California Press Berkeley 1973 p. 269)

20. Mierow, C.C. *The Gothic History of Jordannes* Barnes and Noble Inc., Cambridge 1960 p. 102

21. MacRitchie, David *Ancient and Modern Britons* Vol. I Kegan, Paul and Trench Co., 1884 p. 35 1985 reprint William Preston The volume used by MacRitchie was apparently edited from the Mierow translation of Jordannes.

22. Pritsak, Omeljan *The Origins of Rus* Vol. I Harvard University Press Cambridge, Mass. 1981 p. 243 Between 635-665 A.D., around Lake Maeotis and the Lower Don river, the Magna Bulgaria kingdom was established by the Onogur-Bulgars. The name Onogur (Ugrian, and the origin of the word ogre), has a Turkish equivalent, which is Van (or Vanir) also called "On." "These people were *not Slavs*, but of Hunnic and Turkic origin."

23. Walker, p. 1042 Before dismissing this as a flight of fantasy, let's recapitulate the factual evidence: in Norse tradition, the region between the Don River and the Sea of Azov (where we've already noted Black types), was recognized as the "residence of the gods." Pritsak, p. 198) The Don River emptied into the Black Sea, and the area around it was called "Home of the Vanir." (Dumezil, p. 9) The oldest physical remains suggest that the Vanir, or "some nation preceded the Indo-European nation." Dumezil, Georges *Gods of the Ancient Northmen* University of California Press Berkeley transl. in 1973 p. 9)

24. Liptak, p. 156

25. Chang, Kwang-chih *Art, Myth, and Ritual* Harvard University Press, Cambridge, Mass. 1983 p. 66 In this quotation, we have reference to the dynasty which proceeded the Shang, the Hsia Dynasty. Hai K'ai probably journeyed to a region between China and Tibet.

26. Keightley, David *The Origins of Chinese Civilization* University of California Press Berkeley 1973 p. 221 "According to Cheboksarov, relatively homogeneous communities existed not far from (Anyang) the capital, that were none the less different from the Shang population." The Russian scholar based this in part upon depictions of "Melanesians" on bronze vessels, which he called slaves. We view this an incorrect, as mentioned in the essay.

27. Rogers, p. 67

28. Eberhard, Wolfram *China's Minorities: Yesterday and Today* Wadsworth Publishing Co., 1982 p. 12-13 "Archaeological findings from the time of the Shang Dynasty (?-1022 B.C.), give us a different picture. Excavations of the royal tombs at Anyang . . . have brought out many skeletons, some of which seem to belong to non-Mongol races. Although excavations were done around 1935, the anthropological results have not been fully published, perhaps because the findings were somewhat embarrassing . . . some preliminary comments about the Anyang findings [state evidence] of a Negroid (that is dark-skinned) race of people and of people related to the inhabitants of the South seas (Micronesians).

29. Chang, Kwang-chih *Shang Civilization* New Haven and London Yale University Press 1980 p. 207

30. Chang, *Art, Myth and Ritual* p. 56

31. Maspero, H. *The Kingdom of Khampa* Yale University Press Southeast Asian Studies 1949 p. 42

32. ibid

33. Jackson, John *Introduction to African Civilizations* The Citadel Press Secaucus N.J. 1970 p. 27-273

34. Hulse, Frederick "Physical Types Among the Japanese" *Studies in the Anthropology of Oceania and Asia* Peabody Museum Vol. XX Cambridge, Mass. 1943 p. 22

35. Murdoch, J. *A History of Japan Vol. I* Frederick Ungar N.Y., N.Y. 1964 p. 50-1

36. Ibid., p. 105

37. *ACTA ASIATICA* Bulletin for the Institute of Eastern Culture No. 31 The Toho Gakkai Tokyo 1977 p. 86

CHEIKH ANTA DIOP AND THE SEARCH FOR THE CULTURAL ROOTS OF DALITS

By V.T. Rajshekar

A distinguished Black physicist, historian and linguist, Cheikh Anta Diop was among the first to establish that Egypt was the world's first civilization and that it was Black. He showed that humanity originated in Africa and that the first human being, the first person, was Black. The Blacks migrated from Africa to other parts of the world. The Blacks are also the ancestors of Indian Untouchables (Dalits). That is why the Blacks, wherever they are, belong to one single family. Hence the relevance of Diop's work for India's Black Untouchables. Their African origin and their later founding of the Indus Valley civilization is now widely accepted.

Diop's discoveries, therefore, establish that India's Black Untouchables with their African origin are the ancestors of all humankind. Hence they have to be very proud of their Black Untouchable origin and their glorious cultural past. The whole world owes it origin to Black people—our people. African history laid the foundation of world history.

Collective historical consciousness is a means of survival. If India's Black Untouchables are today hiding their identity, ashamed to own their origin and admit that they are Untouchables, it is because they are not aware of their glorious past. Diop says that the Blacks can regain their personality, can become proud of their past if they are told "who they are," and "what they are." That means we have to discover our roots, our goddesses, our religion, our ancestors, our history.

Cheikh Anta Diop has proven that the core of our problem is cultural rootlessness. The most important task facing us, therefore, is to reconstruct the links that tie us as communities. Humanity was born and developed in Africa. The first human was Black. And Black is beautiful. The Blacks lost their historical memory because we were fed by false history books. The rule of oppression will soon end with the reconstruction of world history, taking the aid of the tools provided to us by authorities like Diop, Runoko Rashidi and Ivan Van Sertima—all world-famous Black scholars.

Figure 1. A Dravidian woman from South India.

THE BLACK UNTOUCHABLES OF INDIA: RECLAIMING OUR CULTURAL HERITAGE

V.T. Rajshekar

The original inhabitants of India were dark-skinned and closely resembled the Africans in physical features. They founded the Indus Valley Civilization which, according to historians, was one of the world's first and most glorious. Aryan tribes invaded India, destroyed the Indus Valley Civilization, and employed a cunning, deceptive religious ideology to enslave the indigenous people. Those who fled to India's forests and hills later came to be called "tribals." As these native Indians were gradually overcome, captured and enslaved they were kept outside village limits and "untouchability" was enforced upon them. These people became "untouchables."

The Black untouchables of today's India try to hide their identities. They are ashamed of themselves. They hate themselves. How can people who hate themselves love others? This self-hatred can vanish only when we reveal to our people our own glorious cultural heritage, our own gods, goddesses and religious traditions, and the great achievements of our own heroes and heroines—our own independent and distinct cultural past. The search for our cultural roots must become our top-most priority.

The native people of India (currently known as "Untouchables, Tribals and Backward Castes") were not Hindus. They were Animists—Nature Worshippers. Since India's Dalits were once autonomous tribal groups, each group was known by its own tribal name. The Aryans created "caste" out of these tribal divisions by hierarchically arranging them in ascending degrees of reverence and descending degrees of contempt. So the Black untouchables have hundreds of tribal names. Aryans based their whole philosophy on color (varna). The four-fold caste system is based on skin (varna) color. The natives are dark-skinned and the Aryans light. So we can say that the untouchables and tribals are India's "Blacks," and that India's Black population is much more than the entire population of Europe. It is also the world's largest Black population living outside of Africa.

The population of India today is about 800-million. Of this, the natives, officially called "Scheduled Castes, Scheduled Tribes, and Dravidian Backward Castes" form about 70%. The break-up is: Scheduled Castes 20%, Scheduled Tribes 10%, and Backward Castes 40%. In addition, India has 15% Muslims (India has the second largest Muslim population in the world, next only to Indonesia), 2.5% Christians and about 2% Sikhs. About 80% of India's

Muslims are native converts. So we can say that over 85% of India's 800-million people are natives, and that the Aryan invaders are less than 10%. Most of the Muslims, Christians and Sikhs are native converts. With untouchability forced on the native population, many sought conversion to these more egalitarian, liberating religions to escape from the rigors of the caste system.

The native "Blacks" are not confined to any one particular area. They are spread all over India. Some of the tribals in Central India closely resemble the African Blacks in their physical features. The Black untouchables of Tamil Nadu, on the southern end of India, perhaps more than any other group retain their original physical features, including dark skins and broad noses. Their language, Tamil, the oldest language of India, was once the language of the whole country. The whole of Bangladesh, a Muslim country today, was once a Dalit stronghold. Pakistan also has a large Dalit population.

"Dalit" is a new name that has come into prominence during the past thirty years. India's Black untouchables and tribals had no common name. They had hundreds of different names, hundreds of tribal languages. The British, who, as we know, formerly ruled India, for the first time made a census of all these castes and put them under a Schedule of Castes. That is how they came to be known as "Scheduled Castes"—the name given them in India's Constitution. But this is an English name which the Black untouchables can't understand. M. K. Gandhi gave them a new name: "Harijan," meaning "children of god." But the leaders of the untouchables of Bombay formed the Dalit Panthers—named after the Black Panthers of the United States.

"Dalit," a Hebrew word, comes out of the root word "Dal"—meaning crushed, broken. It beautifully conveys our anger. This word, found in many native Indian languages, soon caught on, and after we launched *Dalit Voice* it became very popular. Today even the upper caste oppressors use the word Dalit to mean untouchables.

Hinduism: Its Origins, Evolutions And Caste Framework

The word "Hinduism" is not the scientific name of this religion. The real name is Brahminism or Vedic Dharma. It is Aryan imported stuff to India. From the very beginning it has had the suppression of the native population and women, even Aryan women, as its primary principles. India has become the original home of inequality because of Hinduism; whereas the natives respected all humans and assured equal status to women. In fact, the natives of India were matriarchal, under which the women had a higher status. They had only goddesses.

Though castes were already in existence along with untouchability, it was Manu, circa 100 A.D., who codified the laws of caste, invented the different sacrificial rites, and founded the social laws that today constitute the basis of the caste system. That is why Dr. Babasaheb Ambedkar, our greatest leader since the Buddha, burnt the Manu-Smriti, the code of the Hindu law-giver. Manu gave legal sanction to the already existing religious order based on sanctified racism. He inflicted the worst punishments on the Black untouchables, and also women. Even to this day the upper castes hold Manu's code as the essence of the "ideal democratic republic" and defend it to the core. Anybody protesting Manu's Code will be socially ostracized. Both the Indian Penal Code and the Criminal Procedures Code have sections to sentence anybody protesting Manu's Code. Though the whole of Hindu society is a victim of this code of Manu, the Black untouchables and women, including Brahmin women, are its worst victims.

From this we can make out that Hinduism was never the religion of Blacks, though the upper castes (Brahmins, Kshatriyas and Vaishyas—the three Aryan groups who rule India) are claiming that the Scheduled Castes, Scheduled Tribes, and Backward Castes are also Hindus—not out of love for our people but to say that "Hindus" form 85% of India and by that secure our votes and come to power. The second reason for instilling this "Hindu pride" in us is to instigate our people against Muslims, Christians and Sikhs—so that we sufferers and Muslims, our co-sufferers, are kept busy fighting each other.

The non-Aryan (native) people were hostile to the invading Aryans who were both nomads and barbarians. How the caste system originated can be traced to the "Rig Veda," the first and most famous of the four "sacred scriptures" of the Aryans. Brahmins were classified as the topmost caste, controlling the brains of all the rest. A heredity priesthood of Brahmins was formed. The Brahmins arranged a hierarchy of castes, reserving physical and manual labor for others and a life of pleasure and leisure for themselves. The next in order were Kshatriyas (warrior caste) and after that Vaishyas (merchant caste). The Sudras formed the fourth caste. The untouchables were given the fifth and last grade. They refused to compromise and surrender to the Aryan cultural domination, and also refused to join the four-fold caste system. That is why they are outcastes. That means outside the caste system—meaning outside Hinduism. Even today, after thousands of years, our people retain their original identity, refusing to be merged with the Aryans.

Though the Dalits are the agricultural laborers, and without them no agricultural production is possible, they are kept segregated in every village. Every village has its own ghetto and every city its slums. Each caste (jati) and sub-caste was made endogamous. Intermarriage was forbidden. Interdining was prohibited. Native Indians were condemned as untouchables, unseeables, unapproachables, unthinkables, undreamables. They were disarmed and made to live on the carcasses of dead animals. Physically emaciated, mentally wrecked and culturally deprived, the native population hovered between life and death—neither living nor dead. Their women were made prostitutes. No where else in the world is there any parallel to the Aryan persecution of the untouchables of India.

The history of India is full of uprisings by the Dalits, Sudras and other natives of India against the Aryan invaders. The Buddha, a great tribal chieftain with an Afro hairstyle, 2,500 years ago was the first to lead India's Black untouchable's war against Aryan oppressors. Buddhism, India's first really virulent anti-Brahmin philosophy, achieved big successes, and the lower caste people and women became its first adherents. Not only did it become popular all over India, but it spread to Thailand, China, Japan and many other countries. Our revered leader, Dr. Babasaheb Ambedkar, embraced Buddhism and called upon his people to follow him in his conversion. Millions of Dalits all over India followed him.

The Brahmins employed many cunning strategies to destroy Buddhism. They promoted and popularized a Black tribal hero (Krishna) and elevated him to godhood to woo back the Sudras and other masses. Brahmins penetrated the tribal groups, created hundreds of non-Brahmin gods, and changed the name of their religion to "Hinduism." Brahmins, who were the worst gluttons, meat-eaters and liquor-drinkers, for the first time became vegetarians and non-drinkers. They imposed a condition on others that the cow was holy and prohibited beef-eating. By such devices they revived Hinduism. The leader of this Brahminical revivalist movement was Sankara, c. 800 A.D. He infiltrated Buddhism and sabotaged it from both within and without. Sanskrit was revived. Sankara helped divide Buddhism into two schools and made them fight each other. Buddha himself was even called a Hindu god. Although the principle of Ahimsa (non-violence) was incorporated into Hinduism, numerous Buddhist scholars were murdered and vast quantities of Buddhist literature destroyed. The great Buddhist university at Nalanda was physically destroyed. Brahmins virtually took over the country. The inhumanly cruel Devadasi system, based on the forced prostitution of countless Dalit women and girls, was actively introduced and aggressively implemented.

But the religion of Islam however, which was introduced to India during a more recent period, attracted the Dalits. Because of its liberating and egalitarian tendencies Dalits embraced Islam in massive numbers. Islam continues to attract Dalits much more than any other religion, because Christianity and Sikhism got influenced by Hinduism and developed their own internal caste systems, whereas Islam was free from caste. Though the Muslim rulers did not fundamentally interfere with the social system of India, as Brahmins held key positions under Muslim rule, Islam has tended to move undeniably towards the overall liberation of India's Dalits.

The White-controlled world press and the Aryan-controlled (upper caste) Indian press have not disclosed the facts that the Blacks live all over the world

A splendid Buddha with typically distinct Africoid features. Dvaravati Period, Thailand; ninth century. Photo courtesy of Larry Williams.

and that they form the world's largest oppressed group. Once this secret is known and the Blacks of India come to know who they are, what they are, and where they come from, after tracing their roots, they may quickly come together and blow up the white supremacy. That is why the closely guarded secret that Asia also has a large Black population is not made known to the outside world. Not only to the outside world, even Indian Blacks themselves are not aware of it. A strong Black identity is very important because it is necessary to put pride back into the broken hearts of the people and also unite them with the struggle of their brothers and sisters in Africa, America, etc. The Black liberation struggle will get an international dimension only when the Indian Blacks join hands with the Blacks of Africa and America.

The difference between the "class system" and "caste system" is that while the former is mobile, the latter is immobile. There is no promotion or demotion in caste. A person born a Brahmin is only considered a Brahmin. Such a caste system, of which untouchability is a very large part, is given religious sanction. Therefore, the Black untouchables are the world's only victims of a sanctified racism. While South Africa's Apartheid has no theological sanction behind it, Indian Apartheid has religious sanction. We find a lot of Whites also fighting along with Blacks against South African Apartheid. Not so in India, where we can hardly find a single "Hindu" fighting against the caste system.

India's caste system is a unique institution, having no parallel in the whole world. It is a social, cultural and religious institution. Even gods of Hindus belong to a particular caste. The caste structure maintains itself because every member of a particular caste group stands to gain by belonging to that particular caste-group. The caste system helps the exploitation of the weak by the strong. India's constitution not only does not interfere with caste, but fully upholds it.

The Black untouchables are the very bottom of this deathless human pyramid and carry the weight of the entire population. It should be understood very clearly however that in modern India skin-color is not the major problem. It is currently even impossible to make out the caste of a person from his skin color alone. There are any number of fair-skinned untouchables and also dark-skinned Brahmins. The Brahmin stands at the top of the pyramid, enjoying the whole scene. He forms the very apex of the caste pyramid.

Every caste has several sub-castes and the sub-caste bond is much stronger. Even those Hindus living in the United States scrupulously maintain their sub-castes. Since these castes and sub-castes are endogamous, there is no inter-marriage. Caste is based on purity and pollution. One group is considered more pure than the other. The less pure caste group accepts its lower status because it is happy that it has a much larger caste group below it to exploit. As long as there is somebody below it to exploit, it is proud and will not mind somebody always standing on its shoulders. So the entire caste structure is a highly-polished, well-oiled, self-sustaining, automatic, exploitative machine. It needs no external energy to fuel it. That is why India's every Prime Minister except one, for a very brief period, have been Brahmins, and will continue to be Brahmins, because only Brahmins can command everybody's respect.

The Black untouchables of India, even the educated among them, are not aware of the common origin of Africans and Dalits. When they come to know of this and the struggle of the African-Americans and their spectacular achievements, our people will naturally become proud. Putting pride into their broken hearts is our prime task. Tell a slave that he is a slave and he will explode, but until now the Dalit has not even been aware of his slavery. By making him aware of this through acquainting him with the achievements of the American Black struggle, we are going to gain a great deal. It will also attain for us the world's most powerful support and help internationalize our struggle.

The African-Americans also must know that their liberation struggle cannot be complete as long as their own blood-brothers and sisters living in far off Asia are suffering. It is true that African-Americans are also suffering, but our people here today are where African-Americans were two-hundred years ago.

African-Americans and India's Black Untouchables are both the victims of racism. The only difference is that while the Blacks outside are victims of violence, we here are victims of non-violence. The Blacks outside have taken to armed struggle whereas our people don't have even a razor blade to shave with.

African-American leaders can give our struggle tremendous support by bringing forth knowledge of the existence of such a huge chunk of Asian Blacks to the notice of both the American Black masses and the Black masses who dwell within the African continent itself.

No group is better positioned to launch this cultural revolution than India's Dalits. Since we form the foundation of this caste pyramid, we alone are capable of shaking its structure, if not demolishing it altogether. The moment our people come to believe that they are neither Hindus nor obligated to obey the upper castes, the whole caste structure completely collapses.

Bibliography

Ambedkar, Babasaheb. *Annihilation of Caste*. rpt., Bangalore: Dalit Sahitya Akademy, 1987.
Beteille, Andre. "Race And Descent As Social Categories In India." *Color And Race*. John Hope Franklin, Editor. Boston: Houghton Mifflin Co., 1968: pp. 169-185.
Bhagwan, K.S. *Violence In Hinduism*. Bangalore: Dalit Sahitya Akademy, 1986.
Chanana, D.R. *Slavery In Ancient India*. New Delhi: People's Publishing House, 1960.
Hiro, Dilip. *The Untouchables Of India*. London: Minority Rights Group Ltd., 1982.
Kosambi, D.D. *The Culture And Civilization Of Ancient India*. rpt., New Delhi: Vikas, 1981.
Malalasekera, G.P. and K.N. Jayatilleke. *Buddhism And The Race Question*. Paris: UNESCO, 1958.

Rajshekar, V.T. *Apartheid In India.* Bangalore: Dalit Sahitya Akademy, 1983.
_____. *Who Is The Mother Of Hitler?* Bangalore: Dalit Sahitya Akademy, 1984.
Rashidi, Runoko. "The Nile Valley Presence In Asian Antiquity." *Nile Valley Civilizations.* Ivan Van Sertima, Editor. New Brunswick: Transaction Books, 1984: pp. 201-220.
_____. "Dr. Diop On Asia: Highlights And Insights." *Great African Thinkers, Vol. 1: Cheikh Anta Diop.* Ivan Van Sertima and Larry Williams, Editors. New Brunswick: Transaction Books, 1986: pp. 127-145.
Sharma, Ram Sharan. *Sudras In Ancient India.* Delhi: Motilal Banarsidass, 1958.
Sunder, B. Shyam. *They Burn.* Bangalore: Dalit Sahitya Akademy, 1987.
Dalit Voice (Fortnightly, in English, from Bangalore).

DALITS: THE BLACK UNTOUCHABLES OF INDIA

Runoko Rashidi

Ancient India was Africa's Asian heartland. In Greater India during the third millennium B.C. industrious Black men and women erected the powerful Indus Valley Civilization. For more than a thousand years Black rule from the Indus Valley flourished over a territorial expanse larger in size than both dynastic Sumer and Egypt of the pharaohs.

Often referred to as Dravidians, these proud Blacks of the Indus Valley were eventually pushed into the central and southern regions of India by the increasingly aggressive incursions of Indo-European tribes. By 800 B.C. these nomadic Aryan peoples had conquered most of northern India and renamed their newly won dominions "Aryavarta" (the Aryan Land). Throughout Aryavarta a rigid, caste-segmented social order was established with masses of conquered Blacks (Sudras) positioned as the lowest caste and imposed upon for service (in any capacity required) to the higher castes. With the passage of time, this brutally harsh caste system became the basis of the religion which is now practiced throughout all India. This is the religion known as "Hinduism."

The greatest victims of Hinduism have been the "Untouchables." These people are the long-suffering descendants of Aryan-Sudra unions and native Black populations who retreated into the hinterlands of India in their efforts to escape the advancing Aryan sphere of influence to which they ultimately succumbed.

The existence of Untouchability has been justified within the context of Hindu religious thought as the ultimate and logical extensions of karma and rebirth. Hindus believe that persons are born "Untouchable" because of the accumulation of sins in previous lives. Hindu texts describe these people as foul and loathsome things. For caste Hindus any physical contact with an Untouchable was regarded as polluting. Usually, they lived in pitiful little settlements on the outskirts of Hindu communities. During certain periods in Indian history Untouchables were only allowed to enter the adjoining Hindu communities at night. Indeed, the Untouchable's very shadows were considered polluting, and they were required to beat drums and make loud noises to announce their approach. Untouchables had to attach brooms to their backs to erase any evidence of their presence. Cups were tied around their necks to capture any spittle that might escape their lips and contaminate roads and streets. Their meals were consumed from broken dishes. Their clothing was taken from corpses. They were forbidden to learn to read and write, and were prohibited from listening to any of the sacred Hindu texts. Regular access to public wells and water wells was denied them. They could not use ornaments and were not allowed to enter Hindu temples. The primary work of Untouchables included scavenging and street sweeping, emptying toilets, the public execution of criminals, the disposal of dead animals and human corpses, and the clean-up of cremation grounds, all of which were regarded as impure activities by caste Hindus. The daily life of the Untouchables was one of degradation, deprivation and humiliation.

The basic status of India's Untouchables has changed little since ancient times. The general literacy rate, for example, among Untouchables is only about fifteen per cent. Among Untouchable women the literacy rate is below seven per cent. Untouchables in urban India are crowded together in squalid slums, while in rural India, where the vast majority of Untouchables live, they are exploited as landless agricultural laborers and ruled by terror and intimidation. Official Indian figures on violent crimes by caste Hindus against Untouchables have averaged more than 10,000 cases per year. However, Indian human rights workers report that a large number of atrocities against Untouchables, including beatings, rapes, arson and murders, are never recorded. Even when charges are formally filed, justice for Untouchables is seldom dispensed. In one coldly typical case, a state court recently acquitted all persons charged with the brutal mass murder, in bright daylight no less, of fourteen Untouchables in the Central Indian village of Kestara in 1982.

Meeting With The Black Untouchables Of India:
The First All-India Dalit Writers' Conference

Possibly the most substantial percentage of Asia's Blacks can be identified among India's 160 million "Untouchables" or "Dalits." India's "Untouchables" number more than the combined populations of England, France, Belgium and Spain. Frequently they are called "Outcastes." The official name given them in India's Constitution (1947) is "Scheduled Castes." Indian nationalist leader, devout Hindu and social reformer, Mohandas K. Gandhi called them "Harijans," meaning "children of god." "Dalit," meaning "crushed and broken," is a name that has come into prominence only within the last three decades. "Dalit" reflects a radically different response to oppression.

The smoldering anger among Untouchables was fanned into flames almost single-handedly beginning in the 1920s by Dr. B.R. Ambedkar (1891-1956). Born an Untouchable, Ambedkar quickly realized that "there will be outcastes as long as there are castes," and boldly stated that "nothing can emancipate the outcastes except the destruction of the caste system." Under his leadership the Untouchables began political policies of self-help in the educational and social spheres, and launched strident attacks on Hindu orthodoxy. They demanded that the Untouchables be recognized as a separate entity from the caste Hindus and be accorded their own electorate with representa-tion in legislative bodies. In 1956, in a dramatic final break with Hinduism, Ambedkar, with 500,000 of his followers, converted to Buddhism.

India's Dalits are demonstrating a rapidly expanding awareness of their own African roots and have taken much of their heightening inspiration and direc-tion from the recent struggles of African people at home and abroad. The mighty accomplishments of Booker T. Washington, Marcus Garvey and Paul Robeson are raised high and saluted. Slain Black leaders Malcolm X and Dr. Martin Luther King, Jr. are honored as brilliant strategists and shining heroes. Selected works of Black writers Langston Hughes, James Baldwin and Alex Haley are translated and well-read. The courage and strength of Black activ-ists Jesse Jackson and Nelson Mandela are mentioned repeatedly and ap-plauded greatly. The Black Panther Party is absolutely revered.

It was in the refreshing spirit of the new Dalit militancy that the First All-India Dalit Writers' Conference was held in Hyderabad, Andra Pradesh, India on October 8, 9 and 10, 1987. Under the auspices of the Dr. B. R. Ambedkar Memorial Trust, the historic gathering was attended by more than 700 dele-gates: militant Dalit writers, poets, and activists from many parts of India. Journalist V. T. Rajshekar of Bangalore; Indian Supreme Court Advocate Bhagwan Das of New Delhi; Prof. Arun Kamble of Bombay; leading members of the Dalit Panthers (named after the Black Panther Party of the United States); the Dalit Sahitya Akademy, the Dalith Sahitya Sanghatan, and the Dalit Liberation Army made especially noteworthy contributions to the Con-ference. Two African-American delegates, historian Runoko Rashidi and po-litical activist Njeri Khan, attended the Conference and participated extensively. Rashidi formally inaugurated the Conference and delivered a major address on "The Global Unity of African People." Khan documented the Conference's highlights and preserved them on videotape.

The First All-India Dalit Writers' Conference joined together for the initial time the vanguard elements of the Dalit Liberation Movement and effectively accelerated the long overdue assembly of the Black family of mankind. Its sparkling triumph heralds a vital turning point in the liberation efforts of Black and oppressed peoples in India and around the world.

Bibliography

Dalit Voice (The Voice of the Persecuted Minorities). The English language fortnightly newspaper, *Dalit Voice*, edited by the noted activist, author and journalist V.T. Rajshekar, is the best regular publication on the struggling Black Untouchables of India. Annual subscriptions for *Dalit Voice* are $45.00c/o Dalit Sahitya Akademy, 109/7th Cross, Palace Lower Orchards, Bangalore, In-dia—560 003. See also the occasional publications of the Dalit Sahitya Akademy. Lists of their available publications can be obtained free upon request.

Hiro, Dilip. *The Untouchables Of India*. London: Minority Rights Group Ltd., 1982.

Joshi, Barbara R. *Untouchable!* London: Zen Books Ltd., 1986.

Rajshekar, V.T. *Dalit: The Black Untouchables Of India*. Atlanta: Clarity Press, 1987.

THE HISTORICAL UNITY OF AFRICANS AND DALITS: A SELECTED BIBLIOGRAPHY

Compiled by Runoko Rashidi

"African-American Liberation Not Possible Until Dalits Are Free." *Dalit Voice*, 1–15 Apr 1993: 14–15.

"African-Dalit Unity Move." *Dalit Voice* 5, No. 21 (1986): 15.

Akhileshwari, R. "Dalit Writer's Landmark Meeting." *The Deccan Herald* (Bangalore, India), 11 Oct 1987.

"All-India Dalit Writers' Conference: American Black Support to Dalit Struggle." *Dalit Voice*, 1–15 Nov 1987: 15–16.

Ambedkar, B.R. *What Congress and Gandhi Have Done to the Untouchables*. Bombay: Thacker, 1945.

Ambedkar, B.R. *Annihilation of Caste*. Bangalore: Dalit Sahitya Akademy, 1987.

"American Black Scholars Shocked on Hearing About Racism in India." *Dalit Voice* 9, No. 15 (1990): 8–9.

Annamalai, Velu. "Hindu Caste System is the Worst of All." *San Antonio Light*, 9 Apr 1989: L2.

Annamalai, Velu. "Apartheid is Paradise Compared to Caste System." *Voice of Ambedkar* 1, No. 2 (1990): 11–14.

Beteille, Andre. "Race and Descent as Social Categories in India." *Color and Race*. Edited with an Introduction by John Hope Franklin. Boston: Houghton Mifflin, 1968: 166–85.

Bhagat, G. "India Through American Eyes, 1783–1860." Chap. in *Americans in India 1784–1860*. New York: New York University Press, 1970: 115–29.

Clay, Nathaniel. "Blacks of India: A Hidden Race, A Hidden Problem." *The Final Call*, 27 Apr 1986: 3.

"Dalit Writers Call for Literature of Liberation." *Indian Express* (Hyderabad), 10 Oct 1987: 3.

Das, Bhagwan. *Testimony Before U.N.O.'s Human Rights Sub-Commission at Geneva. Switzerland on August 19. 1983*. Jalandhar: Bheem Patrika, 1983.

Dubois, Jean Antoine. *Hindu Manners, Customs and Ceremonies*. Translated from the Author's Later French Manuscript and Edited with Notes, Corrections, and Biography by Henry K. Beauchamp. Preparatory Note by P. Max Muller. 3d ed. 1815; rpt. New Delhi: Asian Educational Services, 1986.

Dutt, Nripendra Kumar. *Origin and Growth of Caste in India*, Vol. 1. Rev. ed. Calcutta: Firma K.L. Mukhopadhyay, 1968.

Dutt, Nripendra Kumar. *Origin and Growth of Caste in India*. Vol. 2, *Castes in Bengal*. 2d ed. Calcutta: Firma K.L. Mukhopadhyay, 1969.

Dutt, Nripendra Kumar. *The Aryanisation of India*. Revised and enlarged edition. Calcutta: Firma K.L. Mukhopadhyay, 1970.

Fineman, Mark. "Creating a Mosaic of India." *Los Angeles Times*, 29 Apr 1991: A1.

Griffith, R.T.H., trans. *Hymns of the Rig Veda*. 2d ed. Benares: E.J. Lazarus, 1897.

Hardiman, W. Joye. "The Liberating Arts and Scientific Methods of Research." *ASCAC Research News Journal* 1, No. 1 (1989): 6.

Hiro, Dilip. *The Untouchables of India*. London: Minority Rights Group, 1982.

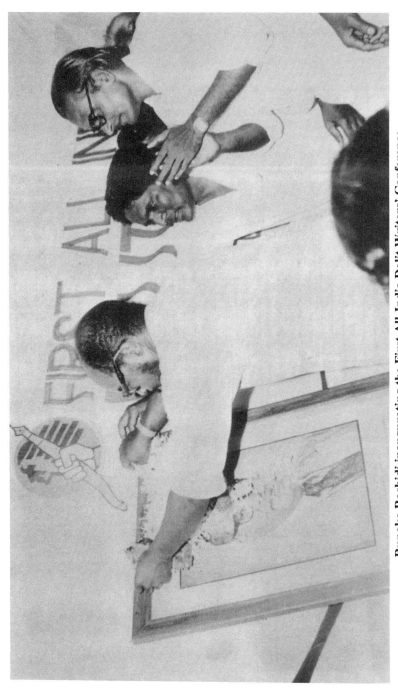

Runoko Rashidi inaugurating the First All-India Dalit Writers' Conference (Hyderabad, India), 8 October 1987.

Joshi, Vijay. "Ancient Traditions Plague the Untouchables." *Los Angeles Times,* 5 Aug 1990: A8.

Keer, Dhananjay. *Dr. Ambedkar: Life and Mission.* 3rd ed. Bombay: Popular Prakashan, 1971.

The Laws of Manu. Translated by Georg Buhler. 1886; rpt. Delhi: Motilal Banarsidass, 1979.

"A Local Custom Called Cruelty." *Time,* 28 May 1990: 37.

Marshall, Tyler. "India's Untouchables Assert Rights." *Los Angeles Times,* 2 May 1981: 1.

Moon, Meenakshi, and Urmila Pawar. "Women in the Early Untouchable Liberation Movement." *Dalit Voice* 10, No. 19 (1991): 19–20.

Rajshekar, V.T. *Apartheid in India: An International Problem.* 2d rev. ed. Bangalore: Dalit Sahitya Akademy, 1983.

Rajshekar, V.T. *Dalit: The Black Untouchables of India.* Foreword by Y.N. Kly. Annexture by Laxmi N. Berwa. Atlanta: Clarity Press, 1987.

Rajshekar, V.T. "Search for Cultural Roots of Dalits." *Dalit Voice* 6, No. 9 (1987): 1–3.

Rajshekar, V.T. *Aggression on Indian Culture: Cultural Identity of Dalits and the Dominant Tradition of India.* Bangalore: Dalit Sahitya Akademy, 1988.

Rajshekar, V.T. "Harmony of Blacks: Dalits and Africans Must Unite." *The Statesman* (published simultaneously from Delhi and Calcutta), 30 Mar 1988.

Rajshekar, V.T. "Black Books to Guide Untouchables." *Dalit Voice,* 16–31 Oct 1991: 6–7.

Rajshekar, V.T. "The Black Untouchables of India: Reclaiming Our African Identity and Cultural Heritage." Appendix to *Introduction to the Study of African Classical Civilizations,* by Runoko Rashidi. London: Karnak House, 1993: 127–34.

Rajshekar, V.T. "What Dalit Voice Did in Fifteen Years For Blacks and Dalits." *Dalit Voice* 13, No. 19 (1994): 3.

Rashidi, Runoko. "Dr. Diop on Asia: Highlights and Insights-Appendix." *Great African Thinkers.* Vol. 1, *Cheikh Anta Diop.* Edited by Ivan Van Sertima and Larry Williams. New Brunswick: Journal of African Civilizations, 1986: 144–45.

Rashidi, Runoko. "Dalits: The Black Untouchables of India." *The African World* 2, No. 3 (1989): 2–3.

Rashidi, Runoko. "The African Presence in Ancient and Modern Asia." *Afro-Synergy* 3, No. 1 (1990): 8.

Rashidi, Runoko. "The Black Presence in Asian Antiquity." *Dalit Voice* 9, No. 24 (1990): 2.

Rashidi, Runoko. "India's Dalits and Africa's Blacks Had a Common Origin." *Dalit Voice* 9, No. 14 (1990): 17–18.

Rashidi, Runoko. "India's Dalits No Longer Stand Alone." *Dalit Voice* 9, No. 13 (1990): 12.

Rashidi, Runoko. "Blacks as a Global Community: Dalits are World's Most Oppressed People." *Dalit Voice* 13, No. 19 (1994): 3–8.

Rashidi, Runoko. *The Global African Community: The African Presence in Asia, Australia and the South Pacific.* Washington, D.C.: Institute for Independent Education, 1994.

Sunder, B. Shyam. *They Burn: The 160,000,000 Untouchables of India.* Introduction by V.T. Rajshekar. Bangalore: Dalit Sahitya Akademy, 1987.

Toure, Yemi. "Horror and Hope." *Final Call,* 6 Feb 1988.

"Untouchables' Leader in India Dies at Age 78." *Times Wire Services,* 8 Jun 1986.

Winters, Clyde-Ahmad. "African Origin of the Glorious Dalits." *Dalit Voice,* 16 Apr 1986.

Wobogo, Vulindlela. "Diop's Two Cradle Theory and the Origin of White Racism." *Black Books Bulletin* 4, No. 4 (1976): 21–29.

RESEARCHING THE AFRICAN PRESENCE IN ASIA: THE CHALLENGE AHEAD OF US

By Chancellor James Williams

I only made passing reference in the work to Blacks scattered outside of Africa over the world—*not from the slave trade,* but dispersions that began in prehistory. This fact alone indicates the great tasks of future scholarship on the real history of the race. We are actually just on the threshold, gathering up some important missing fragments. The biggest jobs are still ahead.

Ancient China and the Far East, for example, must be a special area of African research. How do we explain such a large population of Blacks in Southern China—powerful enough to form a kingdom of their own? Or the Black people of…the Malay peninsula, Indo-China. The heavy concentration of Africans in India…open still another interesting field for investigation. Even the "Negroid" finds in early Europe appear not to be as challenging as the Black population centers in Asia. Our concern is with great and dominant populations. These are the Blacks who have so puzzled Western scholars that some theorize that Asia or Europe may be the homeland of Africans after all. The African populations in Palestine, Arabia, and Mesopotamia are better known, although the centuries of Black rule over Palestine, South Arabia, and in Mesopotamia should be studied and elaborated in more detail. All of this will call for a new kind of scholarship, a scholarship without any mission other than the discovery of truth, and one that will not tremble with fear when that truth is contrary to what one prefers to believe.

Dr. Chancellor James Williams (1893–1992)

TRIBUTE TO A FORERUNNER: A SELECTED BIBLIOGRAPHY OF JOHN GLOVER JACKSON (1 APRIL 1907–13 OCTOBER 1993)

Compiled by Runoko Rashidi

Works by John Glover Jackson

Jackson, John G. Ethiopia and the Origin of Civilization: A Critical Review of the Evidence of Archaeology, Anthropology, History and Comparative Religion— According to the Most Reliable Sources and Authorities. New York: The Blyden Society, 1939; rpt. Baltimore: Black Classic Press, 1985.

Jackson, John G. Pagan Origins of the Christ Myth. New York: Truth Seeker Co., 1941.

Jackson, John G. Introduction to African Civilizations. Introduction and Additional Bibliographical Notes by John Henrik Clarke. Secaucus: Citadel, 1970.

Jackson, John G. Man, God, and Civilization. New Hyde Park: University Books, 1972.

Jackson, John G. Foreword to Gerald Massey's Lectures. New York: Samuel Weiser, 1974.

Jackson, John G. The Mysteries of Egypt. Chicago: MASS, 1980.

Jackson, John G. The African Origin of Christianity. Chicago: L. & P., 1981.

Jackson, John G. "Egypt and Christianity." Egypt Revisited. Edited by Ivan Van Sertima. New Brunswick: Journal of African Civilizations, 1982: 65–80.

Jackson, John G. The African Origin of the Myths and Legends of the Garden of Eden. Chicago: MASS, Inc., 1984.

Jackson, John G. Was Jesus Christ a Negro? Chicago: MASS, Inc., 1984.

Jackson, John G. Christianity Before Christ. Austin: American Atheist Press, 1985.

Jackson, John G. Black Reconstruction in South Carolina. Austin: American Atheist Press, 1987.

Jackson, John G. The Golden Ages of Africa. Austin: American Atheist Press, 1987.

Jackson, John G. Hubert H. Harrison: The Black Socrates. Austin: American Atheist Press, 1987.

Jackson, John G. "Krishna and Buddha of India: Black Gods of Asia." African Presence in Early Asia. Rev. ed. Edited by Runoko Rashidi and Ivan Van Sertima. New Brunswick: Journal of African Civilizations, 1988: 106–111.

Jackson, John G. Ages of Gold and Silver and Other Short Sketches of Human History. Foreword by Madalyn O'Hair. Austin: American Atheist Press, 1990.

Jackson, John G. Introduction to The Story of the Moors in Spain, by Stanley Lane-Poole. Baltimore: Black Classic Press, 1990.

Jackson, John G. "The Empire of the Moors." Compiled, with an Appendix, by Runoko Rashidi. Golden Age of the Moor. Edited by Ivan Van Sertima. New Brunswick: Journal of African Civilizations, 1992: 85–92.

Works by Willis Nathaniel Huggins and John Glover Jackson

Huggins, Willis Nathaniel, and John G. Jackson. *A Guide to the Study of African History: Directive Lists for Schools and Clubs.* New York: New York Federation of History Clubs, 1934.
Huggins, Willis Nathaniel, and John G. Jackson. *An Introduction to African Civilizations With Main Currents in Ethiopian History.* New York: Avon House, 1937; rpt. New York: Negro Universities Press, 1969.

Interviews With John Glover Jackson

Brunson, James E., and Runoko Rashidi. "Sitting at the Feet of a Forerunner: An April 1987 Meeting and Interview with John G. Jackson." *African Presence in Early Asia.* Rev. ed. Edited by Runoko Rashidi and Ivan Van Sertima. New Brunswick: Journal of African Civilizations, 1988: 198–205.
Rashad, Adib. "A Conversation with John G. Jackson." In *A Tribute to John G. Jackson,* by Adib Rashad and H. Khalif Khalifah. Hampton: United Brothers and Sisters Communications Systems, 1991: 15–20.

Works About John Glover Jackson

Ayaga, Odeyo Owiti. "Three Book Reviews: *Introduction to African Civilizations,* by John G. Jackson; *The Destruction of Black Civilization: Great Issues of a Race from 4500 B.C. to 2000 A.D.,* by Chancellor Williams; *Black Man of the Nile,* by Yosef ben-Jochannan." In *Black World* (Aug 1973): 51–52.
"In Honor of Ancestor John G. Jackson (1907–1993)." Association for the Study of Classical African Civilizations Eleventh Annual National Ancient Kemetic Studies Conference Program, 1994.
"John G. Jackson Tribute." *Kemetic Voice: Newsletter of the Institute* 2, No. 1 (Dec 1993): 9.
Muwakkil, Salim. "Whatever Happened to the Great Black Hope." *Chicago Reader,* 25 Jan 1982: Section 1: 9.
Rashad, Adib, and H. Khalif Khalifah. *A Tribute to John G. Jackson.* Hampton: United Brothers and Sisters Communications Systems, 1991.
Rashidi, Runoko. "Notes on Black Scholars of the Moors in John G. Jackson's Life." *Golden Age of the Moor.* Edited by Ivan Van Sertima. New Brunswick: Journal of African Civilizations, 1992: 89–91.
"Remembering John G. Jackson: 1907–1993." *The Knowledge Broker* (Feb 1994): 1.
Sims, Wayne. "African People's Conference A Success." *Tartar Shield,* 10 Mar 1983: 1.
Toure, Yemi. "Elder Statesmen: An Era is Passing for Five Authors Known for Reclaiming the Role of Blacks in History." *Los Angeles Times,* 3 Mar 1991: E1.
"Tribute to the Elders." *Serekh* 5, No. 1 (1994): 2.

A TRIBUTE TO PIONEER CONTRIBUTORS TO THE DOCUMENTATION OF THE AFRICAN PRESENCE IN EARLY ASIA FROM 1883 TO 1918

By Runoko Rashidi and James E. Brunson

Background and Introduction

One of the most fascinating areas in the broad field of the African presence in Asian antiquity is its early documentation by African scholars. In this essay we have chosen to primarily pay tribute to the lives and works of six pioneer African-American scholars who published within the thirty-five year time span from 1883 to 1918—an era that encompassed the greater portion of the Post-Reconstruction period in the United States to the end of World War I.

Interestingly enough, the major scholars discussed here were not the only ones during this turbulent age whose works touched upon and embraced the African presence in early Asia, nor were they the first. As early as 18 July 1827, for example, Samuel E. Cornish (ca. 1795–1859) and Jamaican-born John Brown Russwurm (1799–1851) in *Freedom's Journal* (the first Black newspaper established in the United States) printed an article entitled "European Colonies in America" in which was written that:

> Ethiopia, a country of which the history is almost entirely shrouded in the night of ages and of which we know little or nothing, except that it must have been in its day a seat of high civilization and great power, probably the fountain of the improvement of Egypt and western Asia, was inhabited by Blacks. It then comprehended the country on both sides of the Red Sea, whence the Ethiopians are said by Homer to be divided into two parts. The great Assyrian empires of Babylon and Nineveh, hardly less illustrious than Egypt in arts and arms, were founded by Ethiopian colonies, and peopled by Blacks.[1]

Dr. Edward Wilmot Blyden (1832–1912) argued that "No people can interpret Africans but Africans."[2] In his essay entitled "The Negro in Ancient History," which was the first article written by an African focusing on the Black presence in antiquity to be published in an American literary quarterly (appearing in the January 1869 issue of the *Methodist Quarterly Review*),

---

This essay is dedicated to Dr. John Henrik Clarke and Dr. Charles B. Copher

Blyden referenced the work of Assyriologist Henry Creswicke Rawlinson (1810–1895), concluding "that the early inhabitants of South Babylonia were of a cognate race with the primitive colonists both of Arabia and of the African Ethiopia."[3]

In 1891 Edward Austin Johnson (1860–1944), a lawyer, educator and principal of Washington Public School in Raleigh, North Carolina, published *A School History of the Negro Race in America.* In a section of the work focusing on the "Origins of Race," Johnson pointed out that, "Three million Buddhists in Asia represent their chief deity, Buddha, with Negro features and hair."[4]

Pioneer African Scholars: 1883-1918

The six individuals who are the primary focus of this essay are a representative cross section of the most outstanding Africanist scholars of their era. Although we pay tribute to them here, it is fair to say that in spite of their work, they are not especially well known today in African-centered circles. A pity, for they all led difficult, fascinating and highly remarkable lives. None of them, it must be said, with the possible exceptions of James M. Boddy and Alphonso O. Stafford, made the study of the African presence in Asia the primary focus of their researches. Each of them, however, with varying degrees of significance, made qualitative contributions to the field. All of them were exceptionally brilliant and actively dedicated in their own way to the complete and total emancipation of African people. Reviewing their works today, in some cases more than a century after their initial publication, it is not hard to be critical. However, their work as historians and scholars must be weighed within the context of the times in which they lived, with all of the profound limitations and handicaps imposed upon them by severe economic disabilities and race and gender discrimination. And yet in spite of the innumerable difficulties and staggering obstacles placed in their paths, through their intellect, sacrifice, persistence, determination and the confidence that the work they were doing was a vital, almost sacred mission, they made immense contributions that have served as models, inspiration and guidance. These scholars, these courageous Black men and women, were pioneers and trailblazers whose works, even today and in spite of obvious flaws, merit considerable praise and serious recognition.

George Washington Williams (1849–1891)

Dr. George Washington Williams, a man generally credited as the first African-American to write a "scholarly general history" of Blacks not only in America but antiquity, was born in Bedford Springs, Pennsylvania 16 October 1849. He graduated from Howard University in 1868, and studied at Newton Theological Seminary in Massachusetts, graduating in 1874. In January 1891 Williams visited Cairo, Egypt. Williams was an international traveler, the first Black member of the Ohio legislature, an orator, soldier, minister, journalist, jurist, writer, editor and historian.

In 1883 G.P. Putnam's Sons published Dr. Williams' *History of the Negro Race in America from 1619 to 1880. Negroes as Slaves, as Soldiers, and as Citizens: Together with a Preliminary Consideration of the Unity of the Human Family, an Historical Sketch of Africa, and an Account of the Negro Governments of Sierra Leone and Liberia, in Two Volumes.* In the first volume, in a chapter entitled "The Negro in the Light of Philology, Ethnology, and Egyptology," while dwelling on the antiquity of Blacks in Asia, and utilizing secondary as well as primary sources, Williams wrote that:

> In Japan, and in many other parts of the East, there are to be found stupendous and magnificent temples, that are hoary with age. It is almost impossible to determine the antiquity of some of them, in which the idols are exact representations of woolly-haired Negroes, although the inhabitants of those countries to-day have straight hair. Among the Japanese, black is considered a color of good omen. In the temples of Siam we find the idols fashioned like unto Negroes....Among the Hindus, Kali, the consort of Siva, one of their great Triad; Crishna, the eighth incarnation of Vishnu; and Vishnu also himself, the second of the Trimerti or Hindu Triad, are represented of a black color.[5]
>
> Now, these substantial and indisputable traces of the march of the Negro races through Japan and Asia lead us to conclude that the Negro race antedates all profane history. And while the great body of the Negro races have been located geographically in Africa, they have been, in no small sense, a cosmopolitan people. Their wanderings may be traced from the rising to the setting sun.
>
> Taking the whole southern portion of Asia westward to Arabia, this conjecture—which likewise was a conclusion drawn, after patient research, by the late Sir T. Stanford Raffles—accounts, more satisfactorily than any other, for the Oriental habits, ideas, traditions, and words which can be traced among several of the present African tribes and in the South-Sea Islands. Traces of this black race are still found along the Himalaya range from the Indus to Indo-China, and the Malay Peninsula, and in mixed form all through the southern states to Ceylon.[6]

Rufus Lewis Perry (1834–1895)

Born into slavery in Smith County, Tennessee, African-American scholar and activist Rufus Lewis Perry became a "Ph.D., Editor, Ethnologist, Essayist, Logician, Profound Student of Negro History, Scholar in the Greek, Latin and Hebrew Languages."[7] Like his father before him, "Perry was a Baptist minister. He was editor of the *Sunbeam* (Brooklyn) and the *People's Journal*

Figure 1. Dr. George Washington Williams (1849–1891)

(Columbus, Ohio), coordinate editor of the *American Baptist* (later the *Baptist Weekly,* New York), and editor and publisher of the *National Monitor* (Brooklyn). For ten years, Perry served as corresponding secretary of the consolidated American Baptist Missionary Convention and, later, corresponding secretary of the American Educational Association and of the American Baptist Free Mission Society."[8] In 1887 the State University at Louisville conferred upon Perry, George Washington Williams and James Poindexter, the honorary degree of Doctors of Law.

A dominant theme in Perry's work, and in the work of numerous other scholars as well, was the identification of both an ancient African and Asian land known to the Greeks as Ethiopia and in the Biblical table of nations as Cush. In 1887 the Literary Union published a paper read by Perry before the Brooklyn Literary Union entitled *The Cushite: or, The Children of Ham, (The Negro Race) As Seen by the Ancient Historians and Poets.* In the Introduction to *The Cushite,* T. McCants Stewart (1854–1923), the Union's President, wrote that "'THE CUSHITE,' so ably and learnedly presented in the following pages by a Negro scholar, who has given years to the study of the subject, will prove invaluable to those who desire to know, 'what is truth?' And more; it will aid in the development of a nobler manhood, because of the information which it imparts, and because of the enthusiasm which it will arouse."[9]

In *The Cushite,* heavily referencing the Biblical table of nations, Dr. Perry wrote that:

> The four sons of Ham were Cush, Mizraim, Phut and Canaan. These and their immediate descendants were the founders of great Negro or Cushite nations, traces of whose names and extraordinary deeds exist even unto this day.
> The term 'Cushite' comes directly from Cush whose sons were Nimrod, Seba, Havilah, Sabtah, and Raamah, who begat Sheba, Dedan, and Sabtecha.
> Nimrod founded the city of Babylon and the Babylonian empire.
> Cush and his son Seba are the ancestral heads of the Cushites of southwestern Arabia, Abyssinia and of Nubia, which was originally called *Seba* by the Hebrews, (Isa. xliii. 3,) and Meroe by the Greeks and Romans.[10]
> Canaan, the fourth son of Ham, begat the original inhabitants of Palestine called Canaanites, and was the progenitor of the Sidonians, afterwards called Phoenicians.[11]

In 1893 a far more comprehensive work of Dr. Perry's entitled *The Cushite, Or the Descendants of Ham as Found in the Sacred Scriptures and in the Writings of Ancient Historians and Poets from Noah to the Christian Era* was published, in which separate chapters were devoted to the semi-legendary Queen of Sheba, Nimrod (the Biblical son of Kush and founder of Mesopotamian civilization), and Memnon (the mythical Black warrior-king from southwestern Asia and the most celebrated of the non-Hellenic heroes of antiquity).

By tradition, Memnon was slain by Achilles while defending King Priam's Trojans when they were besieged by the famous coalition of Greek city-states immortalized in Homer's *Iliad*: "To Troy no hero came of nobler line, Or if nobler, Memnon, it was thine." Of this noble hero Dr. Perry pronounced that:

> The distinguished Cushite whom Homer calls Memnon came and went like a meteor in the galaxy of illustrious Ethiopian monarchs. But the poet in classic song and the historian in legendary tradition, have preserved enough of his brightness to indicate his rank and power among the contemporary potentates of the earth. He was king of the Ethiopians. He fought against the Greeks in the Trojan war; and after he had slain Antilochus, son of Nestor, was killed by Achilles.[12]

Dr. Perry expressively concluded that "Though slain by Achilles, Memnon is so embalmed in verse and prose by Homer, Hesiod, Virgil and others, that his name will last as long as the writings of these imperishable authors."[13]

Pauline Elizabeth Hopkins (1859-1930)

Pauline Elizabeth Hopkins has been called the "Dean of African-American women writers." Born in Portland, Maine, she was an editor, journalist, essayist, novelist, poet, publisher, public lecturer, actress, musician, and stenographer for the Bureau of Statistics on the Massachusetts Census of 1895 for four years. From the age of fifteen, after winning a literary contest sponsored by the African-American playwright, novelist, essayist, historian and abolitionist William Wells Brown (1814–1884), Hopkins went on to write prolifically. As stated by Ann Allen Shockley, "She herself also published a thirty-one page booklet entitled *A Primer of Facts Pertaining to the Early Greatness of the African Race and the Possibility of Restoration by its Descendants—with Epilogue* (1905). Listed as Black Classics Series no. 1, she apparently intended to publish additional ones."[14] In *A Primer of Facts* Hopkins wrote that:

> Nimrod first arose to national greatness as a monarch so that until this day his name is great among the princes of the earth. He was the founder of the great Assyrian Empire.[15]

From February to July 1905 Hopkins wrote one of the earliest treatises on the global African community in a four-part series for *The Voice of the Negro*, edited by J. Max Barber, entitled "The Dark Races of the Twentieth Century." In "The Dark Races of the Twentieth Century, Pt. 2: The Malay Peninsula, Borneo, Java, Sumatra and the Philippines" Hopkins' ideas about Blacks in

the Philippines and other parts of Southeast Asia and Australasia were emphasized as follows:

> At the time of Magellan's discovery of these islands lying washed by
> the Pacific Ocean and the China Sea, the country was peopled by the
> tribes of Negritos, or descendants of African tribes. Wars and intermar-
> riage have very nearly obliterated the traces of the original stock, and the
> remaining numbers live in the mountains and cultivate the land. Many
> interesting theories are offered as to the origin of Negroes in this archi-
> pelago. Some scientists say that he was driven from Africa, and others
> that he came from New Guinea.[16]
> The presence of man in all sections is easily explained by migration,
> and there is nothing to show several distinct nuclei. Man started out from
> one point alone, and by the power of adaptation he has finally covered the
> entire habitable globe. Therefore we must conclude that the Negritos of
> the Philippines and the other dark races of Australasia are of the family of
> Ham.[17]

James Marmaduke Boddy (1866–?)

Rev. James Marmaduke Boddy of Troy, New York, was one of the earliest
African-American writers to tackle the issue of an Africoid presence in
ancient China and Japan. In the October 1905 issue of the *Colored American
Magazine*, "the first significant Afro-American journal to emerge in the
twentieth century,"[18] Boddy published the "Ethnology of the Japanese Race,"
which attempted to document a prominent and indelible African strain run-
ning through early Japanese history and that the Japanese are at least in part
"Asian Negroes."

Referencing the work of ethnologist and anthropologist James Cowles
Prichard (1786–1848), Boddy wrote that:

> As to the color of the invaders who gave to the Japanese race their
> crisp hair and dark complexion we have the testimony of Prichard, who
> quotes from ancient Japanese state records of the empire, which speaks of
> the early invaders as 'Black Savages, who were very formidable.' They
> are also described as having 'peculiar features,' 'Crisp hair' and 'dark
> complexion.' Besides their Negro features, which are very observable,
> the early Japanese historians themselves have described for us the 'Black
> Barbarians of the South; the Black savages of the west,' who, in an age
> which antedates authentic history, 'came from the south in ships and
> settled in Japan.' (See 'Prichard's Researches Into the Physical History of
> Mankind,' Vol. IV., p. 492).[19]

It is to be noted that the word "Savage", when used in the context of
Prichard and Boddy, denoted strangers. Rev. Boddy concluded by saying that
"These immigrants mingled and amalgamated one with another and with the
natives, and in time became a homogeneous race, whose predominating

Figure 2. Pauline Elizabeth Hopkins (1859–1930)

Figure 3. Rev. James Marmaduke Boddy (1866–?)

physical characteristics bespeak the unmistakable presence of a large Negro element."[20] In ancient records, wrote Boddy, these Blacks were called, among other things, "'black cinnamon,' 'black barbarians,' and 'dark pygmies,' according to the whims or dictation of the various authors."[21]

Alphonso Orenzo Stafford (1871-1941)

Educator Alphonso Orenzo Stafford was born in Alexandria, Virginia. He studied at Minor Normal School in Virginia, Howard University, the University of Pennsylvania and Columbia University. Stafford taught in Baltimore and Washington, D.C., and served as principle of the Harrison School, also in Washington, D.C. Stafford additionally served on the staff of Chaney Training College for Teachers (which later became Chaney State College in Chaney, Pennsylvania), and assisted Booker T. Washington (1856–1915) and his staff in the study of Africa. Stafford was also an early contributor to Carter G. Woodson's *Journal of Negro History* beginning with "The Mind of the African Negro as Reflected in His Proverbs" published in the inaugural issue in January 1916. An extended essay by Stafford, "Antar, The Arabian Negro Warrior, Poet and Hero," appeared in the second issue of the *Journal of Negro History* in April 1916.
Regarding Antar, Stafford wrote that:

> His fame as a literary character transcends that of the modern authors of black blood, such as Pushkin in Russia, and the elder Dumas in France. After his death the fame of Antar's deeds spread across the Arabian Peninsula and throughout the Mohammedan world. In time these deeds, like Homeric legends, were recorded in a literary form and therein is found that Antar,…has become the Achilles of the Arabian Iliad, a work known to this day after being a source of wonder and admiration for hundreds of years to millions of Mohammedans as the 'Romance of Antar.' The book, therefore, ranks among the great national classics like the 'Shah-nameh' of Persia, and the 'Nibelungen-Lied' of Germany. Antar was the father of knighthood. He was the champion of the weak and oppressed, the protector of women, the impassioned lover-poet, the irresistible and magnanimous knight. 'Antar' in its present form probably preceded the romances of chivalry so common in the twelfth century in Italy and France.[22]

George Wells Parker (1882-1931)

George Wells Parker, along with John Edward Bruce (1856–1924) and the Rev. John Albert Williams (1866–1933), founded the Hamitic League of the World, of which the extraordinary Black bibliophile Arthur Alfonso Schomburg (1874–1938) became a member.[23] Parker was a student at Creighton University in Omaha, Nebraska and a supporter of Marcus Mosiah Garvey (1887–

1940). Robert A. Hill described Parker as "a medical student in Omaha and scion of one of that city's oldest black families."[24]

On 1 April 1917 Parker delivered a speech before the Omaha Philosophical Society entitled "The African Origin of the Grecian Civilization." Still referenced today, "The African Origin of the Grecian Civilization" was published in the *Journal of Negro History* in July 1917.[25]

George Wells Parker was an exceptional scholar, perhaps even ahead of his time, who wrote with a pronounced degree of confidence, clarity and sharpness. In 1918 the Hamitic League of the World published a twenty-nine page pamphlet by Parker entitled *The Children of the Sun* which contained an enlightening section highlighting the ethnic composition of classical Asian civilizations. Of Southwest Asia, Parker wrote that:

> In the great Mesopotamian valley, where flourished Chaldea, Babylon and Assyria, evidences of the rule of African peoples have become so persistent that the most famous scholars simply attribute the glory of these mighty empires to African blood and let it go at that. True, that the ancient writers knew there were black empires and said so, but modern man has always had the habit of believing that the ancients never knew what they were talking about.[26]

After an incisive examination of ancient languages and religions, Persia and Phoenicia, India and Arabia, Parker concludes his comments on Asia as follows:

> And this ends the survey of Asia. Fifty years ago one would not have dreamed that science would defend the fact that Asia was the home of the black races as well as Africa, yet it has done just that thing. Now when we gaze on the ruins of Assyria's palaces or stand in wrapt wonder before the fallen winged beasts which guarded her gates; when we stand silently upon the spot that once was Babylon and ponder upon the mighty walls built by this grand and wondrous mistress of the Euphratean plain or reverently uncover before the tumbled pillars of sanctuaries built in the long ago to forgotten gods; when we marvel at the depth of love and the majesty of grief that built the Taj Mahal or scan the perfumed literatures of India and Persia and Arabia, let us not forget that the secret, like the secret of all things wonderfully and aesthetically beautiful, lies with Africa, the mother of civilization and of nations.[27]

Conclusion

Although the story of the African presence in early Asia has been described as somewhat obscure, its documentation is by no means new, as the admirable and relevant works of the scholars discussed in this essay, Dr. George Washington Williams, Dr. Rufus Lewis Perry, Pauline Elizabeth Hopkins, Rev. James Marmaduke Boddy, Alphonso Orenzo Stafford and George Wells

Figure 4. George Wells Parker (1882–1931)

Parker, effectively demonstrate. More recent historians such as Drusilla Dunjee Houston, Joel Augustus Rogers, John Glover Jackson, Chancellor James Williams and numerous others may be said to have followed in their footsteps. Indeed, their collective works can be credited with having developed and sustained a foundation from which the present generation of scholars can move confidently forward.

Notes

This essay is dedicated to Charles B. Copher and John Henrik Clarke.
  1. Samuel E. Cornish and John B. Russwurm, "European Colonies in America," *Freedom's Journal,* 18 Jul 1827, 1.
  2. Edward Wilmot Blyden, quoted in George Shepperson, "Notes on Negro American Influences on the Emergence of African Nationalism," in Melvin Drimmer, ed., *Black History* (Garden City: Doubleday, 1969), 494.
  3. Edward Wilmot Blyden, "The Negro in Ancient History," *The Methodist Quarterly Review* (Jan 1869), 78.
  4. Edward A. Johnson, *The Negro Race in America* (Raleigh: Edwards & Broughton, 1891), 12.
  5. George Washington Williams, *History of the Negro Race in America,* vol. 1 (New York: G.P. Putnam's 1883), 17.
  6. Williams, 18–19.
  7. William J. Simmons, *Men of Mark, Eminent, Progressive and Rising* (1887; rpt. Chicago: Johnson, 1970), 425.
  8. Sylvia M. Jacobs, *The African Nexus* (Westport: Greenwood Press, 1981), 70.
  9. T. McCants Stewart, Introduction to *The Cushite,* by Rufus Lewis Perry (Brooklyn: The Literary Union, 1887), vi. T. McCants Stewart was a lawyer, pastor, author, editor and educator. He was born of free parents in 1854 in Charleston, South Carolina. In 1898, after attending Howard University and graduating from the University of South Carolina, Stewart move to Honolulu. From 1915 to 1921 he lived in England, and died in St. Thomas, Virgin Islands 7 January 1923.
  10. Rufus Lewis Perry, *The Cushite* (Brooklyn: The Literary Union, 1887), 9–10.
  11. Perry, 10.
  12. Rufus Lewis Perry, *The Cushite, Or the Descendants of Ham as Found in the Sacred Scriptures and in the Writings of Ancient Historians and Poets from Noah to the Christian Era* (Springfield, MA: Willey & Co., 1893), 119.
  13. Perry, 121.
  14. Ann Allen Shockley, *Afro-American Women Writers 1746–1933: An Anthology and Critical Guide* (Boston: G.K. Hall, 1988), 293.
  15. Pauline Elizabeth Hopkins, *A Primer of Facts Pertaining to the Early Greatness of the African Race and the Possibility of Restoration by its Descendants—With Epilogue Compiled and Arranged from the Works of the Best Known Ethnologists and Historians* (Cambridge: P.E. Hopkins & Co., 1905), 10.
  16. Pauline Elizabeth Hopkins, "The Dark Races of the Twentieth Century, Pt. 2: The Malay Peninsula, Borneo, Java, Sumatra and the Philippines," *The Voice of the Negro* (Mar 1905), 190.
  17. Hopkins, 191.
  18. Abby Arthur Johnson and Ronald M. Johnson, "Away from Accommodation:

Radical Editors and Protest Journalism, 1900–1910," *Journal of Negro History* (Jul 1977), 325.

19. James Marmaduke Boddy, "The Ethnology of the Japanese Race," *The Colored American Magazine* (Oct 1905), 582.

20. Boddy, 582.

21. Boddy, 583.

22. Alphonso Orenzo Stafford, "Antar, The Arabian Negro Warrior, Poet and Hero," *Journal of Negro History* 1, No. 2 (1916), 155. Stafford's third article for the *Journal of Negro History*, "The Tarik E' Soudan," was published in April 1917. In November 1940 the *Negro History Bulletin*, which, like the *Journal of Negro History* was founded and edited by Dr. Carter Godwin Woodson (1875–1950), devoted a special issue to the African presence in Asia to which Stafford contributed three brief essays: "Antar," "Africa and Asia," and "Why Study Asia with Respect to Africa."

23. Born in San Juan, Puerto Rico, Schomburg once explained that "The Negro must remake his past in order to make his future. Though it is orthodox to think of America as the one country where it is unnecessary to have a past, what is a luxury of the nation as a whole becomes a prime social necessity for the Negro. For him, a group tradition must supply its compensation for persecution, and race pride is the simple antidote for prejudice." Arthur A. Schomburg, "The Negro Digs Up His Past." In *The New Negro*, ed., Alain Locke (New York: Arno Press and the New York Times, 1968), 231.

24. Robert A. Hill, ed., *The Marcus Garvey and Universal Negro Improvement Association Papers*, vol. 1 (Berkeley: University of California Press, 1983), 522.

25. "This short article in *The Journal of Negro History* is important for its age, 1917! It anticipates George G.M. James' Stolen Legacy and Martin Bernal's *Black Athena* using substantially the same approach." Asa G. Hilliard III, *Free Your Mind: Return to the Source African Origins and Master Keys*, rev. ed. (East Point: Waset Educational Productions, 1991), 86.

26. George Wells Parker, *The Children of the Sun* (Omaha: The Hamitic League of the World, 1918), 12–13.

27. Parker, 22.

Bibliography

Blyden, Edward Wilmot. "The Negro in Ancient History." *Methodist Quarterly Review* (Jan 1869): 71–93.

Boddy, James Marmaduke. "The Ethnology of the Japanese Race." *The Colored American Magazine* (Oct 1905): 577–85.

Brunson, James E. *Africans in Early Asia: An African-Centric Historiography (1827–1991)*. DeKalb: Kara, 1991.

Cornish, Samuel E., and John Russwurm. "European Colonies in America." *Freedom's Journal* 1, No. 18 (18 Jul 1827).

Francis-Monroe, Tonju. "George Washington Williams: Soldier, Preacher and Historian." *Holoman's Black Achievers* 2, No. 6 (Jun 1992): 18.

Franklin, John Hope. *George Washington Williams: A Biography*. Chicago: University of Chicago Press, 1985.

Hill, Robert A., editor. *The Marcus Garvey and Universal Negro Improvement Association Papers. Vol. 1: 1826–August 1919*. Berkeley: University of California Press, 1983.

Hopkins, Pauline Elizabeth. "The Dark Races of the Twentieth Century, Pt. 2: The Malay Peninsula, Borneo, Java, Sumatra and the Philippines." *The Voice of the Negro* (Mar 1905): 186–91.

Hopkins, Pauline Elizabeth. *A Primer of Pacts Pertaining to the Early Greatness of the African Race and the Possibility of Restoration by its Descendants—With Epilogue Compiled and Arranged from the Works of the Best Known Ethnologists and Historians.* Cambridge: P.E. Hopkins & Co., 1905.

Johnson, Edward A. *The Negro Race in America.* Raleigh: Edwards & Broughton, 1891.

Logan, Rayford W., and Michael R. Winston. *Dictionary of American Negro Biography.* New York: W.W. Norton, 1982.

Martin, Tony, compiler and editor. *African Fundamentalism: A Literary and Cultural Anthology of Garvey's Harlem Renaissance.* Dover: The Majority Press, 1991.

Parker, George Wells. *The Children of the Sun.* Omaha: The Hamitic League of the World, 1918; rpt. Baltimore: Black Classic Press, 1978.

Perry, Rufus Lewis. *The Cushite; or, The Children of Ham, (The Negro Race) As Seen by the Ancient Historians and Poets.* Introduction by T. McCants Stewart. Brooklyn: The Literary Union, 1887.

Perry, Rufus Lewis. *The Cushite, Or the Descendants of Ham as Pound in the Sacred Scriptures and in the Writings of Ancient Historians and Poets from Noah to the Christian Era.* Introduction by T. McCants Stewart. Springfield, MA: Willey & Co., 1893.

Schomburg, Arthur Alfonso. "The Negro Digs Up His Past." *Survey Graphic* (Mar 1925): 670–72.

Shockley, Ann Allen. "Pauline Elizabeth Hopkins: A Biographical Excursion Into Obscurity." *Phylon* 33 (Spring 1972): 22–26.

Shockley, Ann Allen. "Pauline Elizabeth Hopkins, 1859–1930." In *Afro-American Women Writers 1746–1933: An Anthology and Critical Guide.* Boston: G.K. Hall, 1988: 289–95.

Stafford, Alphonso Orenzo. "Antar, The Arabian Negro Warrior, Poet and Hero." *Journal of Negro History* 1, No. 2 (1916): 151–62.

Stafford, Alphonso Orenzo. "Africa and Asia." *Negro History Bulletin* 4, No. 2 (1940): 28.

Stafford, Alphonso Orenzo. "Antar." *Negro History Bulletin* 4, No. 2 (1940): 29.

Stafford, Alphonso Orenzo. "Why Study Asia with Respect to Africa." *Negro History Bulletin* 4, No. 2 (1940): 27.

Williams, George Washington. *History of the Negro Race in America from 1619 to 1880. Negroes as Slaves, as Soldiers, and as Citizens; Together with a Preliminary Consideration of the Unity of the Human Family, an Historical Sketch of Africa, and an Account of the Negro Governments of Sierra Leone and Liberia, in Two Volumes.* New York: G.P. Putnam's Sons, 1883.

Williams, Larry Obadele. Book Review of *The Children of the Sun*, by George Wells Parker. In *History, the Bible and the Black Man* 2, No. 2 (1980): 37–38.

Williams, Larry Obadele, comp. *Towards an African Historiography: A Bibliography.* Atlanta: Ipet Isut, 1989.

Figure 1. Temple guard/warrior of South Arabia. Painted by Ludwig Deutsch

EBONY AND BRONZE
RACE AND ETHNICITY IN EARLY ARABIA AND THE ISLAMIC WORLD

By Wayne B. Chandler

Author's Introduction: *The research in this chapter sheds light on the race and ethnicity of Arabia's early inhabitants and, with the aid of Arabian sources, brings historical clarity to the lineage of Muhammed and his family.*

There was, at the inception of Arabian civilization, a powerful matriarchal culture which originated from Kush, now known as Ethiopia. Its influence on Arabia began circa 1500 B.C.E. and dominated the south up to the Islamic era, bequeathing to Arabia several opulent civilizations in the area now known as Yemen. One of the most renowned was the kingdom of Saba or Seba, from which arose the mighty "Queen of Sheba." These Blacks culturally affected the fertile areas of Oman, Yemen, and Hadramaut known as Arabia Felix or "Happy Arabia." Located in the north of Arabia is Arabia Deserta, an arid, barren rocky wasteland, the home of the Semitic Arab. The Semitic Arab descends from Heber of the race of Shem, from which descends the line of Abraham.

Ebony and Bronze is about the racial, social, and cultural politics born from the inevitable interaction between these two groups, the Blacks and Semites of the Arabian peninsula. It closely examines the role of Islam, Muhammed and the jihads, and the mighty Abbassid Empire in the formation and maintenance of what became the Moslem world. The research also explores the calamitous circumstances that would eventually lead to the split of the Islamic world into two camps, the Sunni and Shiite.

The information contained in Ebony and Bronze is pertinent and vital to a clear and comprehensive overview of the major role players in Islamic history, for these very groups would later set the stage for the Moorish movement into Spain and the Iberian peninsula.

[Editor's note] This essay is an edited version of a larger work dealing mainly with the ethnicity of the Moors in Spain. Due to the focus of this anthology, however, Mr. Chandler has graciously allowed us to rearrange it with the original introduction on the Moors in Spain inserted as an appendix.

Chandler   271

> The Copts are a race of Blacks. Khalil Ar-Rahman asked for
> a son from them, so there was born to him a great prophet
> from them, who was Isma'il, the Father of the Arabs. The
> Prophet Muhammed (God bless him and grant him salva-
> tion) also asked them for a son, and Ibrahim was born to
> him, and [the angel] Gabriel made it his surname.
>
> Al-Jahiz, 860 C.E.

*　*　*

We know that Arabia was once a portion of the ancient African Kushite
empire. Most scholars agree that, in an epoch now forgotten, southern Arabia
was originally settled and populated by Blacks who belonged to the Kushite,
or Ethiopian, race. Testimonies in ancient texts fix the geographical origin of
this population in the extreme southwest of the Arabian peninsula, from
where they migrated in a northeasterly direction to areas now known as
Yemen, Oman and Hadramaut. These Ethiopians were the original Arabs,
known in the ancient tongue as Adites or Thamudites, descendants of Ham,
the Father of the Black race. The name Himyar which means dusky, was
given to this Black race. We know the Himyaric language…is African in
origin and character. Its grammar is identical with the African-based Abyssinian.[7] The Encyclopedia Britannica gives a description of the physical qualities
of the original Arabs, as well as a deeper insight into the cultural foundation of
the empire:

> The inhabitants of Yemen, Hadramaut, Omat and the adjoining dis-
> tricts, in the shape of the heat, color, length and slenderness of limbs and
> scantiness of hair, point to an African origin.…The first dawning gleams
> that deserve to be called history find Arabia under the rule of a southern
> race. They claimed descent from Khatan. They were divided anciently
> into several aristocratic monarchies. These Yemenite kings, descendants
> of Khatan and Himyar 'the dusky,' a name denoting African origin,
> whose rulers were called 'Tobba,' of Hamitic etymology, reigned with a
> few dynastic interruptions for about 2,500 years. They demanded the
> obedience of the entire southern half of the peninsula and the northern by
> tribute collectors. The general characteristics of the institutions of Yemen
> bore considerable resemblance to the neighboring ones of the Nile Val-
> ley.[8]

To these great rulers of the Arabian south, we can attribute the finest of that
which constitutes Arabian civilization. Their culture encompassed the vast
accomplishments of those Arabian Blacks and was a direct investment of old
Kushite families as well.

Though the southern Arabian peninsula was generally under Black domination, several different African dynasties succeeded each other for varying

lengths of time. West Asian scholar Runoko Rashidi begins this chronology 8,000 years into Arabia's past, identifying the peninsula's first inhabitants as a group generally classed as Veddoids by anthropologists...whom he says form the region's Africoid Mahra population.9 Knowledge of the chronology of African dynasties in Arabia is imperative to a full understanding of the later cultural developments in Arabia and Spain.

Prior to 1500 B.C.E., the great exploits of these Blacks existed only in legends and tales. The accounts of Ad is one such example. The only proof of the existence of this empire seems to be the region in South Arabia called Aden, which surely took its name from the Adites. Historical accounts of Blacks in Arabia begin in the year 1500 B.C.E., with a civilization known as the Minaean. The Minaeans had trading outlets in Hejaz and Syria for the exportation of incense. Evidence also points to transit trade between the Minaeans and the Blacks of India, Indonesia and East Africa.

In 700 B.C.E., the Black Sabaeans conquered and eventually absorbed the Minaean civilization. The Sabaean empire became an extension of Ethiopia and was ruled by a line of queens or "Kentakes" called candeces by the Greeks. "Before Islam arrived in the 7th century A.D., Arabia was matriarchal for over a thousand years of recorded history. The Annals of Ashurbanipal said Arabia was governed by queens for as long as anyone could remember. The land's original Allah was Al-Lat, part of the female trinity along with Kore, or Q're, the Virgin, and Al-Uzza, the Powerful One, the triad known as Manat....Marriages were matrilocal, inheritance matrilineal. Polyandry— several husbands to one wife—was common."10 The first queen of the Sabaeans to be acknowledged historically was identified as Bilqis in the Quran, as Makeda in Ethiopia's *Kebra Negast* (Glory of Kings) and as the Queen of Sheba in the Christian Bible. The Sabaean civilization flourished under Queen Makeda's reign, setting a standard by which other West Asian empires were measured.

One thousand years later Queen Makeda would be deified in the Shrine of the Black Stone, or Kaaba, worshipped by the Black Arabs. "Shrine of the sacred black anionic stone in Mecca, worshipped as the Goddess Shaybah or Sheba, 'The Old Woman' and formally dedicated to the pre-Islamic Triple Goddess Manat, worshipped by Mohammed's tribesmen, the Koreshites or 'Children of Kore,' the hereditary guardians of the Kaaba. The Black Stone enshrined in the Kaaba at Mecca...was a feminine symbol, no one seems to know exactly what it is supposed to represent today."11

By the year 75 B.C.E., the Sabaeans were followed by another powerful Black empire, the Himyarites. The Himyarites, like the two dynasties that preceded them, established their empire in Yemen, the southern cradle of Arabia. Al-Harith, the first Himyarite monarch, built powerful trade alliances and a military gauntlet which fortified his position and allowed the Himyarites to reign supreme for six-hundred years. During this time, Himyaritic kings in

Yemen extended their dominance over all of Central Arabia, or Nejed, and into Persia.

In the year 24 B.C.E., Rome became politically exacerbated by the power of the Himyarites and launched a substantial campaign under the command of Aelius Gallus to conquer Yemen. However, they had not taken into consideration distance, climate nor terrain. By the time the Roman legion reached Yemen, the soldiers were dying of thirst, exhaustion, hunger and overexposure to the sun and heat. The Roman campaign was a fiasco and most of the soldiers were slaughtered. The remaining survivors were sent back as a warning to Rome.

A catastrophic event, in the year 120 C.E., transformed the entire cultural pulse of Yemen. Life in Yemen had been sustained by an elaborate agricultural irrigation system that was maintained by an ingeniously constructed dam built during Sabaean rule. In 120 C.E., this dam, which had fallen into a state of disrepair, collapsed and caused a tremendous flood—The Flood of Arem— which forced many prominent Yemen families, including the Beni Ghassan and the Lakm, or Lakhmids, to uproot and relocate to the north. Thus, the Himyarite king Asad abu Qarib (200–236 C.E.) extended his reign to include all of Arabia up to the Euphrates. These dynasties ruled for three-hundred years.

The Beni Ghassan erected a powerful dynasty in eastern Syria while the Lakhmids established themselves on the Euphrates in Persia, with Hira as their capital city. These Black dynasties were formidable political and military forces in the north and, indeed, often engaged each other in battle. But both of these dynasties, which had reigned over their respective regions for more than three-hundred years, crumbled in 636 C.E., under the onslaught of the Moslems.

Returning to the chronology of Black dynasties in Yemen, the sixth century began with Dhu Nuwas on the throne. Passionately anti-Christian, he was infuriated that a monk had introduced Christianity to Najran, an area just north of Yemen. Acting on his rage, he ordered an enormous trench dug and filled with branches and other flammable materials, in which the Christians of Najran were thrown and burned alive. Some Christians managed to flee to Constantinople where they appealed to the Byzantine Emperor Justin I. Unwilling to commit his own troops to what would surely be a devastating military defeat, Justin urged the Christian Emperor of Abyssinia to avenge the death of these Christian martyrs. Thus arose the next Black dynasty in Yemen, the Abyssinians.

The Abyssinians marched on Yemen in the year 525 C.E., and with the death of Dhu Nuwas, brought to a close the Himyarite chapter of Arabian history.

Yemen remained under Abyssinian rule for more than fifty years, mostly under the direction of Abraha, who governed from 537 to 570 C.E. The following passage is testimony to their legacy:

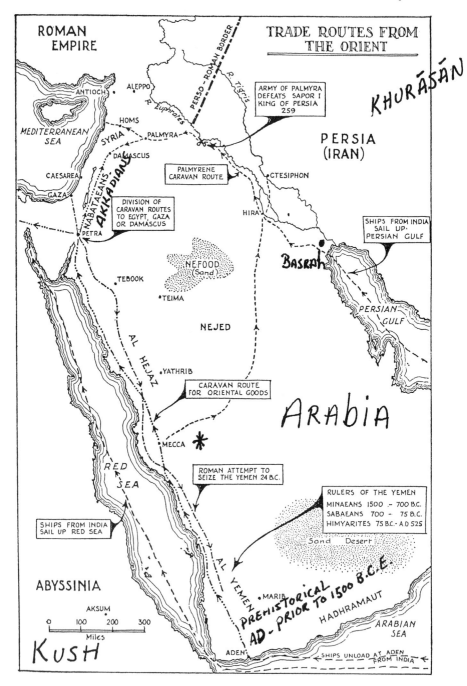

Figure 2. Map of Arabia depicting areas of importance. (courtesy of Wayne B. Chandler)

We possessed the lands from Ethiopia to Mecca, and our rule extended over all that was there. We put Dhu Nuwas to flight, and we killed
the chiefs of Humayr, yet you have never possessed our lands....From
your ignorance you considered us as belonging to you as you considered
your women in the Period of Ignorance. When the justice of Islam came,
you saw this was an evil attitude; yet we have no desire to desert you. We
have filled the country amply through marriage, chieftainship and
lordship....You have made examples of us and have exalted the rule of
our kings, preferring them in many cases over your own kings. If you had
not seen us as preferential over you, you would not have done this.[12]

Through commerce and marriage a constant alliance was maintained between southern Arabian Black empires and the African empire of Ethiopia, or
Kush. After seeing these southern Arabian monarchs grow in wealth and
power, many West Asian rulers began to use matrimony to gain access to the
southern Arabian kingdoms and the prosperity and resources therein. According to ancient literature, these Black kings of southern Arabia preferred to
marry within their own race and chose Ethiopian Kentakes or queens on
numerous occasions. The *Book of the Glory of the Black Race* confirms these
facts: "...the most desirable women to the people of Basra are Indians, Hindu
girls, and those of the valleys. The most desirable women to the people of
Yemen are Ethiopians and Ethiopian girls....It is said the most pleasant of
mouths in fragrance, the strongest in sweetness, and the most wet are the
mouths of these blacks."[13]

By the year 574 C.E., the power and influence of the Abyssinians in Yemen
had begun to wane, and there was widespread social unrest among the
Yemenites. A prince of the deposed Himyarite royal family journeyed to
Persia from Yemen to beg for the Lakhmid's assistance in unseating the
Abyssinian dynasty. The Lakhmid ruler, in cooperation with the King of
Persia, sent troops to Yemen. The Abyssinians refused to retreat and, thus,
began a twenty-year period of war and anarchy. Inevitably, the Persian troops
married locally and were absorbed into the Black Yemenite population, the
final effusion of a kingdom whose influence had spanned over two and a half
millennia, and that was acclaimed as one of the greatest empires of all time.
Yemen never reclaimed its former glory; it remained in a state of perpetual
chaos until its annexation by the Moslems in the year 633 C.E.

So it was, that in the south of the Arabian peninsula there flourished an
ancient civilization which gave birth to magnificent and opulent kingdoms,
legendary even in their own era. Unfortunately, this high quality of life and
level of excellence was not standard in other parts of Arabia. North of Yemen
is the Arabia Deserta, a sterile territory void of the elements necessary for a
highly developed civilization. This sandy, rocky, barren wasteland receives
very little rainfall and would seem uninhabitable yet it is here, from the
earliest periods of north Arabian history, that we find the Semitic Arab.

Born from a geographical melting pot of several different races—labeled

the zone of confluence by Cheikh Anta Diop—the Semitic Arab descends
from Heber of the race of Shem, from whom also descends the line of
Abraham. Biblical history records that Joktan, a son of Abraham, was the first
king of the original homeland of the Semitic Arab, an area that, according to
Herodotus, was located between Colchis and the Medes.

At this point in history, 800 B.C.E., the Semitic Arabs were a veritable
mixture of Black, descended of Africa; White, from the Caucasian extraction,
not Indo-European; and Asiatic races. Their skin hue earned them the appellation "the Red Race." Keeping in line with Cheikh Anta Diop's racial and
ethnic categories of this era, the Semitic presence is that of the Jews and
Arabs, whose traditions identify Yemen as a colony of Kush. In our current
period this term is only indicative of a large family of languages which
include Blacks, as well as Whites.[14] Some suggest that the word Semitic is
derived from the word semi, meaning half or part. Regardless, they lived a
pastoral, nomadic existence in tents, void of cities, abhorring agriculture and
the discipline that characterized civilized life. Because of their arid environment, they were constantly involved in tribal warfare over water and other
scarce resources. Their extreme destitution made them plunder and ravage the
caravans that passed through the land. Although the Semitic Arabs were
fierce fighters—hundreds were maimed and killed in the many bloody battles
they waged among themselves—they were ignorant of the strategies of advanced combat, and would throw themselves upon the sword of their enemies.
Thus, the coining of the phrase: "Ye shall live by the sword and die by the
sword." The Semitic Arabs earned the reputation of being treacherous, un-
trustworthy, and violent. They were also known to be illiterate and ignorant of
cultural refinement.

The relationship between the Semites and the Yemenites went through
several stages of evolution over a period of several centuries. There was
constant tension between these Semitic hordes of the north and the Blacks in
the south. Their geographical and cultural deprivation caused the Semites to
make continual attempts to encroach on the more fertile areas controlled by
the Yemenites. The Semitic Arabs labored under the belief that it was their
curse to be deprived of the wealth of the earth and that they must, at any cost,
struggle to regain their worldly inheritance. The movement of Blacks northward from Yemen, after the devastating Flood of Arem, added pressure to an
already strained relationship between Semitic (Red) and Black Arabs.

Gradually many of the Semitic Arabs were compelled to surrender to the
wisdom and cultural superiority of their Black neighbors and were forced to
adhere to Yemenite law and adopt Yemenite language and custom. Some
subversive factions chafed under foreign rule and were a source of social
unrest and upheaval. In time though, a portion of the Semites became an
integral part of the cultural fabric of this mixed Arab society. The gradual
amalgamation of these Red Arabs with the original Black Arabs produced a

Figure 3. Native fisherman of Yemen (courtesy of Wayne B. Chandler)

Figure 4. Ancient city of Marib in Yemen, South Arabia, built by the female dominated culture of the Sabeans. Dated 700 B.C.E. (courtesy of Wayne B. Chandler)

more culturally refined and civilized Semite. This physiognomical blending also resulted in the development of a darker-skinned Semite with a slender yet muscular build. Uthman Amr Ibn Bahr Al-Jahiz, renowned Islamic historian, theologian and prose writer, recorded the following commentary, in 860 C.E., on this race-mixing: "When they mixed with our groups, they were said to be tan and brownish-black...and their name was derived from ours, at a time when we were the only ones to be called Blacks. They [the Semites] must not be called Black unless they are from us."[15]

The debut of this dark Semite on the Arabian stage caused a change in attitude toward the Blacks who had led them from the darkness of barbarism into the light of civilization. Such is the testimony of the historians in antiquity: "The Semitic Arabs take pride in blackness of color....They say, 'Black is always more striking indeed; 'when the Arabs describe their camels they say, 'Red-brown and fast, but red is plentiful and black is beautiful'....The most noble of spices are musk and ambergris—and they are black...and nothing can overcome the black lion. There is no date sweeter than the black date and none more widely used or lasting over time."[16] This new perspective on black was not held by all Semitic Arab tribes and families; many chose to remain in cultural stagnation—to live and die by the sword. This group of Semites continued to look upon the Arabian Blacks with disdain and malice.

The next change in the relations between the Arabian Blacks and the Red Semites was a result of another pivotal population shift. Black families in the north began to return to their ancestral homes in Yemen and the balance of power rotated again from north to south. The northern Black fortifications were weakened and, eventually, the Semites gained control in the early sixth century and, putting into practice what they had learned from the Yemenites, established the first Semitic hierarchy in Arabia's northern plateau.

This historical period also saw a development that proved to be a cultural metamorphosis for Arabia and that would eventually change the face of the world. From within the womb of the Black Arabian south was born another monarchy, the Koreysh, from the family of Hagar, which was related to the Adites and Mineaens and also was descended from Ham, the Father of the Black race. This is substantiated by tracing the origin of Hagar. The Bible states that to Hagar was born a son called Ishmael who became known as the Father of the Arabs. The families that identified with him called themselves Ishmaelites. From this group arose the tribe of Koreysh, which claimed direct descendence from Ishmael and, therefore, from Hagar. In the King James version of the Christian Bible, Hagar is a slave woman from Egypt. This differs greatly from the role she played in the Quran. Hagar is more than a name; it is a title derived from the Egyptian name Hag, or Heg, a pre-dynastic matriarchal ruler and holy woman of either ancient Kush or Egypt, who spoke the words of hekau, or words of power. Later, this queen's name was used to identify any wise woman or high priestess. "Hag" and "wise, holy woman"

became synonyms.[17] So the biblical portrait of Hagar is completely incongruous with the character her name indicates. A woman bearing that name would
surely be one of substantial power and influence, but oddly enough, she is cast
in the Bible as a helpless, hapless slave girl. Whatever her true identity,
Hagar's importance to history and to this story is undisputed. From the blood
of Hagar, the tribe of Koreysh produced a personality that would unite all of
Arabia and conquer the civilized world. He would be named Abu al-Qasim
Muxammad ibn Abd Allah ibn Abd al-Muttalib ibn Hashim; those who
answered his call would know him as the great warrior of God and would
address him as the Prophet Muhammad, and his sword would be the religion
of Islam.

The Koreysh were several centuries old by 400 C.E., because by that year
they had thirty-six clans established throughout the Arabian peninsula. An
excerpt from one of the oldest documents of Arabian genealogy not only
validates the great age of the Koreysh but relates them to the oldest Black race
in Arabia: "Know, O reader! The great stock of 'Adnan [Aden-Ad], from
which issued the Beni Khandaf, and from these the Beni Koreyash, and from
these latter the Beni Hashim...."[18] This powerful utterance points to a southern Arabian origin for the Koreysh and grants them descendence from the
Black Adites as well.

All of the chronicles that survive intact agree that Ishmael and Muhammad
were of the Black race. Besides Ishmael being the son of Hagar, an Ethiopian,
there is conclusive documentation of his relationship with the Kushites, or
Ethiopians, of that period. Historical annals state that Hagar arranged a
marriage for her son Ishmael to an Egyptian woman. This fact is corroborated
by the Christian Bible in Genesis 21:21: "And Ishmael dwelt in the wilderness
of Paran; and his mother took him a wife out of the land of Egypt."[19] This
marriage produced twelve sons, all Black and, according to the Bible, all
princes of their respective nations.

The most stunning evidence of the race of Ishmael is the rock carving of his
face found near Medina in Arabia. The carving is a colossal head with
powerful Africoid features. Dr. Khalid Abdullah Tariq Al-Mansour, an Islamic historian and author of thirteen books, states that documents and
testimonies of regional Saudi Arabian historians conclusively affirm that this
carving represents the Africoid visage of Ishmael, the Father of the Arabs. A
careful examination of history reveals that the Prophet Muhammad, like
Ishmael, was of the Black race and was black in complexion. D.S. Margoliouth
uncovered an ancient text which sketches a verbal portrait of the Prophet as
"large mouthed, and bluish colored, with hair that was neither straight nor
curly, that is, hair that was probably frizzy, like that of the Fuzzy-Wuzzy."[20]
Many of Islam's more celebrated historians, both ancient and contemporary,
confirm this image.

Information on Muhammad's immediate family gives us the most clear

Figure 5. Youth of Southern Arabia (Yemen). (Photo Runoko Rashidi)

Figure 6. Woman of Yemen (courtesy of Wayne B. Chandler)

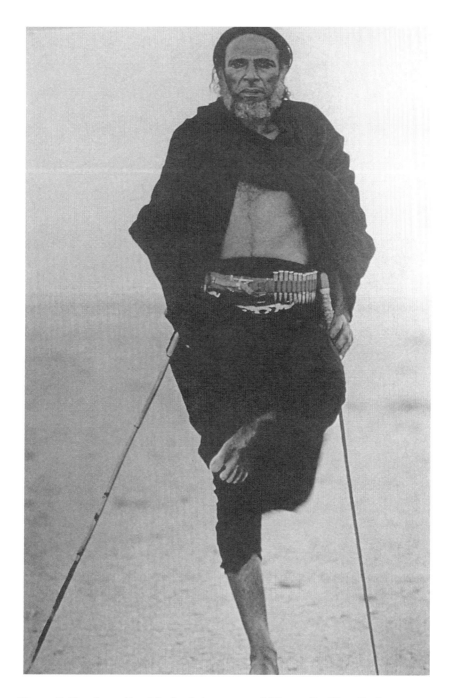

Figure 7. Northern Semitic Arab (courtesy of Wayne B. Chandler)

Figure 8. Semitic Arab woman of the northern tribes (courtesy of Wayne B. Chandler)

evidence of his race and color. Indeed, Muhammad, by his very words, identifies his race. In his appeal to the Blacks of Arabia he called himself an "Arab of the Arabs, of the purest blood of your land, of the family of the Hashim and of the tribe of Qurysh."[21] In professing to be of the "purest blood" of Arabia, he refers to its Black population as the only "pure" and indigenous inhabitants of the peninsula. Muhammad identifies his tribe as the Koreysh, and his family as Hashim, a name which appears in the Prophet's family lineage, for it was the title of his great-grandfather. The Hashim, though not prosperous, was an old and noble southern Arabian family. Al-Jahiz noted in 860 C.E.: "Abd Al-Muttalib fathered ten lords, black as the night and magnificent....Abd Allah Ibn Abbas was blackest in magnificence, and the family of Abu Talib were the most noble of men; and they were black with black skin."[22] Abd Al-Muttalib was Muhammad's grandfather. One of those ten sons was Abdullah, Muhammad's father; another was Abu Talib, Muhammad's uncle.

The Black Koreysh, the tribe in which Muhammad was born, claimed descendence from the lineage of Ishmael. The Koreysh are also identified as being "intimately connected with the southern Cushite tribes that were the originators of the idol worship of the Kaaba at Mecca."[23] The lineage of the Koreysh—the tribe of Muhammad—is a very complex genealogical tree that encompasses many influential Black families of Arabia, some families of the Black Himyarites, and many Semitic ones also.

The Koreysh were an offshoot of a larger family, the Kinana, one of the earlier southern dynasties who resided just north of Yemen. Muhammad's family influence extended throughout Yemen; his grandfather, Abdul Muttalib, was a governor of Yemen.[24] Early in the history of their tribe, a great schism created two major divisions, one of which is known as the lateral branch of the family tree. This group mixed with the Semitic Arabs in the north to create the family of Abid Shems, from which descended the Harb, the Abu Sofian, the Muawiya and the most dominant Semitic family, the Ummayyah. Even though these families had initially renounced their tribal name, their descendence from the Koreysh is verified in the genealogical chronology of the Umaiya or Umeyyah: "As to the last-mentioned family Beni Umeyyah, it gave several Khalifs to Andalus [Spain]....According to Ibnu Sa'id, they were still known in his days under the patronymic of Korashi; for, although they at first called themselves Umawi, from their progenitor Umeyyah, they afterwards changed their patronymic into that of Korashi, from Koraysh, the lateral branch of their parent stock."[25]

According to the family tree, the Hashim consist of Abdul Muttalib, whose son Abdullah is Muhammad's father; Abu Talib, Muhammad's uncle; Al Harith, a Himyarite; Talib; and Jaafar, whose family left Arabia and established themselves in Abyssinia. On the Semitic branch are Abu Lahab, who married a Semitic Arab of Abu Soifan and renounced the name Hashim to

Figure 9. Giant stone head believed to be the visage of Ishmael. (Photo Al-Mansour)

embrace the Semitic clan Umeyya; Zubair; Abdullah, the Prophet's father, who also married a Semitic Arab, Amina, of the Beni Zorah clan descended from Abid Shems and, thus, straddles both sides of the family tree; Hazma; and Abbas, the founder of the mighty Black Abbasid Empire.

Early in the history of the Black families of Koryesh (ca. 400 C.E.) is a character of substantial notoriety. His name was Qusai and it was because of his prior lineage that the Black Koreysh became the ancestral guardians of the Sacred Black Stone of the Kaaba and the most powerful tribe in their valley homeland, that included Mecca. "Qusai was a man of remarkable character and intelligence. He persuaded Quarish to build houses, grouped around the Kaaba....It appears, however, that only the more important clans, or those related to Qusai, built houses around the Kaaba. The others lived further away, still doubtless in tents, while some remained nomadic in the desert."[26] Undoubtedly, it was the Black Arabian families that lived close to the Kaaba, and the Red Semites who were ostracized. This seems to be the cause of the separation within the Koreysh which caused great resentment and malignity between the Black Koreysh and the Semites, who would later become the powerful Umeyyah.

Some Islamic historians state that although Muhammad was Black, he was the lightest in complexion of all the prophets. His father Abdullah, married Amina, a Semitic woman of the clan of Beni Zohrah, who became the Prophet's biological mother. That her clan was Semitic is verified by a short perspicacious sentence from *The Dynastic Chronology of the Arabs*: "There was another family...who pretended to draw their origin form Umeyya, son of Abu Shems; we mean the Beni Zorah...."[27] Born of a pure Black father and a Semitic (racially mixed) mother, Muhammad would no doubt be classified Black by the contemporary American standard. (The global White minority— via its anthropologists, politicians and sociologists—informs the African American that if any one of his sixteen great-great-grandparents was Black, then he is, without a doubt, Black.) Actually Muhammad's two-thirds Black ancestry represents a greater ratio than that of most American Blacks, who are generally a composite of Black African, Native American, and White.

Muhammad's very early years were spent with his mother. After her death, he was raised in the desert by his mother's family, a pastoral Semitic tribe. He then lived from age eight to twenty-five with his father's brother, Abu Talib, who then persuaded him to marry Khadijah, with whom he lived for twenty-four years, until her death, in a marriage absent of the polygamous standard that would later characterize Islam. Muhammad's strong belief in a Black/Semitic alliance, a central theme of Islam which was never well-received by either group, may have been a result of his exposure to these two different worlds. Muhammad always strove to mend this age old animosity: "I was sent to the Reds and to the Blacks."[28] He reminded his followers of both races: "Know that every Moslem is a brother to every other Moslem."[29] Though his foresight was one of universality, his life story reveals that his preference and commitment was to the group that bore him spiritual, cultural and religious fortitude—the Black race.

At the age of forty, Muhammad experienced an event that would consume the remainder of his life. By his own accounts, God appeared to Muhammad to anoint him as His messenger—His prophet. Muhammad began to work in Mecca, discouraging the customary worship of idols housed in the Kaaba and urging a return to the monotheism of Abraham, the father of Ishmael. The general population of Mecca was alarmed at Muhammad's behavior and soon agreed that he was a madman and should be eliminated. Even though Muhammad's following was steadily increasing, it was no match for the ruling majority of Mecca. Word of the threats on his life reached Medina, which issued an invitation of sanctuary to Muhammad. Muhammad fled Mecca on September 20, 622 C.E., and remained in exile for seven years, amassing a formidable army of converts sworn to execute his every command. In 629 C.E., Muhammad, sword in hand, returned to Mecca and conquered it. Meccans were allowed to continue to worship the mystical Kaaba, on the condition that they accept Islam. Thus began Muhammad's quest to unify all of Arabia under the banner of Islam.

Muhammad was aided in his mission by an impressive roster of advisors and warriors, all of Black African descent. There was the great general, Ali, son of Muhammad's uncle, Abu Talib, born into a family historically described by Jahiz as "black-skinned." Bilal-i-Habesh and Zayd bin Harith are two other Black men who are legendary in the Islamic chronicles. Bilal, Muhammad's first convert, achieved the positions of Imam (High Priest), treasurer and confidant. It was he who first uttered the azan, or call to prayer. Muhammad considered Bilal his closest friend and claimed that he would take precedence over the Prophet in paradise. Al-Jahiz states that Islam acknowledges Bilal as being responsible for one-third of the religion's influence and, after Muhammad's death, Bilal was offered the throne, which he declined.[30] Zayd was Muhammad's adopted son and his greatest general and strategist. On a visit to Zayd's home one afternoon, Muhammad caught sight of Zainab, renowned as the most beautiful woman in Islam. Muhammad was hopelessly smitten with this enchanting beauty, who happened to be Zayd's wife. When Zayd discovered Muhammad's infatuation, he dutifully presented his wife to the Prophet, who accepted her as his wife.

In the course of his life, Muhammad married thirteen women, but he was not an advocate of promiscuity. After his calling to Islam, he never even touched the hand of a woman who was not his wife. In his words, "I like women and perfume better than anything else, but the apple of my eye is prayer."[31] The women most intimately involved in Muhammad's life, according to Islamic historical records, were Black women. Khadijah, the Prophet's first wife, was a Black matriarch, born and raised in Mecca when the city was

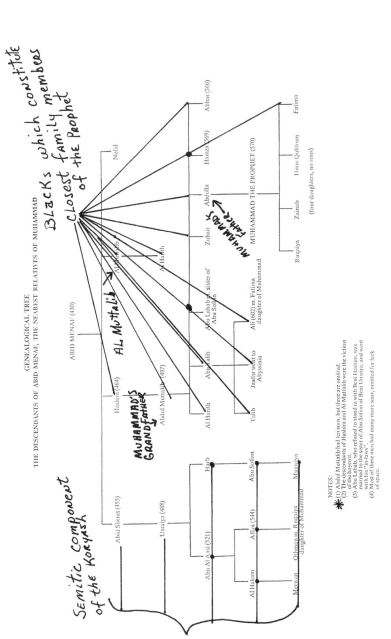

Figure 10. Genealogy tree showing the various branches of the Koreysh.

under Koreysh rule. She was an interesting figure, an heir of the ancient pre-Islamic Arabian tradition of female independence and reverence. "This illustrates the position occupied by women in pre-Islamic Arabia. Khadijah was an independent woman operating her own business; and she, not her future husband, suggested the marriage."[32] Zainab, the former wife of Zayd, was also Black, as was Aisha bint abi Bekr, with whom he is described as having the closest relationship, and Malmoona bint al Harith, the sister-in-law of his uncle Abbas, who married Muhammad in 629 C.E., on the occasion of his pilgrimage to Mecca.

The Islamic texts tell a touching story of Muhammad that involves a Black woman named Umm Habiba, or Ramala. Habiba had been taken by her husband, Ubayd Allah, to Ethiopia which was then completely immersed in Christianity, where the religion made one of its earliest appearances. In Ethiopia, Ubayd renounced Islam and announced his conversion to Christianity. Muhammad greeted this news with great disappointment and contacted the Negus, divine ruler and Christian sovereign of Ethiopia, to ask that Habiba be returned to Arabia. The Negus dissolved Habiba's marriage and allowed her safe passage, with his blessings, back to Arabia where she and the Prophet were wed.[33]

The Negus and the Prophet had an interesting relationship. Though their religious convictions differed, Muhammad had a great deal of respect, admiration and even love for the Ethiopian king. According to Islamic verse, "It was the Negus who arranged the marriage between Umm Habiba...and the Prophet. The Prophet (Blessings of God and salvation be upon him) never prayed for anyone's soul except at a funeral or over a grave—except in the case of the Negus, for whom he prayed at Medina, while the grave of the Negus was in Ethiopia."[34]

The Prophet's personal life followed an orderly pattern. There was dismay concerning the subject of Islam's military might. Muhammad was in need of soldiers to fill his ranks so he looked north. The Semitic Arabs in the north were told that, by accepting Islam, they would be guaranteed a place in eternal paradise filled with beautiful women and shady fruit trees, but what really attracted the north Arabian Semites to join Muhammad's legions was his promise of the spoils of their plunder. From Arabia Deserta and even further north, wild nomadic hordes flocked to the Prophet, bringing their own battle armaments, ready to smite all who stood in their way.

Muhammad was dismayed by the lack of organizational and battle skills of the primitive Semites. He knew that in order to launch his jihad (holy war), he would have to enlist the aid of the great Blacks who had laid the cornerstone of culture and civilization in Arabia. They were master warriors and invaluable to Muhammad's holy quest. Labid wrote: "...when they advanced with their spears, lances, bows, swords, flags, horses and elephants, their black color and incredible strength, you would be seized by a terror the likes of which you have never seen, heard, nor imagined."[35] So the Prophet looked to the kingdom of Yemen in south Arabian to properly consecrate this holy crusade.

He wrote to the Yemenite king, al-Harith, requesting that he and his entire kingdom submit to Islam and join him in the jihads. When he arrived in the capital city of Yemen, Muhammad's messenger was escorted directly to the palace where he presented al-Harith with the Prophet's missive. Al-Harith read the letter intently and, acting on his ministers' advice, flatly rejected Muhammad's offer. Yemen's refusal weighed heavily on Muhammad's mind, as he regretted the one recourse left for him—war!

In the war on Yemen, the Moslem legions were led by the great Ali, a cousin of Muhammad and heir to the royal house of Abu Talib. Ali was heralded as the quintessential warrior, having never seen defeat in the many battles he fought to disseminate the message of Islam. In the *Book of Battles*, the Moors' compilation of the holy wars, Ali's defeats of all his adversaries are recounted in great detail. The battle of Hunayn, 630 C.E., the battle of Asyad and Mecca, in 629 C.E., and the battle of Muhalhil, date unknown, are some of the encounters that elevated Ali to legendary status. Ali once described himself: "I am the killer of millions with license from my Lord…and I am the hero and shedder of blood of the unbelievers.…I am the knight of knights."[36]

The Moslems and the Yemenites clashed and waged a bloody war, yet even after several days and scores of lives lost, neither side succumbed. Muhammad found himself in need of an alternative plan. He had already lost many of his best warriors at the hands of these southern Arabian Blacks and was not willing to sacrifice more. Muhammad ordered Ali to personally join in the battle to expedite victory. Ali learned that among the ranks of the Yemenite forces was a formidable opponent, Amr, who, like Ali, had never been defeated in battle. Amr was also described as the ultimate warrior, "black as cinnabar." Amr had already bested Ali's greatest fighters in hand-to-hand combat, boasting, "I am the one who gives falls. I am decimator of squadrons, victor over champions, ejector of knights to the ground, and the lion of Banu Ghalib."[37]

The next time the two armies faced off for battle, Ali stepped forward and issued a personal challenge to Amr. Amr accepted the invitation and their respective ranks braced themselves for the clash. Both men fought valiantly. At dawn the next day, the combatants respectfully inquired about each other's wounds. Ali suggested that Amr end the duel by making the confession of faith into Islam. Amr indignantly refused and the battle continued for three days. On the morning of the fourth day, Amr's extreme fatigue cost him his advantage. Ali was able to subdue and capture him, admitting that "Amr was the strongest champion he had ever met."[38]

Amr was brought to Mecca to face Muhammad, who demanded that Amr submit to Allah. Once more Amr refused to be threatened into making the confession of faith and the Prophet ordered his decapitation. Because of his great respect for Amr, Muhammad rescinded the order and set him free. Later Amr returned to Mecca and asked whether it was Muhammad or God who had spared his life. Muhammad replied that he had, with God's will. This response pleased Amr and convinced him to make the conversion to Islam. With Amr's power and influence, Muhammad eventually persuaded king al-Harith and the people of Yemen to embrace the faith. Thus, having achieved the unification of Arabia—south and north, Black and Semite—Muhammad prepared to spread the word of Allah to the rest of the world, Quran in one hand and sword in the other.

Three years after he conquered Mecca, Muhammad died in 632 C.E. Before his demise, he saw the fulfillment of his dream; Arabia unified under Islam. With this new and productive cohesiveness, Arabia experienced an unparalleled rate of continental maturity that manifested itself in politics, economics and religion. For a time, Arabia rejoiced in the harmony bequeathed to her by Muhammad and Islam, but a dark cloud of enmity was seething and taking form in the very heart of the country.

Unfortunately, the Prophet had died without naming a successor or establishing a line of succession. This issue created schisms and factions in Islam that remain to this day. Age-old animosity and malice resurfaced between the Arabian Blacks of the south and the Semitic Arabs of the north. Because the Blacks could trace their ancestral lineage back to Ishmael and Kush, they deemed themselves the true Arabians with natural rights to dominion of the land. To these Blacks, the northern Semites still appeared uncivilized, impure, and unworthy of religious, political and social position in Arabia.

Blacks and Semites began to interpret the words of the Prophet in different ways. The following is a Yemenite interpretation of Muhammad's message: "The Prophet (Blessings of God and salvation be upon him) said, 'I was sent to the Reds and to the Blacks.'...we were neither Red nor White to him. Therefore he was sent to us. He was indeed sent to us because of his statement 'the Blacks.' If the Arabs [Semites] are Red, then they are included among...the Romans and the Slavs, Persians and Khurasanis...the Prophet considered the Arabs and us as equals; (Muhammad said, 'Know that every Moslem is a brother to every other Moslem') however, we Blacks are preferable to them. If the name 'Black' characterizes us, then we alone are the pure Blacks, and the Arabs [Semites] only approximate our purity. We were, therefore, the first to be called to Islam..."[39] Because of their racial and tribal affiliation with Muhammad, Yemenite Blacks in the south began to identify themselves as Ishmaelites, or Shi'ites. From within the very bosom of this movement, the mighty Abbasid empire was born and nurtured.

The House of Mudar, that bred the Semitic or northern Arab, began to retaliate against the various denigrating assaults launched by the Abbasids.

Figure 11. Arabs traveling across the Arabian desert reminiscent of the Jihads of the Umayyad. Painted by Jean-Leon Gerome

Figure 12. An interesting mixture of Black Arabian women in the early 1800s traveling across the South Arabian terrain. (Photo courtesy of Wayne B. Chandler.)

Arabia was torn asunder by territorial, racial and religious dissension. Civil war seemed imminent between the southern Shi'ites and the northern Semitic Moslems. The appointment of Abu Bekr as caliph, or ruler, of Mecca (ca. 635 C.E.) deepened the rift. The Shi'ites were opposed to this appointment because they believed that succession to the caliphate should be hereditary, within the lineage of Muhammad. They felt that the rightful heir to the throne was Muhammad's cousin Ali Talib, rather than Abu Bekr who, as Muhammad's father-in-law, was not related by blood to the Prophet. The Semites in the north were naturally opposed to hereditary succession since they had no blood lines that would connect them with the lineage of the Prophet. For the Semites, succession by election would be the only way to guarantee political leverage for themselves. It was this fight for power that created the Sunni Moslem.[40]

In his first action as caliph, Abu Bekr called upon all Moslems to take up arms in the spread of Islam. This could very well have been a diversionary measure by Abu Bekr since he was faced with the prospect of civil war and the possibility of being deposed. Whether or not it was a political move, this call to arms resulted in one of the most epic conquests in all of history.

Like a spring flower pregnant with the prospect of new life, Arabia also flowered anew, pregnant with the Word of Allah. Her legions of God burst forth from the boundaries of the Arabian peninsula and, like a well-spring, overflowed the territories of Syria, Palestine, Persia, Egypt, Tripoli and Tunis, flooding North Africa with the teachings of Islam.

Back in Arabia, the Semitic families of the Umayyad were ruling northern Arabia, Syria and Persia, and the mighty Black Abbasid empire was ruling southern Arabia and Khurasan. Tensions were high between the two groups. The Abbasid empire had been inaugurated by al-Abbas ibn Abd al-Muttalib (566–653 C.E.), an uncle of Muhammad from the family of Hashim. The Abbasid state was a Black nationalist movement. The color black was the political symbol of the Abbasids and they were known by their black hoods and headgear, and by their black flag.

In 656 C.E., Ali, the Prophet's cousin, was elected caliph but Mu'awiyah Ibn Abi Sufyan, the Semitic governor of Syria, refused to acknowledge him, sparking five years of civil war between Blacks and Semites. Ali and the Abbasids launched a series of campaigns throughout Arabia to effect the ejection of the Syrian caliph, who himself had assembled quite a formidable legion. To head his Semitic army against the Abbasids, Mu'awiyah had nominated an outstanding and undefeated Black general named Musa Nosseyr. Musa refused the offer and, when confronted by the Caliph about his reasons, flatly stated: "It is not in my power to assist thee against one to whom I am more indebted than to thee."[41] Mu'awiyah was angry and confused, unable to comprehend the depth of Musa's loyalty to his race.

The Umayyads continued their assault on the family of Muhammad, which was ruling southern Arabia. In 661 C.E., the Umayyads assassinated Ali and, later, his son Husayn, and crucified and impaled both Zayd and his son Yahya. All of these men were heirs to the seat of caliph.[42] The reaction in the caliphate was overwhelming. According to Masudi, one of the greatest Islamic historians of all time, "the Khurasanites kept mourning for seven days for Yahya ibn Zayd in all the regions of Khurasan...and every male child born in Khurasan in that year was named Yahya or Zayd by reason of the grief which descended upon [them]."[43] Having neutralized the threat posed by the Alid and Abbasid families, Mu'awiyah established the Umayyad Dynasty which, for ninety years, ruled all of the Moslem world, except southern Arabia.

The Umayyads continued to be aggressively and violently antagonistic toward the Abbasids, besieging Mecca and burning the Kaaba in 683 C.E. Under this pressure, the Abbasids became incredibly cohesive and consolidated. Moshe Sharon, one of the world's foremost scholars of the Abbasid period of Islamic history, points out, "The identification of the Umayyads as the murderers of the Prophet's family supplied a kind of general Islamic legitimacy for rebelling against them."[44] From Khurasan Al Abbas—a descendant of Muhammad's uncle Abbas—launched an intricate propaganda campaign to convince the rest of the Moslem world that the Umayyads were undeserving of the caliphate and, in fact, were not even following the words of the Prophet. His accusations were grounded in truth—Kumayt Ibn Zayd, a poet contemporary to these times, lamented that the Umayyad caliphs were not swearing allegiance to the Prophet, but rather to themselves.[45] The Abbasids saw themselves as the only champions of the true Islam, as well as the rightful heirs of the Prophet. Ali himself had fueled this war between the Umayyad and Abbasid dynasties with these words: "When thou comest to Marw, dwell in the midst of the tribes of Yaman [Yemen], draw near unto Rabiah [Abbasids] and beware of Mudar [Umayyads]."[46] The Abbasid mission was quite zealous, taking on a messianic nature. According to Abbasid tradition, Muhammad Ibn Ali stated, "The first of my sons will be Ibn al-Harithiyyah and after him they will succeed one another...and from amongst them will be the mahdi [messiah] who will fill the earth with justice, just as it is now full of evil."[47]

By 711 C.E., the Umayyad had taken control of northern Africa and a Black Yemenite named Musa Nosseyr was governor. That Musa was Black and from Yemen is documented in the chronicles of southern Arabian dynastic genealogy. "Arabs of Yemen—Hostile to Beni Mudhar [northern Semitic Arabs]—Khaulan—Ma'afer—*Lakhm*...."[48] Of the various families that arose in the land of Yemen, the clan of Lakhm was held in high esteem. This family produced many great warriors and leaders who became even greater legends. With respect to Musa, in extracts from *The History of the Mohammedan Dynasties in Spain,* written in 1840 by Ahmed Ibn Mohammed AL-Makkari, we find that, "Musa was born...January A.D. 640, and died September A.D.

Figure 13. Bust of Black Arab of old Arabia. 9th century C.E.—during Abbasid period. (Photo courtesy of Wayne B. Chandler.)

715. He was sixty years old when he took possession of the government of Africa...his surname was Abu Abdi-r-rahman. Ibn Khallekan, following Al-homaydi and other ancient historians calls him Musa, son of Nosseyr, of the tribe of Lakhm...and the conqueror of Andalus [Spain]."[49]

In February, 710 C.E., Musa received an invitation from Count Julian to convene at his fortress in Ceuta, on the northern tip of Morocco. Julian had been an ally to King Roderick of Spain and the guardian of the straits which protected Spain from attack. Having successfully fought off all assaults by Musa, he now, for personal reasons switched his allegiance to the very man he had despised only months before. Julian supplied Musa with ships to navigate the straits, as well as details of Roderick's defensive strategies.

Musa, along with two Black Ethiopian generals named Tarif and Tarik, invaded Spain on July 18, 710 C.E., and April 30, 711 C.E. Musa and his Arabian knights now stood upon two continents, Africa and Europe.

Musa passed in 715 C.E., and was succeeded by his brother Suleyman. The Arabian chronicles state that Suleyman died in the bud of his youth; his reign characterized by personal and political upheavals. The Umayyads continued their aggression toward the Abbasids, feeling themselves empowered and secure.

In the year 750, the Abbasids arose from their southern domain and, like an invincible war machine with an unquenchable thirst for vengeance, unseated the Umayyad Dynasty and conquered all of Arabia.

George Wells Parker, an historian writing at the beginning of the twentieth century, summarizes the story of the rise of the Abbasids and their impact on the Moslem world:

The Yemenites...were a Black race akin to the Ethiopians, and between the northern and the southern Arabians there broke out a hatred which they carried to the farthest ends of the world. Early in their national history, two great dynasties [arose]...the House of Mudar and the House of Rabia. They became the Umayyads, or northern Arabians, and the Abbasids, or southern Arabians. The Abbasids were the Black Arabs and their symbol throughout their national existence was a black banner. In early Arabian history the seat of the Umayyad dynasty was at Damascus and for a long period they ruled the whole of northern Arabia unmolested, while the Abbasids ruled the south. But suddenly the Blacks rose, overthrew the Umayyad dynasty, the great Persian empire of the Sasanians, and defeated the Roman legions of the Lower Empire. One burst of enthusiasm, it was but a flash, and these black-skinned warriors went forth to conquer the world. The result of this human convulsion was the total destruction of the northern empire and the rebirth of a new and glorious empire that extended from the Indus to the Atlantic and from the Caspian to the cataracts of the Nile. The capital was removed from Damascus to Baghdad, from which center radiated all that was grand in Arabian history.

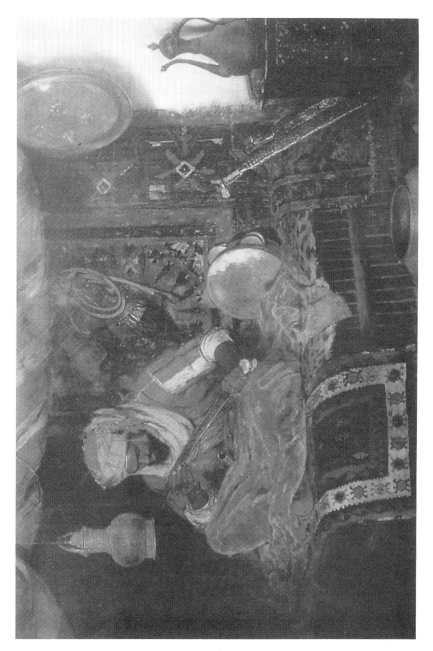

Figure 14. Black warrior of Arabian descent. (Photo courtesy of Wayne B. Chandler.)

For five centuries the caliphs of Baghdad reigned and their rule marked the beginning of a Moslem, as opposed to an Arabic, Empire.[50]

The Abbasid Dynasty ushered in the first true 'golden age' of Islam. The Islamic world exploded in a cultural rebirth of art, science and literature at the same time that Europe was sinking into its "Dark Ages." One author pointedly exclaims: "At a time when even peasants and farmers could read and write in Muslim Spain, kings, princes, and dukes in Christian Europe were mostly illiterate."[51] Sir John Glubb, an Englishman and a world-renowned authority on Muhammad, writes: "During the...Abbasid rule, Baghdad was the wealthiest and the most luxurious city in the world. This was the period when Europe had relapsed into a state of semi-barbarism, and which is contemptuously dismissed in two or three paragraphs in our history books as The Dark Ages. They were dark only for Europe...in the Muslim world, they were brilliantly illuminated."[52] Indeed, this light attracted knowledge and culture seekers. Another English authority proclaims, "It seemed as if the whole world became students, or at least patrons of literature. In quest of knowledge, men traveled over three continents and returned home, like bees laden with honey, to impart the precious stores which they had accumulated to crowds of eager disciples...."[53]

The Abbasids left volumes of classic literature and verse which is still in print to this day, including *The Arabian Nights,* the *Rubaiyat* and one of the most celebrated love stories in history, *The Romance of Antar.* Though the latter is the greatest lyric poem of Arabia, ironically Antar was not Arabian but Ethiopian. A lover and a warrior, Antar describes himself as "Black and swarthy as an elephant," and he is considered by the Arabs around him as a hero, the very embodiment of their ideals.

Besides literature, the Abbasids made tremendous strides in astronomy and medicine. Abbasid astronomers measured the circumference and dimensions of the earth with astounding accuracy (see *Moor: Light of Europe's Dark Age,* p. 159); this was eight-hundred years before Europe recognized that the earth was not flat! The format currently followed in contemporary medical schools was set during this golden age in the Islamic world. "Medical schools were extremely active in Baghdad in the ninth century under the Abbasid Khalifs. Medical students underwent four years of training, at the end of which they were obliged to pass their final examinations before they were allowed to practice....Arabic textbooks on medicine and ophthalmology were standard works in European universities until the sixteenth century."[54]

From ancient Egypt and India, the Abbasids acquired an insatiable desire for the study of mathematics. It was the Abbasids who rediscovered the use of zero and introduced it to Western civilization along with the place value system of writing numbers in tens, hundreds, thousands, and so on. All of our current mathematical principles are based on the use of this system. Algebra, trigonometry, logarithms, trigonometric ratios, sine, cosine, tangent and cotangent are also inventions attributed to the Blacks of south Arabia.[55]

Though the Black Abbasids made advances in all areas of culture and knowledge, their greatest contribution to Islam was in the organization and structure of the religion itself. The Abbasids shaped Islam. According to Moshe Sharon, "with the advent of the Abbasids, the whole nature of Islam was revolutionized. During the period of this dynasty...Islam achieved glory in almost every known field of human endeavor, and succeeded in creating and consolidating the ideological, theological and material foundations of its religious and administrative institutions."[56]

Of the many caliphs who guided the ascent of the Abbasid Caliphate, there are three who were particularly instrumental in creating and maintaining the grandeur of this period. In 750 C.E., Abu Jafar al-Mansur transferred the Eastern Caliphate from Damascus to Baghdad—which was known in the Moslem world as Dar-al-Salam, or City of Peace—where he established the Abbasid Caliphate. It was Al-Mansur who set the stage for municipal reform and helped to transform Baghdad into a great metropolis. Though he promoted all of the sciences, Al-Mansur had a keen interest in astronomy and erected Baghdad's first astronomical observatory. Al-Mansur also founded schools of medicine and law, enhancing the educational and cultural magnetism of Baghdad.

The fifth caliph of the Abbasids was Al-Mansur's grandson, Harun al-Rashid ibn Muhammad al-Mahdi ibn al-Mansur al-Abbasi (763–809 C.E.). He shared his grandfather's passion for education and decreed that a school should be attached to every mosque. Harun-al-Rashid still lives through the character of Aaron the Just in *The Arabian Nights*.

Baghdad reached its zenith under the legendary caliph Abu al-Abbas Abd Allah al-Mamun (786–833 C.E.), the son of Harun-al-Rashid and the seventh sovereign of the Abbasids, who ruled during the historical period designated as the Golden Age of Baghdad (813–832 C.E.). Al-Mamun extended the Abbasid Caliphate to include all of the land from the Oxus River to Tripoli and from the Arabian Desert to the Caucasus Mountains. Al-Mamun's passion was astronomy—he stated that Aristotle appeared to him in a dream—and he commissioned seventy scholars to produce an image of the earth and the first stellar map in the Islamic world.

Al-Mamun's obsession with astronomy and astronomical equations inevitably led him to the Great Pyramid in Egypt in which, legend has it, existed a secret chamber that housed maps and tables of the celestial and terrestrial spheres. This chamber is also reputed to harbor a myriad of ingenious devices, such as weapons that could not rust and glass that could be bent and stretched but would not shatter. In 820 C.E., Al-Mamun assembled an amalgam of the greatest engineers, architects, stonemasons, and builders in the ancient world to locate the secret passageway into the pyramid. They searched in vain for several days and, finally, Al-Mamun, with insane determination, ordered his workers to bore a hole directly into the pyramid. This was a veritable nightmare; hammers and chisels would not even dent or scratch the huge sixteen ton blocks of limestone that encased the smaller two and a half ton blocks. With an ancient method of applying intense heat and vinegar, Al-Mamun did crack the stone and upon entering, discovered the so-called Queen's and King's Chambers in the pyramid, but did not find the secret chamber of treasures. According to the chronicles, in the King's Chamber, Al-Mamun discovered a highly polished, dark, chocolate-colored, granite sarcophagus, that contained a stone statue of a man wearing a gold breastplate inlaid with precious stones. On his chest lay a priceless sword and upon his head was a ruby the size of an egg, "which shone as with the light of day." Mysterious characters were inscribed on the statue in writing that was unrecognized and never deciphered. Though there is no historical evidence to substantiate this discovery, it retains a strong presence in Arabian legend.[57]

The tales of *The Arabian Nights* bear much of the lore of Arabia and, of those many fables and phantasmagoric legends, probably none is more recognizable than the tale of Aladdin. The actual historical story of Aladdin differs greatly from his mythical portrait in *The Arabian Knights,* but, nonetheless, his story carries a boundless mystique that has endured through the ages. The authentic episodes of Aladdin began in the south of Arabia, in Yemen, during the Abbasid Caliphate, with an invincible fighting task force of Black Ismaili Shi'ites known as the Brotherhood of the Hashimiyyah.

Modern dictionaries and encyclopedia will report that the name Hashimiyyah, or Hashishim, means "hashish-takers," yet these warriors actually took their name from the family name of the Prophet, Hashim, who they were sworn to protect; then, subsequently gave their name to the substance they allegedly consumed before a battle. These Blacks, described by Marco Polo as fanatical, were the first true ninja warriors, invulnerable and unconquerable.

Marco Polo also provides the link between the Hashimiyyah and the historical Aladdin. The name Aladdin comes from the word Ala-ud-den, "the Bloody One," which was a title taken by the first chief of the Hashimiyyah— the Shi'ite leader Hasan Ibn al-Sabbah, meaning the "Son of the Goddess"— and by all successive leaders of this brotherhood.[58] According to the legend, Aladdin was the master of a secret cave filled with treasure. In fact, this cave and others like it did exist. During Marco Polo's time, a string of caverns, located in the fortified valley of Alamut near Kazvin, served as strongholds for the Hashimiyyah in the Elburz Mountains of northern Persia. The Shi'ite Hashimiyyah had seized and fortified these mountain fortresses and, from them, had launched a devastating war of terror against the Christian Crusaders and the Semitic orthodox Sunni Moslems.[59] Christians mispronounced their name, calling them "assassins." The victims of the Hashimiyyah were often prominent individuals, hence our use of the word "assasinate" to describe politically motivated murders.

Figure 15. Aladdin's Lamp. (Photo courtesy of Wayne B. Chandler.)

Aladdin's legendary lamp also has roots in historical reality. This sect of Aladdin, the Hashimiyyah, worshipped the moon as a symbol of the Goddess. They used the energy of this celestial body to create a talisman, a symbol of power, which produced djinni (genie), forms of the "spirits of the ancestors."[60] These spirits were contained within the Vessel of Light, which became known as Aladdin's Lamp. The lamp was the source of the djinni just as the moon was the source of all human souls. This was the belief that the Hashimiyyah shared in the most ancient of African traditions, in which the moon is the realm of death and rebirth since its influence seems to be directly connected with the gestation of all mammalian life forms.

The influence of this Brotherhood of the Hashimiyyah was widely felt. Their power was either life-threatening or life-sustaining, depending on one's religious persuasion. The mystique of the Hashimiyyah and the tales spun about them, inadvertently and ironically, were the genesis of a Christian order of knights, the "Knights Templar," or "The Order of the Knights of the Temple." This order was founded in Jerusalem in 1118 C.E., by a Burgundian knight named Hugues de Payens, or Hugh of the Pagans. As one author states, "...its organization was based on that of the Saracen fraternity of the hashishim, 'hashish-takers,' whom Christians called Assassins."[61] The symbol used by the Templars was a Triple Head of Wisdom, depicting three Black Saracen heads which were, more than likely, Hashimiyyah.

The Templars held these Blacks in such high esteem that their first headquarters was a wing of the royal palace in Jerusalem next to the al-Aqsa mosque which was revered by the Hashimiyyah Shi'ites as the central mosque of the Goddess Fatima. Historian H.A. Gueber, writes of the legends which grew around the Templars: "Western romances, inspired by Moorish Shi'ite poets, transformed this Mother-shrine into the Temple of the Holy Grail, where certain legendary knights called Templars gathered to offer their service to the Goddess, to uphold the female principle of divinity and to defend women. These knights became more widely known as Galahad, Perceval, Lohengrin, etc."[62]

The real, historical Templars were Christians who assumed the duty of protecting Christian pilgrims and merchants traveling through the Holy Land. Members of this brotherhood were also sent to the homelands of Christian travelers to protect their property: their castles, lands and monies. The Templars were respected and exalted, even by Moslems who ordinarily despised Christians.

The Hashimiyyah thrived until 1273 C.E., working for the Egyptian-based Fatimid Caliphate from 1094 to 1273. One arm of the Hashimiyyah that survives to this day is the sect of the Sufi Moslem. The Sufis represent the deeply mystical aspects of Islam, with their trance-like whirling dervish dance and their tantric [sexual] rituals that invoke spiritual energy. The fanaticism of the Hashimiyyah began to mitigate in the thirteenth century, and they were eventually destroyed in Persia, by the Mongols, in 1256 and in Syria, by the Mameluks, in 1273.

The mighty Abbasid Empire came to its end during this period (1258 C.E.), too, with Baghdad being destroyed in a two-year siege by the Mongol hordes. Technically, the Abbasid Caliphate reigned from 750 to 861 C.E., but the Abbasids retained control of Baghdad until 1258. With their death came the birth of another Black caliphate; this one in Egypt. The Fatimids, who reigned in Egypt from 973 to 1171 C.E., were originally descended from Muhammad's daughter Fatima, who reigned from 616 to 633 C.E., and Ali, who had become her husband. Fatima was a great religious figure in her own right and helped to create a majestic Arabian empire in Egypt.

Though some individual Blacks would succeed to the throne as caliph and many others would rise to national prominence, with the demise of the Abbasid and the Fatimid Empires, came the end of the Black as a national force in West Asia. The Semites had finally descended upon them and would eventually engulf them.

As George Wells Parker wrote, "…and between the northern and southern Arabian there broke out a hatred that they carried to the farthest ends of the world." For one and a half millennia, the Black and Semitic Arabs had battled on the Arabian peninsula and throughout most of West Asia. Ironically, their final, decisive battle would not be fought anywhere on the Asian continent, rather it was fought in Europe, on a land mass known to the Arabs as Andalus and known to us as Spain.

So it is in Spain that we will begin the final chapter. The powerful Black dynasties which had faded into the dust of Arabia were resurrected in the fertile valleys of Andulus. Also reborn was their nemesis, the Semitic Arab. Though the names were changed, the game remained the same. Now the players were known as the Mudarites, the Yemenites and the Moors.

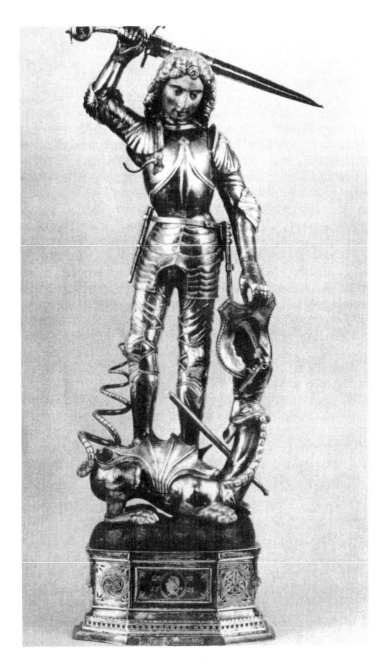

Figure 16. An image depicting the visage of the Templar. Found in the "House of the Blackheads" Germany. Notice black face on his shield. (Photo courtesy of Wayne B. Chandler.)

Figure 17. Former minister of finance in Arabia. (Photo Al-Mansour)

APPENDIX
EBONY AND BRONZE: RACE AND ETHNICITY OF THE MOORS IN SPAIN

By Wayne B. Chandler

Spain extends from the southwest corner of Europe as a flower from its stem. The French Pyrenees to the north, the Straits of Gibraltar to the south, the Mediterranean to the east, and the Atlantic Ocean to the northwest allow Spain an isolation unique to Europe, and provide its inviting terrain, highly fertile soil and diverse climate. Historical records maintained by scholars past and present show that between 2000 B.C.E. and 1492 C.E., Spain was conquered, colonized and occupied by at least eight various groups. Among those that exerted noted cultural influence in Spain are the Phoenicians, Carthaginians, Romans, Jews, Vandals (a Germanic tribe that ruled for about twenty years), Visigoths, and the Arabians and Moors.

Our focus will be on the Arabs and Moors, for it was during their eight-hundred year reign that the veil of darkness—idolatry, superstition and cultural deprivation—was lifted from Spain, redefining for all of Europe the very meaning of civilization. Though scarcely recorded, Moorish influence extended into the very fundamentals of art, science, hygiene, medicine, technology and philosophy. Arabian and Moorish influence in Spain ushered in the era of European history known as the Renaissance.

Until the arrival of the Moor—literally, "the Black"—Europe was entangled in a web of cultural decomposition characterized by ignorance, rampant disease due to hygienic neglect, starvation and slavery. Many Moslem chroniclers have left living testimonies to the primitive state of Europe in this dark age. The geographer and philologist al-Bakri (d. 1094 C.E.) describes the Galatians: "They are treacherous, dirty, and bathe once or twice a year; then with cold water. They never wash their clothes until they are worn out because they claim that the dirt accumulated as the result of their sweat softens their body."[2] Usamah Ibn Munqidh, an official and historian, describes his encounter with Crusaders in the Holy Land:

> I saw Franks as like animals possessing courage and fighting prowess though their character is rude. Their medical knowledge is in a crude state for I saw a Frankish physician cut off a leg on which an abscess had grown, causing the man's death. A woman afflicted with imbecility was diagnosed as possessed by the devil, the physician recommended for her the shaving of her head, and as her case worsened, he made a deep

cruciform incision [a cross] on her head, to chase the devil away, but the woman died in the process.[3]

Moslem historians made keen observations which they recorded. The following is an interview between Suleyman and Musa, the conqueror of Spain, during which Suleyman probes Musa's reflections on the nature of the various infidels with which he had engaged in war and other transactions. Of the Greeks, Musa said: "They are lions behind the walls of their cities, eagles upon their horses, and women in their vessels. Whenever they see an opportunity, they seize it immediately." According to Musa: "The Berbers are the people who most resemble the Arabs in activity, strength, courage, endurance, love of war, and hospitality, but they are the most treacherous of men. They have no faith, and they keep no word." On the Goths, he commented: "The Goths are lords living in luxury and abundance, but champions who do not turn their backs to the enemy." He describes the Franks as "people of great courage and enterprise, their numbers are considerable, and they are amply provided with weapons and military stores."[4]

In contrast to the detail and objectivity of the records kept by Moslem chroniclers, the historical records of Europeans are full of neglect, blatant omission and fabrication. As S.S. Ahmad points out: "the historical records in very many cases have been tampered with, just to suit the whims of a particular ruler and also to pollute the people's mind against the forerunners."[5] Blacks are conspicuously absent from European historical accounts of the Arabian and Moorish conquests of Spain and North Africa, and European historians go so far as to assert that the Moors, whose name literally means "black," were everything but Black!

A leading American encyclopedia defines the Moors: "In ancient history, the Romans called the people of northwestern Africa Mauri and the region they lived in Mauritania. These peoples belonged to a larger group, the Berbers. The Berbers became Muslims, and many of them adopted Arabic in addition to their own Berber language. They joined the Arabs in conquering Spain during the 700s....A common but incorrect belief that Moors are black was spread by William Shakespeare's play Othello. Moors belong to the European geographical race."[6]

This erroneous statement not only seeks to reinforce the fallacy that the Moors are not Black but ventures to claim that they are, of all things, White! By the conclusion of this chapter, the reader will be able to fully understand the absurdity of this statement.

Endnotes

7. Drusilla Dunjee Houston. *Wonderful Ethiopians of the Ancient Cushite Empire.* Black Classic Press, Baltimore, 1985, pp. 112–113.

8. Ibid. pp. 113 and 120.
9. Runoko Rashidi. *Africans in Early Asian Civilizations; African Presence in Early Asia.* Edited by Runoko Rashidi and Ivan Van Sertima, Transaction Publishers, Rutgers University, New Jersey, 1988, pp. 22–23.
10. Amaury de Riencourt. *Sex and Power in History.* Dell Publishing Co., New York, 1974, pp. 187–189 and 193.
11. Idris Shah. *The Sufis.* Octagon Press, London, 1964, p. 390.
12. Al-Jahiz. pp. 39–40.
13. Ibid. p. 55.
14. Cheikh Anta Diop. *Great African Thinkers.* Edited by Ivan Van Sertima and Larry Williams, Transaction Books, Rutgers University, New Jersey, 1992, pp. 40, 48 and 58.
15. Al-Jahiz. pp. 50–51.
16. Ibid. p. 45.
17. *Egyptian Book of the Dead.* Translated by E.A. Wallis Budge, Bell Publishing Co., 1960, p. 351.
18. AL-Makkari. p. 20.
19. *The Holy Bible.* King James Version, American Bible Society, New York, 1816, p. 18.
20. J.A. Rogers. *Sex and Race.* Vol. 1., Helga Rogers Publishers, 1967, pp. 95–96. Author's note: Professor D.S. Margoliouth was the reigning authority on Muhammad in the West. Sir John Glubb, one of the world's foremost experts on the subject, makes constant reference to Margoliouth's works on Muhammad and Islam.
21. George Wells Parker. *The Children of the Sun.* Black Classic Press, Baltimore, (first published 1918, reprinted 1978), p. 22.
22. Al-Jahiz. p. 50.
23. Robert Briffault. *The Mothers.* Vol 1., Macmillan, New York, 1927, pp. 3 and 80.
24. Moshe Sharon. *Black Banners From the East: The Establishment of the Abbasid State.* Institute of Asian and African Studies, The Magnes Press, Jerusalem, 1983, p. 25.
25. Al-Makkari. p. 23.
26. Sir John Glubb. *The Life and Times of Muhammad.* Scarborough House Publishers, 1970, p. 62.
27. Al-Makkari. p. 23.
28. Al-Jahiz. p. 50.
29. Ibid. p. 51.
30. Ibid. p. 23.
31. Glubb. p. 238.
32. Ibid. p. 74.
33. Al-Jahiz. p. 44n.
34. Ibid. p. 44.
35. Ibid. p. 43.
36. *Book of Battles.* Translated by Edward Nolan, Semar Publishers, London, 1926, p. 144. Authors note: Though this story is told in great detail with what seems to be historic authenticity, many contemporary Islamic scholars maintain that Muhammad's legions never engaged the kingdom of Yemen in battles of any kind. Stating that Yemen willfully embraced Islam, as well as the jihads.
37. Ibid. p. 145.
38. Ibid.
39. Al-Jahiz. pp. 50–51.

40. John G. Jackson. *Ages of Gold and Silver.* American Atheist Press, Austin, 1990, p. 121.
41. Al-Makkari. Vol. 2, p. 298.
42. Sharon. pp. 177–178.
43. Ibid. p. 177.
44. Ibid. p. 178n.
45. Ibid. pp. 79–81.
46. Ibid. p. 158.
47. Ibid. p. 187n.
48. Al-Makkari. Vol. 2, p. 20.
49. Ibid. p. 27.
50. Parker. pp. 20–21.
51. Glubb. p. 372.
52. Ibid. p. 371.
53. Parker, p. 21.
54. Glubb. p. 372.
55. Ibid.
56. Sharon. p. 19.
57. Peter Tompkins. *Secrets of the Great Pyramid.* Harper Colophon Books, 1971, pp. 6–7.
58. Heinrich Zimmer. *Myths and Symbols in Indian Art and Civilization.* Princeton University Press, Princeton, 1946, p. 54.
59. Marco Polo. *Travels.* Abaris Books, Inc., New York, 1982, pp. 53–54.
60. Eithne Wilkens. *The Rose-Garden Game.* Victor Gallancz Ltd., London, 1969, p. 58.
61. Norman MacKenzie. *Secret Societies.* Holt, Rinehart & Winston, 1967, p. 117.
62. H.A. Guerber. *Legends of the Middle Ages.* American Book Co., 1924, pp. 186–187 and 200.

Endnotes to Race and Ethnicity of the Moors in Spain

2. Anwar G. Chejne. *Islam and the West: The Moriscos.* State University of New York Press, Albany, 1983, p. 77.
3. Ibid.
4. Ahmed Ibn Mohammed Al-Malekari. *The History of the Mohammedan Dynasties in Spain.* Printed in India and London for the Oriental Translation Fund, 1840, p. 297.
5. S.S. Ahmad. *The Moorish Spain.* Farooq Kitab Ghar, Karachi, 1972, Preface p. i.
6. Vernon Robert Dorjahn. *New Age Encyclopedia.* Vol. 12., Lexicon Publishing, New York, 1988, p. 287.

RESEARCH NOTES
ANCIENT CITIES BENEATH THE ARABIAN SANDS: UBAR AND SAFFARA METROPOLIS

By Runoko Rashidi

In 1992, Ubar—a fortress city celebrated in *A Thousand and One Arabian Nights* and the Koran—was identified buried under the shifting sands of a section of Oman so barren that it is known as the Rub'al Khali or Empty Quarter. Ubar was identified by a Los Angeles based team led by filmmaker Nicholas Clapp with the aid of high-tech satellite imagery employed by NASA's Jet Propulsion Laboratory. Clapp persuaded JPL scientists to scan the region with a special shuttle radar system flown on a Challenger space mission. The radar was able to see through the overlying sand and loose soil to detect subsurface geological features and picked out the outlines of ancient trade routes. Reputedly built nearly five thousand years ago, Ubar was a processing center for frankincense.

Filmmaker Clapp was inspired in the project after reading a book entitled *Arabia Felix* by Bertram Thomas. In a related work, *The Arabs,* Thomas wrote that:

> The original inhabitants of Arabia, then, according to Sir Arthur Keith, one of the world's greatest living anthropologists, who has made a study of Arab skeletal remains, ancient and modern, were not the familiar Arabs of our own time, but a very much darker people. A protonegroid belt of mankind stretched across the ancient world from Africa to Malaya. This belt, by environmental and other evolutionary process, became in parts transformed, giving rise to the Hamitic peoples of Africa, to the Dravidian peoples of India and to an intermediate dark people inhabiting the Arabian peninsula.[1]

Shortly after identifying Ubar, the long-lost "Queen of the Frankincense Trade," the same Los Angeles-based team identified an even larger city, Saffara Metropolis, fifty percent larger than Ubar but with many of the same architectural characteristics. Saffara Metropolis, or the "Main City of Dhofar," was apparently an administrative center for the incense trade and possessed at least eleven crenelated towers similar to those found at Ubar. Saffara Metropolis is on the southern coast of Oman, across the Qara Mountains from Ubar and near the port of Moscha, from which frankincense was shipped to Yemen and Iraq.

The Incense Trade

At the base of the ancient prosperity of Ubar and Saffara Metropolis were the region's greatest natural resources—frankincense and myrrh—two highly desirable gum resins which from the earliest historical periods were much prized and sought after. The world's purest and most abundant sources of frankincense and myrrh were grown in Somalia (ancient Punt?) in East Africa and southern Arabia, just across the Red (Erythraean) Sea from the Horn of Africa.

Frankincense—an aromatic resin derived from tree sap, brought great wealth to those who controlled its harvest and distribution. Frankincense occupied a tremendously vital place in the ancient world. In the pharaonic civilization of Africa's Nile Valley it was burned as an offering to the gods, carried in royal processions, extensively employed in ancient funerary rites, and while extensively utilized for its perfume-like fragrance, it was equally valued for its medicinal properties. It was used both in the stoppage of bleeding and as an antidote for poisons. In Rome, for the funeral of Nero's wife, an entire year's frankincense harvest was consumed. Biblical traditions assert that frankincense was so valued that it was presented as a gift to the Christ child. Myrrh was employed for cosmetics and ointments, and formed an essential element in the mummification process.

Notes

1. Bertram Thomas, *The Arabs* (Garden City: Doubleday, 1937), 339.

Bibliography

Doe, Brian. *Southern Arabia*. New York: McGraw-Hill, n.d.
Horton, Sue. "Arabian Adventure." *Los Angeles Times,* 12 Sep 1990: E1.
Maugh II, Thomas H. "Ubar, Fabled Lost City, Found by L.A. Team." *Los Angeles Times,* 5 Feb 1992: A1.
Maugh II, Thomas H. "L.A.-Based Archeology Team Finds Second Arabian City." *Los Angeles Times,* 11 Oct 1992: A3.
McAlpine, Ken. "Atlantis of the Sands." *American Way,* 1 Sep 1992: 39–42.
Thomas, Bertram. *The Arabs*. Garden City: Doubleday, 1937.
Tindel, Raymond D. "Zafar: Archaeology in the Land of Frankincense and Myrrh." *Archaeology* (Mar/Apr 1984): 40–45.
Wilford, John Noble. " 'Atlantis of the Sands' Believed found". *San Francisco Chronicle,* 5 Feb 1992: 1–2.

THE AFRICAN PRESENCE IN ARABIA AND THE EARLY ISLAMIC WORLD IN ASIA: A SELECTED BIBLIOGRAPHY

Compiled by Runoko Rashidi

Abdul-Rauf, Muhammad. *Bilal Ibn Rabah: A Leading Companion of the Prophet Muhammad.* n.p.: American Trust Publications, 1977.

Cerulli, E. "Ethiopia's Relations with the Muslim World." Chap. in *UNESCO General History of Africa.* Vol. 3, *Africa from the Seventh to the Eleventh Century.* Edited by M. El Fasi. Berkeley: University of California Press, 1988: 575–85.

Drake, J.G. St. Clair. "The Black Experience in the Muslim World." Section in *Black Folk Here and There: An Essay in History and Anthropology,* Vol. 2. Los Angeles: Center for Afro-American Studies, UCLA, 1990: 77–184.

Fleming, Beatrice J., and Marion J. Pryde. "Antar of Arabia." Chap. in *Distinguished Negroes Abroad.* Washington, D.C.: Associated Publishers, 1946: 10–20.

Fleming, Beatrice J., and Marion J. Pryde. "Bilal, Black Muezzin." Chap. in *Distinguished Negroes Abroad.* Washington, D.C.: Associated Publishers, 1946: 21–30.

Hakim, Musa Abdul. "Diop on Cultural Kinship Between Arabs and Africans." *The Challenger* 24, No. 6 (1988): 15.

Hayes, John R., ed. *The Genius of Arab Civilization: Source of Renaissance.* Second Edition. Foreword by Bayly Winder. Introduction by John Stothoff Badeau. Cambridge: The MIT Press, 1983.

Hitti, Philip K. *History of the Arabs from the Earliest Times to the Present.* New York: St . Martin's Press, 1970.

Houston, Drusilla Dunjee. *The Wonderful Ethiopians of the Ancient Cushite Empire.* 1926; rpt. Introduction by W. Paul Coates. Afterword by Asa G. Hilliard III. Commentary by James Spady. Baltimore: Black Classic Press, 1985.

Hunwick, John O. "Black Africans in the Islamic World: An Understudied Dimension of the Black Diaspora." *Tarikh* 5, No. 4 (1978): 20–40.

Irwin, Graham W., ed. *Africans Abroad: A Documentary History of the Black Diaspora in Asia, Latin America, and the Caribbean During the Age of Slavery.* New York: Columbia University Press, 1977.

al-Jahiz, Uthman Amr Ibn Bahr. *The Book of the Glory of the Black Race.* Translated by Vincent J. Cornell. Los Angeles: Preston, 1981.

Keith, Arthur, and Wilton Marion Krogman. "The Racial Character of the Southern Arabs." Appendix to *The Arabs,* by Bertram Thomas. London: Jonathan Cape, 1932: 301–33.

Khalidi, Omar. "African Diaspora in India: The Case of the Habashis of the Dakan." *Islamic Culture* 53, Nos. 1–2 (1989): 85–107.

Lewis, Bernard. *Race and Slavery in the Middle East: An Historical Enquiry.* Oxford: Oxford University Press, 1990.

al-Mansour, Khalid Abdullah Tariq. *The Destruction of Western Civilization as Seen Through Islam, Christianity and Judaism.* San Francisco: First African Arabian Press, 1982.

al-Mansour, Khalid Abdullah Tariq. *Seven African Arabian Wonders of the World:*

The Black Man's Guide to the Middle East. San Francisco: First African Arabian Press, 1991.

al-Mansour, Khalid Abdullah Tariq. *The Lost Books of Africa Rediscovered: We Charge Genocide.* San Francisco: First African Arabian Press, 1995.

Mekasha, Getachew. "Ancient Ethiopia. Pt. 3, Islam and Ethiopia.' *Ethiopian Review* 1, No. 3 (1991): 18–22.

Pellat, Charles, trans. and ed. *The Life and Works of Jahiz.* Berkeley: University of California Press, 1969.

Rao, Vasant D. "The Habshis: India's Unknown Africans." *Africa Report* 18, No. 5 (1973): 35–38.

Rao, Vasant D. "Siddis: African Dynasty in India." *Black World* (Aug 1975): 78–80.

Rao, Vasant D. "Unknown African Dynasty in India." *India News,* 24 Apr 1978: 6.

Richmond, Diana. *Antar and Abla.* London: Quartet Books, 1978.

Rogers, J.A. "Al-Jahiz, Lord of the Golden Age of Arab Literature." Chap. in *World's Great Men of Color,* Vol. 1. New York: Macmillan, 1972: 163–71.

Stafford, Alphonso Orenzo. "Antar, The Arabian Negro Warrior, Poet and Hero." *Journal of Negro History* 1, No. 2 (1916): 151–62.

Stafford, Alphonso Orenzo. "Africa and Asia." *Negro History Bulletin* 4, No. 2 (1940): 28.

Stafford, Alphonso Orenzo. "Antar." *Negro History Bulletin* 4, No. 2 (1940): 29.

Stafford, Alphonso Orenzo. "Why Study Asia with Respect to Africa." *Negro History Bulletin* 4, No. 2 (1940): 27.

Talib, Y., based on a contribution by F. Samir. "The African Diaspora in Asia." *UNESCO General History of Africa. Vol. 3, Africa from the Seventh to the Eleventh Century.* Edited by M. El Fasi. Berkeley: University of California Press, 1988: 704–33.

BLACK SHOGUN: THE AFRICAN PRESENCE
IN JAPANESE ANTIQUITY

By James E. Brunson, Runoko Rashidi and Wallace Magsby, Jr.

Although the island nation of Japan, occupying the extreme eastern extensions of Asia, is assumed by many to have been historically composed of an
essentially homogeneous population and culture, the accumulated evidence
(much of which has been quietly ignored) places the matter in a vastly
different light, and though far more study needs to be done on the subject, it
seems indisputable that Black people in Japan played an important role from
the most remote phases of antiquity through at least the eighth century.

Meaningful indications of an African presence in ancient Japan have been
unearthed from the most remote ages of the Japanese past. To begin with, and
as a significant example, a 15 February 1986 report carried by the *Associated
Press,* chronicled that:

> The oldest Stone Age hut in Japan has been unearthed near
> Osaka....Archeologists date the hut to about 22,000 years ago and say it
> resembles the dugouts of African bushmen, according to Wazuo Hirose
> of Osaka Prefectural Board of Education's cultural division.
> 'Other homes, almost as old, have been found before, but this discov-
> ery is significant because the shape is cleaner, better preserved' and is
> similar to the Africans' dugouts.[1]

The Physical Anthropology of Ancient Japan

In 1911 Professor Neil Gordon Munro, described as "one of the foremost
students of Japanese life and culture," wrote that:

> The Japanese people are a mixture of several distinct stocks. Negrito,
> Mongolian....That the Japanese have inherited an infusion of Mongolian
> characters goes without saying, but breadth of face intraorbital width, flat
> nose, prognathism, and bracheephaly might be traced to the Negrito stock
> as dolichocephaly in Europe appears to have been derived from that of
> the Negro.[2]

In 1923 anthropologist Roland B. Dixon wrote that "this earliest population
of Japan were in the main a blend of Proto-Australoid and Proto-Negroid
types, and thus similar in the ancient underlying stratum of the population,
southward along the whole coast and throughout Indo-China, and beyond to
India itself."[3] Dixon pointed out that, "In Japan, the ancient Negrito element

may still be discerned by characteristics which are at the same time exterior and osteologic."[4]

In his last major text , *Civilization or Barbarism: An Authentic Anthropology* (published posthumously in English in 1991), the brilliant Dr. Cheikh Anta Diop (1923–1986) pointed out that:

> In the first edition of the *Nations negres et culture* (1954), I posited the hypothesis that the Yellow race must be the result of an interbreeding of Black and White in a cold climate, perhaps around the end of the Upper Paleolithic period. This idea is widely shared today by Japanese scholars and researchers. One Japanese scientist, Nobuo Takano, M.D., chief of dermatology at the Hammatsu Red Cross Hospital, has just developed this idea in a work in Japanese that appeared in 1977, of which he was kind enough to give me a copy in 1979, when, passing through Dakar, he visited my laboratory with a group of Japanese scientists.
>
> Takano maintains, in substance, that the first human being was Black; then Blacks gave birth to Whites, and the interbreeding of these two gave rise to the Yellow race; these three stages are in fact the title of his book in Japanese, as he explained it to me.[5]

As to linguistics, in 1987 former Senegalese president Leopold Sedar Senghor noted that, "The peoples who populate the island of Japan today are descendants from Blacks....Let us not forget that the first population of Japan was Black...and gave to Japan their first language."[6]

Sakanouye Tamuramaro: Sei-I Tai-Shogun of Early Japan

Of the Black people of early Japan, the most picturesque single figure was Sakanouye no Tamuramaro, a warrior symbolized in Japanese history as "a paragon of military virtues," and a man who has captured the attention of some of the most distinguished scholars of twentieth century America (see appendix). Perhaps the first such scholar to make note of Tamuramaro was Alexander Francis Chamberlain (1865–1914). An Anthropologist, Alexander Francis Chamberlain was born in Kenninghall, Norfolk, England, and was brought to America as a child. His family first settled in New York State near Rochester, but soon moved to Peterborough, Canada. In 1868 Chamberlain graduated from the University of Toronto with honors in languages and ethnology. In 1892 he received a Ph.D. from Clark University in Worchester, Massachusetts—the first such degree given for work in anthropology at an American university. Dr. Chamberlain was an assistant professor of Anthropology at Clark, and the department editor for the *American Anthropologist* and the *American Journal of Archaeology*. In April 1911 the *Journal of Race Development* published an essay by Chamberlain entitled "The Contribution of the Negro to Human Civilization." While discussing the African presence in early Asia, Chamberlain stated in an exceptionally frank and matter of fact manner:

> And we can cross the whole of Asia and find the Negro again, for, when, in far-off Japan, the ancestors of the modern Japanese were making their way northward against the Ainu, the aborigines of that country, the leader of their armies was Sakanouye Tamuramaro, a famous general and a Negro.[7]

The Sakanouye Family

In E. Papinot's *Historical and Geographical Dictionary of Japan*, the Sakanouye (also written Sakanoue) are described as an ancient family of warriors descended from Achi no Omi.[8] An account of the family's ancestors move from Korea to Japan is found in the chronicle of *Shoku nihongi* in a petition for higher official rank made by Tamuramaro's father, Sakanouye no Karitamaro (728–786). Considered the most illustrious branch of the Aya family of immigrant descent, the Sakanouye maintained a long tradition of expertise in archery and horsemanship, becoming hereditary court generals in Japan beginning in the seventh century. Later members of the Sakanouye family, until the early fourteenth century, distinguished themselves as poets, scholars and legal experts.[9]

In 672 C.E., a civil war referred to as the *Jinshin Disturbance* ensued between the forces of the brother of Emperor Tenchi, Prince Oama, and the former's son, Prince Otomo. Passed over in the royal succession, Prince Oama angrily went into the eastern provinces of Yamato to enlist the military support of local influential families. Among the families solicited is the first mention of a Sakanouye—Okina (d. 699), great-grandfather of Karitamaro. Okina was a close associate of Prince Oama. Serving as a general to Oama, Okina was instrumental in crushing the forces of Prince Otomo, who ultimately committed suicide. With the uprising suppressed, Prince Oama acceded to the throne as the Emperor Temmu.

> It is said that the Emperor Temmu was so impressed by the bravery of the warriors of the east that he even thought of transferring the capital to that district.[10]

After the Jinshin Disturbance, the region to the east of Heiankyo became associated with the Azumabito, or "Men of the East."

> This refers to a recognizable type, somewhat uncouth by Kyoto's standards, but courageous and skilled in the use of the bow, spear and sword...Heian Japan's frontier country could be called the 'Wild East', meaning the north as well as east of the Fuji Lakes.[11]

By the eighth century C.E., this group of private warriors dominated the country. According to George Sansom, there was no one to match these warriors, particularly the Imperial troops, who were not nearly of the same mettle:

> They were known as Azumabito or Men of the East, and their praises were sung in early Japanese literature. The regular government forces in the eastern provinces were not of this mettle. Their commanders were so notably unsuccessful that in 783 the Emperor publicly rebuked them for cowardice and ordered a new campaign to be undertaken under competent leadership.[12]

The spread of Buddhism at this time by some Japanese emperors, put an incredible burden upon the general population. In 757 Tachibana no Nakamaro, under the pretext of assisting these people, staged a coup. Sakanouye no Karitamaro (728–786), father of Tamuramaro, helped suppress their revolt. In 764 Karitamaro assisted the Empress Koken Shotoku in crushing the rebellion of Fujiwara no Nakamaro. During this turbulent period Karitamaro demonstrated great bravery and military leadership, and later on became Chinjufu-Shogun.[13] Sakanouye no Tamuramaro continued this tradition, and followed his ancestors in service to the court.

Sakanouye Tamuramaro: Paragon of Japanese Military Virtues

Sakanouye no Tamuramo is regarded as an outstanding military commander of the early Heian royal court. The Heian Period (794–1185 C.E.) derives its name from Heian-kyo, which means "the Capital of Peace and Tranquility," and was the original name for Japan's early capital city—Kyoto. It was during the Heian Period that the term *samurai* was first used. According to Papinot, the "word comes from the verb *samurau,* or better *saburau,* which signifies: to be on one's guard, to guard; it applied especially to the soldiers who were on guard at the Imperial palace."[14]

The *samurai* have been called the knights or warrior class of Medieval Japan and the history of the samurai is very much the history of Japan itself. For hundreds of years, to the restoration of the Meiji emperor in 1868, the samurai were the flower of Japan and are still idolized by many Japanese. The samurai received a pension from their feudal lord, and had the privilege of wearing two swords. They intermarried in their own caste and the privilege of samurai was transmitted to all the children, although the heir alone received a pension.

The "paragon of military virtues," Sakanouye no Tamuramaro (758–811) was, in the words of James Murdoch:

Figure 1. Black Buddhist deity Fudo Myo-o depicted on a suit of armor traditionally believed to have belonged to Ashikaga Takaugi (1305–1358), the founder of the Ashikaga shogunate.

In a sense the originator of what was subsequently to develop into the renowned *samurai* class, he provided in his own person a worthy model for the professional warrior on which to fashion himself and his character. In battle, a veritable war-god; in peace the gentlest of manly gentlemen, and the simplest and most unassuming of men.[15]

According to his biographers, Tamuramaro steadily worked his way up through the military ranks, first serving as a lieutenant of the inner palace guards, advancing to minor captain, and then to middle captain. Tamuramaro, whose career began in the Nara Period (710–794 C.E.), was elevated to the rank of major captain and the office of major counselor by Emperor Saga. He was granted this promotion because of his knowledge of both civil and military codes.

As late as the Nara Period, the Ainu, who were possibly distributed throughout the whole of Japan thousands of years ago, held a considerable portion of northeastern Honshu, Japan's main island. By the eighth century the Ainu had become a formidable enemy of the expanding Japanese rulers. Unsuccessful commanders in 783 were sharply rebuked by the Emperor Kammu for their cowardice and inability to drive out the Ainu, and were summarily dismissed. In 788 the emperor had the government assemble a mighty army and arsenal to confront this powerful enemy. Kammu demanded tribute from the provinces in the form of military armament. Kanto would provide adequate armor, Dazifu in Kyushu the iron helmets, and Tokaido and Tosando thousands of arrows. In that same year Japanese Imperial troops began fighting a series of bloody battles against mounted Ainu soldiers. This series of campaigns resulted in few victories, and in 791 the emperor summoned a 'man of the east,' appointing him to the title of "Envoy for the Pacification of the East." The deputy of this individual, who would go on to achieve far greater fame than his nominal superior, was Sakanouye no Tamuramaro. As stated by Sansom:

> At length in 791 a commander was appointed, and given the title of Seito Taishi, or Envoy for the Pacification of the East; his deputy was one Sakanouye Tamura Maro, celebrated in Japanese history as a paragon of military virtues. Tamura Maro preceded his superior officer to the front in 793, and in 795 they both returned to the capital in triumph. But for a decade or more it was necessary to keep up the pressure against the Ainu and to encourage farmers to settle near the effective frontier so as to provide a permanent defence against raids and sallies, which Tamura Maro's successes had not entirely checked. In order to finish the affair he was given a new commission in 800 and sent off again. In a series of campaigns lasting until 803 he finally accomplished his purpose, and was able to push the frontier as far north as Izawa and Shiba, where strongholds were built and garrisoned. So important was his task in the eyes of the Court that the title of Sei-i Tai-Shogun or Barbarian-subduing Generalissimo, which he was the first to hold, was sought after by the highest military officers in the land for the next thousand years.[16]

Figure 2. Black Buddha from the ancient temple at Nara, Japan.

Throughout his career, Tamuramaro was rewarded for his services with high civil as well as military positions. In 797 he was named "barbarian-subduing generalissimo" (Sei-i Tai-Shogun), and in 801–802 he again campaigned in the north, establishing fortresses at Izawa and Shiwa and effectively subjugating the Ainu. In 810 he helped to suppress an attempt to restore the retired emperor Heizei to the throne. In 811, the year of his death, he was appointed great counselor (dainagon) and minister of war (hyobukyo).

> Tamuramaro founded a shrine in the district of Izawa in Mutsu dedicated to Hachiman in which he hung up his bow and arrows. As has been said, this Tamuramaro was one of the very few soldiers whom military exploits had sufficed to raise to power and place in the councils of the State, and it was he that furnished the model on which successive generations of aspiring warriors endeavored to form themselves. Before starting on their expeditions, later Shoguns (Generals) invariably went to worship at his tomb and invoke the aid of his spirit.[17]

Sakanouye no Tamuramaro "was buried at the village of Kurisu, near Kyoto, and it is believed that it is his tomb which is known under the name of Shogun-zuka. Tamuramaro is the founder of the famous temple Kiyomizu-dera. He is the ancestor of the Tamura daimyo of Mutsu."[18] Tamuramaro "was not only the first to bear the title of Sei-i-tai-Shogun, but he was also the first of the warrior statesmen of Japan."[19] In later ages he was revered by military men as a model commander and as the first recipient of the title shogun—the highest rank to which a warrior could aspire.[20]

Notes

1. "African-Like Stone Age Hut is Unearthed in Japan," *Associated Press,* 15 Feb 1986.
2. Neil G. Munro, *Prehistoric Japan* (Yokohama, 1911), 676–78.
3. Roland B. Dixon, *The Racial History of Man* (New York: Scribner's, 1923), 288.
4. Dixon, 287–92.
5. Cheikh Anta Diop, *Civilization or Barbarism,* trans. Yaa-Lengi Meema Ngemi, eds. Harold J. Salemson and Marjolijn de Jager (Westport: Lawrence Hill, 1991), 55.
6. "Senghor Presents 'Actual Facts' on Japanese: They're Descendants from Blacks," *The Final Call* 6, No. 5 (1987).
7. Alexander Francis Chamberlain, "The Contribution of the Negro to Human Civilization," *Journal of Race Development* (Apr 1911), 484–85.
8. E. Papinot, *Historical and Geographical Dictionary of Japan,* vol. 2 (New York: Frederick Ungar, 1964), 532.
9. William R. Carter, "Sakanoue Family," *Kodansha Encyclopedia of Japan,* vol. 6 (Tokyo: Kodansha, 1983), 379.
10. "In Japan, East is East, and West is West," *The East Magazine* 33 (1988), 7.
11. Richard Storry, *The Way of the Samurai* (New York: G.P. Putnam's Sons, 1978), 91.

12. George Sansom, *A History of Japan to 1334* (Stanford: Stanford University Press, 1958), 105.
13. Papinot, 532.
14. Papinot, 536.
15. James Murdoch, *A History of Japan,* vol. 1 (London: Kegan Paul, Trench, Truhner & Co., 1925), 917.
16. Sansom, 106.
17. Murdoch, 273.
18. Yagi Atsuru, "Sakanoue no Tamuramaro (758-811)," *Kodansha Encyclopedia of Japan,* vol. 6 (Tokyo: Kodansha, 1983), 379.
19. Murdoch, 221.
20. Papinot, 532-33.

APPENDIX
REFERENCES TO SAKANOUYE TAMURAMARO
IN THE WORKS OF TWENTIETH CENTURY
AFRICAN SCHOLARS

By Runoko Rashidi

William Henry Ferris (1873-1941) attended Yale Graduate School, Harvard Divinity School, and Harvard Graduate School. He rose to assistant president general of the Universal Negro Improvement Association and became the literary editor of Marcus Garvey's *Negro World* newspaper. Ferris was the author of the highly popular *The African Abroad: Or, His Evolution in Western Civilization, Tracing His Development Under Caucasian Milieu,* published in two volumes in 1913. In volume two of *The African Abroad,* Ferris referenced Alexander Francis Chamberlain's article and reproduced his comments on Tamuramaro word for word.[1]

Among the greatest scholars in all of American history stands W.E.B. Dubois. A towering figure, a brilliant scholar and a prolific writer, William Edward Burghardt Dubois (1868-1963) was born 23 February 1868 in Great Barrington, Massachusetts. In 1896 Dubois became the first Black person to receive a Ph.D. from Harvard University. After teaching at Wilberforce University in Ohio and the University of Pennsylvania, he went on to establish the first department of sociology in the United States at Atlanta University. In his book, *The Negro* (first published in 1915), which significantly influenced the lives and careers of Drusilla Dunjee Houston and William Leo Hansberry, among others, Dr. Dubois placed Sakanouye Tamuramaro of Japan within a list of some of the most distinguished Black rulers and warriors in antiquity.[2]

Dubois actually visited Japan in 1937. Dr. Dubois also authored *The World and Africa: An Inquiry Into the Part that Africa has Played in World History,* first published in 1946, and in which mention is made of the Black presence in Japanese antiquity. Dubois was invited to Ghana in 1961 in the twilight of his life by President Kwame Nkrumah to head up a secretariat for an *Encyclopedia Africana.* W.E.B. Dubois died in Accra, Ghana 27 August 1963 as a Ghanaian citizen.

In 1922 Carter Godwin Woodson and Charles Harris Wesley (1891-?), in a chapter called "Africans in History with Others," in their book *The Negro In Our History,* quoted Chamberlain on Tamuramaro verbatim.[3] Born in New Canton, Virginia, Carter Godwin Woodson (1875-1950) obtained a B.A.

from the University of Chicago in 1907. In 1908 he attended the Sorbonne for
one semester where he became fluent in French, and received a Ph.D. from
Harvard University in 1912. Woodson taught briefly and held educational
administrative posts in the Philippines, at Howard University and West
Virginia State College. Woodson was a member of the Niagara Movement
and a regular columnist for Marcus Garvey's weekly *Negro World.* In addition, he was the author of 16 books about African people (including the *Mis-
Education of the Negro*), initiator of the annual February observation of
Negro History Week, founder of the Association for the Study of Negro Life
and History, and founder and editor of the *Journal of Negro History.* As a
contributing writer for the *Journal of Negro History,* Dr. Woodson wrote
more than a hundred articles and 125 book reviews. Woodson was also the
founder of Associated Publishers, and the founder and editor of the *Negro
History Bulletin.*

In the November 1940 issue of the *Negro History Bulletin,* Lois Mailou
Jones contributed a brief article entitled "Sakanouye Tamura Maro." Lois
Mailou Jones, born in Boston, Massachusetts, was an illustrator, artist, de-
signer and water colorist. Jones was on the editorial board of the *Negro
History Bulletin* and served as a professor in the College of Fine Arts at
Howard University from the 1930s to the 1970s. In her article Jones pointed
out that:

> The probable number of Negroes who reached the shores of Asia may
> be estimated somewhat by the wide area over which they were found on
> that continent. Historians tell us that at one time Negroes were found in
> all of the countries of southern Asia bordering the Indian Ocean and
> along the east coast as far as Japan. There are many interesting stories
> told by those who reached that distant land which at that time they called
> 'Cipango.'
> One of the most prominent characters in Japanese history was a Negro
> warrior called Sakanouye Tamura Maro.[4]

Very similar themes were expressed in 1946 "In the Orient," the first
section in *Distinguished Negroes Abroad,* a book by Beatrice J. Fleming and
Marion J. Pryde in which was contained a small chapter dedicated to "The
Negro General of Japan—Sakanouye Tamuramaro."[5]

Joel Augustus Rogers (1883-1966) was a scholar unequaled in assembling
data about African people. A real giant, Rogers probably did more to popular-
ize African history than any single scholar of the twentieth century. Rogers
was born in Nagril, Jamaica 6 September 1883. In 1906 he moved to the
United States and spent most of his life in Harlem. Largely self-trained,
Rogers was an anthropologist, historian, journalist and a prolific writer. He
covered the Marcus Garvey trial, and though never a member of the Universal
Negro Improvement Association, wrote for Garvey's *Negro World.* In 1930
Rogers was elected to membership in the Paris Society of Anthropology. Also

in 1930, in Ethiopia, he attended the coronation of Haile Selassie as a correspondent for the *Amsterdam News*. Beginning in 1935, Rogers served as war correspondent for the *Pittsburgh Courier* during the Italian aggression in Ethiopia. He contributed to such publications as the *Crisis, American Mercury* and *Survey Graphic*. W.E.B. DuBois wrote that, "No man living has revealed so many important facts about the Negro race as has Rogers."[6]

In 1940 Rogers devoted several pages of the first volume of his *Sex and Race* to the Black presence in early Japan. He cites the studies of a number of accomplished scholars and anthropologists, and even goes as far as to raise the question of "were the first Japanese Negroes?" In the words of Rogers:

> There is a very evident Negro strain in a certain element of the Japanese population, particularly those of the south. Imbert says, 'The Negro element in Japan is recognizable by the Negroid aspect of certain inhabitants with dark and often blackish skin, frizzly or curly hair....The Negritos are the oldest race of the Far East. It has been proved that they once lived in Eastern and Southern China as well as in Japan where the Negrito element is recognizable still in the population.'[7]

Rogers mentioned Tamuramaro briefly in the first volume of *World's Great Men of Color*, also published in 1946. Regrettably, Rogers was forced to confess that "I have come across certain names in China and Japan such as Sakonouye Tamuramaro, the first shogun of Japan but I did not follow them up."[8]

Sakanouye Tamuramaro was a warrior symbolized in early Japanese history as a "paragon of military virtues." Could it be that this was what Cheikh Anta Diop was alluding to in 1954 in his first major book, *Nations negres et culture*, when he directed our attention to the tantalizing and yet profound Japanese proverb: "For a Samurai to be brave he must have a bit of Black blood."[9]

Gabriel K. Osei was born in Ghana during the late 1930s. He studied law at the University College and founded the African Publication Society. In 1968 in his book entitled *Europe's Gift to Africa* Osei, like Ferris, Woodson and Wesley before him, cited Chamberlain's remarks on Tamuramaro.[10]

Adwoa Asantewaa B. Munroe referenced Tamuramaro in the 1981 publication *What We Should Know About African Religion, History and Culture* and cites Gabriel K. Osei's *African Contributions to Civilization* as the source. Of Tamuramaro, Munroe wrote that "He was an African warrior. He was prominent during the rule of the Japanese Emperor Kwammu, who reigned from 782-806 A.D."[11]

In 1989 Mark Hyman, a doctoral candidate at Temple University, authored a booklet entitled *Black Shogun of Japan*. Hyman concluded his remarks on Tamuramaro by stating that "The fact remains that Sakanouye Tammamura Maro was an African. He was a Japanese. He was a great fighting general. He was a Japanese Shogun."[12]

However the most comprehensive assessment to date of the Black presence in early Japan and the life of Sakanouye no Tamuramaro is art historian and University of Chicago doctoral candidate James E. Brunson's *The World of Sakanouye No Tamuramaro: Black Shogun of Early Japan* published in 1991. Brunson had previously published a series of detailed articles, monographs and books on the African presence in early Asia. In *The World of Sakanouye No Tamuramaro* Brunson accurately noted that "In order to fully understand the world of Sakanouye Tamuramaro we must focus on all aspects of the African presence in the Far East."[13]

Notes to Appendix

1. William Henry Ferris, *The African Abroad*, vol. 2 (New Haven: Tuttle, Morehouse & Taylor Press, 1913), 541-42.

2. W.E.B. DuBois, *The Negro* (1915; rpt. London: Oxford University Press, 1970), 84.

3. Carter G. Woodson and Charles H. Wesley, *The Negro In Our History*, 12th ed. (Washington, D.C.: Associated Publishers, 1972), 45. Historian, educator and administrator, Charles Harris Wesley was born in Louisville, Kentucky in 1891. Wesley attended Columbia University and Guilde International in Paris; received a B.A. from Fisk in 1911, an M.A. from Yale in 1913 and a Ph.D. from Harvard in 1925. In 1930-31 he was the recipient of a Guggenheim Fellowship. In 1913 Wesley joined the faculty of Howard University, eventually becoming a professor, department chairman and dean. Wesley served as editor of the *Negro History Bulletin* and in 1965 became the Director of the Association for the Study of Negro Life and History.

4. Lois M. Jones, "Sakanouye Tamura Maro," *Negro History Bulletin* 4, No. 2 (1940), 31.

5. Beatrice J. Fleming and Marion J. Pryde, *Distinguished Negroes Abroad* (Washington, D.C.: Associated Publishers, 1946), 3-9.

6. W.E.B. DuBois, *The World and Africa: An Inquiry Into the Part that Africa Has Played in World History* (1946; rpt. New York: International Publishers, 1965), xi.

7. J.A. Rogers, *Sex and Race*, vol. 1 (New York: Rogers, 1940), 68-70.

8. Rogers, *World's Great Men of Color*, vol. 1 (1946; rpt. New York: Macmillan, 1972), 20.

9. Cheikh Anta Diop, *The African Origin of Civilization*, trans. Mercer Cook (Westport: Lawrence Hill, 1974), 281. Another recording of the proverb, documented by Maget and cited by Eugene Pittard, professor of Anthropology at the University of Geneva, in 1926 reads: "Half the blood in one's veins must be black to make a good Samurai." Eugene Pittard, *Race and History* (New York: Alfred A. Knopf, 1926), 408.

10. Gabriel K. Osei, *Europe's Gift to Africa* (London: African Publication Society, 1968), 23.

11. Adwoa Asantewaa B. Munroe, *What We Should Know About African Religion, History and Culture* (London: African Publication Society, 1981), 50.

12. Mark Hyman, *Black Shogun of Japan* (Philadelphia: Mark Hyman Associates, 1989), 5.

13. James E. Brunson, *The World of Sakanouye No Tamuramaro* (DeKalb: Kara, 1991), 4.

SAKANOUYE TAMURAMARO AND THE BLACK PRESENCE IN JAPANESE ANTIQUITY: A SELECTED BIBLIOGRAPHY

"African-Like Stone Age Hut is Unearthed in Japan." *Associated Press,* 15 Feb 1986.

Atsuru, Yagi. "Sakanoue no Tamuramaro (758-811)." In the *Kodansha Encyclopedia of Japan,* Volume 6. Tokyo: Kodansha, 1983: 379.

Boddy, James Marmaduke. "The Ethnology of the Japanese Race." *The Colored American Magazine* (Oct 1905): 577-85.

Brunson, James E. "Japanese Racism and Self-Inferiority." *Mo Better News* (Summer 1991): 6.

Brunson, James E. *The World of Sakanouye No Tamuramaro: Black Shogun of Early Japan.* DeKalb: KARA, 1991.

Carter, William R. "Sakanoue Family." In the *Kodansha Encyclopedia of Japan,* Volume 6. Tokyo: Kodansha, 1983: 379.

Chamberlain, Alexander Francis. "The Contribution of the Negro to Human Civilization." *Journal of Race Development* 2 (Apr 1911): 458-71.

Diop, Cheikh Anta. *The African Origin of Civilization: Myth or Reality.* Translated from the French and edited by Mercer Cook. Translator's Preface by Mercer Cook. Westport: Lawrence Hill, 1974.

Diop, Cheikh Anta. *Civilization or Barbarism: An Authentic Anthropology.* Translated from the French by Yaa-Lengi Meema Ngemi. Edited by Harold J. Salemson and Marjolijn de Jager. Foreword by John Henrik Clarke. Westport: Lawrence Hill, 1991.

Dixon, Roland B. *The Racial History of Man.* New York: Scribner's, 1923.

Ferris, William Henry. *The African Abroad: Or, His Evolution in Western Civilization: Tracing His Development Under Caucasian Milieu.* Volume 2. New Haven: Tuttle, Morehouse & Taylor Press, 1913.

Fleming, Beatrice J., and Marion J. Pryde. "The Negro General of Japan—Sakanouye Tamuramaro." Chap. in *Distinguished Negroes Abroad.* Washington, D.C.: Associated Publishers, 1946: 3-9.

Hulse, Frederick S. "Physical Types Among the Japanese." In *Studies in the Anthropology of Oceania and Asia.* Edited by Carleton S. Coon and James M. Andrews IV. Cambridge, MA: Peabody Museum of American Archaeology and Ethnology, Harvard University, 1943: 122-33.

Hyman, Mark. *Black Shogun of Japan and Sophonisba: Wife of Two Warring Kings: Other Events from Ancient Times.* Introduction by Edward Sims, Jr. Philadelphia: Mark Hyman Associates, 1989.

Jones, Lois Mailou. "Sakanouye Tamura Maro." *Negro History Bulletin* 4, No. 2 (Nov 1940): 31.

Munro, Neil Gordon. *Prehistoric Japan.* Yokohama, 1911.

Munroe, Adwoa Asantewaa B. *What We Should Know About African Religion, History and Culture.* London: African Publication Society, 1981.

Murdoch, James. *A History of Japan, Volume 1: From the Origins to the Arrival of the Portuguese in 1542 A.D.* London: Kegan Paul, Trench, Trubner & Co., 1925.

Osei, Gabriel K. *Europe's Gift to Africa.* London: African Publication Society, 1968.

Osei, Gabriel K. *African Contributions to Civilization.* London: African Publication Society, 1973.

Papinot, E. *Historical and Geographical Dictionary of Japan,* Volume 2. New York: Frederick Ungar, 1964.

Person-Lynn, Kwaku. "First Japanese Were Black." *Los Angeles Sentinel,* 14 Mar 1991: A-8.

Pittard, Eugene. "The Japanese." Chap. in *Race and History: An Ethnological Introduction to History.* New York: Alfred A. Knopf, 1926: 403-10.

Rogers, Joel Augustus. *Sex and Race. Vol. 1, The Old World.* New York: Rogers, 1940.

Sansom, George. *A History of Japan to 1334.* Stanford: Stanford University Press, 1958.

"Senghor Presents 'Actual Facts' on Japanese: They're Descendants from Blacks." *The Final Call* 6, No. 5 (1987).

Suzuki, Hiroe. "September Meeting Report." *JAFA News: Japan Afro-American Friendship Association Dedicated to Friendship and Mutual Understanding Between Japanese People and the Black Community in Japan* (Dec 1993): 5-6.

Williams, George Washington. *History of the Negro Race in America from 1619 to 1880. Negroes as Slaves, as Soldiers, and as Citizens; Together with a Preliminary Consideration of the Unity of the Human Family, an Historical Sketch of Africa, and an Account of the Negro Governments of Sierra Leone and Liberia, in Two Volumes,* Vol. 1. New York: G.P. Putnam's Sons, 1883.

Winters, Clyde-Ahmad. "Further Thoughts on Japanese Dravidian Connections." *Dravidian Linguistics Association News* 5, No. 9 (Sep 1981): 1-4.

Woodson, Carter Godwin, and Charles H. Wesley. "Africans in History with Others." Chap. in *The Negro In Our History.* 12th ed. Washington, D.C.: Associated Publishers, 1972.

THE BLACK PRESENCE IN CLASSICAL SOUTHEAST ASIAN CIVILIZATION

By Runoko Rashidi

For the complexion of men, they consider black the most beautiful. In all the kingdoms of the southern region, it is the same.

Nan Ts'i Chou

The most prominent and enduring kingdom of early Southeast Asia was Angkor (802–1431). The builders of Angkor were an Africoid people known as Khmers, a name that loudly recalls Kmt (ancient Egypt). It is also interesting to note that the genealogies of Angkor, like Kmt, were matrilineal in character. In remote antiquity the Khmers established themselves throughout a vast area that encompassed portions of the modern countries of Myanmar, Thailand, Kampuchea, Malaysia, Vietnam and Laos.

Much of our knowledge of early Southeast Asia is derived from Chinese and Indian sources. Chinese historical documents speak of the Funanese (the builders of the earliest kingdom in Southeast Asia) as "ugly and black. Their hair is curly."[1] The Khmer men, essentially the same as the Funanese, were described by the Chinese as "small and black."[2] In 1923 Harvard University anthropologist Roland Burrage Dixon noted that the ancient Khmers were physically "marked by distinctly short stature, dark skin, curly or even frizzly hair, broad noses and thick negroid lips."[3]

The Kingdom of Chenla

By the midpoint of the sixth century, extensive agricultural reversals combined with the loss of cardinal trade routes had led to a drastic deterioration in Funan's stature and prestige. The focal point of regional domination was then transferred northwards to Chenla, where stone was in great abundance, and utilized as a major building material for the first time in the history of Southeast Asia. The Kingdom of Chenla, initially a vassal state of Funan, was the second significant Khmer kingdom and was divided into two parts— Upper Chenla and Lower Chenla. The southern state (Lower Chenla), bordering on the sea, was covered with lakes and waterways, and was called *Water Chenla*. The northern state (Upper Chenla), which consisted of mountains and valleys, extended northward to the present Chinese province of Yunnan, and was called *Land Chenla*. The Chinese called Upper Chenla *Wen Tan* and *Po-lieu*. In 722 Upper Chenla joined in a war against the Chinese governor of Chiao-chou (Tonkin). The leader of the revolt defeated the Chinese forces, conquered Chiao-chou and proclaimed himself Hei-ti, "Black Emperor."[4] The chronicle of the Khmer Kingdom of Chenla is much the same as that of Funan. After many decades of prosperity, late during the eighth century trade with India was disrupted, resulting in a severe administrative break down and Chenla's descent into darkness.

The Kingdom of Angkor

Early in the ninth century Jayavarman II (802–850) unified the Khmer kingdom and identified himself with the powerful Hindu deity Shiva. The Khmers of Angkor were sophisticated agriculturalists, advanced engineers, aggressive merchants and intrepid warriors. They developed a splendid irrigation system (with some canals extending forty miles in length), and created grandiose hydraulic works. The hydraulic system of Angkor was used for transportation and for rice cultivation to support a surrounding population estimated at one million people. During the reign of King Indravarman I (877–889), for example, the vast artificial lake known as the *Indratataka* was completed. It was also during the reign of Indravarman that inscriptions began to refer to the kingdom of the Khmer as *Kambuja,* or *Kambujadesa*—the origin of the modern name of Kampuchea (the country formerly called Cambodia). The Chinese continued to call the whole country Chenla, and the Khmers engaged in extensive international trade with both India and China. For the harsh purposes of war the Khmer engineers designed machines to launch fearsome arrows and hurl sharp spears at their enemies, and rode boldly into battle atop ornately outfitted elephants.

In the Khmer language, Angkor means *the city* or *the capital.* In 889 King Yasovarman I (889–900) constructed his capital on the current site of Angkor, and over the centuries Khmer monarchs augmented the city with their own distinct contributions. Notably, it was during the reigns of Rajendravarman II (944–968) and Jayavarman V (969–1001) that the East Mebon, Pre Rup, Banteay Srei, Phimeanakas and Ta Keo temples were constructed.

Angkor eventually covered an expanse of seventy-seven square miles and was designed to be completely self-sufficient. The Khmers were magnificent builders in stone, and for more than six-hundred years successive dynasties commissioned the construction of meticulously detailed temples, such as Banteay Samre, marvelous artificial lakes, like the Indratataka, and incomparable temple-mountains, including Angkor Wat—the crown jewel of Angkor and estimated to contain as much stone as the Dynasty IV pyramid of King Khafre in Old Kingdom Kmt.

Figure 1. Colossal Africoid figure from early Southeast Asia. Photo courtesy of Wayne B. Chandler

Angkor Wat

Called "the largest stone monument in the world,"[5] Angkor Wat, the most famous of the Khmer stone structures, took thirty-seven years to build. During this period millions of tons of sandstone used in its construction were transported to the site by river raft from a quarry at Mount Kulen, located twenty-five miles to the northeast. Angkor Wat rises in three successive flights to five central towers that represent the peaks of Mount Meru—the cosmic or world mountain that lies at the center of the universe in Hindu mythology and considered the celestial residence of the Hindu pantheon. The towers of Angkor Wat, the tallest of which rises about two hundred feet above the surrounding flatlands, are Kampuchea's national symbol. The temple's outer walls represent the mountains at the edge of the world, while the moat surrounding the temple represents the oceans beyond.

The Angkor Wat temple dates from the twelfth century reign of Suryavarman II (1113–1150) when the Khmer dominion over Southeast Asia was at its zenith, with an empire "stretching from the South China Sea to modern Thailand, as far north as the uplands of Laos and as far south as the Malay Peninsula. King Suryavarman II built it as a funerary temple for himself, and dedicated it to the Hindu god Vishnu, whom the king represented on Earth and with whom he integrated on his death."[6] Called "the most powerful king in the country's history," Suryavarman II was the first Angkorean king since Jayavarman II to send missions to China.

Angkor Wat is decorated throughout with intricate bas-reliefs depicting stories from the epic Hindu poems, the *Mahabharata* and the *Ramayana* (narrating the myths of Krishna, Vishnu and Rama), with marching armies and more than 1,700 vivid and sensual depictions of the celestial female dancers of the Khmers known as *apsaras*. French architect and archaeologist Henri Parmentier gave his opinion of the apsaras of Angkor Wat in 1923 when he said that, "To me they are Grace personified, the highest expression of femininity ever conceived by the human mind."[7] To the members of the Khmer court, a walk to the center of Angkor Wat was a metaphorical trip of the spirit to the center of the universe.

The Kingdom of Champa

Angkor was not the only significant kingdom of its time in Southeast Asia. Another major Southeast Asian power and sometimes rival of Angkor was the Kingdom of Champa. While Champa, like Angkor, was a substantially Indianized kingdom, the Cham are believed to have settled along the coastal plains of mid-southern Vietnam (Annam) more than two millennia ago, and essentially dominated the area from about the fourth through the thirteenth

Figure 2. The Buddha. 10th Century Bronze, Thailand. Janake Collection.

centuries. According to one account, the Kingdom of Champa was born of a victory by the Blacks "over the Chinese province of Je-Nan in +137; later, it frequently demonstrated its unruliness and spirit of conquest, including against China, of which it had become theoretically a tributary."[8]

Chinese dynastic records from as early as 192 C.E. reference a kingdom of Lin-yi, which meant the "land of Black men."[9] The kingdom of Lin-yi was known as *Champa* in Sanskrit documents. Its inhabitants possessed "'black skin, eyes deep in the orbit, nose turned up, hair frizzy' at a period when they were not yet subject to foreign domination and preserved the purity of this type."[10] These records expressly state that:

> For the complexion of men, they consider black the most beautiful. In all the kingdoms of the southern region, it is the same.[11]

Chinese scribes added that the Cham adorned themselves:

> In a single piece of cotton or silk wrapped about the body....They are very clean; they wash themselves several times each day, wear perfume, and rub their bodies with a lotion compounded with camphor and musk.[12]

H. Otley Beyer believed that between 900 and 1200 C.E. a group of sea-farers made their exodus from Southern Annam and found their way to the Philippines. They were called the *"Orang Dampuans* or Men of Champa." "The *Orang Dampuans,"* wrote Beyer, "were the first civilized foreigners to establish a settlement in Sulu, according to the most reliable of pre-Moham-medan histories."[13] During this same period Cham ships, known to the Chinese by the appellation *kun-lun bo* (the "vessels of Black men"), were navigating the currents of the Indian Ocean ranging from Southeast Asia to Madagascar.[14]

Among the major centers of Champa were those based near Dong Duong, Tra Kieu and Pandulanga (Phan-Rang). The great southern capital was Vijaya (Binh Dinh), and the early northern capital and religious center was Mi Son. From its inception in the fifth century, Mi Son was a cardinal center of Brahminic worship. More than seventy temples were constructed at Mi Son from the seventh through the twelfth centuries. The masterpiece of Cham architecture at Mi Son was an enormous, seventy-foot-high stone tower that was destroyed by U.S. Army commandos in August 1969.

By the beginning of the tenth century the Cham were being aggressively pressured and gradually absorbed by Sinicized Vietnamese. By the end of the tenth century, Sinicized Vietnamese had annexed the northern provinces of Champa. In 1225 the Vietnamese once again followed a course of aggression, and in 1283 the Mongols under Kublai Khan desolated the entire coast. All told, however, more than a hundred temples and a multitude of exquisite statuary have survived to remind us of the former splendor of the traders, artisans and royalty of the realm of the Cham.

During the eleventh and twelfth centuries Champa, whose ethnic character was being rapidly transformed by the influx of Sinicized Vietnamese, was engaged in intense martial conflicts with Angkor. In 1177 a Cham fleet sailed up the Mekong River and sacked Angkor—an event chronicled in a bas-relief at the Bayon. In defense of Angkor, an exiled Khmer prince who would come to be known as Jayavarman VII, gathered formidable armies, shattered the Cham forces and drove them from Angkor.

King Jayavarman VII: Angkor's Most Prolific Builder

The reign of Jayavarman VII (1181–1220) marks the height and the beginning of the decline of the kingdom of Angkor. Jayavarman VII (the prefix of whose name, *Jaya*, in Sanskrit, means "victory") was so successful in his military campaigns with Champa, in fact, that during the last seventeen years of his reign Champa was virtually a Khmer province. Jayavarman VII lived more than nine decades, ruling with strength and wisdom. Almost all of the earlier kings of Angkor had been Hindus, but Jayavarman VII was a devout Buddhist monarch whose second wife, Indradevi (described as "intelligent by nature, scholarly, very pure, devoted to her husband"), became chief lecturer at a Buddhist foundation.[15]

In 1181 Jayavarman VII was proclaimed king in the battled-scarred and essentially devastated Khmer capital, and many of the monuments of Angkor reflect his Herculean reconstruction efforts and seemingly ceaseless building projects. Jayavarman VII built more than any other Khmer king. Indeed, it is calculated that he built more than all the others put together. In fact, as magnificent as it is, Angkor Wat is only one of 215 sites in the immediate region. Other famous sites include the Bayon, the sculptured stone mountain at the center of the six-square-mile walled city of Angkor Thom, about a mile northeast of Angkor Wat, and the capital of the Khmer empire from the late tenth through the early thirteenth century. "To protect Angkor Thom, Jayavarman constructed a moated stone wall around the city, with five monumental bridges."[16]

The Bayon

The Bayon, an Angkor temple second in size only to Angkor Wat, is an intricate, eight hundred-year-old shrine celebrated for the gigantic stone faces of its builder, Jayavarman VII. In 1297 a Chinese diplomat named Chou Ta-kuan described the Bayon as shining with gold, and exclaimed that:

> On the eastern side is a golden bridge, guarded by two lions of gold, one on each side, with eight golden Buddhas spaced along the stone chambers. North of the Golden Tower, at a distance of about two hundred

Figure 3. Map of Southeast Asia.

Figure 4. Africoid figure from early Vietnam (Champa). Photo courtesy of Wayne B. Chandler

Figure 5. Africoid figure from early Vietnam (Champa). Photo courtesy of
Wayne B. Chandler

yards, rises the Tower of Bronze (Baphuon), higher even than the Golden Tower: a truly astonishing spectacle, with more than ten chambers at its base. A quarter of a mile further north is the residence of the King. Rising above his private apartments is another tower of gold. These are the monuments which have caused merchants from overseas to speak so often of 'Cambodia the rich and noble.'[17]

An inscription on the Bayon temple pertaining to Jayavarman states that, "He suffered from the sicknesses of his subjects more than from his own: for it is the public grief which makes the grief of kings and not their personal grief."[18]

The Ta Prohm and Preah Khan Temples

The Ta Prohm and Preah Khan temples, monuments almost as large as Angkor Wat, were also erected by the prolific Jayavarman VII and were designed by him as mausoleums for his mother and his father (Dharanindravarman II), respectively. The inscription of Ta Prohm reveals that there were 102 hospitals in the Khmer empire when Jayavarman VII reigned. The medical personnel in each hospital consisted of two doctors, two pharmacists, fourteen guardians, eight male nurses, six female nurses, six orderlies, two cooks, two clerks and sixty general assistants.

The Preah Khan temple, a veritable labyrinth of pavilions, halls and chapels, immerses about a square mile of ponderously wooded land just north of the enclosed city of Angkor Thom. According to the dedicatory stele dating to 1191, the site sheltered 515 pietistic portraits, which were embellished with immense quantities of silk veils and golden jewelry set with diamonds, emeralds and pearls.

The Decline and Fall of Angkor and Champa

After the death of Jayavarman VII Angkor began to decline, and no great monuments were constructed after his reign. Jayavarman VII was succeeded by Indravarman II (1219–1243). His successor, Jayavarman VIII (1243–1295), reestablished Brahminic dominance at the Khmer court, and by the beginning of the fifteenth century the entire kingdom was on the verge of total collapse. During the fifteenth century the Khmers endeavored to repulse a steady series of Thai invasions and preserve the last vestiges of Classical Khmer civilization.

Although the early people of the country now known as Thailand clearly reflect a pronounced Africoid phenotype (based on numerous depictions of Buddhas and Bodhisattvas), the people referred to here as Thai (sometimes called *Siamese*) were originally a tribal people without writing or an organized state. The Thai invaders of Angkor were Sinicized or Mongoloid types generally believed to be ethnically related to modern Chinese. In any case, they, or at least a large group or groups of them, lived in the southern and southeastern portions of the country now known as China. Similar peoples. Sinicized Vietnamese, brought about the final destruction of the kingdom of Champa in 1471.

The invasion of the Thais was a life or death struggle for the Khmers. Able-bodied Khmer men and the last remnant of the Khmer intelligentsia were abducted as captives and carried away, and the intricate irrigation system of Angkor, which required constant innovation and vigilance, ceased to work effectively. Archaeological excavations have shown that the Thais blocked the canals at Angkor, so that Kingdom of Angkor's complex and elaborate irrigation system was virtually ruptured. In 1431, after a seven month siege, the Thais occupied and ravaged Angkor and pilfered many of its statues. By the end of 1432 came the physical abandonment of Angkor by the Khmer court and the removal of the capital, first to the province of Srei Santhor and later to Phnom Penh and Oudong.

The Ruins of Angkor

Angkor was eventually retaken from the Thais and even experienced a brief renaissance in the late sixteenth century, but soon afterwards slipped into obscurity. However even as late as 1860 a young French scholar and scientist, Henri Mouhot, recorded in his diary that "It is grander than anything left to us by Greece or Rome."[19] Visiting the site for the first time, Mouhot was able to write that:

> In the province still bearing the name of Ongcor [Angkor], there are…ruins of such grandeur, remains of structures which must have been raised at such an immense cost of labor, that at first view one is filled with profound admiration and cannot but ask what has become of this power-ful race, so civilized, so enlightened, the authors of these gigantic works.[20]

The ruins of the 124-square-mile archaeological district of Angkor consists of several hundred monuments built of laterite, brick and sandstone, ranging in size from small pavilions to massive temples. Unfortunately, however, the famed temples of Angkor, alternately consumed by man, vegetation and neglect, are in danger of quietly disintegrating. Although Angkor Wat itself remains in use as a Buddhist temple and has been spared some of the more extreme ravages of other parts of the complex, it has not gone entirely unscathed. Headless statues abound at Angkor Wat. At Angkor Wat, damage to the region's ancient irrigation system over the centuries has drained the underlying water table, and the weight of the central towers has caused them

Figure 6. The Standing Shiva. 10th Century C.E. Vietnam (Champa). Photo courtesy of Gaynell Catherine

Figure 7. Depiction of Shiva. Vietnam (Champa), date unknown. Photo
courtesy of Wayne B. Chandler

Figure 8. Colossal Buddha head. From Dong-Duong, Vietnam (Champa), 875
C.E. sandstone, Musee Guimet, Paris.

to subside, leaving large cracks between giant carved stone blocks, while fungi consumes the stone itself. According to the Reuters news agency, "The work could take twenty years and cost up to $100 million."[21] The disused Ta Prohm temple, also from the twelfth century, has been taken over by fast-growing banyan trees, and creepers dozens of yards long enmesh its friezes.

Art thieves and plunderers have also engaged in relentless and rampant destruction at Angkor. During the French occupation of Kampuchea untold numbers of artworks were physically taken out of the country. More recently, after the Vietnamese overran Kampuchea in 1978 and replaced the Khmer Rouge government, an underground sculpture trade flourished. UNESCO has estimated that artworks are being stolen from Angkor at the rate of one per day. A famous statue at the royal city of Angkor Thom, called the *Leper King,* was removed to the museum of Preservation d' Angkor after it had been decapitated. Afterwards, the museum replaced the statue with a replica made of cement. Only a few weeks later, however, thieves made off with the replacement head of the substitute *Leper King,* reinforcing rods and all.

Figure 9. Figures of divinities from the Banteay Samre temple at Angkor. Constructed by Suryavarman II in the 12th century.

Figure 10. Central portion of the Bayon temple, Angkor. Constructed by Jayavarman VII in the 12th century.

Figure 11. Central portion of the Bayon temple, Angkor. Constructed by Jayavarman VII in the 12th century.

Notes

1. Quoted in Lawrence Palmer Briggs, *The Ancient Khmer Empire* (Philadelphia: American Philosophical Society, 1951), 16.
2. Quoted in Briggs, 50.
3. Roland B. Dixon, *The Racial History of Man* (New York: Scribner's, 1923), 226.
4. Quoted in Briggs, 59.
5. Russell Ciochon and Jamie James, "The Battle of Angkor Wat," *New Scientist,* 14 Oct 1989, 52.
6. Ciochon and James, 52.
7. Henri Parmentier, quoted in Michael Freeman and Roger Warner, *Angkor: The Hidden Glories,* ed. David Larkin (Boston: Houghton Mifflin, 1990), 182.
8. B. Domenichini-Ramiaramanana, "Madagascar," in *UNESCO General History of Africa, Vol. 3. Africa from the Seventh to the Eleventh Century,* ed. M. El-Fasi (Berkeley: University of California Press. 1988), 696.
9. Xu Yun-qiao, quoted in Domenichini-Ramiaramanana, 697.
10. Quoted in Georges Maspero, *The Kingdom of Champa* (New Haven: Yale University Press, 1949), 8.
11. *Nan Ts'i Chou,* quoted in Maspero, 8.
12. Quoted in Russell Ciochon and Jamie James, "Land of the Cham," *Archaeology* (May/Jun 1992), 52.
13. Quoted in Pedro A. Gagelonia, *The Filipinos of Yesteryears* (Manila: Star Book Store, 1967), 82.
14. Domenichini-Ramiaramanana, 697.
15. Christopher Pym, *The Ancient Civilization of Angkor* (New York: Mentor-New American Library, 1968), 145.
16. Russell Ciochon and Jamie James, "The Glory that was Angkor," *Archaeology* 47, No. 2 (1994), 43.
17. Chou Ta-Kuan, *The Customs of Cambodia,* trans. Paul Pelliot and J. Gilman d'Arcy Paul (Bangkok: The Siam Society, 1987), 1.
18. Quoted in Christopher Pym, 153.
19. Henri Mouhot, quoted in Freeman and Warner, 9.
20. Henri Mouhot, quoted in Russell Ciochon and Jamie James, "The Glory that was Angkor," *Archaeology* 47, No. 2 (1994), 40.
21. Reuters, "U.N. Seeks to Save Fabled Khmer Temples," *Los Angeles Times,* 1 Oct 1991.

References

Briggs, Lawrence Palmer. *The Ancient Khmer Empire.* Philadelphia: American Philosophical Society, 1951.
Chou, Ta-Kuan (Zhou Daguan). *The Customs of Cambodia.* Translated into English from the French Version by Paul Pelliot of Chou's Chinese Original by J. Gilman d'Arcy Paul. Bangkok: The Siam Society, 1987.
Ciochon, Russell, and Jamie James. "The Battle of Angkor Wat." *New Scientist* 124 (14 Oct 1989): 52–57.
Ciochon, Russell, and Jamie James. "Land of the Cham." *Archaeology* (May/ Jun 1992): 52–55.

Ciochon, Russell, and Jamie James. "The Glory That was Angkor.' *Archaeology* 47, No. 2 (Mar/Apr 1994): 38–49.

Dixon, Roland B. *The Racial History of Man.* New York: Scribner's, 1923.

Domenichini-Ramiaramanana, B. "Madagascar." In *UNESCO General History of Africa, Vol. 3. Africa from the Seventh to the Eleventh Century.* Edited by M. El-Fasi. Berkeley: University of California Press, 1988: 681–703.

Freeman, Michael, and Roger Warner. *Angkor: The Hidden Glories.* Edited by David Larkin. Boston: Houghton Mifflin, 1990.

Gagelonia, Pedro A. *The Filipinos of Yesteryears.* Manila: Star Book Store, 1967.

Maspero, Rene Gaston Georges. *The Kingdom of Champa.* Preface by John G. Embree. New Haven: Yale University Press, 1949.

Pym, Christopher. *The Ancient Civilization of Angkor.* New York: Mentor-New American Library, 1968.

Reuters. "U.N. Seeks to Save Fabled Khmer Temples." *Los Angeles Times,* 1 Oct 1991.

ANCIENT MONUMENTS OF ANGKOR, CHAMPA AND THAILAND—THE BLACK PRESENCE IN EARLY SOUTHEAST ASIA: A SELECTED BIBLIOGRAPHY

Compiled By Runoko Rashidi

Boisselier, Jean. *The Heritage of Thai Sculpture.* New York: Weatherhill, 1975.
Briggs, Lawrence Palmer. *The Ancient Khmer Empire.* Philadelphia: American Philosophical Society, 1951.
Brunson, James E. "Black Kingdoms of Southeast Asia." Chap. in *Black Jade: The African Presence in the Ancient East.* Introduction by Runoko Rashidi. DeKalb: KARA, 1985: 63–104.
Brunson, James E. *Kamite Brotherhood: African Origins in Early Asia.* DeKalb: KARA, 1989.
Brunson, James E. *Image of the Black in Eastern Art.* Pt. 3, *Kingdoms in Southeast Asia.* DeKalb: KARA, 1990.
Chakravarti, Adhir K. "The Caste System in Ancient Cambodia." *Journal of Ancient Indian History* 4, Pts. 1–2 (1970–71): 14–59.
Chandler, Wayne B. "Jayavarman VII: Ruler of the Khmer Empire." In *A Journey Into 365 Days of Black History.* Petaluma: Pomegranate Calendars & Books, 1993.
Chou, Ta-Kuan (Zhou Daguan). *The Customs of Cambodia.* Translated into English from the French Version by Paul Pelliot of Chou's Chinese Original by J. Gilman d'Arcy Paul. Bangkok: The Siam Society, 1987.
Ciochon, Russell. "Jungle Monuments of Angkor." *Natural History* (Jan 1990): 52–59.
Ciochon, Russell, and Jamie James. "The Battle of Angkor Wat." *New Scientist* 124 (14 Oct 1989): 52–57.
Ciochon, Russell, and Jamie James. "Land of the Cham." *Archaeology* (May/Jun 1992): 52–55.
Ciochon, Russell, and Jamie James. "The Glory That was Angkor." *Archaeology* 47, No. 2 (Mar/Apr 1994): 38–49.
D'Argenee, Rene-Yvon Lefebvre. "Buddhist Sculpture in the Indianized States of Southeast Asia." *Apollo* (Aug 1980): 78–86.
Freeman, Michael, and Roger Warner. *Angkor: The Hidden Glories.* Edited by David Larkin. Boston: Houghton Mifflin, 1990.
Garrett, Wilbur E. "The Temples of Angkor: Will They Survive?" *National Geographic* 161, No. 5 (1982): 548–51.
Gerini, G.E. *Researches on Ptolemy's Geography of Eastern Asia (Further India and Indo-Malay Archipelago).* London: Royal Asiatic Society and the Royal Geographical Society, 1909.
Gray. Denis D. "Angkor Wat: Restoration on Cambodia Shrine Begins. *Los Angeles Times,* Pt. 1, 6 Aug 1989: 2.
Majumdar, B.K. "Cambodia and Indian Influence (Circa 200–1432 A.D.)." *Indo-Asian Culture* (Jan 1965): 36–41.
Majumdar, R.C. *Kambuja-Desa, or An Ancient Hindu Colony in Cambodia.* Madras: University of Madras, 1944.

Majumdar, R.C. *India and South East Asia.* Edited by K.S. Ramachandralt and S.P. Gupta. Delhi: B.R. Publishing, 1979.

Maspero, Georges. *The Kingdom of Champa.* Preface by John G. Embree. New Haven: Yale University Press, 1949.

Matics, K.I. "Introduction to Khmer Monuments in Present-Day Thailand." *Arts of Asia* (Sep/Oct 1984): 45–55.

Mazzeo, Donatella, and Chiara Silvi Antonini. *Monuments of Civilization: Ancient Cambodia.* Foreword by Han Suyin. New York: Grosset & Dunlap, 1978.

Myrdal, Jan, and Gun Kessle. *Angkor: An Essay on Art and Imperialism.* Translated by P. Austin. New York: Random House, 1971.

Pym, Christopher. *The Ancient Civilization of Angkor.* New York: Mentor-New American Library, 1968.

Pym, Christopher, ed. *Henri Mouhot's Diary.* Oxford: Oxford University Press, 1967.

Rashidi, Runoko. "Kingdom Builders: The African Presence in Early Southeast Asia." *A Journey Into 365 Days of Black History.* Edited by Wayne B. Chandler. Petaluma: Pomegranate Calendars & Books, 1990: 4.

Rashidi, Runoko. "African People: The First to Inhabit Asia." *Color* 1, No. 5 (1992): 4.

Rashidi, Runoko. "The African Presence in Asia: A Brief Update." *The Challenger,* 19 Feb 1992: 18.

Rawson, Philip. *The Art of Southeast Asia: Cambodia, Vietnam, Thailand, Laos, Burma, Java and Bali.* New York: Praeger, 1967.

Reuters. "U.N. Seeks to Save Fabled Khmer Temples." *Los Angeles Times,* 1 Oct 1991.

Shenon, Philip. "Washing Buddha's Face." *New York Times Magazine,* 21 Jun 1992: 18–21.

White, Peter T. "The Temples of Angkor: Ancient Glory in Stone." *National Geographic* 161, No. 5 (1982): 552–89.

DIMINUTIVE AFRICOIDS: FIRST PEOPLE OF THE PHILIPPINES

By Runoko Rashidi

Although they presently exist in limited numbers and are generally only found in heavily forested, barren, isolated or similarly forbidding terrains, the widely dispersed groups of people we are calling *Diminutive Africoids,* who can be described very generally as exceptionally small, unusually short, dark-skinned, spiral-haired and broad-nosed, are probably the closest representatives and remnant populations of the world's earliest modern humans. Moving slowly and sporadically from their original African homeland, beginning perhaps 100,000 years ago and continuing through the millennia, untold numbers of Diminutive Africoids (the first waves of Black people), in the course of their migrations, began to gradually filter into and populate Asia. This view is consistent with DNA studies, for as Oxford University's Jim Wainscoat observed:

> It seems likely that modern man emerged in Africa and...that subsequently a founder population left Africa and spread throughout Europe, Asia and the Americas.[1]

It is no less than tragic that the exact contributions of Diminutive Africoids to monumental high-cultures characterized by urbanization, metallurgy, agricultural science and scripts remain essentially unassessed. Diminutive Africoids are minority populations in Asia and have been overwhelmingly presented as such in anthropological, ethnographic and linguistic studies by most Asian and European writers, and while an abundance of anthropological studies are available, it is exceedingly difficult to glean anything of significance from them in the form of clear historical data.

Although the great majority of the people of the Philippines are Tagalog, the country is not ethnically homogeneous. The original inhabitants of the Philippines are the Agta (Diminutive Africoids), who still live there in some numbers and are commonly and pejoratively called *Pygmies, Negritos* and *Aeta,* and a variety of other names based upon their specific locale.

Very similar groups of Black people in Asia reside (in relatively small numbers) in the Andaman Islands in the Bay of Bengal in the Indian Ocean north of the Indonesian island of Sumatra, and in northern Malaysia and southern Thailand in Southeast Asia. In Thailand they are commonly called *Sakai.* In Malaysia they have been called Orang Asli (*Original Man*); pejoratively they are known as *Semang,* with the connotation of savage.

The presence of Diminutive Africoids (whom Chinese historians called "Black Dwarfs") in early southern China during the period of the Three Kingdoms (ca. 250 C.E.), is recorded in the book of the *Official of the Liang Dynasty* (502–556 C.E.).[2] In Taiwan there are recollections of a group of people now said to be extinct called "Little Black Man."

> They were described as short, dark-skinned people with short curly hair....These people, presumably Negritos, disappeared about 100 years ago. Their existence was mentioned in many Chinese documents of the Ching Dynasty concerning Taiwan.[3]

Other Diminutive Africoid populations in Asia have been identified, at least tentatively, in Kampuchea, Myanmar, Pakistan, Indonesia, Vietnam and ancient Japan.

In stark contrast to the Agta (The *People*), the Tagalog seem to have only entered the Philippines during the last several thousand years, and while almost nothing is known of the early history of the Agta in the Philippines, it has been well documented that they engaged in bitter martial conflicts with the Spanish invaders of the Philippines, whose presence in the islands began in the sixteenth century. Indeed, the country was named by the Spanish navigator Ruy Lopez de Villalobos for Prince Philip of Asturias, who, as Philip II, became the king of Spain in 1542. It was also the Spaniards who named the native people of the Philippines "Negritos" (*Little Blacks*).

The Spanish observed that "The Negritos, which our first conquerors found were, according to tradition, the first possessors of the islands of this Archipelago."[4] Another account observed that "There are black Negroes in this island who pay tribute to no one."[5] Similar documents affirm the widespread presence and distribution of the Agta in the Philippines at the time of the Spanish intrusion. "If we are to believe later historians, the shores of some of the islands fairly swarmed with Negritos when the Spaniards arrived."[6] The Bisayan island of Negroes derives its name from having been an Agta population center.[7] Today, however, the Agta probably comprise less than one per cent of the national population.

Although the accuracy of the report is questionable, it is said that the Agta were "such enemies to the Spaniards, that if they happen to kill one, they invite all their kindred, and rejoice for three days, drinking out of the skull, clear'd for that purpose; by which means, they afterwards get wives the easier, as being more courageous."[8]

Dr. Pedro A. Gagelonia, a Filipino scholar, citing the commentaries of the European colonizers of the Philippines regarding the Agta, wrote that:

> They were the aborigines of the Philippines, and for a long time been masters of Luzon. At a time not very far distant, when the Spaniards conquered the country, the Aetas levied a kind of blackmail from the

Tagalog villages situated on the banks of the lake of Bay (Laguna de Bay). At a fixed period they quitted their forests, entered the village, and forced the inhabitants to give them a certain quantity of rice and maize....After the conquest of the Philippines by the Spaniards, the latter took upon themselves the defense of the Tagalogs, and the Aetas, terrified by their firearms, remained in the forests, and did not reappear among the Indians.[9]

The Eruptions of Mt. Pinatubo

The violent eruptions of Mt. Pinatubo in June 1991 were particularly devastating for the Agta. Alternately ignored and discriminated against, many Agta lived on the slopes of the long-dormant volcano that is regarded as the center of their cosmology. Forced down the mountain slopes by the eruptions, numbers of Agta, who have historically relied on the herbal medicines now buried under tons of mud and ash, have perished from dreadful epidemics of measles, diarrhea and pneumonia.[10]

Notes

1. Jim Wainscoat, "Out of the Garden of Eden," *Nature* 325 (1 Jan 1987), 13.

2. Li Chi, *The Formation of the Chinese People* (1928; rpt. New York: Russell & Russell, 1967), 245.

3. Chen Kang Chai, *Taiwan Aborigines* (Cambridge: Harvard University Press, 1967), 33.

4. Quoted in Pedro A. Gagelonia, *The Filipinos of Yesteryears* (Manila: Star Book Store, 1967), 82.

5. Francisco Combes, *Historia de las Islas de Mindanao, Joly y sus Adjacentes* (Madrid, 1667). Quoted in Gagelonia, 103.

6. William Allan Reed, *The Negritos of Zambales* (Manila, 1940).

7. A.L. Kroeber, *Peoples of the Philippines,* 2d ed. (New York: American Museum of Natural History, 1943), 39.

8. Gagelonia, 111.

9. Gagelonia, 113–15.

10. Bob Drogin, "Pinatubo's Agonizing Aftermath," *Los Angeles Times,* 9 Oct 1991, 1.

DIMINUTIVE AFRICOIDS IN SOUTHEAST ASIA: A SELECTED BIBLIOGRAPHY

Compiled by Runoko Rashidi

Bennagen, P.L. "The Negrito: A Rallying Call to Save a Filipino Group from Cultural Extinction." In *Filipino Heritage: The Making of a Nation*. Manila: Lahing Pilipino, 1977.

"Black People are Catching Hell in the Philippines." *Zamani* 9, No. 3 (1990): 10.

Brandt, John H. "The Negrito of Peninsular Thailand." *Journal of the Siam Society* (Nov 1961): 123–143.

Brandt, John H. "The Southeast Asian Negrito: Further Notes on the Negrito of South Thailand." *Journal of the Siam Society* (Jan 1965): 27–38.

Branigin, William. "'Angry' Mt. Pinatubo Evicts Aboriginal Tribe." *San Francisco Chronicle,* 14 Jul 1991.

Chai, Chen Kang. *Taiwan Aborigines: A Genetic Study of Tribal Variations*. Cambridge: Harvard University Press, 1967.

Chi, Li. *The Formation of the Chinese People: An Anthropological Inquiry*. 1928; rpt. New York: Russell & Russell, 1967.

Drogin, Bob. "Pinatubo's Agonizing Aftermath." *Los Angeles Times,* 9 Oct 1991: 1.

Drogin, Bob. "Under the Volcano." *Los Angeles Times Magazine,* 11 Aug 1991: 22–26.

Evans, Ivor H.N. *The Negritos of Malaya*. London: Cambridge University Press, 1937.

Evrard, Alain. "Encounter with a Vanishing Forest People: The Pugot of Isabela." *Orientations* 10, No. 11 (1979): 34–39.

Gagelonia, Pedro A. "Negritos." Chap. in *The Filipinos of Yesteryears*. Manila: Star Book Store, 1967: 101–33.

Griffin, P. Bion, and Agnes Estioko-Griffin, eds. *The Agta of Northeastern Luzon: Recent Studies*. Cebu City: San Carlos Publications, 1985.

Headland, Thomas N. "Agta Negitos of the Philippines." *Cultural Survival Quarterly* 8, No. 3 (1984): 29–31.

Hutchcroft, Paul. "This is Whose Land?: The 'Squatter Problem' at Clark." *Southeast Asia Chronicle* (Apr 1983): 20–26.

Kingdon, Jonathan. "Eve's Descendants." Chap. in *Self-Made Man: Human Evolution from Eden to Extinction?* New York: John Wiley, 1993: 255–93.

Lebar, F.M. *Ethnic Groups of Insular Southeast Asia, Vol. 2: Philippines and Formosa*. New Haven: HRAF, 1975.

Maceda, Marcelino N. *The Culture of the Mamanua (Northeast Mindanao) as Compared with that of the Other Negritos of Southeast Asia*. 2d ed. Cebu City: University of San Carlos, 1975.

Noval-Morales, Daisy, Y., and James Monan. *A Primer on the Negritos of the Philippines*. Preface by Rudolf Rahmann. Manila: Philippine Business for Social Progress, 1979.

Orang Asli Studies Newsletter. Hanover: Department of Anthropology, Dartmouth College (Jan 1983-Dec 1993).

Peterson, Jean Treloggen. *The Ecology of Social Boundaries: Agta Foragers of the Philippines.* Urbana: University of Illinois Press, 1978.

Reed, William Allen. *The Negritos of Zambales,* 1905; rpt. Manila: Bureau of Public Printing, 1940.

Warren, Charles P. "Minority Student Response to the Anthropology of Asian Black Populations." Chicago: Department of Anthropology, University of Illinois at Chicago, 1982.

Figure 1. Agta family in the Philippines

THE PRINCIPLE OF POLARITY

By Wayne Chandler

Author's Introduction: It is the general consensus that the I-Ching originated in China and is Chinese by design—this could not be further from the
truth. The historical origins of the I-Ching or Book of Changes, as it is
commonly called, are to be found in the vicinity of West Asia. Here, in the
region now known as Mesopotamia, we find this oracle complete and well
utilized by the inhabitants of the area. To these individuals, as recorded in the
Library of Ashurbanipal (700 B.C.E.), the I-Ching was addressed as the
"Tablet of Destiny," known and utilized by the great antediluvian monarch
Enmeduranki, the seventh of the aboriginal kings of Sippar. One of the oldest
oracles of antiquity, the I-Ching was constructed by the Black Akkado-
Sumerians of Elam-Babylonia and is dated circa 2800 B.C.E. This is substantiated by philologist Terrien De Lacouperie in his translation of West Asian
language, Chinese cultural custom and various historical documents.

Although the I-Ching may be traced to a West Asian origin it is the opinion
of this author that its rudimentary genesis may be based in Ifa, the divine
oracle conceived in the geographical region of West Africa. Chinese historians state that, like Ifa, the I-Ching was originally designed in a rectilinear
format. Both oracles connect the genetic patterns of DNA and RNA, linking
the past of the human family to its current expression. Ifa, like the I-Ching,
tells one of a potential future if we do not act to change our present circumstances. More importantly, both Ifa and I-Ching are expressed in a binary
formula, the key to their power, insights and foresights. Thus, it is probable in
my opinion that the Ifa oracle was taken into West Asia, expounded upon and
refined by the Akkadians of Accad, creating, in time, the "Tablet of Destiny,"
known as the I-Ching.

Establishing the cultural transmission for Ifa into West Asia is a relatively
simple process. Please see endnotes 3 & 4 for the details of this hypothesis.

> Everything is dual; everything has poles; everything has its
> pair of opposites; like and unlike are the same; opposites are
> identical in nature, but different in degree; extremes meet;
> all truths are but half-truths; all paradoxes may be recon-
> ciled.
>
> —*Kybalion*

"The ancient Africans...believed the world to be founded upon
contradictions...and this belief was expressed in the form of the Principle or
Doctrine of Opposites."[1] This principle—probably the most visible, most
employed and most widely known of the seven—is found still at the basis of
many African societies: the *Dogon of Mali,* the *Fon of Dahomey,* the *Bambara
of Eastern Guinea,* and the ancient *Ife* of West Africa. The Ife employ this law
today in the form of an oracle known as the *Ifa.* They profess the genesis of
the Ifa system of divination to be 20,000 B.C.E., and speak to its pervasive
influence in the dissemination of the concept of polarity in various cultures
and lands outside of Africa. (endnotes 2 and 3)

African cultures of antiquity as well as contemporary hold this principle
paramount in the formation and maintenance of creation and universal order.
Nigerian born Dr. C. Kamalu defines life itself "with the duality of being and
becoming...the product of being and becoming is the Life Force, that which
gives rise to change and motion....The Life Force is also the organizing
power bringing to order to the primeval chaos. This organizing power, this
force of life and motion, is sometimes described as the first created [thing]."[2]

Here in the West, the notion of an ever-present cosmological duality is
slowly becoming commonplace. Influenced by the metaphysical iconagraphy
of the Far East, the Western hemisphere is inundated with the two primary
symbols on which Chinese philosophical tradition was conceived: *yin/yang*
and the oracle of the *"I-Ching."* The concept of yin/yang essentially translates
into the positive and negative duality which permeates the material Universe;
it is the absolute or ultimate reality of all existence, which existed from the
beginning. Introduced into China during the Xia Dynasty by the cultural hero
Hwang-Ti (2697–2597 B.C.E), it soon became the hereditary symbol of
Taoist philosophy. The I-Ching or *Yih King* entered China at an earlier period
(2852–2738 B.C.E.), and is reported to have been the invention of a man the
Chinese called Fu-Hi Based on an arrangement of eight trigram figures, the I-
Ching oracle was reputed to hold the key to creation. Though these two
systems of divination are considered synonymous with Chinese ironically,
their origins are not Chinese.

Paul Carus, in his book *Chinese Thought,* discusses a Babylonian tablet
found in the Library of *Ashurbanipal* (700 B.C.E.) called the *"Tablet of
Destiny,"* said to "contain the Mystery of Heaven and Earth." Carus speculates that not only are the I-Ching and the Tablet of Destiny one and the same,

Figure 1. I-Ching surrounding the symbol of the Tao. (Photo courtesy of Wayne B. Chandler.)

but since the tablet predates the I-Ching by several centuries, the latter may have evolved from the former. A translation of a fragmented text from the Library of Ashurbanipal, identified as the *Text of Enmeduranki*, states: "Enmeduranki, king of Sippar, is the seventh of the *aboriginal* kings, and he declares that he received the divine tablet from Anu."[3] Sippar is located in the region of Mesopotamia known now as Iraq and is one of the most ancient cities in that area which, prior to the Indo-European incursions, was controlled and culturally dominated by some of the oldest Black populations of West Asia. Carus goes on to say, "Chinese sages have their own interpretation of the phrase 'the mystery of heaven and earth.' They would at once associate the words 'heaven' and 'earth' with the two opposing principles yang and yin....It seems not to be impossible that the Chinese tablet in the hands of Fuh-Hi is the same as the 'Tablet of Destiny' of the [Mesopotamians]."[4]

One of the most outstanding contributors to the history and origins of the Chinese people and their philosophies was Professor Albert Etienne Terrien de Lacouperie. The work Lacouperie did in this area of investigative study has never been rivaled, let alone surpassed. He was a scholar's scholar holding several prestigious positions in the field of historical academia. Terrien De Lacouperie held appointments as Professor of Indo-Chinese Philology at the University of London, President of Council of the Royal Asiatic Society and Philological Society, and board member of the Peking Oriental Society. He authored 25 books, among them the provocatively titled *The Languages of China Before the Chinese, West Asian Origins of Chinese Civilization, The Black-Heads of Babylonia and Ancient China, The YH-King and Its Authors.* It is this last volume which documents those who introduced to the Chinese people the concept of duality (yin/yang) and the oracle of the I-Ching.

An accomplished philologist, Lacouperie used language and various historical documents to launch what seems to be an impenetrable defense for a West Asian origin of China's I-Ching. Lacouperie begins by identifying a group of families known as the Bak which immigrated into China carrying with them the beginnings of civilization—a well-defined sociopolitical structure, writing, philosophy, and economic fortification. Culturally, this group was intimately related to the Meso-Sumerians of West Asia. Racially and ethnically the Bak were descendent from the Black *Akkadians* and *Elamites* of Mesopotamia.

"The language of the Bak families, which under the leadership of Yu Nai Hwang-ti (Hu Nak-Kunte) arrived about 2282 B.C. on the banks of the Loh river in Shensi, [and] was deeply connected with that of the Akkado-Sumerians of Elam-Babylonia. This alone might be sufficient to show that previously to their migration to the East and the Flowery Land [China] they were settled in the vicinity of these populations and, therefore, in proximity of Chaldean civilization, with which we have shown them to have been well-acquainted. The relationship of their language with that of the Akkado-Sumerians was pointed out and exemplified by me in 1880...an extensive comparison has shown me that the Akkado-Sumerian words in Chinese belong [to] the Bak families from the Elamo-Babylonian civilization in which they were current terms."[5] These statements by Lacouperie are extremely significant for three reasons. First, the identification of Yu Nai Hwang-ti as a family of languages removes the shroud of ambiguity from China's first Emperor Hwang-ti. We know that the name does not refer to an individual but to a group or entire population. Second, the transliteration of Yu Nai Hwang-ti into Hu Nak-Kunte is very revealing. The fact that Kunte is a common clan name among West African Mande speakers suggests a link between the linguistic patterns of the two geographically distinct regions. Finally, the mention made by Lacouperie to the Akkado-Sumerians indicates that the Akkadians play a very significant role in the transmission of culture from West Asia to the Far East. Their influence is acknowledged more than once by Lacouperie. Shedding more light on the Bak culture he remarks: "The language of the...invading Bak tribes was entirely distinct from that of the Aborigines of China....The result of this advance was for a time an intermingling of the language of the conquerors with that of the previous inhabitants."[6] What is evident among the Bak tribes is that though they spoke a language derived from a common source, there were various dialectical branches which included syntaxes, syllabaries, and polyphonics of a different origin.

Dr. Lacouperie documents that the Yh-King appears in early texts of the Xia dynasty (2000 B.C.E.), whose writing and language "correspond to linguistic features peculiar to the *Tagalo-Malayan* languages, and cannot be mistaken."[7] This language group was and to some extent is still found on various islands throughout Melanesia and South East Asia which are presently inhabited by the Blacks who originally spoke the languages. Currently these dialects fall within the category of the Austronesian family of languages.

Focusing more specifically on the origin of the I-Ching, Terrien de Lacouperie writes: "...before their emigration to the Far East, the Bak families had borrowed the pre-cuneiform writing...from South-Western Asia. A most interesting feature of the literature embodied in the cuneiform characters in the numerous vocabularies of several kinds giving the different meanings, [and] various sounds,...[they are] Sumerian, Akkadian descriptive names of the characters, single and compound."[8] Lacouperie goes on to say, "...the Yh-King is the oldest of the Chinese books...some of the Yh-King's chapters, would suggest that some of the Yh-King's vocabularies are imitated from old pre-Cuneiform ones...what is pretty sure is that the Chinese vocabularies have been framed in obedience to the same principles, with the same materials, and undoubtedly according to the [same] tradition of the old syllabaries of South-Western Asia."[9]

Lacouperie has skillfully utilized the instruments of his profession. Through

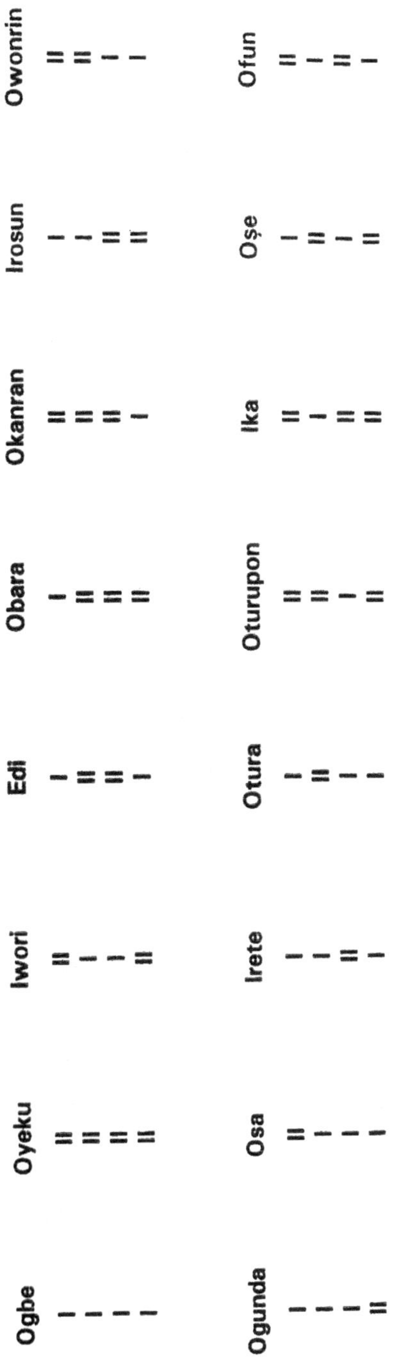

Figure 2. Ifa oracle of West Africa. Like the I-Ching it is based on the binary principle. (Photo courtesy of Wayne B. Chandler.)

Figure 3. Tieguai—one of the nine immortals of Taoism who lived during China's "Golden Age." An accomplished martial artist, Tieguai was known as the "Iron-Staff Immortal." Hand painted on silk, early Yuan Dynasty thirteenth century C.E. (Photo courtesy of Wayne B. Chandler.)

writing and language, he has unraveled the important roots of a system whose originators are not only forgotten, but have become strangers in their own land. Lacouperie's evidence both supports and is corroborated by the words of world-renowned historian and theosophist Helena Petrova Blavatsky:

> One of the oldest known Chinese books is the Yih King, or Book of Changes. It is reported to have been written 2850 B.C., in the dialect of the Accadian black races of Mesopotamia. It is a most abstruse system of Mental and Moral Philosophy, with a scheme of universal relation and divination. Thus a circle represents YIH, the Great Supreme; a line is referred to YANG, the Masculine Active Potency; two half lines are YIN the Feminine Passive Potency....[10]

The linguistic trail blazed by Lacouperie was not only daring but at times brilliant. Though he meticulously dissected the I-Ching, he was never able to perceive it as anything more than a codex which recorded historical events. Lacouperie believed that its functions as an oracle were unfounded and therefore dismissed them. This is unfortunate, for to the Black Akkado/ Elamite races of West Asia the I-Ching was a scepter of power which contained the secrets of the solar cosmology as well as the biopsychic unfolding of the Human Race, all of which was contained within its principle of duality—yin and yang.[11] The I-Ching like Ifa, reflects the fundamental reality in the material Universe based on the primordial binary elements f positive and negative, dark and light, or yin and yang. The term binary simply indicates something which is compounded or consists of two parts. In respect to numerics, binary signifies any mathematical system which has two at its base. And so it is with the I-Ching or Book of Changes. Yes/No, On/Off, Positive/Negative are all encounters of a binary nature. Several examples will dramatize the power of polarity as it is represented in the I-Ching. At the base of the individual lines of the eight binary triplet figures are the units of duality expressed as—and—or yang and yin respectively. These two lines are then arranged in three line structures, enclosed in a circle, and read from the bottom up. The binary trigram configurations in the upper hemisphere of the circle correspond to the energy which emanates from the Earth's electromagnetic field, while those at the bottom of the circle pertain to the Earth or the gravitational field rotating in time. When the two are combined they produce the 64 *permutations,* or *hexegrams.* These 64 six-line structures comprise the Changes and correspond to the *biopsychic field,* energy which surrounds every human being.

In 1675, German mathematician and philosopher Gottfried Von Leibniz was given credit for the discovery of Differential and Integral Calculus. Leibniz had begun work on a theory involving the concept of *binary mathematics* but encountered great difficulty finding evidence to prove his theory. Through a Jesuit priest who had travelled extensively throughout the Far East,

Figure 4. Akkadian ruler, thought to be the great Naram-Sin, grandson of Sargon. Naram-Sin ruled virtually all of West Asia for 37 years (2270–2233 B.C.E.). Naram-Sin is depicted here with the false beard and crown of West Asian kingship. (Photo courtesy of Wayne B. Chandler.)

Figure 5. West Asian population of Blacks known as Elamites whom Lacouperie identifies as the Bak. Limestone relief ca. 900 B.C.E. (Photo courtesy of Wayne B. Chandler.)

Leibniz was introduced to the I-Ching. After close study of this oracle, he was able to confirm his system of binary mathematics, which has became the basis of present-day computer science.

Less than 200 years ago, another German philosopher and historian, G.F. Hegel, had acquainted himself with the binary system of Leibniz. Hegel would go on to construct the *dialectical theory of history* which equates the rational and real and uses dialectic to comprehend an absolute idea. This theory of dialectical history would have a profound impact on the great social philosopher Karl Marx who would use this concept of binary to espouse his theory of *dialectical materialism.* [12] Thus, in the course of several centuries, three men who would radically effect the philosophical direction of Western civilization, inherited from his predecessor and accepted as fact the fundamental reality of binary law as postulated and espoused by the I-Ching.

Carl Jung was attracted to the I-Ching for what he perceived as its psychological applications. Jung stated that it confirmed many suspicions concerning the "archetypes" of human consciousness as well as the notion of synchronicity, the idea that events gain significance from their simultaneous occurrence. So impressed was Jung with the I-Ching that he would eventually write the forward to the most authentic translation of this book in the Western hemisphere, the 1949 Wilhelm/Baynes edition.

Though the validity of the I-Ching was confirmed and embraced by four of the most influential minds of this era, the most stunning revelation was yet to come. In 1953, two scientists, James Watson and Francis Crick, announced to the world their discovery of the genetic code, consisting of 64 BINARY TRIPLET FIGURES called DNA codons, which correspond directly to the 74 binary triplet hexagrams of the I-Ching oracle. The genetic code is written with four nucleic acid letters, each one represented by the two basic linears units of binary language (—, -), yin and yang. Like the hexagram of I Ching, there are 64 condons, and only 64 such structures possible. From these codons, the 20 amino acids are derived which make possible every biochemical and physiological action in the human organism. Thus, we are able to say that the I-Ching contains the key to unlocking the very mystery of life itself. Whether identified as *The Book of Changes,* the *Tablet of Destiny,* or the *I-Ching,* one thing is certain: the power of this oracle has been used consciously to mold specific periods in the history of humankind. That it derives this power from the principle of duality or polarity is the radical but undeniable lesson here. Ironically, that which the West has learned and used from this axiom is far less than what it has to offer. Though many have acknowledged the reality of opposites, there is a tendency to overlook or neglect the countless levels between the two extremes. The Hermetists of ancient Egypt had a thorough understanding of the functional dynamics of the Law of Polarity.

This, the fourth great axiom, from the Hermetic perspective, embodies the truth that all things manifested in the mental Universe have two sides, two aspects, two poles, and a pair of opposites with multi-phasic degrees between them. Thus, everything has inherent duality or poles which manifest the multitudes of opposites which we encounter on a daily basis. Dry cell batteries have an anode and a cathode, or positive and negative aspects which, when properly connected, will generate power or electrical force. Electrical current is actually two currents, AC (alternating current) and DC (direct current). AC-DC is also English slang to describe someone who alternates their sexual poles, bisexual. Manic depressives, who exhibit wide mood swings from the depressive pole to the manic pole, are called "bi-polar." Love and hate, hot and cold, good and bad, not to mention male and female, are all manifestations of universal opposites that consistently prove to us, whether or not we acknowledge it, that everything in creation has its pair of opposites.

All of these opposites may at any time be transmuted provided the practitioner understands the law. Things belonging to different classes cannot be transmuted into one another, but elements of the same class may have their polarity transformed. For example, love can never become east or west but it may become hate; hard things may be rendered soft, hot things become cold, and sharp things may become dull.

The principle of polarity states that like and unlike are the same, that opposites are identical in their nature and different only in their degree. This can easily be substantiated: Hermetists proclaim that spirit and matter are but two poles of the same element, the intermediate planes are various degrees of vibration. Infinite mind and finite mind are the same in their nature, that nature being mind, and are different only in that the two are among the many planes of correspondence comprised of myriads of vibratory frequencies. Heat and cold are identical in nature, their nature being temperature, and are different only in degree. A thermometer registers many degrees of temperature, the lowest point or pole being cold and the highest hot. Between these two points are many variances of the two and in the absolute sense there is no place on the thermometer where heat ceases and cold begins. Such is the case with short and tall or high and low, all height; large and small, both size; wide and narrow, both breadth; and day and night, which in a 24-hour period exhibit many degrees which gradually shade into one another.

What is imperative to understand is that all of these varying degrees become extremely relative. We are compelled to use these terms in a descriptive context so that others may understand us, but they are relative from person to person let alone in the absolute sense. If you travel around the world in an eastward direction, you will eventually arrive in the west. If you go far enough south you will find yourself in the north. That which we deem good and bad is not an absolute. The term "the lesser of two evils" refers to a thing which is "less good" than the thing higher in the scale; but that thing which is "less good" in turn, is better or "more good" than the thing below it.

Love and hate are emotions that humans categorize as diametrically op-

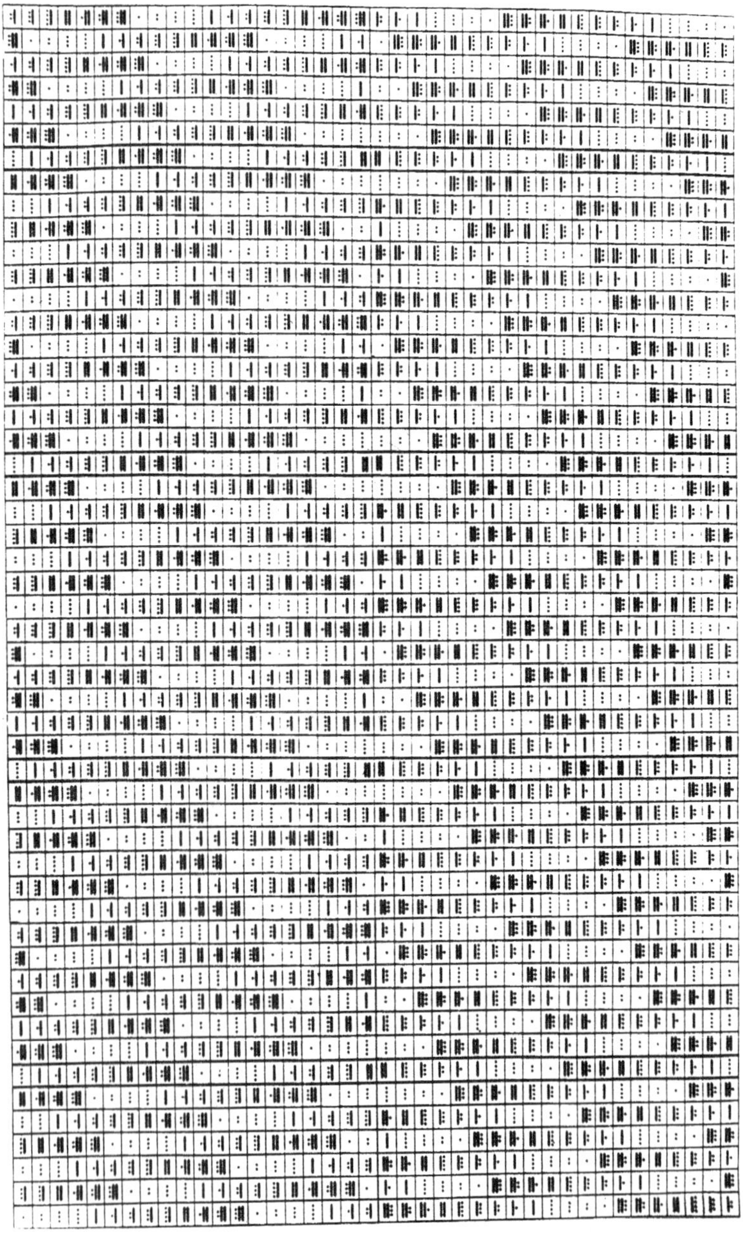

Figure 6. Computer language chart derived from binary configurations as those found in I-Ching via the great German mathematician Leibniz. (Photo courtesy of Wayne B. Chandler.)

ELECTROMAGNETIC FIELD

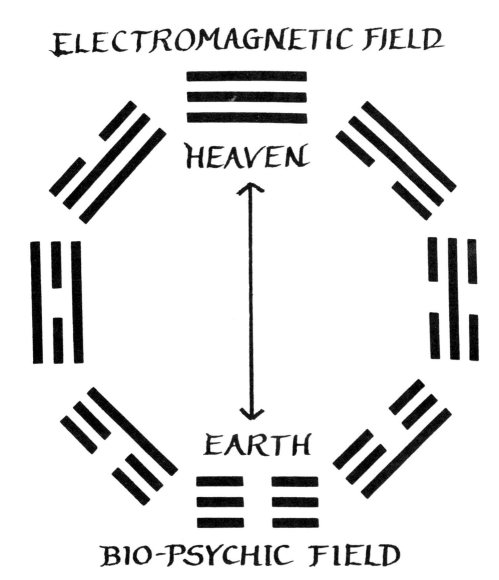

BIO-PSYCHIC FIELD

Figure 7. The eight hexagrams which comprise the I-Ching, the oracle said to unravel the mystery of Heaven and Earth. The upper portion of this oracle corresponds to Heaven or the electromagnetic field, while the lower relates to Earth and the biopsychic field which envelopes each individual human being. Blending the various hexagrams one is able to obtain 64 combinations and no more. This correlates to the 64 combinations found within the genetic code. (Photo courtesy of Wayne B. Chandler.)

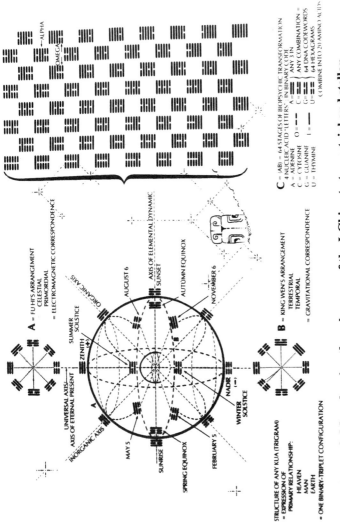

Figure 8. Map showing the relevance of the I-Ching to terrestrial and stellar phenomena. It also demonstrates the two different arrangements of the oracle. Fu-Hi's original arrangement utilized by the Xia and Shang dynasties, pertains to heaven while King Wen's of the later Zhou relates to Earth. In the far right we find the chart (LETTER C) which corresponds to the code of genetic dialect. (Photo courtesy of Wayne B. Chandler.)

posed, or unreconcilable. But, according to the principal of polarity, there is no such thing as absolute hate. Envision a polar scale which measures the two extremes of this emotion. At any point on the scale, there will be more love or less hate or vice versa. As we ascend the scale we encounter less hate and more love, but if we descend the scale we find just the opposite. These intermediate areas are the jurisdiction of like, dislike, disdain, fondness, amiability....Therefore there are no absolutes which introduce the next sub-category.

The proclamation of this axiom that "all truths are but half truths" and all paradoxes may be reconciled echoes many ancient philosophical aphorisms: "everything is and isn't at the same time," "every truth is half false," and "there are two sides to everything." The reality is that all truths are but half truths, simply because there are no definitive absolutes, though humans are forever trying to create them.

Though much of this axiom has been explicated in the preceding paragraphs, the best way to understand that which remains of this principle is through your own experience. In the human promenade through life, there is a continuous parade of new lessons which inevitably create perspectives, convictions, and directions in and about life. These personal realities become our truths and we live and relive them daily. As we grow and mature, many, if not most, of our notions about our realities change, and that which we held to be hallowed or divinely consecrated is modified, sometimes radically, demonstrating that our truths and realities are in a constant state of flux. Those of us who are too rigid to see change on our paths eventually succumb to a fixed view of the world, making ourselves and those around us miserable.

The two poles characteristic of all things can be classified as positive or negative. Thus, love is positive and hate is negative, and the positive pole is considered a higher degree of vibration than the negative pole and constantly dominates it. The ancient Hermetists stated that the tendency of nature is to move in the direction of the positive pole which is forever increasing in its vibratory capacity. Here we see that the laws of Vibration and Correspondence work intimately with the law of Polarity.

With the comprehension of this, one may see its transmutive ability. When properly applied, it can, like the two laws which precede it, allow a greater sense of self-awareness and clarity.

THIS CHAPTER ON POLARITY IS A SEGMENT FROM THE UP-COMING BOOK *BLACK PHOENIX RISING* BY WAYNE B. CHANDLER ON THE SEVEN PRINCIPLES OF ANCIENT EGYPT, TO BE PUBLISHED BY BLACK CLASSIC PRESS.

Notes

1. Chukunyere Kamalu. *Foundations of African Thought.* (Karnak House, Great Britain, 1990), p. 31.
2. Ibid. p. 36—Chinese historians state that, like Ifa, the I-Ching was once designed in a rectilinear fashion. It is not known exactly when, but the forerunners of Chinese civilization later discovered that these trigrams could be rearranged into a circular form. The oracle of Ifa, like the I-Ching, is said to connect the genetic patterns of DNA and RNA, linking the past of the human family to its current expression. Ironically, geneticists have just recently established this fact known to West African culture for millennia. But Ifa again in line with the I-Ching, professes to go beyond the physical and connects the race with a "road of energy" and "power" that is available to those who know and practice the oracle. This "road" in I-Ching is the ever present interplay between the Earth's electromagnetic field and the biopsychic field of the human race. Ifa, like the I-Ching believes these patterns of energy are established prior to our birth in the world but does not lend itself to predestination. Through the divination of Ifa, the cultures of West Africa believe it is possible to know something about our future and "the outcome of all our undertakings." Ifa, as the I-Ching, tells one of a potential future if we do not act to change our present circumstances. Thus, the older features which comprise the Ifa oracle can arguably be said to have comprised the basis of thought now identified in the I-Ching.
3. Paul Carus. *Chinese Thought.* (Open Court Press, 1907) p. 34—Considering the possible antiquity of Ifa and its geographical point of origin, it is plausible that this "Tablet of Destiny", now referred to as the I-Ching, evolved out of the older system of Ifa. If we examine the biblical "Table of Nations" we are informed that, "The sons of Ham: [father of the Black race] were Cush, Mizraim [Egypt], Phut, and Canaan. Then Cush begot Nimrod; he became a mighty one on the earth. The beginning of his kingdom was Ba'bel, Erech, and Accad, all of them in the land of Shinar [Mesopotamia]." This is the biblical lineage of the Black race; its dawning rooted in the soil of the African continent, originating from a common point, and eventually spreading to West Asia. There is no denying the cultural and linguistic affinities which show a cultural interconnectedness. There are also those parallels which pertain to the systems of writing between the Cuneiform and Egyptian. Thus, it is probable in my opinion that the Ifa oracle was taken into West Asia and expounded upon and refined by the Akkadians of Accad creating, in time, the Book of Changes, known as the I-Ching. This common point of origin yet diverse cultural expression is substantiated by current archaeology. The findings of the UNESCO International Scientific Committee states that ca. 20,000 B.C.E., most of West to East Africa was an inland sea which began to recede and drain leaving by, 10,000 B.C.E., large lakes, streams, rivers, and swamps. The various cultures and people which inhabited this area used these waterways as a mode of travel and cultural exchange, and became known as the "Aquatic civilization."
    This civilization, which once lived around the perimeter of the inland sea, then inhabited an area which spread across the continent, from the Atlantic coast to the Nile Basin. Numerous archaeological sites have been unearthed in the Saharan highlands and the southern fringe of the desert from the upper Niger, through the Chad Basin, to the middle Nile, and south as far as the East African Rift Valley. These aquatic people of West and East Africa varied in their physical type but skeletal remains recovered indicate that they were most certainly a Negroid people, harmoniously living and trading with one another. Evidence shows that they were master ship builders and traveled the lakes and rivers from one part of the continent to the other. This

civilization thrived for several millennia until adverse climate began to dehydrate and reduce the aquatic size and productivity of the region. I believe it was at this point in history, ca. 5000–4000 B.C.E., that extensive migrations took place out of Africa into West Asia carrying with it the vestiges of West African culture as seen with the Ifa.

Some of the Ifa principles are as follows: There is one God and there is no devil except that which we make for ourselves; except for birth and death there is no single event in our lives that cannot be forecast and changed; we grow and obtain wisdom through life and are reborn through life's revelations; what we call Heaven is home and Earth the proving ground or a marketplace where we learn the lessons of life, and we are in constant passage between the two; we are part of the Universe in a literal, not figurative way; we must never initiate harm to another human being or the Universe of which we are apart; temporal and spiritual capacities must work together for we are born with a specific path and it is our goal to travel it.

4. Ibid. p. 34.

5. Terrien de Lacouperie. *The Ya-King and its Authors.* (London, 1892) p. 106.

6. Terrien de Lacouperie. *The Language of China Before the Chinese.* (Reprinted by Che'eng-wen Publishing Company Taipei, 1966) pp. 14–15.

7. Ibid. p. 15.

8. T. de Lacouperie. *The Ya-King.* p. 96.

9. Ibid. pp. 100–101.

10. Helena Petrova Blavatsky. *The Theosophical Glossary.* (Cunningham Press Inc., Los Angeles, California, 1982) p. 81.

11. Jose Arguelles PhD. *Earth Ascending.* (Shambhala, Boulder and London 1984), p. 21—Arguelles, matriculated at the University of Chicago, he has a background in history and philosophy. Having gone abroad to study in Paris and London, Arguelles returned to teach at Princeton University, University of California, Davis; The Naropa Institute, California State University, San Francisco; and the University of Colorado, Denver. He is considered a leading edge thinker advancing new concepts in resonant harmonics and the principles of cosmic science.

12. Ibid. p. 42.

RESEARCH NOTES
BODHIDHARMA: FOUNDER AND FIRST PATRIARCH
OF ZEN BUDDHISM

By Wayne B. Chandler

The martial arts have been a part of Chinese civilization for more than three thousand years, but they did not originate in China. Although the first traces of a martial influence may be recognized as early as 1500 B.C.E., the martial traditions typically recognized as purely Chinese began in the fifth century A.D. under the influence of a great Indian sage known in Chinese chronicles as Bodhidharma or Talmo, and in Japan as Dharuma. Bodhidharma, founder and first patriarch of Ch'an (Zen) Buddhism, introduced the foundations of the martial disciplines to the Shaolin monks of southern China's Songshan Province.

Bodhidharma was born in A.D. 440 in the southern Indian kingdom of Pallava and resided in Kanchi, one of its largest cities. He was Dravidian, a member of the Black aboriginal population that during his time dominated most of Asia.

As an adult Bodhidharma journeyed to China, bringing with him the ancient Indian martial arts that once permeated Indian society. India's oldest epics—the *Ramayana*, the *Rig Veda* and the *Mahabharata*—recount fierce, colorful battles of a warrior epoch when "it was a sin to die in bed." This was the tradition that Bodhidharma carried into China.

Bodhidharma redefined the Chinese approach to Buddhism. His contribution, now known as Zen, required long periods of meditation rather than adherence to a particular doctrine or scripture. He also taught the monks breathing exercises to help them develop their mystical power base, or *chi*, and movement techniques to foster strength and self-defense skills. Thus was born the Shaolin *ch'uan fa,* or "temple boxing," one of the most renowned of the Chinese martial arts.

RESEARCH NOTES
THE AFRICAN PRESENCE IN THE ART AND ARCHI-
TECTURE OF EARLY CENTRAL ASIA

By Runoko Rashidi and James E. Brunson

Around the fourth century, the ancient central Asian bastion of Toprak Kala in Khwarizm, embracing portions of modern Uzbekistan, Kazakhstan and Afghanistan, contained towered battlements which encompassed an area 1,900 feet by 1,400 feet. The palace itself, which was assembled about an enclosure situated on a elevated platform, ascended to a height of three stories and was overlooked by three tremendous towers. The palace possessed three enormous halls. The decoration of the designated "Hall of Kings" was a consolidation and melding of stucco sculptures and paintings with effigies of the aristocracy of Chorasmia and their families. Benjamin Rowland notes that the "Hall of Victories" was lined with statues of princes attended by the molded figure of Nikes, and the "Hall of Warriors" was brilliantly decorated with reliefs of men-at-arms painted black with Africoid features. The wavy hair of the figures is perhaps an indication that Dravidian soldiers were affiliated in an important way with the ruling lords of Chorasmia.[1]

John M. Rosenfield contends that another sort of indication of the presence of Dravidian physical types in the portrait assemblies in the Toprak Kala palace are "guards with small stature, dark skins, thick lips, and straight hair. This suggests the presence of armed contingents from South India....Skeletal remains have substantiated the fact that Indians were in the area."[2]

Notes

1. Benjamin Rowland, *The Art of Central Asia* (New York: Crown, 1974), 54.
2. John M. Rosenfield, *The Dynastic Arts of the Kushans* (Berkeley: University of California Press, 1967), 168.

RESEARCH NOTES
THE AFRICAN PRESENCE IN ASIA IN THE WORKS OF
JAMES COWLES PRICHARD

By Runoko Rashidi

James Cowles Prichard, M.D. (1786–1848) was an early and influential British ethnologist described as "one of the founders of the science of anthropology." Prichard was the author of the massive text, *Researches Into the Physical History of Man*, originally published in London in 1813. George W. Stocking, editor of a revised reissue of the work, pointed out that, "To Prichard, the continued existence of tribes of 'wooly-haired blacks' from the Andaman Islands east to the South Pacific suggested the early diffusion of a black race over a much wider area."[1] James M. Boddy referenced Prichard in his 1905 article on the "Ethnology of the Japanese Race," which sought to demonstrate a discernible African presence in early Japan.[2]

Although Prichard was distinctly biased in his views about race and ethnicity, an examination of his work indicates that many of the European scholars of his era were well aware of the position, stature and prominence of Black people in antiquity. In a notable section of his work "On the Physical Characters of the Ancient Indians," Prichard acknowledged that for a long time, both physically and culturally, the dominant people in ancient India were Black. In support of this he cites, for example, the observations of a number of well-known classical (Greek and Roman) authors. He points first to Herodotus (ca. 450 B.C.E.), and notes that "It is remarkable that Herodotus, in his enumeration of the forces of Xerxes, mentions a tribe of Ethiopians from the eastern parts of Asia, who were drawn out in the same division of the army with the Indians."[3] Another notable historical source was the Greek historian Arrian (ca. 150 B.C.E.). In his work called the *Indica,* Arrian said of the people of India that, "Those farther to the south are somewhat more like the Ethiopians, and they are black in their complexion, and their hair is black, but they are not likewise flat nosed, nor is their hair woolly; but those who live farther northward most resemble the Egyptians in their persons."[4] In more recent times, Prichard cites one of his contemporaries, Francis Wilford, an officer in the Indian Army, whose writings appeared in the monumental, twenty volume *Asiatick Researches,* first published in Calcutta from 1788 to 1839. The initial twelve volumes of *Asiatick Researches* were reprinted in London from 1806 to 1812. A widely recognized scholar during his day, Wilford ultimately concluded that "it cannot reasonably be doubted, that a race of Negroes formerly had pre-eminence in India."[5] And then, after examining the art of early India, Prichard himself concluded that, "There can be no doubt that the prototypes from which they were designed, were either Negroes properly so called, or that they were possessed of physical characteristics similar to those of the natives of Africa."[6]

Notes

1. George W. Stocking, Jr., "From Chronology to Ethnology: James Cowles Prichard and British Anthropology 1800–1850." In *Researches Into the Physical History of Man,* by James Cowles Prichard, rev. ed. (Chicago: University of Chicago Press, 1973), liv.
2. James Marmaduke Boddy, "The Ethnology of the Japanese Race," *The Colored American Magazine* (Oct 1905), 582.
3. James Cowles Prichard, *Researches Into the Physical History of Man* (Chicago: University of Chicago Press, 1973), 389.
4. Prichard, 390.
5. Prichard, 391.
6. Prichard, 395.

GLOSSARY

Compiled By Runoko Rashidi

Aboriginal: Being the first of its kind present in a region. Aboriginal people are the first inhabitants of a country.

Absolute/Relative age: An absolute date applies to a specific time in calendar or radiocarbon years, whereas a relative age only indicates whether an item is younger or older than other items.

Adivasis: Original inhabitants of India.

Agriculture/Domestication: Practice of cultivating the soil and bringing animals under human control.

Akkadian: An important language of ancient Iraq, significantly influenced by Sumerian.

Anthropology: The study of humankind.

Archaeology: Study of the material traces of the human past.

Artifact: Any object made by human agency.

Aryan: A member of the Indo-European speaking tribes which invaded Pakistan, India and Iran in ancient times; Nordic.

Asparas: The celestial female dancers depicted in the art of Angkor.

Assyrians: An ancient people who lived approximately in the area of modern-day Iraq from the mid-third millennium B.C.E., and who invaded the Nile Valley twice in the seventh century B.C.E.

Bas-relief: A carving or sculpture that projects slightly from the background on which it is carved.

B.C.E.: Before the common era.

Beringia: Refers to the ancient land mass that formerly connected Siberia with Alaska.

Bodhisattva: A person destined for enlightenment, a future Buddha, who embodies the ideals of compassion by assisting or caring for others. The Bodhisattva ideal is a characteristic feature of Mahayana Buddhism.

B.P.: Before the present, 1950 taken as the zero year.

Brachycephalic: Short-headed or broad-headed with a cephalic index of over 80.

Brahmin: The highest ranking Hindu caste.

Ca: Approximately.

Caliph: "Chief executive officer of the Islamic religion (Successor or Representative of Muhammad)."

Carbon-14: A heavy radioactive isotope of carbon of mass number 14 used especially in tracer studies and in dating archaeological and geological materials.

Caste System: A hierarchical system of classification of peoples by which social privileges, duties and prohibitions are rapidly assigned. In India caste is determined by birth, but was originally ethnically based.

City-State: An autonomous state consisting of a city and the surrounding territory.

Cranial: Of, or relating to the cranium or skull, which forms the enclosure of the brain, excluding the lower jaw.

Craniometric: The comparison and contrast of crania and cranial features based on metric measurements.

Cuneiform: A West Asian system of writing with wedge-shaped characters incised on clay tablets.

Cyclopean Architecture: Architecture characterized by the use of very large close-fitting irregular stones.

Dalits: The only name which India's Black Untouchables have given themselves. Presently designated as Scheduled Castes, the Dalits are descended from the original Black founders of the Indus Valley civilization, who were subjugated and kept in conditions of enslavement and apartheid called untouchability, from the time of conquest until the abolition on paper of "untouchability" in 1951.

Diminutive Africoids: The sub-division of African people phenotypically characterized by: unusually short statures; skin-complexions that range from yellowish to dark brown; tightly curled hair; and, in frequent cases (like many other Blacks), steatopygia. The Diminutive Africoids are also known by such pejorative terms as Aeta, Negritos, Semang and Pygmies.

DNA: Deoxyribonucleic acid; an essential component of all living matter and a basic material in the chromosomes of the cell nucleus. It transmits the hereditary pattern.

Dolichocephalic: Having a skull long in proportion to its breadth; having a skull whose width is less than 80% of its length.

Dravidian: An autonomous family of languages which spread in antiquity from Southern India to Eastern Iraq. It was likely the language of Harappa. The best-known representatives of the family are Tamil and Telegu, which continue to thrive in Southern India, and Elamite, the language of the ancient Elamite high-culture of Iran.

Dynasty: A line of rulers belonging to the same family; also the period during which a certain family reigns.

Elam: The ancient civilization of Southwestern Iran. The chief city of Elam was Susa.

Empire: A major political unit having a territory of great extent or a number of territories or peoples under a single sovereign authority; also the period during which such a government prevails.

Epicanthic Fold: A skin fold on the eyelid that, when the eye is open, comes down over and runs on a line with the edge of the upper eyelid.

Eponym: A real or mythical person from whose name the name of a nation, community or institution is derived or supposed to have derived.

Erythraean Sea: The term applied by Greek and Roman geographers to the Indian Ocean, including its adjuncts, the Red Sea and the Persian Gulf.

Fossil: Any hardened remains or traces of plant or animal life of some previous geological period, preserved in rock formations in the earth's crust.

Genotype: The fundamental constitution of an organism in terms of its hereditary factors.

Greater India: "Outer India": A broad geographic region encompassing at various periods what is now Bangladesh, India, Pakistan and Sri Lanka (Ceylon) and sometimes parts of Southeast Asia.

Hadith: a hadith is a reliably transmitted report of what Muhammad said, did, or approved.

Hajj: The annual pilgrimage to Makkah.

Harappan Civilization: The high culture of the Indus Valley in what is now Pakistan and related centers in northwest India dating from ca. 2700 B.C.E. to 1500 B.C.E.

Harijans: "Children of God", a term applied by M.K. Gandhi to the Untouchables.

Hijra: The migration in the year 622 by Muhammad and his followers from Makkah to the city of Madinah some 260 miles to the north. The Hijra marks the beginning of the Muslim calendar.

Hominid: A member of the family Hominidae, which includes Homo (mankind) and Australopithecus but excludes the apes.

Homo: The generic name given to the hominid group containing fossil and modern man.

Homo erectus: A species of humans that preceded modern humans.

Homo habilis: A group of fossil hominids and the earliest Homo. The population named 'Handymen.'

Homo sapiens sapiens: Modern human beings.

Hydraulic: Operated, moved, or effected by means of water.

Hyksos: Translated both as 'Shepherd Kings' and 'Rulers of Foreign Lands,' the Hyksos were the Asiatic invaders of Africa who occupied Kmt and formed dynasties XV and XVI.

Interglacial: Warmer period between colder glacial periods.

Interstadial: Short, relatively warm interlude within a longer glacial period.

Islam: The Arabic word 'Islam' simply means 'submission', and derives from a word meaning 'peace'. In a religious context it means complete submission to the will of God.

Isthmus: A narrow strip of land connecting two masses of land that would otherwise be separated by water.

Jati: Sanskrit term for caste.

Ka'ba: The sanctuary at Makkah; of very ancient date. It was a small square temple of black stones what had for its corner-stone a meteorite.

Koran (Quran): Believed to be the exact words revealed by God through the Angel Gabriel to the Prophet Muhammad.

Laterite: A red, porous, iron-bearing rock that is easy to quarry but extremely hard when dried.

Linguistics: The study of human speech including the units, nature, structure, and modification of language.

Lithic: Of, or pertaining to stone.

Littoral: Near, or along a coastal region.

Mahabharata: Classical Sanskrit epic probably composed between 200 B.C.E. and 200 C.E. The *Bhagavad-Gita,* a religious classic of Hinduism, is contained in the *Mahabharata.*

Material Culture: The tangible objects produced by a society.

Matrifocal: The strong presence and importance of the mother.

Megalithic: Constructed of large stones.

Mesolithic: The Stone Age period between the Paleolithic and the Neolithic. The prefixes indicate 'Old', 'Middle', and 'New' Stone Ages.

Mesopotamia: A Greek term denoting "the land between the rivers [the

Tigris and Euphrates]." In 1921 the British changed the name from Mesopotamia to Iraq, an Arabic word which means "well-rooted country."

Mongoloid: Term commonly used to describe Eastern Asians.

Monolith: A single gigantic stone or similarly huge object, often in the form of an obelisk or column.

Natufian: A ancient tool industry and culture in western Asia named for settlements extending from Turkey to the Egyptian Delta.

Paleo: Ancient, historically early or prehistoric.

Paleolithic: The 'Old Stone Age'. The Paleolithic is the pre-agricultural era beginning with the emergence of humankind and the manufacture of the earliest tools.

Paleontology: A science dealing with the life of past geological periods as known from fossil remains.

Pancharma: M.K. Gandhi's name for a suggested fifth lowest caste, which he proposed be created for the purpose of incorporating the Dalit into the caste system, purportedly to correct the ill of defining and maintaining them outside it as Untouchables.

Periplus: The name applied to a class of writings which answered for both a sailing chart and traveler's handbook.

Phenotype: The visible characteristics of an organism that are produced by the interaction of the genotype and the environment.

Physical Anthropology: Study of the physical nature of humankind.

Platyrrhine: Denoting a short broad nose.

Pleistocene Age: The first epoch of the Quarternary Period in the Cenozoic Era; characterized by the rise and recession of continental ice sheets and by the appearance of human beings.

Pluvial: Prolonged periods of high rainfall marked by major changes in lake levels, flora and fauna.

Prehistoric: The period before written history.

Prognathous: Jaws projecting beyond the upper face.

Proto: The first in time, original, principal.

Pseudo: False, pretended, spurious or illusory.

Ramayana: Classical Sanskrit epic of India, probably composed in the third century B.C.E. The *Ramayana* relates the adventures of Rama.

Reflex-bow: The much-feared weapon of the horse nomads of the Eurasian steppes. It was made of wood or other organic material reinforced by bone. At rest, it curved outward and had to be bent back to string. The reflex-bow possessed had great range and penetrating force.

Rig Veda: The oldest and probably the most important of the Hindu sacred texts.

Riverine: On, or near, the banks of a river.

Rockshelter: A naturally formed hollow or overhang in a more or less vertical rock face.

Saba: Biblical Sheba, with its capital at Marib in South Arabia.

Samurai: Literally, 'those who serve'; the knights of Medieval Japan.

Sanskrit: An ancient Indo-European language regarded by many as "the sacred and classical language of India and Hinduism."

Scheduled Castes: Indian bureaucratic designation for the Dalit, replacing their previous label accorded by Hinduism of "Untouchable."

Scheduled Tribes: Indian bureaucratic designation for tribal peoples. "Tribespeople in India, minorities in a dominant Hindu population, are officially classified as 'scheduled tribes', meaning that they appear on a schedule of tribal communities enjoying a legal status distinct from that of other Indians. They number nearly 40 million and not long ago were referred to as 'aboriginals', a term justified by the well-founded belief that in all probability they had dwelt in their present habitat long before the first Aryan had set foot on Indian soil."

Semitic: Related to a subfamily of Afro-Asiatic languages including Arabic, Hebrew, Ethiopic, Amharic, Aramaic and others.

Shang: The first historical dynasty of China, ca. 1700–1060 B.C.E.

Shari'a: 'The Divine Law'; the detailed code of conduct comprising the precepts, governing modes and ways of worship and standards of morals and life.

Shogun: Name given to the military governor of Japan prior to the Meiji era.

Steatopygia: A physical trait characterized by an excessive accumulation of fat on the buttocks.

Stela: A stone column or upright slab decorated with carvings or inscriptions.

Steppe: Vast grasslands capable of supporting herds of grazing animals, but generally too cold and arid for the growing of crops.

Sudras: Originally the lowest of the four castes of Hinduism; now divided into hundreds of subcastes. In Hindu tradition, a Sudra who intentionally reviles twice-born men by criminal abuse, or criminally assaults them with blows, shall be deprived of the limb with which he offends. If he has criminal intercourse with an Aryan woman, his organ shall be cut off, and all his property confiscated. If the woman had a protector, the Sudra shall be executed. If he listens intentionally to a recitation of the *Veda,* his tongue shall be cut out. If he commits them to memory his body shall be split in twain.

Sumer: The oldest known civilization of Western Asia, located in the Tigris-Euphrates river valley and flourishing during the third millennium B.C.E.

Sumerian: The earliest recorded language of the southernmost part of Mesopotamia, used during the third millennium B.C.E., and later preserved as the language of religion and ritual.

Suttee: The rite recorded from India of a widow taking her own life in order to accompany her deceased husband.

Taxonomy: Classification of living things into groups.

Tundra: A level or undulating treeless plain that is characteristic of arctic and subartic regions where the subsoil is frozen.

Varna: Classical division of Hindu society; Sanskrit term denoting color or complexion.

Vedas: The four religious books that instruct Brahmanic ritual, of which the most famous is the *Rig Veda*.

Wadi: An Arabic word meaning dried-up river-bed.

Ziggurat: Massive rectangular shaped, step-temple structures or stage-towers in early Western Asia, generally composed of mud bricks.

BIOGRAPHICAL NOTES

Runoko Rashidi (Editor)

Runoko Rashidi is an historian, research specialist, writer and public lecturer focusing on the African foundations of world civilizations. As a lecturer, he has made major presentations at sixty-six different colleges and universities in the United States, as well as in Belize, Egypt, England, France, India and Japan. From 1981 to 1984, he was employed as an African History Research Specialist at Compton Community College. From 1985 to 1987, Rashidi was the History Editor for the National Black Computer Network. Since 1983, he has been an active member of the Board of Directors and the Board of Editors of the *Journal of African Civilizations*. In August 1993, he taught the first ever graduate level course on Comparative Civilizations at the University of Hawaii at Manoa. Currently he is a Social Sciences Consultant at McClymonds High School in Oakland, California, Scholar-in-Residence at Amon-Rah (African People's Community Church) in Los Angeles, California, and United States Representative of *Dalit Voice: The Voice of the Persecuted Nationalities Denied Human Rights*.

As a writer, Rashidi's articles have appeared in more than twenty community, national and international publications. He has been a regular contributor to the *Journal of African Civilizations* and editor of *African Presence in Early Asia* (Tenth Anniversary Edition).

He has been described as "the world's foremost authority on the African presence in Asia." He is the author of *Introduction to the Study of African Classical Civilizations*, published in 1993 by Karnak House of London, England, and *The Global African Community: The African Presence in Asia, Australia, and the South Pacific*, published by the Institute of Independent Education in Washington, D.C. in 1994. He is currently preparing major works on *The Nile Valley and Beyond, The African Presence in Ancient and Modern Asia*, and *The Black Presence in Ancient and Modern India*.

For information write to: Rashidi, 4140 Buckingham Road, Suite "D", Los Angeles, CA 90008. Or call (213) 293-5807.

Ivan Van Sertima (Co-Editor)

Ivan Van Sertima was born in Guyana, South America. He was educated at the School of Oriental and African Studies (London University) and the Rutgers Graduate School and holds degrees in African Studies and Anthropology. From 1957–1959 he served as a Press and Broadcasting Officer in the Guyana Information Services. During the decade of the 1960s he broadcast weekly from Britain to Africa and the Caribbean.

He is a literary critic, a linguist, and an anthropologist and has made a name in all three fields.

As a literary critic, he is the author of *Caribbean Writers,* a collection of critical essays on the Caribbean novel. He is also the author of several major literary reviews published in Denmark, India, Britain and the United States. He was honored for his work in this field by being asked by the Nobel Committee of the Swedish Academy to nominate candidates for the Nobel Prize in Literature from 1976–1980. He has also been honored as an historian of world repute by being asked to join UNESCO's *International Commission for Rewriting the Scientific and Cultural History of Mankind.*

As a linguist, he has published essays on the dialect of the Sea Islands off the Georgia Coast. He is also the compiler of the *Swahili Dictionary of Legal Terms,* based on his field work in Tanzania, East Africa, in 1967.

He is the author of *They Came Before Columbus: The African Presence in Ancient America,* which was published by Random House in 1977 and is now in its twenty-first printing. It was published in French in 1981 and in the same year was awarded the Clarence L. Holte Prize, a prize awarded every two years "for a work of excellence in literature and the humanities relating to the cultural heritage of Africa and the African diaspora."

Professor of African Studies at Rutgers University. Van Sertima was also Visiting Professor at Princeton University. He is the Editor of the *Journal of African Civilizations,* which he founded in 1979 and has published several major anthologies which have influenced the development of a new multi-cultural curriculum in the U.S. These anthologies include *Blacks in Science: Ancient and Modern; Black Women in Antiquity; Egypt Revisited; Egypt: Child of Africa; Nile Valley Civilizations; African Presence in Early American; African Presence in Early Europe; Great Black Leaders: Ancient and Modern; African Presence in the Art of the Americas, Great African Thinkers* (co-edited with Larry Obadele Williams) and *Golden Age of the Moor.* He is also co-editor, with Runoko Rashidi, of *African Presence in Early Asia.*

Professor Van Sertima has lectured to more than 100 universities in the U.S. and has also lectured in Canada, the Caribbean, South America and Europe. He defended his highly controversial thesis on the African presence in pre-Columbian America before the Smithsonian which published his address in March, 1995. He also appeared before a Congressional Committee on 7 July 1987 to challenge the Columbus myth.

Jamal Ali

Drawing on more than twenty years of design engineering experience in the aerospace industry, Jamal Ali has focused his research on the sacred architecture of Nile Valley civilizations. An eclectic blend of scientist, esotericist, historian and artist, he has made several contributions to the *Encyclopedia of Vernacular Architecture of the World*, which is being published out of the Oxford Brookes University in England.

James E. Brunson

African centered art historian James Edward Brunson III is a native Chicagoan, who currently lives in DeKalb, Illinois. He has taught in the Northern Illinois University Art Department where he received his Master of Fine Arts degree. Brunson is presently a doctoral candidate at the University of Chicago. As an artist, Brunson has exhibited his work throughout the Midwestern and Southern United States. He has recently completed a lithographic series on the African Presence in Kemetic (Egyptian) Mythology, and is currently completing documentation for an educational course on The African Image in World Art.

Brunson is a prolific writer and has been a significant contributor to the *Journal of African Civilizations*. These contributions include: "The African Presence in the Ancient Mediterranean Isles and Mainland Greece" in 1985, "The African Presence in Early China" and "Unexpected Black Faces in Early Asia: A Photo Essay" in 1988, "Ancient Egyptians: The Dark Red Race Myth" and "Ethnic or Symbolic: Blackness and Human Images in Ancient Egyptian Art" in 1989, and "The Moors in Antiquity" (co-authored with Runoko Rashidi) in 1992.

In 1985 Brunson wrote and published *Black Jade: The African Presence in the Ancient East and Other Essays*. Other works by Brunson include: *Black Roots in Most Ancient China* and *Kamite Brotherhood: African Origins in Early Asia* in 1989, *The Black Canaanites from the Earliest Times, Blacks of the Early Steppe, Kingdoms in Southeast Asia , Image of the Black in West Asian Art* in 1990, *Africans in Early Asia: An African-Centric Historiography (1827–1991), The World of Sakanouye No Tamuramaro: Black Shogun of Early Japan* and *Predynastic Egypt: An African-centric View* in 1991, and *Frat and Soror: The African Origin of Greek-Lettered Organizations* in 1992. For information write to: James E. Brunson, P.O. Box 0962, DeKalb, IL 60115–0962.

Wayne B. Chandler

Wayne B. Chandler is an anthrophotojournalist with a background in anthropology, history, and photography. He is co-founder of *What's A Face Productions,* a business dedicated to the research and dissemination of information on the historical growth of all races and cultures, in particular the Black and African cultures throughout the Diaspora with attention to their positionality in various world civilizations. He has also co-founded the Inu Gallery in Takoma Park, Maryland, an art space dedicated to intercultural contact and exchange.

Mr. Chandler is an historian and lecturer specializing in Asian civilization, philosophy, and culture and the African presence therein. In 1991, he visited the ruins of the Indus Valley (now known as Pakistan) in South Asia, and has done extensive research into the African presence and influence in this area. He is a board member of *Afriasia,* a national organization dedicated to the historical study of the impact and unition of African and Asian world populations. He has lectured throughout the United States, Canada, Western Europe, and Britain.

Mr. Chandler has appeared on numerous television and radio programs, including a television program produced in London by the BBC. Through the photo-archives of *What's A Face,* Mr. Chandler and his business partner, Mr. Gaynell Catherine, have created and continue to produce *New World Visions,* a television series which explores many aspects of the international Black cultural experience from the ancient to the contemporary. *What's A Face's* current project is a feature film on the life of Hannibal, Rome's North African nemesis.

Mr. Chandler has published widely in his area of expertise. Since 1985, he has been a regular contributor to the *Journal of African Civilizations,* edited by Ivan Van Sertima and published by Rutgers University. His *JAC* articles have been recommended by reviews in historical journals published by Yale, Harvard, and Cambridge. In association with *What's A Face Productions,* Mr. Chandler designs and produces annually via Pomegranate Publishers *A Journey into 365 Days of Black History,* a teaching calendar highlighting and explicating events and people often obscured by standard American and world history. His latest book, *Black Phoenix Rising,* is due for release in 1995 by Black Classic Press (Baltimore). Mr. Chandler is presently at work on a book of fine art photographs and text on the divine and mundane nature of women, to be published by Pomegranate.

Charles B. Copher

The Reverend Dr. Charles B. Copher is a distinguished and eminent scholar of the Old Testament and minister of the Gospel of Jesus Christ in the United Methodist Church. Formerly Vice President for Academic Affairs and Dean of the Faculty, he now serves as Professor Emeritus and Adjunct Professor Old Testament at the Interdenominational Theological Center in Atlanta, Georgia, lecturing on Black Biblical history.

Dr. Copher's educational and theological credentials include a B.A. from Clark College, a M.Div. from Gammon Theological Seminary, and a B.D. in Biblical Literature from Boston University. His writings have appeared in numerous textbooks, religious publications, scholarly journals and the *Encyclopedia Britannica*. During the second semester of the 1987–1988 school year, Dr. Copher served as Distinguished Visiting Professor at the Howard University School of Divinity.

Widely respected and highly regarded, Dr. Copher has been working on a major book entitled *Black People in and of the Bible*. He is the author of *Black Biblical Studies: Biblical and Theological Issues on the Black Presence in the Bible*. His travels have included Egypt, Sudan, Ethiopia and Israel.

Walter A. Fairservis, Jr.

Professor of anthropology at Vassar College. Received Bachelor's degree at Columbia University; Doctorate at Harvard University. He has led expeditions to Afghanistan, Pakistan, Iran and India, some of them under the auspices of the American Museum of Natural History. He has held appointments at New York University and the University of Washington, and is the author of numerous works on the Indus Valley civilization, including *Roots of Ancient India* (University of Chicago, 1975).

Charles S. Finch III, M.D.

Charles S. Finch III, M.D. is a board-certified family physician who is currently Assistant Director of International Health at the Morehouse School of Medicine. Dr. Finch completed his undergraduate training at Yale College, his medical training at Jefferson Medical College, and his Family Medicine Residency at the University of California, Irvine Medical Center. He has worked as an epidemiologist for the Center of Disease Control and was formerly a clinical preceptor at the Duke-Watts Family Medicine Clinic in Durham, North Carolina. He was founder and chairman of the Raleigh Afro-American Life Focus Project between 1981 and 1982 and is a co-founder and Co-Convener of Bennu, Inc. of Atlanta.

Dr. Finch is an Associate Editor of and regular contributor to the *Journal of*

African Civilizations. These contributions include: "The African Background of Medical Science" 1983, "The Nile Valley Conference: New Light on Kemetic Studies" and "The Kemetic Concept of Christianity" in 1984, "Race and Evolution in Prehistory" in 1985, "Black Roots of Egypt's Glory," "Imhotep the Physician: Archetype of the Great Man," and "The Great Queens of Ethiopia" (co-authored with Larry Obadele Williams) in 1987, "Science and Symbol in Egyptian Medicine: Commentaries on the Edwin Smith Papyrus" and "The Works of Gerald Massey: Studies in Kamite Origins" in 1989, and "Nile Genesis: Continuity of Culture from the Great Lakes to the Delta" in 1994.

His own works include: *The African Background to Medical Science: Essays on African History, Science and Civilizations* (London: Karnak House, 1990), *Echoes of the Old Darkland: Themes from the African Eden* (Decatur:L Khenti, 1991), and *Africa and the Birth of Science and Technology: A Brief Overview* (Decatur: Khenti, 1992). Dr. Finch has regularly visited Senegal, West Africa where he has begun studies on the empirical basis of traditional West African medicine.

Joseph E. Harris

Joseph E. Harris received his B.A. and M.A. degrees from Howard University and his Ph.D. in History from Northwestern University. He was formerly chairman of the Department of History at Howard University and has taught at the University of Nairobi. Prior to coming to Howard, Harris was professor of history at Williams College. Dr. Harris is the author of *Africans and Their History* (New York: Penguin, 1972) and *The African Presence in Asia: Consequences of the East African Slave Trade* (Evanston, IL: Northwestern University Press, 1971). Harris is the editor of the *William Leo Hansberry African History Notebook* and *Global Dimensions of the African Diaspora.*

Drusilla Dunjee Houston (1876–1941)

Teacher, journalist and historian, Drusilla Dunjee Houston was born in Winchester, Virginia in 1876, and spent most of her life in Oklahoma and Phoenix, Arizona. As a journalist, Houston aggressively covered numerous cases of white atrocities committed against Black people in the state of Oklahoma. But it is as a bold and uncompromising historian that Houston comes to our attention here, the crowning achievement of which was the publication of the *Wonderful Ethiopians of the Ancient Cushite Empire; Nations of the Cushite Empire.*

Wonderful Ethiopians was originally published in 1926 in Oklahoma City, Oklahoma by the Universal Publishing Company and was intended as the first volume of a three volume work. *Wonderful Ethiopians*—a bold and pioneering work, not only contains comprehensive chapters devoted to African civilizations along the Nile, but continues the survey eastward into Asia where it examines and illuminates the strong African presence and influence on classical Asian civilizations.

Wonderful Ethiopians was favorably reviewed in a number of newspapers buy Arthur Alfonso Schomburg, in the *Amsterdam News* by Joel Augustus Rogers and in the *Pittsburgh Courier* by Robert L. Vann. Houston was also the author of a syndicated column entitled the "Wondrous History of the Negro," which appeared in the *Louisiana Weekly*.

Graham W. Irwin

Graham W. Irwin is the editor of *Africans Abroad: A Documentary History of the Black Diaspora in Asia, Latin America, and the Caribbean During the Age of Slavery* (New York: Columbia University Press, 1977), and Associate Dean of Columbia University in the City of New York.

John Glover Jackson (1907–1993)

John Glover Jackson was born on 1 April 1907 in Aiken, South Carolina. At the age of fifteen he moved to Harlem, New York, where he entered Stuyvesant High School. During his student days Jackson began to do active research, and was soon writing short essays about African-American culture and history. These essays were so impressive that in 1925, while still a high school student, Jackson was invited to write articles for the Honorable Marcus Garvey's *Negro World.*

In addition to his growing activities as a writer, in 1930 Jackson became a lecturer at both the Ingersoll Forum and the Harlem Unitarian Church. Among his teachers and associates during this period were such immortal figures as Hubert Henry Harrison, Arthur Alfonso Schomburg, Joel Augustus Rogers and Willis Nathaniel Huggins.

In 1932 Jackson became the Associate Director of the Blyden Society. Named after the great Pan-Africanist Edward Wilmot Blyden, the Blyden Society played an outstanding role as an African-American support group for Ethiopia, after Italy's brutal 1935 invasion of that country. The Blyden Society was then under the leadership of Dr. Willis Nathaniel Huggins, the organization's founder, and an absolutely brilliant scholar and Pan-Africanist. Among the very early and, as Jackson is quick to point out, most talented students to come out of the Blyden Society is the now highly respected Dr. John Henrik Clarke.

Although these were difficult years for John G. Jackson, with race-prejudice, poverty and illness his frequent companions, he continued to produce well-researched, informative and controversial works. In 1934 Jackson co-authored with Dr. Huggins *A Guide to the Study of African History,* and in 1937—also with Dr. Huggins—*Introduction to African Civilizations.* In 1939 he authored *Ethiopia and the Origin of Civilization,* and *Pagan Origins of the Christ Myth* in 1941. His contributions to *The Truthseeker Magazine* continued regularly from 1930 until 1955.

John G. Jackson authored several major books relevant to the African presence in Asia. These works include *Man, God, and Civilization* in 1972, *Introduction to African Civilizations* in 1974, and *Ages of Gold and Silver* in 1990. He taught and lectured at colleges and universities throughout the U.S. and resided for many years in Chicago, Illinois. He died on 13 October, 1993.

Rafique Ali Jairazbhoy

Indian born scholar Rafique Ali Jairazbhoy is an independent researcher who has devoted more than thirty years in tracing the rise and spread of civilizations, and has written extensively on the interconnections between the primary world civilizations. He is the author of several books. These include *Foreign Influence in Ancient India* (New York, 1963), *Ancient Egyptians and Chinese in America* (London, 1974), *Ancient Egyptians in Middle and South America* (London, 1981) and *Egyptian Survivals in the Pacific* (London, 1990).

Omar Khalidi

Omar Khalidi was born in Hyderabad, Deccan, India in 1957. He obtained his Masters in Liberal Arts from Harvard University School of Extension Studies in 1991, and Ph.D. in Islamic Studies from the University of Wales in 1994. His doctoral thesis on the Muslim experience of Indian democracy is to be published in June 1995. Currently he is on the staff of Aga Khan Program for Islamic Architecture and Urban Studies at Massachusetts Institute of Technology.

Wallace Magsby, Jr.

Wallace Magsby, Jr. is a graduate of Los Angeles City College and a student at California State University, Dominguez Hills majoring in Africana Studies led by Dr. William Little, and Asian-Pacific Studies led by Dr. Donald T. Hata. He was selected outstanding student for the academic year 1994–1995 by both the Africana and Asian-Pacific Studies Department. At California State University, Dominguez Hills he also became student President of the National Council for Black Studies for the academic year of 1994–

1995. From 1986 to 1990 he served in the United States Air Force. Magsby is the author of a recent paper entitled "Unexpected Faces in Early Japan."

Jacqueline Patten-Van Sertima

Jacqueline L. Patten-Van Sertima, Photographic consultant, art director and cover designer for the Journal of African Civilizations, also established the Journal's audio arm, Legacies, Inc. in 1987.

Her 23-year track record has won her national and international acclaim for her hand-painted photography, not only for its technical excellence, but for its sociological significance to social awareness. Since 1983 she has been listed in the Cambridge World Who's Who of Women for "distinguished achievement," their International Register of Profiles and their International Who's Who in America for "outstanding artistic achievement and contribution to society." Some of her work appears in: *The Black Photographer's Annual, Black Photographers: An Illustrated Bio-Bibliography 1940–1987* (Garland Publishing) and *Race, Discourse, and the Origin of the Americas* (Smithsonian Institution Press). To name just a few, her awards include Lincoln Center's award for photographic excellence for 1980 and 1982 and first prize in Mademoiselle's Fourteenth Annual Photography Competition, 1978. Exhibitions include: The Museum of the City of New York, the National Urban League, Columbia University, Washington Square East Galleries, the Ziegfield Gallery, and various college throughout the country.

Mrs. Patten-Van Sertima received her B.S. degree in Psychology and M.S. in Education from Hunter College, New York.

V.T. Rajshekar

V.T. Rajshekar has been described as "one of India's foremost original thinkers." From India's west coast district of South Kanara, Karnataka, he is a noted journalist and writer with more than 25 books to his credit. Until 1979, he was the deputy chief reporter of the *Indian Express,* Bangalore—India's largest circulated English daily. He was dismissed from the *Indian Express* for taking up the cause of India's Black Untouchables and other national minorities. He is now the editor of the *Dalit Voice (The Voice of the Persecuted Nationalities Denied Human Rights).* Established in 1981, the powerful *Dalit Voice* has been the only English journal for the Black Untouchables of India and its other oppressed nationalities.

Mr. Rajshekar is the founder of the Dalit Sahitya Akademy, an institution that has developed an international reputation for publishing books on India's social, cultural, religious and ethnic problems. Widely travelled internationally, Rajshekar led delegations in 1980 and 1983 to the People's Republic of

China. He has also journeyed to Japan to study the plight of Japan's Untouchables—the Burakumin. In 1986 Rajshekar represented India's Black Untouchables at the World Mathaba Conference against Fascism, Racism, and
Colonialism in Tripoli, Libya. Upon his return to India he was arrested under
India's dreaded Terrorist Act. Following national and international protests
and appeals, he was released with an apology. His passport, however, has
remained impounded since 1986 on the charge that he was making "anti-
national" speeches outside India. For information contact: V.T. Rajshekar,
109/7th Cross, Palace Lower Orchards, Bangalore, India—560 003.

Gershom Williams

Gershom Williams is a cultural historian, writer, lecturer, Black history
consultant, teacher, and community activist. He attended Indiana University
Northwest majoring in Afro-American History and Sociology. For almost
two decades Mr. Williams has conducted extensive study and research into
"pre and post Slavery" heritage of African Americans. His special areas of
interest and concentration have been in the African origins of humanity, the
African influence and impact on Nile Valley and Western Civilizations, and
the role of African people in world religion and spirituality. His articles and
historical essays have appeared in *History, the Bible and the Black Man, The
Village Runner,* the *Journal of African Civilizations, Odyssey West,* and the
Arizona Informant Newspaper.

Chancellor James Williams (1893–1992)

Chancellor James Williams, probably best known as the author of *The
Destruction of Black Civilization: Great Issues of a Race from 4500 B.C. to
2000 A.D.,* was born in Bennetsville, South Carolina, on 22 December 1893.
His father had been a slave; his mother a cook, a nurse, and evangelist.
Williams' elementary education was completed in Bennetsville at the Marlboro
Academy. After moving to Washington, D.C. (where he lived for more than
seventy years), he attended Paul Laurence Dunbar High School and Armstrong
High School (graduating from the latter). Williams received a Bachelor of
Arts degree in Education from Howard University in 1930 and a Master of
Arts degree in History from the same institution in 1935. He did post-
graduate, non-resident studies at the University of Chicago and the University
of Iowa. Williams obtained a Ph.D. in Sociology from American University
in Washington, D.C. in 1949.

In 1945, Chancellor Williams joined the faculty of the Howard University
History Department. He retired in 1966, and returned in the early 1970s as a
distinguished lecturer. It was while at Howard University, first as a student

and later as a teacher, that Williams came under the guiding influence of one of the finest Africanist scholars of the twentieth century—William Leo Hansberry. Dr. Williams was a Visiting Research Scholar at Oxford University, England and the University of London in 1953 and 1954. In 1956, he began direct field studies in African history, based at University College, which later became the University of Ghana. Williams was actually in Ghana when it gained independence from Britain on 6 March 1957 under the leadership of Kwame Nkrumah. The final phase of the field studies, which covered twenty-six countries and 105 language groups, was completed in 1964.

The career of Chancellor Williams was spacious and varied: university professor; President of the Log Cabin Baking Company; Vice President and General Manager of Cooperative Industries; Editor of *The New Challenge*; U.S. Government economist; high school teacher and principal; historical novelist and author-historian. He was the father of fourteen children. Blind and in poor health, the last years of Dr. Williams' life were spent in a nursing home in Washington, D.C. Dr. Chancellor Williams, the man, died on 7 December 1992. His legacy, however, remains distinct, vibrant and alive.

A Series of Historical Classics

The Journal of African Civilizations, founded in 1979, has gained a reputation for excellence and uniqueness among historical and anthropological journals. It is recognized as a valuable information source for both the layman and student. It has created a different historical perspective within which to view the ancestor of the African-American and the achievement and potential of black people the world over.

It is the only historical journal in the English-speaking world which focuses on the heartland rather than on the periphery of African civilizations. It therefore removes the "primitive" from the center stage it has occupied in Eurocentric histories and anthropologies of the African. The Journal of African Civilizations is dedicated to the celebration of black genius, to a revision of the role of the African in the world's great civilizations, the contribution of Africa to the achievement of man in the arts and sciences. It emphasizes what blacks have given to the world, not what they have lost.

Books

Add $8.00 per book
foreign airmail

___African Presence in Early America $15.00
___African Presence in Early Asia (out of print)
___African Presence in Early Europe $20.00
___Black Women in Antiquity $15.00
___Blacks in Science: ancient and modern $20.00
___Egypt Revisited $20.00
___Egypt: Child of Africa $20.00
___Golden Age of the Moor $20.00
___Great African Thinkers - C.A. Diop $15.00
___Great Black Leaders: ancient and modern $20.00
___Nile Valley Civilizations (cancelled)

Postage for above books:
$1.75 per order of single book.
.75 more for each additional book.

___They Came Before Columbus $23.00
(**For this particular book, please make checks payable to**   postage $ 3.00
"**Ivan Van Sertima**".)

Date_____

Name_____
Address_____
City/State_____
Zip_____Tel. No._____

Check and money orders should be made payable to:

"Journal of African Civilizations"
Ivan Van Sertima (Editor)
Journal of African Civilizations
African Studies Department
Beck Hall
Rutgers University
New Brunswick, New Jersey 08903

A Listener's Library of Educational Classics

Legacies, Inc., the audio arm of the Journal of African Civilizations, was established by Mrs. Jacqueline L. Patten-Van Sertima in answer to a genuine need and many requests from parents and teachers across the country. They needed a widespread, easily accessible and responsible medium of communication. It not only had to serve as a learning tool, but as an informational vehicle for educational strategies that hold promise for our youths. They also needed a dynamic and expedient way to absorb and disseminate information as well as a bridge to parents whose time for relearning and participation in the educational process was limited. So, in keeping with the highly controversial needs of the times, Legacies, Inc. was born.

In most of our audio cassette tapes, you will be hearing the voice of Dr. Ivan Van Sertima, founder and editor of the Journal of African Civilizations. His untiring fervor has made learning for everyone an exciting adventure through time. The lectures, by a variety of speakers, are brilliant, stimulating, passionate and absorbing. It is the drama of forgotten peoples and civilizations, brought to you through an unusually fresh and liberating vision of the human legacy.

AUDIO TAPES

___African Presence in Early America & Address to the Smithsonian	$10.00
___African Presence in Early Asia - R. Rashidi & Van Sertima	$10.00
___African Presence in Early Europe	$10.00
___African Presence in World Cultures	$10.00
___The Black Family - J.H. Clarke & Van Sertima	$10.00
___Black Women in Antiquity	$10.00
___Blacks in Science: ancient and modern	$10.00
___Egypt Revisited	$10.00
___Golden Age of the Moor - R. Rashidi & Van Sertima	$11.00
___Great African Thinkers - C.A. Diop	$10.00
___Great Black Leaders: ancient and modern	$10.00
___The Legacy of Columbus - Jan Carew	$10.00
___Re-Educating Our Children	$10.00
___Socialization of the African-American Child - Asa G. Hilliard	$10.00
___They Came Before Columbus	$10.00
___Van Sertima Before Congress	$10.00
___Egypt: Child of Africa	$10.00

Date_____

Name_____

Address_____

City/State_____

Zip_____Tel. No._____

Check and money orders should be made payable to:

"Legacies"
Jacqueline L. Patten-Van Sertima
347 Felton Ave.
Highland Park, New Jersey 08904

Please include postage:

1 tape 1.50
2 tapes 2.00
3 tapes 2.50
4–10 tapes 3.50
11–18 tapes 5.00

ORDER FORM FOR BOOKS

Journal of African Civilizations

Books Now Available:

❑ African Presence in Early Asia $20.00
❑ African Presence in Early Europe $20.00
❑ Blacks in Science: Ancient and Modern $20.00
❑ Black Women in Antiquity $20.00
❑ Egypt Revisited $20.00
❑ Golden Age of the Moor $20.00
❑ Great Black Leaders: Ancient and Modern $20.00
❑ African Presence in Early America $20.00
❑ Great African Thinkers (Reprinting Fall '95) $20.00
❑ Egypt: Child of Africa $20.00

Name_____

Address_____

_____

City/State/Zip _____

Checks and Money Orders should be made payable to
Journal of African Civilizations and sent to:

Ivan Van Sertima (Editor)
Journal of African Civilizations
African Studies Department
Beck Hall, Rutgers University
New Brunswick, New Jersey 08903

They Came Before Columbus

by IVAN VAN SERTIMA

Winner of The 1981 Clarence L. Holte International Prize

"Comprehensive and convincing evidence of links between Africa and America in the Pre-Columbian Period. Ivan Van Sertima takes the subject out of the 'Lost Worlds' category and brings together all the known facts established by various disciplines . . . He makes an impressive case for contact . . . A big boost to Black Cultural History."
—*Publishers Weekly*

"The theory has been argued for years. Usually supported by enthusiasts claiming far too much on very little information. Professor Van Senima is no such romantic. . He has pursued it with good judgement and persuasive evidence drawn from a wide variety of sources. A facinating case worth the attention it demands. . ."
—*The Atlantic Monthly*

"The majority of Afro-American and White Americans accept the slave version as the definitive story of Black presence in this land. . . . This book will place Afro-American History in a much more important dimension than *Roots*. . . . A remarkable work. . ."
—*Los Angeles Sentinel*

"This is a pioneering work that will help to bring about a reassessment of the place of African people in world history. . . . A scholarly achievement. . . . Calls attention to Africa's ages of grandeur and the great adventurous spirit of the Africans that brought them to the worlds beyond their shores. . . . After the excitement over Alex Haley's *Roots*, I hope a popular and scholarly reading public will turn to this book where the roots are much deeper. . ."
—John Henrik Clarke, *Africa*

"The great stone heads of Mexico are by far the most spectacular evidence that, as civilization was dawning in the New World more than 2,000 years before Columbus, black people from Africa had already reached these shores. . . . The leading proponent of an African presence in the New World is Ivan Van Sertima. . . . Van Sertima marshals many other kinds of evidence."
—*Science Digest* (September 1981)

"As one who has been immersed in Mexican archeology for some forty years, and who participated in the excavation of the first of the giant heads, I must confess that I for one am thoroughly convinced of the soundness of Van Sertima's conclusions . . ."
—Dr. Clarence W. Weiant (Professor of Archeology) *The New York Times Book Review* (Letters)

"The French translation of *They Came Before Columbus* has been very well received by the French-speaking intellectual and academic community. Already it is highly regarded as a fundamental contribution by a young Afro-American scholar to universal histoncal knowledge . . ."
—Dr. Cheikh Anta Diop *Director, Radio Carbon Laboratory, IFAN University, Dakar, Senegal.*

To order a copy, please send $23.00 plus $3.00 postage to: Ivan Van Sertima, 347 Felton Avenue, Highland Park New Jersey 08904. Checks or money orders should be made out to "Ivan Van Sertima."

NOTES

NOTES

NOTES